THE PICKY EAGLE

THE PICKY EAGLE

How Democracy and Xenophobia
Limited U.S. Territorial Expansion

RICHARD W. MAASS

CORNELL UNIVERSITY PRESS

Ithaca and London

First published 2020 by Cornell University Press

Library of Congress Cataloging-in-Publication Data

Names: Maass, Richard W., author.
Title: The picky eagle : how democracy and xenophobia limited U.S. territorial expansion / Richard W. Maass.
Description: Ithaca : Cornell University Press, 2020. | Includes bibliographical references and index.
Identifiers: LCCN 2019025912 (print) | LCCN 2019025913 (ebook) | ISBN 9781501748752 (hardcover) | ISBN 9781501748769 (epub) | ISBN 9781501748776 (pdf)
Subjects: LCSH: Democracy—United States—History. | Xenophobia—Political aspects—United States— History. | United States—Territorial expansion— History. | United States—Foreign relations.
Classification: LCC E179.5 .M124 2020 (print) | LCC E179.5 (ebook) | DDC 320.0973—dc23
LC record available at https://lccn.loc.gov/2019025912
LC ebook record available at https://lccn.loc. gov/2019025913

For Etuna

Contents

ACKNOWLEDGMENTS

"Ask big questions." If there is one piece of advice I've taken to heart, this is it. Big questions concern important subjects; their answers profoundly shape how we understand the evolution and operation of the world around us. Furthermore, big questions end in big question marks. We genuinely don't know the answers when first undertaking to study them. As a result, big questions offer both the opportunity to make a scholarly contribution and the intellectual motivation for a curious mind to persevere through an objectively daunting amount of research. This book was born from my nagging unease that the modern world would look very different if its first unrivaled superpower had continued pursuing conquest instead of outlawing it. It stemmed as well from my curiosity about why the most powerful country in the history of the world had lost interest in something that many other great powers as well as its own early leaders found so appealing.

After devoting a decade of work to this book, I am deeply grateful for the support of mentors, colleagues, friends, and family who have helped me see it through. Mike Desch's genuine interest in this question and his open-mindedness in pursuit of accurate answers reinforced my own, and his consistently thoughtful guidance helped me navigate through early drafts. This book has also benefited immensely from Dan Lindley's unceasing skepticism and ruthless attention to detail, Sebastian Rosato's infectious ambition and "read everything" thoroughness, and Walter Nugent's enthusiasm and care for historical research.

Mike Desch, Dan Lindley, Walter Nugent, George Herring, and Josh Shifrinson each read a heavily revised and expanded draft manuscript, providing valuable feedback at a book conference made possible thanks to funding from the Notre Dame International Security Center and an Alumni Research and Scholarly Activity Fellowship from the University of Evansville. After its submission to Cornell University Press, two anonymous reviewers (who turned out to be Peter Liberman and Scott Silverstone) each read multiple iterations of the full manuscript. Their diligence and insightful recommendations were everything peer review should be, and they played a crucial role in helping me hone the book's strengths. I am grateful to Emily Andrew for being a wonderful editor to work with, to Bethany Wasik for her efficient editorial assistance, to Roger Haydon for his early support of the project, and to members of the editorial board at Cornell University Press for their own comments, which helped strengthen the manuscript in its final stages.

Richard Bensel, Daniel Bessner, and Henry Nau each read draft portions of the manuscript and offered generous comments, as did William Ayres, Jonathan Caverley, Dale Copeland, Colin Elman, Holley Hansen, Christopher Layne, David Mayers, Andrew Radin, Marybeth Ulrich, and John Vasquez in conference panels. I thank Matt Evangelista, Taylor Fravel, Jeff Friedman, Paul Huth, Peter Katzenstein, Jonathan Kirshner, Sarah Kreps, Kyle Lascurettes, John Mueller, Barry Posen, Ashim Subedee, and William Wohlforth for thoughtful conversations related to this book. Equally helpful were attendees at related presentations at the annual conferences of the American Political Science Association, the International Studies Association, the APSA and ISA international security sections, the Midwest Political Science Association, the Indiana Political Science Association, the Ivane Javakhishvili Tbilisi State University International Scientific Conference, the Cornell University PSAC series, and the Institute for Qualitative and Multi-Method Research. At Notre Dame, both the book and its author benefited from a vibrant community of young international relations scholars, including Paul Avey, Bobby Brathwaite, Peter Campbell, Ben Denison, Charles Fagan, Kirstin Hasler, Rita Konaev, Soul Park, Ji Hye Shin, and John Stringer. Keir Lieber helped lay its groundwork by emphasizing big questions in early conversations.

Big questions take time to answer, and I owe that time to institutional support from the University of Notre Dame, Cornell University, and the University of Evansville. An Art, Research, and Teaching Grant and an Alumni Research and Scholarly Activity Fellowship from the University of Evansville funded the map, which was designed by Mike Bechthold, as well as the index, which was created by Lisa DeBoer. Related research was funded in part by a Global Scholar Award from the Institute for Global Enterprise at the University of Evansville. Librarians at all three universities greatly facilitated my research as did those at archival collections, including the William Henry Seward Papers at the University of Rochester, the John Bigelow Papers at the New York Public Library, and the National Archives in Washington, DC. Immeasurable credit is due to the numerous librarians and historians nationwide who have worked to preserve and digitize documentary collections—I shudder to think how long my research would have taken in a prior age.

Finally, I owe the most profound debt of gratitude to my family: Bill and Shelagh, whose love and support enabled me to build any life I chose; Adele and Charlie, whose companionship shaped me more than they know; Ani and Lily, whose future deserves that we improve upon the past; and especially Etuna, who has shared every step of this journey. This book is for her.

Abbreviations

AC	*Annals of Congress*
AG	*The Writings of Albert Gallatin*, ed. Henry Adams, 3 vols. (Philadelphia: J. B. Lippincott, 1879)
AH	*The Papers of Alexander Hamilton*, ed. Harold C. Syrett, 27 vols. (New York: Columbia University Press, 1961–87)
AIC	House of Commons, *Correspondence between the United States, Spain, and France, concerning Alleged Projects of Conquest and Annexation of the Island of Cuba* (London: Harrison and Son, 1853)
AJ	*The Correspondence of Andrew Jackson*, ed. John S. Bassett, 4 vols. (New York: Kraus Reprint, 1969)
ASP:FR	*American State Papers: Foreign Relations*
ASP:IA	*American State Papers: Indian Affairs*
ASP:MA	*American State Papers: Military Affairs*
BF	*The Writings of Benjamin Franklin*, ed. Albert H. Smyth, 10 vols. (New York: Macmillan, 1905–7)
CG	*Congressional Globe*
CR	*Congressional Record*
CS	*Speeches, Correspondence and Political Papers of Carl Schurz*, ed. Frederic Bancroft, 6 vols. (New York: G. P. Putnam's Sons, 1913)
DC:CR	*Diplomatic Correspondence of the United States: Canadian Relations, 1784–1860*, ed. William R. Manning, 4 vols. (Washington, DC: Carnegie Endowment for International Peace, 1940–45)
DC:IA	*Diplomatic Correspondence of the United States: Inter-American Affairs, 1831–1860*, ed. William R. Manning, 12 vols. (Washington, DC: Carnegie Endowment for International Peace, 1932–39)
DC:ILN	*Diplomatic Correspondence of the United States Concerning the Independence of the Latin-American Nations*, ed. William R. Manning, 3 vols. (New York: Oxford University Press, 1925)
FRUS	*Foreign Relations of the United States*
GC	*Letters of Grover Cleveland: 1850–1908*, ed. Allan Nevins (Cambridge, MA: Riverside Press, 1933)

GW   *The Writings of George Washington from the Original Manuscript Sources, 1745–1799,* ed. John C. Fitzpatrick, 39 vols. (Washington, DC: Government Printing Office, 1931–44)

HC   *The Papers of Henry Clay, 1797–1852,* ed. James F. Hopkins, Mary W. M. Hargreaves, Robert Seager II, and Melba Porter Hay, 10 vols. (Lexington: University of Kentucky Press, 1959–91)

JB   *The Works of James Buchanan,* ed. John B. Moore, 12 vols. (Philadelphia: J. B. Lippincott, 1908–11)

JBP   *John Bigelow Papers,* Manuscripts and Archives, New York Public Library, Astor, Lenox, and Tilden Foundations

JC   *The Works of John C. Calhoun,* ed. Richard K. Crallé, 6 vols. (New York: D. Appleton, 1851–56)

JCC   *Journals of the Continental Congress*

JMa:H   *The Writings of James Madison,* ed. Gaillard Hunt, 9 vols. (New York: G. P. Putnam's Sons, 1900–1910)

JMa:RF   *Letters and Other Writings of James Madison,* ed. William C. Rives and Philip R. Fendall, 4 vols. (Philadelphia: J. B. Lippincott, 1865)

JMo   *The Writings of James Monroe,* ed. Stanislaus M. Hamilton, 7 vols. (New York: G. P. Putnam's Sons, 1898–1903)

JP   *The Diary of James K. Polk during his Presidency, 1845 to 1849,* ed. Milo M. Quaife, 4 vols. (Chicago: A. C. McClurg, 1910)

JPC   *Correspondence of James K. Polk,* ed. Herbert Weaver, Wayne Cutler, Tom Chaffin, and Michael D. Cohen, 13 vols. (Nashville: Vanderbilt University Press and Knoxville: University of Tennessee Press, 1969–2017)

JQA:A   *Memoirs of John Quincy Adams,* ed. Charles F. Adams, 12 vols. (Philadelphia: J. B. Lippincott, 1874–77)

JQA:F   *The Writings of John Quincy Adams,* ed. Worthington C. Ford, 7 vols. (New York: Macmillan, 1913–17)

MPC   *A Compilation of the Messages and Papers of the Confederacy,* ed. James D. Richardson, 2 vols. (Nashville: United States Publishing Company, 1906)

MPP   *A Compilation of the Messages and Papers of the Presidents, 1789–1897,* ed. James D. Richardson, 11 vols. (Washington, DC: Government Printing Office, 1896–1913)

RD   *Register of Debates*

RDC   *The Revolutionary Diplomatic Correspondence of the United States,* ed. Francis Wharton, 6 vols. (Washington, DC: Government Printing Office, 1888)

SH	*The Writings of Sam Houston, 1813–1863*, ed. Amelia W. Williams and Eugene C. Barker, 8 vols. (Austin: University of Texas Press, 1938–43)
SL	*U.S. Statutes at Large*
TJ:F	*The Works of Thomas Jefferson*, ed. Paul L. Ford, 12 vols. (New York: G. P. Putnam's Sons, 1904–5)
TJ:LB	*The Writings of Thomas Jefferson*, ed. Andrew A. Lipscomb and Albert E. Bergh, 20 vols. (Washington, DC: Thomas Jefferson Memorial Association, 1903–7)
TJ:W	*The Writings of Thomas Jefferson*, ed. H. A. Washington, 9 vols. (Washington, DC: Taylor and Maury, 1853–54)
TPUS	*The Territorial Papers of the United States*, ed. Clarence E. Carter and John P. Bloom, 28 vols. (Washington, DC: Government Printing Office, 1934–75)
UG	*The Papers of Ulysses S. Grant*, ed. John Y. Simon, 31 vols. (Carbondale: Southern Illinois University Press, 1967–2009)
USSS	*U.S. Serial Set*
WHH	*Messages and Letters of William Henry Harrison*, ed. Logan Esarey, 2 vols. (Indianapolis: Indiana Historical Commission, 1922)
WHS	*The Works of William H. Seward*, ed. George E. Baker, 5 vols. (Boston: Houghton, Mifflin, 1887–90)
WHSP	*The Papers of William Henry Seward*, Department of Rare Books and Special Collections, University of Rochester

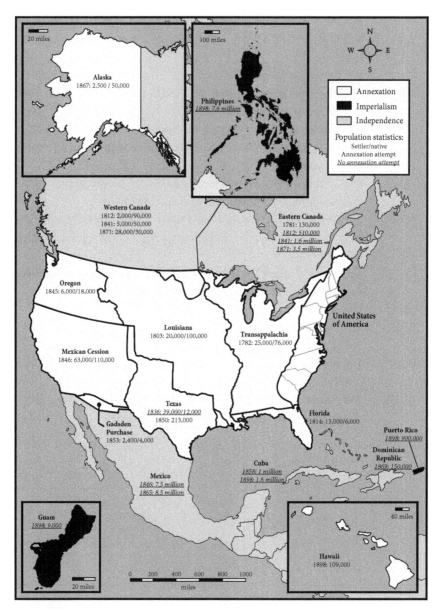

MAP 1. Map of U.S. territorial expansion. Territorial population data sources cited in chapters 3–7.

CHAPTER 1

The Limits of U.S. Territorial Expansion

> Robbery by European nations of each other's
> territories has never been a sin, is not a sin today.
>
> To the several cabinets the several political
> establishments of the world are clotheslines; and a
> large part of the official duty of these cabinets is to
> keep an eye on each other's wash and grab what they
> can of it as opportunity offers.
>
> All the territorial possessions of all the political
> establishments in the earth—including America, of
> course—consist of pilferings from other people's wash.
>
> Mark Twain, 1897

Why did the United States stop annexing territory? Mark Twain's country was ten times larger than the colonies that declared independence in 1776, the result of expansionism by Thomas Jefferson, James Polk, William Henry Seward, and countless other U.S. leaders.[1] Yet since Twain's death in 1910 the United States has made no major annexations. Political scientists and historians alike have highlighted the U.S. shift from territorial expansion to commercial expansion, arguing that transformations in the sources of economic wealth and military power undercut the profitability of further annexations after the mid-nineteenth century. However, this conventional wisdom overstates the importance of material constraints on U.S. expansionism and neglects the main reason U.S. leaders rejected the annexation of their remaining neighbors: its domestic political and normative consequences.

By absorbing external territory into the state, annexation necessarily changes the state. Some of those changes are positive—for example, increasing its future wealth and security by gaining natural resources and population or controlling strategic terrain. These potential benefits may stoke leaders' expansionist ambitions. Yet annexation may also change the state in ways that leaders consider negative—for example, distorting its institutions and demographics in ways that undercut their domestic political influence or their normative goals for the state. Even opportunities to pursue annexation that appear profitable in material terms may be undesirable for leaders who fear these domestic costs.

Two factors made the presidents, secretaries, and congressmen who shaped U.S. foreign policy during the nineteenth century especially sensitive to annexation's domestic costs: democracy and xenophobia. First, they were acutely aware that their democratic institutions left them vulnerable to domestic political shifts resulting from the assimilation of new populations or the admission of new states. At the same time, they valued those democratic institutions enough to grant all major territorial acquisitions an eventual path to statehood, rejecting endless imperialism and militarized rule as threats to democracy at home (at least until 1898). Second, their xenophobia fueled widespread opinions of neighboring peoples as undesirable candidates for U.S. citizenship. As a result, virtually all viewed large foreign populations as deterrents, sources of moral and cultural corruption that would degrade the United States and undermine the popular sovereignty of their existing constituents if annexed.

Together, democracy and xenophobia raised the potential for annexation to impose formidable domestic costs from the moment the Constitution was ratified. This notion—that the factors most profoundly limiting U.S. territorial expansion were in place from the earliest days of the Union—is a provocative one. After all, scholars usually search for the cause of some effect by asking what else changed when that effect appeared. Most previous studies have followed this approach, explaining the end of U.S. annexation by asking what else changed by the late nineteenth century and identifying economic changes like industrialization and globalization or military transformations like nationalism and regional hegemony as the most likely culprits.

Yet in this case it turns out that the answer was present all along: the U.S. pursuit of annexation came to an end not because of any new development but because an old process had run its course. U.S. leaders did not fundamentally change their expansionist calculus in the mid-nineteenth century; rather, they confronted the prospect of annexing neighboring territories episodically as opportunities arose, deciding whether or not to pursue each specific territory based on its material, political, and normative merits. Once they had rejected a neighboring territory, their successors rarely reversed that decision, and one by one each remaining neighbor was either annexed or understood to be better left independent.

In this way U.S. leaders pursued annexation throughout the nineteenth century by picking and choosing from among their potential options until they ran out of desirable targets. Congressional majorities supported presidential efforts to annex areas like Louisiana and California, but they delayed similar efforts in Florida and Texas and defeated efforts to gain more of Mexico and Cuba. Time and again they raised objections to the domestic costs of annexation, and as they crossed their remaining neighbors off their list of viable targets, the practice gradually disappeared from U.S. foreign policy. To recognize that annexation has domestic consequences and that those consequences bear on leaders' decision making is to recognize that in international politics, as in the human diet, you are what you eat. And the United States has always been a picky eater.

What Is Annexation?

Like many terms, "annexation" has often been used in vague and contradictory ways. In this book, consistent with its dictionary definition, annexation refers to the absorption of territory into a state. The most straightforward way to think about annexation is as a subset of territorial expansion, which is itself a subset of the expansion of international influence (table 1.1). Expansionism, or states' pursuit of influence abroad, has attracted consistent interest from international security scholars due to its role in causing wars and shaping the international system.[2] While most forms of expansionism simply aim to increase one state's leverage over another's policies, territorial expansion sees a state claim Westphalian sovereignty over an area beyond its previous borders, declaring itself to be the highest political authority there and proscribing foreign interventions.[3] Territorial expansion may increase the state's economic and military power more efficiently than other forms of expansionism—depending on its administrative and technological abilities to utilize its new territory—which explains why it is simultaneously a coveted foreign policy goal and a potent source of international conflict.[4]

Territorial expansion, in turn, comes in two forms, annexation and imperialism, distinguished by whether the state fully absorbs its new territory or rules it separately and subordinately. A state in international relations, as opposed to U.S. states, is an institutional order that exercises paramount

Table 1.1   Forms of international expansion

Expansion *(of influence beyond the state's borders)*		
Territorial expansion *(claims sovereignty over new territory)*		Nonterritorial expansion *(involves no sovereignty claim)*
Annexation *(absorbs territory into the state)*	Imperialism *(foreign control over effective sovereignty)*	Informal imperialism, regime change, alliances, diplomacy, etc.

political authority and a monopoly on legitimate violence within its borders.[5] Annexation expands that order by integrating new territory within its core protective, extractive, and legislative institutions. This doesn't mean that states are internally homogeneous—no state entirely is—but rather that a state's relationship with the annexed territory comes to mirror its relationship with its other constituent territories. By merging the new territory into the state itself, annexation enables leaders to redefine their national homeland, molding local identities, institutions, and cultural politics to reduce the likelihood of future unrest and maximize deterrent credibility in the eyes of international rivals who might desire to gain that territory for themselves.[6]

In contrast, imperialism establishes "foreign control over effective sovereignty," in Michael Doyle's phrasing.[7] It too involves a new sovereignty claim, but the state rules its empire externally through institutions separate from and subordinate to those governing itself. Imperialism thus represents a state's deepest method of expanding its influence abroad without expanding the institutional order that defines the state itself. Like nonterritorial forms of expansionism, imperialism may function as a precursor to annexation. For example, the United States pursued diplomacy, economic and cultural penetration, regime change, and imperialism in Hawaii before annexing it. But leaders may also pursue imperialism without any intention to annex territory. Those primarily concerned with extracting resources from a territory may prefer imposing institutions designed to streamline that process via imperialism rather than extending their state's more cumbersome legal institutions via annexation. Similarly, leaders whose authority depends on ethnic nationalism may prefer to subordinate areas inhabited by other ethnicities via imperialism rather than compromise the perceived purity of their nation by annexing them.

Distinguishing between annexation and imperialism is crucial to understanding why the United States lost its early appetite for territorial expansion. U.S. leaders tended to think of territorial expansion and annexation as one and the same, imperialism being valid only on a transitional basis to prepare territories for integration into the Union. Leading a country born through anti-imperial revolution and infused with liberal ideology, they widely assumed that any territories they acquired would eventually gain representation either by enlarging existing states within the Union or, as quickly became the norm, by admitting new states to the Union. Most leaders rejected the notion of perpetual imperialism as fundamentally incompatible with American democracy. It emerged as a serious proposition during their debates only when there was widespread agreement that potential statehood was unthinkable, notably with regard to southern Mexico in 1848 and the Philippines in 1898. In other words, when U.S. policymakers considered opportunities for territorial expansion, they considered them first and foremost as opportunities for annexation.

This book seeks to explain why U.S. leaders pursued annexation when and where they did, not why their efforts succeeded or failed. Since annexation extends a state's institutional order over new territory, it cannot occur without conscious implementation by state leaders. There are no accidental annexations. Unlike a balance of power, which may persist for centuries despite great powers' frequent attempts to overturn it and dominate each other, the pursuit of annexation is necessary for its occurrence.[8] Explaining why the United States stopped pursuing annexation can therefore tell us why it stopped annexing territory.

U.S. foreign policy today continues to feature other forms of expansionism, including diplomacy, foreign aid, sanctions, military occupation, regime change, and (in a mostly informal way) imperialism. Its military reaches all corners of the globe, yet the U.S. domestic political system remains limited to part of North America, seemingly invalidating Joseph Stalin's mantra that "everyone imposes his own system as far as his army can reach."[9] For all their rhetoric about creating an "empire of liberty" and fulfilling their "manifest destiny," U.S. leaders annexed far less territory than was feared by neighbors who quaked before the "northern colossus" and European leaders who assumed that further U.S. territorial expansion was "written in the Book of Fate."[10] Why did U.S. leaders stop pursuing annexation?

Why Abandoning Annexation Matters

The reasons why the United States stopped pursuing annexation should interest scholars and students of international relations, diplomatic history, American history, and American politics as well as members of the broader international public. By choosing to pursue only the territories they did, U.S. leaders contradicted typical patterns of great power behavior throughout history, offering intriguing puzzles to theories of international politics. Moreover, their decisions fundamentally shaped the geopolitical, economic, demographic, institutional, and ideological development of the United States across the centuries that followed, with repercussions that continue to echo through its current flaws and virtues. Finally, their rejection of further annexations enabled the creation of the modern international order, and understanding why they did so can help us understand why that order looks the way it does and how long we should expect it to last.

U.S. territorial pursuits differed from typical great power behavior in two major ways: (1) by targeting land rather than people, and (2) by declining as U.S. power grew. Most great powers in history have spent their blood and treasure trying to absorb nearby population centers and their workforces, which could be taxed and conscripted, rather than uninhabited lands requiring extensive settlement in order to yield a profit.[11] They did so with good reason, since population and wealth are the building blocks of military might. Yet U.S. leaders preferred to annex sparsely populated lands like Louisiana and California, expelling many of the inhabitants they found there. Moreover, they intentionally declined opportunities to absorb population centers in eastern Canada, southern Mexico, and the Caribbean despite the impressive material benefits those territories offered. In short, when the United States pursued annexation, its choice of targets reversed the usual great power appetite.

U.S. leaders also broke from historical precedent by abandoning territorial ambitions as their power grew. International politics used to be defined by a quest for conquest: from Alexander and Qin Shi Huang to Genghis Khan and Napoleon, the list of historical conquerors "could go on almost ad infinitum."[12] Those leaders saw increases in their own power as opportunities to conquer and absorb their neighbors, making history trend "toward greater accumulation and concentration."[13] The United States helped reverse that trend, rejecting further annexations even as it rose toward an unprecedented position of global unipolarity. Robert Gilpin's maxim that "as the power of a state increases, it seeks to extend its territorial control" may hold true for the United States if broadly conceived to include spheres of influence and alliances, but it is squarely defied by the pattern of U.S. annexation.[14] In short, the United States converted its wealth into power but stopped translating that power into further territory.[15]

U.S. leaders' decisions to depart from great power precedent in these ways had profound consequences for the development of both the United States and the international system. The course of race relations in the United States is inseparable from early U.S. leaders' decisions to pursue land rather than people, which ensured that they could engineer the demographic future of territories they annexed.[16] Successive generations of U.S. leaders manipulated federal land policies to recreate racial hierarchies on the frontier, promoting the Anglo-American domination of local politics before each new state was admitted to the Union.[17] Denying representation to Native Americans and refusing to annex populous territories like Quebec and Cuba reinforced those hierarchies within the federal government by preventing its early racial, religious, linguistic, and cultural diversification. Those racial hierarchies, in turn, informed the development of virtually all aspects of U.S. society, from civil rights and labor relations to partisanship and liberal ideology, to say nothing of the controversy over the spread of slavery into annexed territories, which ignited sectionalism and the Civil War.[18]

In addition to its demography, U.S. leaders intentionally molded the geopolitical, economic, institutional, and ideological development of their country to match their normative visions. Controlling New Orleans and Florida secured the seaborne trade of the Mississippi River valley, fueling early settlement and economic development, while conquering California ensured U.S. regional hegemony and facilitated trade with Asia. Decisions to pursue or reject annexation shaped the development of executive power (e.g., Jefferson's annexation of Louisiana despite questionable constitutional authority), legislative power (e.g., Congress's annexation of Texas by joint resolution), and judicial power (e.g., the Insular Cases), as well as the relationships among the three branches.[19] U.S. leaders' deliberate refusal to conquer neighboring societies despite their growing wealth and power also fed their self-images as an exceptional nation acting on a higher moral plane than the old empires of Europe.[20]

Beyond their domestic significance, these decisions had global consequences. By removing annexation from the U.S. foreign policy agenda, nineteenth-century U.S. policymakers laid the groundwork for their twentieth-century successors to condemn the practice of conquest internationally. From positions of power after both world wars, U.S. leaders advocated a new international order prohibiting forcible annexation. The United Nations Charter reads, "All members shall refrain . . . from the threat or use of force against the territorial integrity or political independence of any state."[21] This principle came not from nature, heaven, nor international consensus—it came from the United States. Declaring that "no right exists anywhere to hand peoples about from sovereignty to sovereignty as if they were property," President Woodrow Wilson insisted over British objections that the League of Nations Covenant feature a territorial guarantee.[22] Three decades later President Franklin Roosevelt's advisers composed the UN Charter and painstakingly choreographed the San Francisco conference where it was signed.[23] Subsequent presidents gave teeth to the norm against conquest by punishing violators, from the Korean War, when Harry Truman saw "the principles of the United Nations . . . at stake," to the Gulf War, when George H. W. Bush reaffirmed that "the acquisition of territory by force is unacceptable."[24]

The prohibition of conquest drives many other characteristics of the modern world, from how many countries are on the map to how we think about national security and what day-to-day diplomacy looks like. Europe consolidated "from some five hundred more or less independent political units in 1500 to twenty-odd states in 1900," but after World War II that trend reversed, and the number of countries ballooned.[25] In contrast to previous eras, scholars have meaningfully spoken of "trading states" whose diplomacy focuses mostly on peaceful economic coordination rather than hostile security competition.[26] Weak states with valuable resources like oil have been able to translate those resources into wealth and influence instead of being conquered by stronger neighbors, and many countries enjoy sovereignty today despite lacking the institutional and military strength that was once its prerequisite.[27]

Most important of all, the decline of U.S. annexation and the subsequent construction of this international order laid a stronger foundation for international peace than the world had ever seen. Alexander Hamilton observed in *Federalist*, no. 7 that "territorial disputes have at all times been found one of the most fertile sources of hostility among nations," and numerous studies have confirmed his assessment.[28] As other countries joined the United States in renouncing territorial ambitions, those disputes disappeared from entire regions of the world, diminishing the fear of foreign invasion among their inhabitants to an all-time low and allowing leaders to reorient military spending toward counterterrorism and distant interests rather than border defense.[29]

None of these developments was inevitable. The international order as we know it would not exist if twentieth-century U.S. leaders had used their immense resources to pursue conquest instead of outlawing it. Norms and institutions are not physical objects but social constructions, which means they thrive only if powerful advocates abide by them, rally support for them, and keep potential violators in line.[30] It is hard to imagine U.S. leaders spearheading a movement against forcible annexation had they not already ruled out further annexations of their own, a fact which should not be taken for granted given the land hunger of the early United States. As Nuno Monteiro has written, "When the world has a preponderant power, its grand strategy is the most important variable."[31] The world would be a very different place today if annexation remained on the U.S. foreign policy agenda, so the decline of U.S. territorial ambitions should feature prominently in any account of the origins of the modern international system.

Things that are rare are often forgotten. As the great power politics of the Cold War gave way to preoccupations with ethnic conflict and terrorism in the 1990s and 2000s, many people forgot about annexation, which for all its historical importance seemed of little relevance in the modern world.

Then, in the spring of 2014, Russia annexed Crimea, shocking those who had assumed such behavior was a thing of the past. Secretary of State John Kerry exclaimed, "You just don't in the 21st century behave in 19th century fashion."[32] The United States and the European Union levied sanctions against Russia as punishment, confirming expectations that any international territorial aggression would "put pressure on the United States as the dominant state in the system to respond and enforce shared norms against conquest."[33] Such expectations feel natural to us now, but when viewed in historical context they beg the question: Why does the dominant state in the system punish conquerors rather than pursuing conquests of its own?

The Picky Eagle

My central argument is that the domestic consequences of annexation can strongly affect its desirability. U.S. leaders repeatedly rejected the annexation of otherwise attractive targets for fear of their domestic political and normative fallout, even where they saw substantial material benefits ripe for the taking. When debating whether or not to pursue a territory, they often worried about whether its future population would favor themselves or their domestic political rivals once granted representation in federal elections. When they saw that population as fundamentally alien and too dense to be realistically Americanized, they rejected annexation rather than sharing their self-government with people they considered unfit for it. U.S. presidents, secretaries, and congressmen consistently targeted land rather than people because they feared the domestic impact of absorbing large alien populations into their democratic institutions, and they gradually abandoned annexation as they ruled out the desirability of their remaining neighbors. In other words, U.S. territorial ambitions were selective from the start.

Surrounded by weaker Native American tribes and outposts of distant European empires, early U.S. leaders enjoyed remarkable freedom of choice regarding where to expand and when (if ever) to stop. Although they were freer from external constraints than most great powers in history, their authority was based on democratic institutions which guaranteed that adding new states to the Union would alter the balance of power within the federal government, especially if those new states brought sizable populations with them. Accordingly, policymakers quickly began judging territorial opportunities on the basis of their domestic political consequences, and the hardening sectional divide gave rise to an explicit "balance rule" whereby each northern state added to the Union was counterbalanced by a corresponding southern state.

U.S. leaders interpreted the diverse racial, linguistic, cultural, and religious characteristics of nearby populations as evidence of their alien identities, distinguishing them from the Protestant, Anglo-American nation they envisioned and marking them as unfit to share in its self-government. As a result, abnormally for a great power and hypocritically for a nation of immigrants, the United States deliberately rejected the annexation of nearby population centers. Its leaders pursued Transappalachia, Louisiana, Florida, Texas, Oregon, and California specifically because they expected future Anglo-American settlement to overwhelm the relatively few Native Americans living in those territories. In contrast, U.S. leaders balked at opportunities to annex large alien societies in eastern Canada, southern Mexico, Cuba, and the Philippines that were ill-suited to comprehensive resettlement, afraid that assimilating their alien populations would corrupt the United States rather than improve it. Even the few who favored annexation in those cases did so not because they welcomed the inhabitants of those territories, but because they were more optimistic than their opponents about the prospect of Americanizing them.

Contrary to how the decline of U.S. annexation is often represented, nineteenth-century U.S. leaders did not suddenly and categorically abandon territorial expansion in favor of commercial expansion. Instead, they considered opportunities to annex neighboring territories on a case-by-case basis, seizing some and rejecting others, until eventually they had ruled out all of their remaining neighbors. Although their successors would champion an international order outlawing conquest, the history of U.S. territorial expansion is no tale of an altruistic Captain America fighting to make the world a better place. It is a selfish history. For all their talk of liberty and a civilizing mission, the thing most conspicuously absent from U.S. leaders' annexation debates was any genuine interest in sharing self-government with the people they encountered. In the end, the strongest deterrents to U.S. territorial expansion were not formidable militaries but cities full of people that policymakers didn't want in their country.

Nevertheless, U.S. leaders were neither greedy conquerors targeting everything in sight nor calculating materialists seizing every profitable opportunity. Explaining the decline of U.S. annexation requires appreciating that they were driven by a mix of power, institutions, and ideas: excitement about geopolitical opportunities, desires to increase their wealth and power, concerns about the domestic political balance and their own enduring influence over federal policy, visions of the grand republic they sought to build, and colored perceptions of other peoples' identities relative to their own. The history of U.S. territorial expansion is one of leaders expanding where they could while still governing themselves the way they wanted, its limits set largely by their own limited visions for their country's future and their fear of losing control of that future. The eventual result was something truly exceptional in world history: a preeminent global power disinterested in annexing its neighbors. Yet sometimes exceptional results emerge from the basest of causes.

Theories of International Expansionism

Political scientists have largely refrained from studying the pursuit of annexation, preferring to focus on the broader concept of expansionism and implicitly assuming no meaningful causal differences among its various forms. Existing theories have tended to focus on three factors that may limit states' territorial ambitions: capability, security, and profitability. Some theories assume that leaders always desire more territory, expecting them to pursue annexation whenever their capabilities allow and to stop only when forced by internal or external constraints. Others assume that leaders' primary objective is national security, expecting them to pursue annexation only insofar as it advances that goal. The most common view assumes that leaders judge annexation's desirability on the basis of its material profitability, pursuing it whenever the benefits outweigh the costs. Yet despite much productive scholarship on great power politics and increasing interest in the U.S. rise to power, none of these theories offers a compelling explanation for the pattern of U.S. annexation.

Annexing territory is often the most efficient way for states to increase their relative power. This incentive leads some scholars to argue that international leaders should constantly harbor territorial ambitions, pursuing annexation except when prevented from doing so by internal or external constraints. Externally, powerful rivals may constrain leaders by threatening a costly war if they try to seize new territory.[34] Internally, administrative costs resulting from overexpansion may drain too many resources for the state to afford further pursuits.[35] Institutional checks and balances may also deny leaders the capacity to undertake ambitious foreign policy ventures by decentralizing control of foreign policy.[36]

Capability-based arguments are often persuasive where severe constraints exist. After all, no leader can pursue annexation without having the capacity to do so. Compared to their international peers, though, U.S. leaders have been remarkably unconstrained. The United States has almost always been much stronger than its neighbors, becoming comparable to the European great powers by the mid-nineteenth century and surpassing them in the twentieth (fig. 1.1). That U.S. leaders rejected further annexations as their

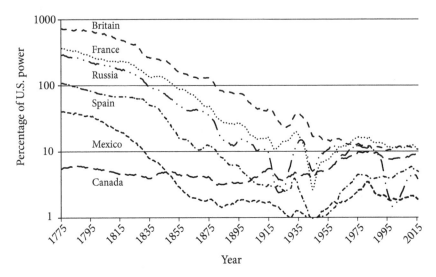

FIGURE 1.1. Adversaries' power as a percentage of U.S. power. Power proxied by net resources (GDP*GDP per capita), using estimated Maddison data from Christopher J. Fariss, Charles D. Crabtree, Therese Anders, Zachary M. Jones, Fridolin J. Linder, and Jonathan N. Markowitz, "Latent Estimation of GDP, GDP per capita, and Population from Historic and Contemporary Sources," https://arxiv.org/pdf/1706.01099.pdf (accessed 11/2/2018); cf. Michael Beckley, "The Power of Nations: Measuring What Matters," *International Security* 43, no. 2 (Fall 2018): 7–44.

relative power grew to such heights makes little sense from the perspective of external constraints. Moreover, European great powers were reluctant to seriously contain U.S. expansion even in its early decades, preferring to conserve their resources for higher priorities in their own region.[37] As British Prime Minister Palmerston wrote in November 1855, "Britain and France would not fight to prevent the United States from annexing Mexico, 'and would scarcely be able to prevent it if they did go to war.'"[38] Since other great powers consistently pursued territory in the face of far more formidable and committed adversaries, it is hard to believe that military deterrence significantly limited U.S. annexation.

Overexpansion did not significantly constrain the United States either. The U.S. economy has never suffered a prolonged decline owing to the maintenance of too broad an empire. On the contrary, U.S. power has grown with remarkable consistency, both during and since its early territorial expansion (table 1.2). Like any other country, the United States has experienced periodic recessions that have temporarily limited the resources available for foreign policy, but such momentary hindrances offer little rationale for a lasting end to U.S. annexation.

Given their prominent role in U.S. domestic politics, institutional checks and balances are a more likely reason, and numerous studies have examined

Table 1.2   Growth in U.S. power, 1775–2015

ERA	GROWTH IN U.S. POWER (%)
1775–1795	58
1795–1815	68
1815–1835	156
1835–1855	175
1855–1875	165
1875–1895	196
1895–1915	188
1915–1935	56
1935–1955	382
1955–1975	275
1975–1995	205
1995–2015	164

Source: Power proxied by net resources (GDP * GDP per capita), using estimated Maddison data from Christopher J. Fariss, Charles D. Crabtree, Therese Anders, Zachary M. Jones, Fridolin J. Linder, and Jonathan N. Markowitz, "Latent Estimation of GDP, GDP per capita, and Population from Historic and Contemporary Sources," https://arxiv.org/pdf/1706.01099.pdf (accessed 11/2/2018).

their impact on U.S. foreign policy. Scott Silverstone describes how the United States refrained from using military force or pursuing territory during numerous crises between 1807 and 1860 because its federal democratic institutions and the diversity of interests they represented made it hard to rally support for ambitious foreign policies, leading Congress to constrain presidential ambitions and presidents to exercise self-restraint.[39] Fareed Zakaria recounts how U.S. leaders failed to translate growing national wealth into broader foreign policy goals between 1865 and 1889 because of "decentralized, diffuse, and divided" institutions, but shifting authority from the states to the federal government and from the legislative to the executive branch meant that between 1889 and 1908 "the executive branch was able to bypass Congress or coerce it into expanding American interests abroad."[40] Jeffrey Meiser describes U.S. foreign policy between 1898 and 1941 as marked by "delay, limitation, prevention, backlash, and retrenchment" due to restraints imposed by the "separation of powers, elections/public opinion, and federalism" as well as anti-imperialist norms.[41] Jack Snyder argues that democratic "checks on concentrated interests that would promote overexpansion" and "public scrutiny of strategic justifications for global intervention" limited U.S. overstretch during the Cold War.[42]

The breadth of historical research contained in these studies persuasively shows that institutional checks and balances have often affected U.S. foreign policy, but it is striking how poorly they explain the country's behavior when the focus is narrowed from expansionism in general to annexation specifically. The federal executive was most constrained (by the state governments) in the early 1800s, precisely during the heyday of westward expansion, and the rise of the "imperial presidency" during the Cold War prompted no revival of U.S. territorial ambitions.[43] If institutional constraints on executive power are primarily responsible for the decline of U.S. annexation, history books should be filled with tales of thwarted presidential plans to annex Canada and Mexico. Yet the record of presidential ambitions on the continent is largely consistent with the annexations that actually occurred. Moreover, institutional checks and balances cannot explain why majorities in Congress enthusiastically supported some potential annexations but rejected others.

Some political scientists have explained why leaders do not always want annexation by assuming that their primary goal is to ensure their state's survival in the anarchic international system. As Sean Lynn-Jones writes, "States attempt to expand when expansion increases their security."[44] Leaders who prioritize national security should pursue annexations that mitigate strategic vulnerabilities while making sure their actions do not provoke costly retaliation or balancing coalitions.[45] John Mearsheimer goes further, arguing that states best ensure their survival by maximizing their own relative power and hence that their leaders should be "bent on establishing regional hegemony."[46] In this view, the marginal security benefits of territorial expansion decline precipitously once regional hegemony is achieved, as leaders shift from conquering nearby rivals to deterring distant adversaries from projecting power against them. Although they disagree how much power makes a state most secure, these perspectives agree that U.S. policymakers lost interest in annexation once their conquest of California prevented Mexico from developing into a peer competitor, effectively guaranteeing long-term national security.

Regional hegemony has been a boon for the United States, yet U.S. leaders were neither consistently expansionist prior to 1848 nor content with refraining from expansion thereafter. Instead, they were reliably picky expansionists, primarily for domestic reasons. The War of 1812 is an especially problematic case for security-driven explanations: rather than work resolutely to eliminate their greatest security threat by driving British forces from Quebec, U.S. leaders proved disinterested in annexing the province despite the fact it represented both the greatest potential source of relative gains and the primary obstacle to U.S. domination of North America. Decades later, they similarly refused to annex southern Mexico and Cuba despite recognizing their geopolitical and economic value. Thus security-based arguments are built on the dubious notion that U.S. policymakers rejected the territories that would have contributed most to their presumed motivation. Moreover, even if regional hegemony diminishes annexation's marginal security returns, a regional hegemon may still benefit from additional resources and geopolitical control. This explains why U.S. leaders continued to pursue Mexican border areas, the Pacific Northwest, and Hawaii after 1848, though not why they refused to annex Cuba (a future base for Soviet power projection against the United States) and opted for imperialism in Puerto Rico and the Philippines.

Why else might leaders lose interest in annexation? The best existing theories hold that modern economic and military transformations have made conquest less profitable.[47] On the economic side, political scientists have identified several transformations that make it harder for conquerors to extract resources from a captured economy. Stephen Brooks describes how the global dispersal of production "means that conquering an advanced country may only result in possession of a portion of the value-added chain," limiting the returns on its annexation.[48] Modern economies are increasingly driven by human capital and information technologies, enabling workers to slash their conqueror's profits by organizing dissent, scuttling their own economies, or fleeing.[49] Conquest also brings greater economic oversight and less available risk capital, stifling innovation and hence productivity.[50] Growing international trade and foreign direct investment have increased access to raw materials across borders, raising the opportunity costs of annexation by making more achievable without it.[51] As Erik Gartzke writes, "If modern production processes de-emphasize land, minerals, and rooted labor in favor of intellectual and financial capital . . . then states can prefer to buy goods rather than steal them."[52]

On the cost side of the ledger, military transformations have made conquest prohibitively expensive. Occupying forces struggle to pacify insurgencies that are not only inspired by nationalism to zealously resist foreign rule but also increasingly lethal due to the spread of small arms.[53] The astronomical deadliness of major war has congealed into a deterrent through memories of past carnage and the potential for even limited aggression to escalate.[54] Nuclear proliferation has purified that deterrence by raising the price of aggression against a nuclear-armed state to annihilation.[55] The unprecedented military power of the United States presents potential aggressors with a more formidable adversary than ever before.[56] Whether or not annexation's economic benefits have decreased, these increased military costs may deter states from pursuing it.

Profitability arguments are not immune to criticism, however. Conquest may impair the productivity of a modern economy, but it is far bolder to claim that this has made conquest entirely undesirable given how much higher productivity is today than ever before.[57] Peter Liberman observes that modern information technologies may facilitate repression as well as dissent, and "industrial societies are cumulative enough that conquerors can greatly increase their mobilizable economic base through expansion."[58] Moreover, globalization may actually proliferate opportunities for annexation by heightening great powers' capabilities and destabilizing less-developed countries.[59]

Major war is a terrifying prospect (especially nuclear war), but that possibility may make small-scale conquests like Russia's 2014 annexation of Crimea easier by deterring forcible retaliation.[60] Even nationalist populations remain conquerable, as in western Europe during World War II, and nationalism can sometimes be manipulated to incite expansionism aimed at unifying a nation across borders or asserting the dominance of one nation over others.[61] The most compelling modern deterrent is the prospect of fighting the formidable U.S. military, but that prospect cannot deter the United States itself from pursuing annexation; if anything, its leaders should be emboldened by their overwhelming might. When it comes to conquest, why don't the watchmen seem to need watching?

Most important, nearly all of the phenomena highlighted by these profitability arguments emerged in the late twentieth century, and thus could not have caused the nineteenth-century decline of U.S. annexation. Nevertheless, the logic of profitability remains viable as a potential explanation thanks to its dependence on leaders' perceptions and calculations. If nineteenth-century U.S. leaders primarily based their decisions on the material benefits and military costs of each opportunity, they may have rejected further annexations as unprofitable well before globalization or nuclear weapons entered the scene. This does not mean that every annexation must have generated a profit; leaders may misjudge opportunities due to misperceptions, biases, or incomplete information.[62] Instead, profitability theory predicts that U.S. leaders facing an opportunity to pursue annexation should have based their decisions on its material profitability as they understood it at the time. This logic represents the current conventional wisdom among scholars of international relations. As Randall Schweller writes, "States expand when . . . it [is] profitable to do so."[63] As a result, profitability theory is the intellectual starting point of this book and the standard against which its contributions must be measured.

The History of U.S. Territorial Expansion

Historians have paid substantial attention to the roles of domestic factors like racism and sectionalism in limiting U.S. territorial expansion, though that attention remains largely confined to studies of specific periods like the Mexican–American War. Broader histories of U.S. expansionism, from the Wisconsin School of the 1960s–1970s to the more recent American Empire literature, have tended to downplay the decline of annexation, stressing instead the continuity of U.S. foreign policy across two centuries. As the newest generation of diplomatic historians focuses largely on twentieth-century phenomena like the Cold War, this tendency continues to overshadow the historiography of U.S. territorial expansion.

Although it has become a problematic generalization, the notion of U.S. foreign policy as continuously expansionist originated with a valuable insight, namely, that imperialism in the Philippines was not a "great aberration" from an otherwise innocent track record of U.S. foreign policy.[64] William Appleman Williams's revision of that prevailing view in the late 1950s inspired numerous students to understand the U.S. shift from territorial to commercial expansion as one of "form" rather than substance.[65] Critics warned that this was oversimplifying. As Stuart Creighton Miller wrote, "Some scholars have not only refused to differentiate between continental and overseas expansion, but also make no distinction between formal empire and the more informal one involving indirect, largely economic, controls that the United States has long exercised in Latin America."[66] Nevertheless, the tendency to conflate diverse forms of expansionism proliferated after 9/11, with a wave of books labeling the Bush administration's War on Terror as the latest symptom of an ever-expanding "American Empire."[67] The United States has never been truly isolationist, and demolishing that pernicious myth has been a valuable contribution, but by overselling continuity in the history of U.S. foreign policy, the American Empire literature has helped obscure meaningful variations within that history.[68]

When historians of U.S. expansionism have offered explanations for the shift from territorial to commercial expansion, they have tended to share political scientists' emphasis on profitability logic.[69] Williams himself argued that that shift was driven by profit: "The agricultural majority . . . was the dynamic element in the shift from continental to overseas empire. . . . The American farmer was a capitalist businessman whose welfare depended upon free access to a global marketplace, and who increasingly demanded that the government use its powers to ensure such freedom of opportunity."[70] Walter LaFeber similarly held that U.S. leaders pursued annexation until industrialization made them "almost entirely interested in markets (not in land)."[71] Others such as Walter McDougall and Frank Ninkovich have more recently highlighted globalization's role in reinforcing the turn to commercial expansion.[72]

In contrast, specialists in the era of Manifest Destiny recognized long ago that racism and sectionalism had limited U.S. leaders' territorial appetites.

As far back as 1963 Frederick Merk argued that westward expansion was not inevitable nor was public opinion united behind it, highlighting the "roadblocks of slavery and race" that prevented the annexation of all Mexico in the 1840s.[73] Reginald Horsman reached a similar conclusion in his 1981 study of Anglo-Saxon racism, noting that the Treaty of Guadalupe Hidalgo "obtained the largest possible area from Mexico with the least number of Mexicans. It was not the problem of the extension of slavery but the Hobson's choice of racial amalgamation or imperial dominion that finally frustrated those who were prepared to take most or all of Mexico."[74] Four years later Thomas Hietala reiterated "the dilemma of desirable lands encumbered by undesirable peoples," recounting, "When a more concentrated nonwhite population inhabited an area, as in Mexico below the Rio Grande or in Cuba, enthusiasm waned because of fears about amalgamation and racial conflict."[75]

These insights have echoed across recent landmark histories emphasizing the role of identity in U.S. foreign policy.[76] Eric Love rebukes prevailing narratives of a late-nineteenth-century "white man's burden" in *Race Over Empire*, arguing that "political and legal questions of alien, nonwhite citizenship . . . unsettled imperialists and made many anti-imperialists."[77] David Hendrickson highlights the centrifugal forces unleashed by potential expansion into Canada, Texas, and Mexico while examining debates over U.S. identity in *Union, Nation, or Empire*.[78] Analyzing federal land policies that encouraged Anglo-Saxon settlement, Paul Frymer observes in *Building an American Empire* that "fighting over the domestic institutional balance" and "white racism ultimately served to limit American expansion almost as frequently as it promoted it."[79] As implied by these studies of racism and sectionalism in U.S. history, but contrary to enduring myth, the United States did not transition cleanly from an early period of territorial expansion to a later focus on commercial expansion.[80] The limits of U.S. territorial expansion fell into place episodically as leaders faced opportunities to annex neighboring territories and decided to seize some but reject others.

The Structure of the Book

This section offers a roadmap to the chapters that follow, including brief surveys of the historiographical state of the art for each of the five case study chapters, highlighting theory-relevant areas of established consensus that those chapters reaffirm as well as enduring debates or gaps where they make fresh historiographical contributions. Chapter 2 lays out my theory of annexation, suggesting that leaders often decide whether or not to pursue annexation on the basis of its domestic consequences as well as its material benefits and military costs. Although leaders usually like to increase their state's relative power, doing so would be counterproductive if it undermines their control of state policy or their goals for the state itself. These domestic costs are particularly severe for democratic leaders annexing large alien societies, driving U.S. leaders to routinely view them as undesirable targets. The chapter concludes by deriving testable predictions and discussing the methodology used in the chapters that follow, which investigate why U.S. leaders chose to pursue the annexation of some territories but not others across twenty-three case studies between 1774 and 1898.

Chapter 3 examines the successful efforts to acquire European titles to Transappalachia, Louisiana, and Florida. As theoretical tests, these cases offer within-case evidence for the importance of domestic considerations in the sectional divisions over Louisiana and Florida, which promised domestic benefits to the Virginia Dynasty but costs to Northern Federalists, in contrast to the broadly popular pursuit of Transappalachia, which threatened minimal domestic costs under the loose institutional structure of the Articles of Confederation. These acquisitions are well documented, resulting in scholarly consensus on key findings like the risks U.S. negotiators took in demanding Transappalachia over their allies' objections, President Thomas Jefferson's economic and geopolitical motivations for pursuing New Orleans and Florida, and Northern Federalists' opposition to those annexations.[81] As a result, the greatest historiographical contributions of the chapter lie in emphasizing certain theory-relevant factors that often go underappreciated. For example, many histories of U.S. expansion begin in 1783 or later, overlooking expansionism during the Revolution.[82] Even studies that address Transappalachia often undersell the contrasting domestic implications of its acquisition, which occurred prior to the Constitution's ratification, and those of the other territories that followed.[83] Treatments of the Louisiana Purchase and the Florida cession disagree as to whether presidents Thomas Jefferson, James Madison, and James Monroe deserve substantial credit for orchestrating those annexations or whether they were primarily driven by local or foreign actors.[84] Although both acquisitions were notably facilitated by events beyond their control, I read all three presidents as uncompromising in their long-term southward ambitions and opportunistic in their expansionist policies.

Chapter 4 studies the U.S. pursuit of Native American lands between the administrations of George Washington and Andrew Jackson. As theoretical tests, these cases reveal how federal leaders' domestic incentives shifted with the rise of frontier states, driving later administrations to abandon their predecessors' plans for tribal assimilation and instead enforce removal.

Historians have thoroughly examined federal civilization and removal policies, but the timing and causal responsibility for the change from one to
the other remains subject to debate.[85] Whereas many accounts emphasize
removal as Jackson's legacy, this chapter follows those that take a longer view
of its emergence, locating removal's origin as a concept with Jefferson, as
common practice with Madison's deference to frontier leaders, and as federal
policy with Monroe.[86] In contrast to accounts that describe removal as an
inevitable consequence of U.S. military dominance over the tribes, this chapter sees U.S. power as an enabling factor rather than a deterministic one.[87]
It locates the driving cause of removal in the domestic costs of assimilation
for frontier leaders, which lay dormant in the early federal government but
boiled over once a critical mass of frontier states had been admitted to the
Union.

Chapter 5 considers six major opportunities to annex territory in Canada:
the revolutionary pursuit of Quebec, the War of 1812, the crises of 1837–42,
the Oregon controversy, the Fenian raids, and the push for the Pacific Northwest. As theoretical tests, these cases cast doubt on profitability theory by
revealing how U.S. leaders pursued sparsely populated western Canada while
repeatedly declining to annex populous eastern Canada. Historians have not
neglected the 1775 Quebec campaign, but this chapter pays particular attention to the endurance of U.S. northward ambitions throughout the Revolutionary War and the domestic political differences between this case and
those that follow.[88] The War of 1812 is frequently misrepresented as expansionist despite the opposite consensus among period specialists, and this
chapter highlights its significance as the first time U.S. leaders consciously
declined a profitable opportunity to pursue annexation.[89] The chapter also
offers a useful contrast between President James Polk's Oregon diplomacy,
which has received substantial attention, and U.S. reactions to the crises of
1837–42, which have gone relatively understudied as a negative case of U.S.
territorial expansion.[90] That said, its greatest historiographical contributions
fall in the post–Civil War period, which, except for the purchase of Alaska,
is often ignored. In contrast, this chapter scrutinizes U.S. responses to the
Fenian raids and the Red River rebellion, and it contributes new archival
research on Secretary of State William Henry Seward's ambitions for British
Columbia.[91]

Chapter 6 turns to six major opportunities to annex territory in Mexico: the Texas Revolution, the annexation of Texas, the Mexican–American
War, the all-Mexico debate, the antebellum period, and the Maximilian affair.
As noted above, specialists in these cases have led the way in revealing how
domestic considerations limited U.S. territorial pursuits. Northern opposition

to the spread of slavery delayed and nearly prevented the U.S. annexation of Texas, circumscribed U.S. ambitions during the Mexican–American War, and curtailed southern expansionism in the 1850s.[92] Xenophobia took center stage in deterring the annexation of densely populated southern Mexico, solidifying U.S. perceptions of Mexico as a distinct nation that should remain independent.[93] This chapter gives greater consideration to the expansionist ambitions of independent Texas than most studies, but the wealth of previous research on these cases means that its greatest historiographical contributions fall in the Civil War period, where my archival research uncovered more overt opportunities for expansion into Mexico than are typically recognized.

Chapter 7 investigates the potential annexations of Cuba before the Civil War, the Dominican Republic afterward, and Cuba, Hawaii, Puerto Rico, the Philippines, and Guam in 1898. The first case study builds on Robert May's impressive research on southern expansionism, reinforcing his initial observations of sectionalism and racism as obstacles to the annexation of Cuba in the 1850s.[94] Whereas many studies emphasize institutional checks and balances in recounting how Congress prevented President Ulysses Grant from annexing the Dominican Republic, my second case study builds on Eric Love's work to highlight the xenophobia that fueled congressional opposition.[95] Period specialists agree that it was neither yellow journalism nor the explosion of the U.S.S. *Maine* that drove U.S. leaders to declare war on Spain in 1898, as is often caricatured, but scholars continue to debate whether the resulting expansionism was more a product of the war itself or of the culmination of long-gestating pressures for penetration into Asia and the Caribbean.[96] The chapter's third case study challenges histories that emphasize continuity between earlier continental expansion and 1898 by questioning why Congress specifically refused to target Cuba for annexation, despite its being the primary cause and theater of the war as well as an attractive target for early U.S. leaders. Where many histories of Hawaiian annexation discuss racism as a justification, via social Darwinism or white man's burden ideologies, the fourth case study goes further than most studies in examining how xenophobia fueled annexation's opponents in Congress.[97] Finally, the fifth case study builds on inquiries into the role of racism in U.S. policy toward the Philippines as well as the explosion of scholarship on Puerto Rico's legal status, which has produced a strong consensus that U.S. leaders manufactured the category of unincorporated territories to retain sovereignty over islands inhabited by people they viewed as unfit for U.S. citizenship.[98]

Chapter 8 summarizes the book's findings and explores its implications for U.S. foreign policy and international relations. The accumulated evidence strongly suggests that democracy and xenophobia worked together to undercut U.S. leaders' interest in annexing their remaining neighbors, a conclusion which should inform our debates regarding American exceptionalism, benign hegemony, informal imperialism, and the apparent contradiction between U.S. liberal ideals and illiberal policies. These dynamics likely extend to other countries beyond the United States—a fruitful area for further research—with consequences for how we think about the sources of international territorial ambitions, the democratic peace, and the origins and sustainability of the norm against conquest. In the end, this book resolves a central puzzle of international relations: why did the United States stop annexing territory? And it does so in a way that contributes to our understanding of American history, undercuts enduring myths of U.S. altruism, and bridges a key logical gap in prominent histories of U.S. expansionism by explaining why U.S. foreign policy has continued to expand since 1898 but U.S. territory has not.

CHAPTER 2

Explaining Annexation

> Victory as well as defeat can set off undesired domestic changes within the state.
>
> Robert Jervis, 1978

Why did U.S. leaders stop annexing territory? My answer is that annexation's domestic consequences heavily influenced its desirability. I develop that argument here into a theory of annexation that I call *domestic impact theory*. In its broadest form domestic impact theory suggests that leaders will take any significant domestic consequences into account when deciding which foreign policy to pursue. More specifically, if a certain policy is likely to change the state's institutions or demographics in ways that affect a leader's domestic political influence or normative goals for the state, that leader will treat those changes as costs or benefits of that policy when deciding whether or not to pursue it. A policy's domestic impact is not the only factor driving leaders' decisions, but it should weigh heavily on their deliberations over any foreign policy that carries meaningful domestic consequences, as annexation often does. U.S. leaders' concerns about domestic costs, heightened by the interaction of democracy and xenophobia, limited their pursuit of annexation by rendering many profitable opportunities undesirable.

This chapter proceeds through five sections. The first describes why leaders find annexation appealing in the first place: it is often the most efficient way to increase state power. Assuming leaders would generally like to increase their power, the interesting question is not why they have territorial ambitions but why they would ever reject opportunities for annexation.

The second section explores why even leaders who desire annexation cannot always pursue it: the military costs of overcoming local and international opposition. Together, these two sections illustrate the conventional wisdom, which explains the causes and limits of annexation as rooted in its material profitability.

The third section adds domestic consequences to this calculus, explaining why even profitable annexation may be undesirable. Annexation may generate domestic costs for leaders in two major ways: by weakening their influence over state policy and by worsening the state vis-à-vis their envisioned ideal. The fourth section examines two factors that exacerbate those domestic costs: democracy, which increases leaders' vulnerability to demographic changes and concern for popular sovereignty, and xenophobia, which drives leaders to disdain the traits and interests of people they see as alien. Democracy and xenophobia are each capable of generating formidable domestic costs from annexation. When combined, they transform otherwise attractive opportunities into an impossible choice between corrupting society and undermining democracy.

The fifth section derives specific predictions from domestic impact theory regarding how U.S. leaders should behave when facing opportunities to pursue annexation, contrasting them with profitability theory's predictions and setting the stage for the chapters that follow.

Annexation and Power

Annexation has been endemic throughout human history because leaders value power, defined here as the ability to employ resources in pursuit of goals. They exercise power through the state, commanding a portion of society's resources in its name as authorized by its domestic political institutions. Controlling state policy enables leaders to pursue far grander goals than any individual could hope to achieve acting alone, but the finiteness of state resources necessarily limits their practical ambitions. As Theda Skocpol writes, "State officials are most likely to try to do things that seem feasible with the means at hand."[1] Leaders who wish to pursue grander goals with a reasonable hope of success must find a way to further increase their power, and hence amassing power itself is often a central goal of state leaders.[2] Increasing state power does not guarantee that all of a leader's goals will be achieved, but it does enlarge the set of goals that leaders can hope to achieve—the strongest states can profoundly shape international relations within their region and beyond.[3]

Power-hungry leaders have two options: they can either extract more wealth from their existing society or extract the same percentage from a wealthier society. The former is more immediate but may carry dangerous long-term costs. Extracting a higher percentage of private wealth for state use diverts resources away from future economic development; a larger slice of the pie today means a smaller pie tomorrow. Higher taxation also risks provoking unrest and undermining leaders' authority. Extracting more is therefore best reserved for emergencies, when an urgent threat warrants sacrificing future growth and persuades the public to willingly contribute.

Prudent leaders increase their power by making their society wealthier, simultaneously increasing the government budget, domestic political support, public happiness, and resources available for future emergencies. Since leaders always have this incentive, though, opportunities for additional gains through internal efforts are usually few and far between.[4] Domestic strategies aimed at encouraging childbirth, modernization, worker productivity, or military spending are inherently limited by state capacities and require decades to produce significant results. Instances of the most rapid internal development can be found in states with large populations lagging behind the frontier of modernity, which succeeded by copying the technologies and practices of their more highly developed peers. For example, Stalin forced the Soviet Union through industrialization before World War II, bearing terrible human costs to quadruple the size of the Soviet industrial economy in ten years.[5] Similarly, China's rise into the twenty-first century was fueled by the decades-long modernization of its enormous population.[6]

In contrast to internal efforts, annexing external territory offers the prospect of enhancing state power rapidly and with lasting effect. Sovereignty is based on territorial borders, limiting the physical resources leaders can harness and hence their state's maximum potential power.[7] Annexing new territory adds its population to the state's workforce and its natural resources to the state's warehouse, increasing its potential power beyond previous limitations. Moreover, this growth can be achieved as swiftly as administrative control is extended over the new territory. Annexation can raise state power to previously unattainable heights, and the leaders who pursue it can expect to wield that power themselves.

Historically, population rather than natural resources has been the primary target of international territorial ambitions.[8] Populous lands are more valuable than sparsely populated ones because they offer a preexisting taxable economy and an employable labor force, whereas extracting resources from lands with few people requires extensive settlement and investment beyond the cost of acquisition. This pattern has been visible in regions of sparse population and low development, where the scarcity of agency heightens its value. Precolonial Africa saw power defined explicitly in terms of controlled population, and international boundaries shifted with the operational range of militaries.[9] Similarly, James Scott writes that in precolonial Southeast Asia "wars were more often about rounding up captives and settling them near the central court than asserting a territorial claim."[10] Dense societies are even more valuable. China's concentrated population was prized by would-be conquerors from Kublai Khan in the thirteenth century to Toyotomi Hideyoshi in the sixteenth, and Europe's tremendous development between the seventeenth and twentieth centuries made it the ultimate prize until it was joined by the industrializing North America, Russia, East Asia, and the Middle East.[11]

The Profitability of Annexation

Given its potential benefits, why doesn't annexation always top every leader's foreign policy agenda? The most common answer relies on the notion that "the strong conquer the weak because it pays."[12] If the strong do not always conquer the weak, the thinking goes, then it stands to reason that conquest must not always pay. If the main lures of annexation are material benefits like population and natural resources, leaders should reject annexation where they anticipate losing more in its pursuit than they would gain by its achievement. In other words, annexation is desirable only where it is profitable.

Attempts at annexation often generate military costs from two sources: local leaders unwilling to sacrifice their sovereignty and rival states bristling at their peer's sudden growth. Since territory is scarce, one state's expansion is another's contraction, and local leaders in the target territory usually face domestic and international incentives to preserve their independence by any means necessary. A territorial loss would not only spark accusations of weakness from their political opponents but also impair their ability to resist greater predations in the future.[13] Local resistance to perceived foreign rule may also impose ongoing military costs after annexation. Moreover, rival states may fight to prevent annexation rather than allow an enlarged adversary to wield greater resources against them in the future. Where states have competing interests, after all, one state's empowerment is another's impediment. Between local and international resistance, pursuing annexation often requires formidable military costs.

If leaders think annexation's military costs exceed its material benefits, they should reject it as a game not worth the candle. This is the central insight of profitability theory, though a fair reading leaves room for individual leaders to disagree about the size and salience of many factors that may bear on their decisions. How leaders value a territory's population, natural resources, current wealth and productivity, future economic potential, and strategic geography; how they assess the scope of local resistance, the likelihood of foreign intervention, their own military prowess, and the long-term costs of alienating other countries by their actions—these considerations and more may be grounds for debate, so empirical tests should pay attention to leaders' perceptions in addition to physical realities.[14] Yet despite the fact that leaders' perceptions may be muddled or misinformed or may change over time, profitability theory is clear in predicting that their decisions whether or not to pursue a territory should be based on how they weigh its material benefits against the costs of acquisition. This logical clarity makes profitability theory an attractive conventional wisdom. After all, why would leaders decline easy opportunities to gain valuable territory?

Annexation's Domestic Consequences

This conventional wisdom overlooks the fact that even profitable annexations may be undesirable for domestic reasons. Domestic impact theory relaxes profitability theory's assumption that leaders primarily concern themselves with national material interests—in other words, that the state resembles a unitary rational actor. Instead, it recognizes that leaders often pursue goals that are subnational or ideational. In doing so, my theory helps unravel the paradox of how annexation may simultaneously increase state resources yet make it harder for leaders to achieve their goals. To repeat the warning of Robert Jervis cited in the epigraph to this chapter, "Victory as well as defeat can set off undesired domestic changes within the state."[15]

Annexation necessarily changes the state in ways that some leaders may desire but others may not, and these domestic costs and benefits influence whether leaders find annexation itself desirable. Two types of domestic costs, weakening and worsening, may override annexation's material benefits in leaders' minds. The severity of these costs—and hence the likelihood that leaders will reject a potential annexation for fear of them—depends on their state's domestic political institutions and their perceptions of the target population's identity.

Weakening

If a potential annexation threatens to weaken a leader's influence over state policy, even while promising to increase state power, that leader may prefer retaining control of the state as it is rather than handing over a more power-ful state to domestic political opponents. Who controls state policy depends on domestic political institutions that warp as they stretch over annexed territory, and these distortions strengthen some leaders while weakening others. As Rogers Smith writes, "Political struggles can be won by altering existing civic boundaries in ways that add or strengthen friends and expel or weaken foes."[16]

Some leaders may expect that annexing a certain territory will bolster their control of the state. If its population shares core interests with their existing constituents, annexation may expand the size of their domestic polit-ical base. It may also reinforce their existing domestic support by generating spoils for their constituents, such as access to resources or land. If the terri-tory features in their nationalist mythology, leaders might hope to translate its annexation into a broader wave of nationalist support. Leaders in fragile domestic political positions should especially value annexations that promise to reunify a fractured governing coalition or prevent their impending fall from power. Annexations that promise such domestic political benefits may thus have a similar appeal to diversionary wars, possibly with longer-lasting effects.[17]

On the other hand, leaders may be reluctant to annex a certain territory because it would weaken their domestic political position. Sizable annexa-tions tend to increase the number of territorial subunits within the state and hence the number of officials overseeing them, mathematically reduc-ing the relative influence of each. More domestic political actors may also represent more diverse interests, threatening increased competition for any one agenda and rendering the government a less cohesive corporate actor. As Dietrich Rueschemeyer and Peter Evans write, even powerful states can be brought to a standstill "when strong and divergent forces in civil society are bent on capturing parts of the state apparatus and using them for their purposes."[18] More significantly, if leaders expect the territory's population to harbor interests incompatible with their own, they may fear that annexa-tion would allow local elites to undermine their rule. Fragile leaders should especially dread the prospect of local elites teaming up with their domestic political opponents to drive them from office.

Since these considerations play out in the minds of leaders who are deciding whether or not to pursue annexation, they concern the territory's population not as it currently is but as leaders expect it to be in the future, including any voluntary or compulsory postannexation migrations. For example, U.S. leaders frequently anticipated removing Native Americans, legalizing slavery, or expelling foreign laborers as they weighed the domestic consequences of annexing particular territories.

In short, leaders may reject annexation because they fear ending up like the sorcerer's apprentice, whose pursuit of power caused him to lose control of that power.[19] Rational leaders should pursue annexation where it promises to increase state power while reinforcing their domestic political authority, but not where it threatens to weaken their influence over state policy. After all, leaders can usually advance their goals better by governing their current state than by losing control of a stronger one.

Worsening

Unlike weakening, which concerns leaders' control of the state, worsening concerns their goals for it. If leaders value power as a means to pursue their goals, and if those goals include a vision for the future of their state itself, then potential annexations may carry positive or negative normative value. Leaders should oppose annexations that threaten to impose changes that move it further away from their envisioned ideal, preferring to maintain their current better state rather than create a stronger but worse state.[20]

One way annexation can have normative effects is by distorting the state's domestic political institutions. As discussed above, annexation stretches the state's domestic institutions over new territory, and leaders may frown on the associated institutional changes if they undermine previous notions of legitimacy, distributions of authority, or traditional domestic hierarchies. Even changes of scale alone may raise objections. For instance, early U.S. leaders who had read Montesquieu's *Spirit of the Laws* worried that the sheer size of the United States would undermine its republican government, which they ideologically revered, especially as it absorbed vast Transappalachia and Louisiana.[21] If leaders expect annexation to worsen their state's social and political institutions, they should weigh those changes as meaningful costs when deciding whether or not to pursue it.

Ideologies speak not only to what the ideal state should look like but also to how it should behave. Accordingly, annexation may generate normative costs both by its institutional consequences and by the way it is achieved. Where the pursuit of annexation would involve behavior that leaders consider immoral, that moral weight may factor into their decision making. John Quincy Adams and William Henry Seward famously opposed the practice of military conquest, preferring to annex territory after a popular referendum favoring such action. Growing abolitionism in the decades before the Civil

War similarly inspired many northern leaders to reject on moral grounds any annexations that would spread the practice of slavery.

Annexation may also generate normative costs if leaders see their state as embodying the will of a particular nation. Leaders have strong incentives to arouse nationalism within domestic society because it motivates citizens to support their policies and enables impressive capabilities, such as a mass army.[22] Nationalism is inherently exclusive, however, defining at once who belongs to a nation and who does not. Its core tenet, that the borders of nation and state should align, implies that annexation improves the state only when it brings those borders closer together, a normative view that may reduce the appeal of annexing other nations.[23] Jerry Muller attributes the territorial stability of Western Europe after World War II to its consolidation of relatively coherent ethnonational borders during the preceding centuries.[24] Since annexing a territory entails absorbing its population into domestic society, leaders who see no place for that population in their ideal state may reject the prospect of annexing that territory.

As in the case of weakening, this mechanism can be reversed: leaders may favor an annexation because they expect it to contribute to the fuller realization of their ideal state. Nationalism may drive leaders to target territories that feature prominently in their national mythology or are populated by those who share their defining national characteristics.[25] For example, the Anschluss movement after World War I aimed to unify German-speaking peoples, and Adolf Hitler exploited its ideology to legitimize his annexation of Austria. Similarly, Vladimir Putin explained his annexation of Crimea by saying, "Crimea has always been an integral part of Russia in the hearts and minds of people."[26]

In summary, the logic of worsening asks why leaders would want to annex a territory that would move their state further away from their own vision for it. If annexation's appeal lies in empowering leaders to pursue their goals more effectively, then they should shun any annexation that would inherently undermine those goals. Therefore, any normative effects leaders see in potential annexations should factor into their decision making.

The Severity of Domestic Costs

The severity of annexation's domestic costs for leaders depends both on their state's domestic political institutions, which dictate the form of integration between the state and annexed territory, and on how they perceive the target population's identity, which informs their expectations regarding its future political behavior and their judgments of its normative appeal.

Both democracy and xenophobia increase the likelihood that leaders will fear weakening themselves and worsening their state through annexation. In combination, these two factors can make even highly profitable acquisitions a nonstarter.

Democracy

Although it is widely respected for making leaders accountable to their citizens, democracy has a hotly debated relationship with foreign policy. Many scholars argue that it affects the methods states use to pursue foreign policy, most prominently in the assertion that democracies rarely if ever fight wars with each other.[27] Others argue that it affects states' foreign policy success, claiming, for example, that democracies are better than autocracies at choosing or fighting wars.[28] Some scholars think democracies tend to choose wiser policies due to institutional checks and public debate, while others echo George Kennan's quip that democracies resemble "one of those prehistoric monsters with a body as long as this room and a brain the size of a pin."[29]

This book examines democracy's effect on a state's foreign policy goals rather than its methods or success. For present purposes, democracies are states in which leaders' authority to command state resources depends on regular, free and fair public elections, while autocracies are states in which leaders' authority is not subject to regular public checks. This definition follows previous research on the relationship between regime type and foreign policy behavior in being relatively minimalist.[30] Other characteristics such as universal suffrage, freedoms of speech, assembly, religion, etc. affect the breadth and quality of democratic representation, but all leaders who are subject to genuine elections should face more profound domestic costs from annexation than those who are not. Annexation changes the makeup of society and hence of the electorate, thereby altering democratic politics in ways that autocratic leaders can more easily mitigate. As a result, democratic leaders should be particularly concerned with potential domestic costs when considering opportunities to pursue annexation.

First, annexation is more likely to weaken democratic leaders than autocratic leaders. Owing their office to elections, democratic leaders' continuing authority depends on maintaining favor among their constituents. Moreover, their ability to effectively wield state resources requires a coalition of like-minded leaders across institutional veto points that are themselves subject to electoral politics. Therefore, demographic changes which alter the electorate directly affect democratic leaders' ability to maintain control of the state.

Since annexation by a democracy extends domestic political representation to the territory's population, democratic leaders may anticipate domestic political benefits if that population seems likely to support their bloc. If it appears likely to support rival candidates, however, pursuing annexation may put their continued rule at risk.

In contrast, autocratic leaders are institutionally equipped to annex territory without weakening their domestic political authority. Autocratic governments centralize policymaking at the highest level, allowing their leaders to subordinate annexed populations under existing hierarchical structures while maintaining tight control over state policies. Ruling at the pleasure of a relatively narrow selectorate, autocratic leaders can more easily delegate authority over annexed territories and divide spoils among their lieutenants, thereby strengthening their domestic control.[31] When problems arise, autocratic leaders frequently resort to persecuting political challengers and repressing disobedient groups. Since they are less vulnerable to demographic changes than their democratic counterparts, autocratic leaders have less reason to fear that annexation will weaken their rule.

Second, democratic leaders are more likely than autocratic leaders to fear that annexation will worsen their state. If they subscribe to a liberal ideology, for example, they are more likely to value democracy itself and hence more likely to have genuine concern for popular sovereignty.[32] This concern may make them reluctant to pursue annexation via undemocratic means, such as where a local majority opposes it (violating that population's self-determination) or where it would require long-term martial law (threatening democracy at home). Democratic leaders' preoccupation with popular sovereignty may also make them reluctant to annex populations they see as belonging to different nationalities, since allowing those populations to share in their self-government would dilute the popular sovereignty of their own perceived nation.

Autocratic leaders are less likely to fear that annexation will worsen their state because they can more aggressively coerce society without compromising the institutions underwriting their authority. Unconcerned with popular sovereignty, their ideologies are more likely to facilitate the subordination of peoples and the forcible maintenance of local order. They may even look to achieve domestic political benefits when cracking down on local uprisings by rallying the nation against a purported rebel threat. By following annexation with subjugation rather than with domestic political representation, even autocratic leaders who look down on foreign nationalities may be less concerned than democratic ones that their annexation would worsen the state. Ideologies of superiority, which seek to legitimize the domination of one nationality over others within the same state, are institutionally consistent with autocratic hierarchies but fundamentally inconsistent with democracy. This mismatch does not preclude their use within democratic states, but it does make democratic leaders more likely to see them as carrying real normative costs and long-term domestic risks.

This discussion is not meant to suggest that all autocracies are cut from the same cloth or that autocratic leaders are free from domestic constraints. An important emerging literature demonstrates the opposite.[33] Rather, it is to observe that autocratic leaders share institutional abilities and incentives that democratic leaders do not, enabling them to minimize the risk of weakening and worsening as a result of annexation. They may therefore calculate annexation's desirability more purely in terms of profitability than democratic leaders, who have more to lose from domestic costs.

Skeptics may suggest that democracy should make annexation easier. After all, people who find themselves absorbed into a democracy should be freer, happier, and less likely to rebel than people conquered by a dictator who will brutally punish them for stepping out of line.[34] This argument returns to the logic of profitability, speculating that annexation's military costs (not domestic ones) should be lower for democracies welcoming eager newcomers than for autocracies oppressing unwilling subjects. Moreover, it is unconvincing for three reasons. First, in an age of widespread nationalism, we should expect most states to resist annexation by a foreign power regardless of that power's regime type. Second, local elites can usually guarantee their privileged status better by remaining independent, but they may prefer becoming an autocrat's lieutenant rather than losing power through elections. Third, even if a population happily joins a democracy, the same mechanism that reduces annexation's military costs (political representation) also produces the domestic costs described above. Indeed, the notion that domestic costs can outweigh material factors is the very crux of domestic impact theory.

Others may suspect that this focus on democracy remains incomplete without more attention to federalism, which profoundly shaped U.S. leaders' institutional powers as well as the domestic political role of territories annexed by the United States. The U.S. government's federal structure dictated how much geographic representation was required to exercise veto power over federal policy, that is, the number of congressmen and senators required to pass or block foreign policy legislation as well as the anticipated nationwide electoral support won or lost for a president or political party by pursuing a given foreign policy venture. Federal institutions also shaped the domestic political salience of each new state for leaders of the others by dictating its effects on the distribution of interests in Congress and in presidential elections. As Scott Silverstone writes, "This federal principle defines the character of its competing interests and provides the institutional mechanisms necessary for the expression of diverse territorial interests at the national level."[35]

Federalism undeniably shapes how weakening and worsening manifest themselves. Through the lens of domestic impact theory, however, its effects were more a matter of form than of function: helping determine where the lines of domestic political contention were drawn and what interests and ideas resonated with particular leaders. Like the separation of powers, the traditional two-term limit on the presidency, and the independent press, sectional economic interests and moral convictions helped determine how each potential target appealed to specific leaders and which domestic political coalitions could be formed in response to each annexation opportunity. That said, the causal logic of domestic impact theory hinges on the domestic political representation of annexed populations, so we should not expect leaders of a federal autocracy to worry about annexation's domestic costs nearly as much as leaders of a nonfederal democracy.

This contention—that democratic leaders may find even profitable opportunities for annexation undesirable due to their domestic consequences—is distinct from previous theories of democratic foreign policy restraint. As I noted in chapter 1, several prominent books have argued that democratic checks and balances constrain executive power, preventing leaders from translating their territorial ambitions into foreign policy.[36] In contrast, domestic impact theory suggests that democratic leaders frequently harbor no territorial ambitions at all and that those who do are highly selective regarding their targets. Institutional constraints may explain why policy does not reflect a specific leader's personal ambitions, but domestic costs can explain why that leader holds limited ambitions in the first place.

Domestic impact theory also offers a relatively fresh twist on the relationship between ideology and foreign policy, proposing that the normative value U.S. leaders assigned to democracy helped generate annexation's domestic costs by molding their domestic goals. Most previous studies relating liberalism to foreign policy argue that it shapes leaders' views of acceptable behavior, driving liberal leaders to respect other nations' sovereignty as the international equivalent of individual freedom, which liberalism values above all else.[37] Such arguments are vulnerable to prominent counterexamples, however, including the overseas empires of democratic Britain and France as well as U.S. regime change operations targeting democracies, pursued covertly, and executed by presidents as liberal as Woodrow Wilson.[38]

Moreover, it is far from philosophically clear why liberalism should champion sovereignty. Major works of liberal political theory have repeatedly treated international sovereignty as analogous to individual liberty, yet the two are logically at odds: if all states have equal influence over global affairs, then the liberty of each individual is diluted proportionate to its state's population.[39] Thus the principle of individual liberty would be best realized not by a world of independent democracies, but by a unified global democracy with internal institutions protecting minorities against a tyranny of the majority.[40] Far from prohibiting it, liberalism justifies annexation by democracies in order to broaden the scope of political representation.[41] We take it for granted today that U.S. leaders want to spread democracy to other countries rather than absorb other countries into their democracy, but from the perspective of individual liberty this is logically backward. Domestic impact theory suggests that this paradox stems not from their ideological respect for other countries' sovereignty, but from the institutionally and ideologically rooted domestic costs of assimilating others.

Xenophobia

The second factor that exacerbates annexation's domestic costs is xenophobia, fear and disdain for people seen as foreign.[42] When deciding whether or not to annex a territory, xenophobia drives leaders to gauge its domestic costs by examining the number and identity of its inhabitants, distinguishing between kindred people—those who share their salient characteristics, principles, and practices—and others whom they see as alien. Xenophobic leaders expect kindred people to assimilate seamlessly into their vision for the state, but they treat alien societies with suspicion as threatening formidable long-term political and normative challenges.

One way to think about identities is as inherent indicators of expected action: we identify who people are by categorizing them on the basis of relatively stable, observable characteristics, and we use those categories to predict how people are likely to behave in a given situation.[43] We expect Catholics but not Buddhists to attend Mass; Americans but not Brazilians to sing along when "The Star-Spangled Banner" is played; and policemen to move toward the sound of a gunshot but civilians to move away. In other words, we expect ourselves and others to act in ways that are appropriate to our various identities.[44] States, too, are expected to act consistently with their identities. For example, we expect a rogue state to flout international conventions and a rising power to demand recognition of its higher status.[45] As these examples suggest, identities are socially constructed by how we represent ourselves to others and how others perceive us, and they can vary in the extent to which they are internally aspired to or externally assigned. Identities are not perfect predictors of behavior—a self-identified Republican may occasionally vote for a Democratic candidate or vice versa—but they are useful tools that help people form reasonable expectations of the complex world around them.

Leaders have more to fear from both weakening and worsening when they annex alien societies than when they annex kindred ones. Assessing the target people's identity helps them anticipate what kinds of policies they might support after annexation, and thus whether they are likely to become political allies or rivals. Leaders who consider annexing kindred societies should expect them to supplement their existing constituents and reinforce their domestic influence, while leaders who face alien societies should see them as more likely to back domestic political opponents. By breeding disdain for alien peoples, xenophobia drives leaders to view their interests as incompatible with their own and hence to write off any chance of gaining their support, thereby solidifying annexation's domestic political costs. Leaders who incite xenophobia among their constituents for domestic political gain face similar incentives regardless of their personal beliefs.

Xenophobia has an even greater effect on annexation's normative costs. Leaders who see alien peoples as fundamentally inferior are more likely to brand them as unfit to join their state. Psychological experiments have shown that individuals consistently favor their own group over others regardless of how group identities were formed, and those identities grow more salient when facing important decisions.[46] Where annexation would alter the demographic future of their country, xenophobia drives leaders to judge kindred populations as bettering their state but alien populations as worsening it. Domestic impact theory thus parallels Stephen Saideman's and William Ayres' argument that xenophobia obstructs irredentism. In their words, "Hate may actually produce peace."[47]

Xenophobia's effect on the domestic costs of annexation depends not only on a target population's identity but also its size, which determines whether leaders can anticipate remaking it. Postannexation policies marginalizing, enslaving, or exterminating local inhabitants can have dramatic consequences in sparsely populated territories, where a relatively small influx of new settlers can transform local demographics. Dense populations are far less malleable, forcing leaders to confront their preexisting identities. Accordingly, we should expect xenophobic leaders to assess a territory's future population rather than its current one when anticipating the domestic consequences of its annexation.

Xenophobia often spurs objections to immigration. For example, a wave of thirty-seven thousand German immigrants to English Pennsylvania in the early 1750s prompted Benjamin Franklin to voice his fear that the region would become "a colony of *aliens*." He was convinced they could "never adopt our language or customs, any more than they can acquire our complexion."[48] Yet xenophobia poses an even greater obstacle to annexation because large societies are harder to assimilate than individual immigrants. U.S. leaders explicitly addressed this difference during several congressional debates. Advocating Cuba's annexation in 1858, Congressman Augustus Wright of Georgia observed, "The Irish and Dutch, and general foreign immigration, when not carried on by the governments for purposes of colonization, sympathize with our people and institutions, rather than their own."[49] Unlike immigration, which "leaves one united American people," Senator Carl Schurz of Missouri opposed the proposed annexation of the Dominican Republic in 1871 because "the Anglo-Saxon appearing as a mere exotic plant, *they* will not be the assimilating force."[50] Congressman William Howard of Georgia opposed the 1898 annexation of Hawaii because of its "heterogeneous population," insisting that "it is no reply to say that annually we have taken into the United States immigrants exceeding in number the entire population of the islands and of as many distinct and different types as exist there, because in the case of immigration to the United States the immigrants are absorbed by diffusion throughout the mass of 70,000,000 people, and their identity is as completely lost as the waters of the Mississippi as they empty into the Gulf."[51]

Annexation's domestic costs are doubly dangerous when both democracy and xenophobia are in play. Xenophobic democratic leaders see the absorption of a large alien population as subjecting their nation to partial governance by foreigners they disdain, thereby diluting their constituents' popular sovereignty and undercutting their domestic political influence. Such leaders might avoid those undesired outcomes by denying political representation to the annexed population, but doing so would undermine their democratic institutions. Rather than force themselves to choose between their identity and their ideology, xenophobic democratic leaders prefer to avoid both Scylla and Charybdis by rejecting opportunities to annex alien societies.

Xenophobia poses less of a dilemma to autocratic leaders, who may control annexed territories by coopting local elites rather than by granting representation to alien peoples. They may also implement draconian post-annexation policies without undermining their domestic authority. Stalin maintained tight political control even as he ethnically cleansed Soviet border regions and "routinely replaced [their former inhabitants] with demobilized Red Army soldiers."[52] Xenophobic autocratic leaders may decimate even dense alien societies to promote their ideological agenda, as when Hitler murdered millions of Jews, Slavs, and others to furnish *Lebensraum* (living space) for the Aryan race exalted by his *Weltanschauung* (ideology).[53] Such draconian policies may allow autocratic leaders to exchange the long-term domestic costs of annexing dense alien societies for the short-term military costs of large-scale repression, expulsion, or extermination, a trade-off that is feasible for their democratic counterparts only in sparsely populated territories.

If leaders fear that annexation will weaken their domestic influence or worsen their state, those domestic costs should bear heavily on their decision whether or not to pursue it. Democracy and xenophobia each raise the potential domestic costs of annexation; in combination, they transform population centers from the golden apples that have lured conquerors throughout history into scarecrows.

Testing Predictions

Domestic impact theory suggests that leaders who consider pursuing annexation weigh its likely domestic consequences—in other words, that the "second image reversed" plays a role in policymaking.[54] In doing so, it revises the conventional wisdom that leaders desire annexation wherever it is profitable in a way that makes sense if leaders care about their ability to pursue their goals more than their state's relative power. Geopolitical events may generate an opportunity to pursue annexation, but leaders' responses to that opportunity depend on how institutional and ideational factors shape its appeal. As Gideon Rose writes, "Systemic pressures must be translated through intervening variables at the unit level."[55] Leaders who fear annexation's domestic costs may reject even profitable opportunities to pursue it, and those domestic costs are especially severe where democracy and xenophobia interact (fig. 2.1).

Accounting for domestic costs sacrifices some theoretical parsimony, but the best reason to complicate a theory is also the simplest one: important questions cannot be answered persuasively by anything less. In Stephen Van Evera's words, "We can tolerate some complexity if we need it to explain the world."[56] Does domestic impact theory explain the pattern of U.S. annexation better than profitability theory? To answer this question, we must determine which theory better predicts why U.S. leaders chose to seize some opportunities for annexation but reject others.

Profitability Theory

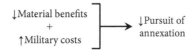

Domestic Impact Theory

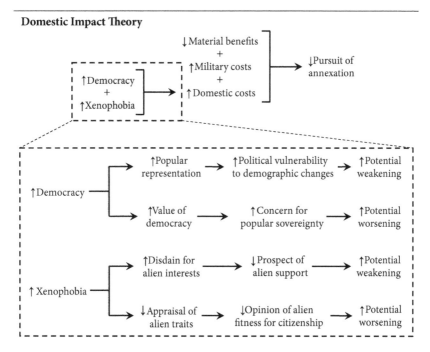

FIGURE 2.1 Theory arrow diagram

Profitability theory predicts that U.S. leaders should have evaluated each opportunity primarily by weighing its material benefits and military costs. Leaders make decisions on the basis of imperfect information, so they may misjudge factors like the risk of foreign intervention or the effectiveness of U.S. forces. Their knowledge of a territory may also be flawed or incomplete, especially with regard to unexplored wildernesses like 1803 Louisiana or 1867 Alaska. Therefore, reasonable tests should not measure profitability with the benefit of hindsight: all costs and benefits in question must be assessed as they would have been seen by leaders at the time. As William Wohlforth writes, power influences international politics, "largely through the perceptions of the people who make decisions on behalf of states."[57]

When U.S. leaders considered whether or not to pursue a specific territory, then, profitability theory predicts that their speeches and correspondence should focus on appraising material benefits like its population size, economic development, natural resources, strategic geography, and commercial significance and comparing them against its likely military costs, such as the probability of encountering local resistance or foreign intervention, the balance of forces between the United States and any adversaries, the likelihood of winning a potential war, and the human and monetary costs required to secure the territory. When debating the issue, proponents should focus on persuading their hesitant colleagues that the material benefits of annexation will exceed its military costs, and most leaders should favor annexation if the available evidence supports those arguments. When U.S. leaders reject opportunities for annexation, they should do so because they judge its military costs to be unaffordable or its material benefits insignificant (table 2.1).

Table 2.1   Competing predictions regarding U.S. annexation

THEORY	PROFITABILITY THEORY	DOMESTIC IMPACT THEORY
Arrow diagram	↓Material benefits + ↑Military costs → ↓Pursuit of annexation	↓Material benefits + ↑Military costs + ↑Domestic costs → ↓Pursuit of annexation
Predicted process	(1) Geopolitical events present an opportunity for U.S. leaders to annex a certain territory.	(1) Geopolitical events present an opportunity for U.S. leaders to annex a certain territory.
	(2a) Leaders evaluate annexation's material benefits by examining the territory's population size, economic development, natural resources, strategic geography, commercial advantages, etc.	(2a) Leaders evaluate annexation's material benefits, as described at left.
		(2b) Leaders evaluate annexation's military costs, as described at left.
	(2b) Leaders evaluate annexation's military costs by examining the probability of local resistance or foreign intervention, the balance of forces between the United States and any adversaries, the likelihood of winning a potential war, human and monetary costs, etc.	(2c) Leaders evaluate annexation's domestic consequences by appraising the size and identity of the territory's future population (anticipating any postannexation changes), predicting demographic and institutional effects on the domestic political balance of power and their normative goals for their country, assessing their constituents' support for annexation and the availability of spoils, etc.
	(3) Leaders weigh annexation's material benefits against its military costs to determine whether it would be profitable.	(3) Leaders weigh annexation's material benefits against its military costs and domestic consequences to gauge its desirability.
	(4a) Leaders who expect annexation to be profitable pursue it with an eye toward maximizing its profitability.	(4a) Leaders who expect annexation to be profitable and domestically beneficial pursue it with an eye toward maximizing both.
	(4b) Leaders who expect annexation to be unprofitable reject it.	(4b) Leaders who expect annexation to generate prohibitive military or domestic costs reject it.

In contrast, domestic impact theory predicts that U.S. leaders should base their decisions on annexation's domestic consequences as well as its profitability. When evaluating the desirability of a potential annexation, they should not only employ a material cost-benefit analysis but also gauge how it would affect their domestic politics and society. Highlighting the territory's population as a demographic modifier, they should use its size and identity (accounting for any anticipated postannexation changes) to predict its effects on their country's domestic politics and normative quality. Where kindred populations promise to reinforce their political support and vision for the state or where sparsely populated territories can be molded to achieve similar results, leaders should anticipate domestic benefits and hence desire annexation. Where populous alien societies threaten to undercut those domestic priorities, leaders should recoil from annexation regardless of its profitability. They should also consider annexation's popularity among their existing constituents, especially where it might reinforce their support by generating spoils. In sum, domestic impact theory predicts that U.S. leaders' correspondence and debates about annexation should focus on its domestic consequences as well as its material benefits and military costs, with leaders promoting it when they judge it to be both profitable and domestically beneficial but rejecting it when they expect either its military or domestic costs to be unpalatable.

In the chapters that follow, I test these predictions against the historical record across twenty-three case studies. Why case studies? Of the various research methods in the political scientist's toolkit, they are the best choice because they offer the strongest tests of this book's competing theories. Those theories make specific, unique predictions regarding U.S. leaders' decision-making, so case studies that examine what kinds of information they focused on and which arguments carried the day can decisively corroborate one theory while undermining the other.[58] In Andrew Bennett's words, "What is important is not the number of pieces of evidence within a case that fit one explanation rather than another, but the likelihood of finding this evidence if the alternative explanations are true."[59] We would be very unlikely to see domestic political or xenophobic concerns playing a major role in leaders' decision-making if profitability theory sufficiently explains the pattern of U.S. annexation. On the other hand, we would be very unlikely to see U.S. leaders emphasizing profitability and ignoring severe domestic costs if domestic impact theory makes a valuable contribution.

These theories could also be tested by using statistical methods—comparing the pattern of U.S. annexation attempts with territories' economic production, population characteristics, military casualties, partisanship, and so on—but doing so would pose relatively weak tests because their predictions become less specific and unique as our analytical lens dilates. For example, if we discovered that the United States tended not to pursue populous territories, how would we know whether its leaders were deterred from doing so because they feared domestic costs or military costs? As I discussed above, leaders' perceptions play a central role in the causal logic of both theories, leaving them relatively ill-suited to quantitative testing but offering rich opportunities to test their predictions against the historical documentary record.

Why these twenty-three cases in particular? When approaching case-study research, as Bennett and Colin Elman observe, "It is vital that cases be selected self-consciously and with a view to maximizing inferential leverage."[60] There are four reasons these cases offer our best opportunity to understand the decline of U.S. annexation. First, they include all major annexation opportunities U.S. leaders confronted between the Revolution, when the United States was founded, and the Spanish–American War, when U.S. leaders made their last major annexation and formally embraced imperialism. In other words, they offer a comprehensive set of occasions when U.S. leaders seriously considered pursuing annexation, including both opportunities they seized and those they declined. Several of these are paradigm cases that belong in any study of U.S. annexation, for example, Texas, California, and Hawaii; others, like the Canadian and Caribbean cases, are lesser known but just as important for theoretical testing.[61] Although some readers may find the reintegration of the Confederacy during the Civil War a notable omission, we should expect the dynamics behind a decision to reassert control over a secessionist region to differ from those driving decisions to absorb external territory. The former is complicated by the interdependence of identities, economics, and geopolitics involved coupled with psychological incentives to prevent major losses.[62] The inclusion of all major U.S. annexation opportunities affords these cases a firm foundation on which to reach conclusions about why the United States stopped annexing territory.

This book's central research question concerns why U.S. leaders stopped pursuing annexation, not why their efforts succeeded or failed. Accordingly, the case studies focus on U.S. leaders' pursuit or nonpursuit of annexation rather than on U.S. state admissions, which would shed relatively little light on our theories since the decisions to place territories on a path to statehood had already been made. Although some territories were admitted quickly while others spent decades under imperial stewardships, most U.S. leaders equated territorial acquisition with annexation until 1898. As a result, the logic of both theories operates at the moment of potential acquisition, when leaders decided whether a territory should join the United States or remain independent.

Second, these twenty-three cases feature large variations in the theories' independent and dependent variables, offering a firm basis for us to judge whether causation occurred as they predict.[63] Decisions varied when different leaders confronted the same territory, when the same leaders confronted different territories, and even when the same leader considered annexing the same territory at different times. The result is rich variation over time and space, offering fertile ground for comparisons both within and across cases. Within cases, we can observe whether annexation's most vocal opponents were those most skeptical of its material value or most fearful of military costs, those from a particular section or political party, or those most xenophobic with regard to the territory's population. Across cases, the chapter format facilitates most-similar-case comparisons as U.S. leaders confronted comparable targets at different times or different targets at the same time. Examples include U.S. policies regarding Native American lands post-Transappalachia versus post-Louisiana versus post-Florida; regarding Canada during the Revolution versus the War of 1812; regarding California versus southern Mexico during the Mexican–American War; and regarding Cuba versus Hawaii versus Puerto Rico versus the Philippines in 1898. Finally, this structure helps us compare across chapters, as U.S. leaders from distinct eras facing different territories home to diverse populations rejected annexation for similar reasons.[64]

Third, either the pursuit or rejection of annexation was possible in every case, so leaders' reasons for choosing one or the other should be observable within each case rather than predetermined by structural constraints. In every case, the United States faced a weaker potential target or one held by a distant empire, and in every case geopolitical events gave U.S. leaders pretexts to pursue annexation.[65] Lacking formidable structural constraints, U.S. leaders were consistently free to pursue their territorial ambitions. States cannot annex territory unwillingly or accidentally—annexation is a voluntary foreign policy goal that leaders are free to decline if they find it undesirable, as U.S. leaders often did. In all twenty-three cases, then, the decision to pursue or reject annexation was up to U.S. leaders, and all negative cases or nonannexations satisfy the "possibility principle."[66]

Fourth, most of these cases offer strong tests, as our theories predict different behaviors driven by leaders' differing perceptions of annexation's costs and benefits. Even when both theories predict the same overall policy—that is, whether the United States should have pursued annexation or not—the case study method allows for fine-grained testing of their divergent within-case predictions, such as who should have opposed that policy and why or how leaders should have gone about pursuing it. Moreover, most of these cases represent relatively hard tests for domestic impact theory and easy tests for profitability theory.[67] Most potential targets offered considerable economic and geopolitical advantages, and U.S. leaders rarely saw military costs as an obstacle. Profitability theory confidently expects U.S. leaders to seize such golden opportunities. The interesting question is thus why the United States did not seize every opportunity, and profitability theory's failure to explain these relatively easy cases should raise grave doubts about its sufficiency. In contrast, we should consider domestic impact theory especially persuasive if it can explain why leaders defied such strong material incentives.[68]

The central purpose of the case studies is to investigate the predicted connections between our theories' proposed causes and effects, using process-tracing methodology and historical research based on primary and secondary sources.[69] Direct observation of intervening steps is impossible where causal processes involve decision-making within the human mind; instead, the case studies aim to assemble a structured, evidence-based argument that causation occurred. Specific pieces of evidence hold unique meaning, and each theory's persuasiveness rests on how convincingly the collected evidence shows its logic at work. As John Gerring writes, "Process tracing is akin to detective work. . . . It is the quality of the observations and how they are analyzed, not the quantity of observations, that is relevant in evaluating the truth claims of a process-tracing study."[70]

The form of process tracing employed here follows a two-level inquisitive framework. First, each case study poses case-specific questions regarding why U.S. leaders acted the way they did. For instance, why did U.S. leaders decline Texan requests for annexation in the late 1830s? These case-specific questions highlight key empirical puzzles and frame the historical analysis, supplying a lens through which relevant decisions, actions, and contextual information can be identified. Second, the case studies investigate a shared set of theoretically informed questions that focus attention within them and provide connective tissue across them: (1) How did U.S. leaders perceive the material benefits, military costs, and domestic consequences of annexation? (2) How did those considerations inform whether U.S. leaders pursued or rejected annexation and how they went about doing so?[71]

This two-level structure of analysis frames a compelling historical story that both explains U.S. behavior and is attentive to our theories' predictions. In a sense, the research process is like panning for gold: the questions act as pans which can help us separate out nuggets of theory-relevant evidence from the infinity of irrelevant information. The case-specific questions accentuate the key decisions and actions in each case, while the theoretically informed questions connect them to the theoretical variables. One advantage of this approach is that the application of the shared questions within each specific context leads to additional questions that can help indicate which theory's logic more closely resembles leaders' actual thought processes. For example, how did they choose which territories to pursue when they faced multiple options? When they pursued annexation, did they go about it in ways that prioritized profitability or domestic benefits?

All of these questions focus on U.S. leaders, but which leaders matter most varies on a case-by-case basis depending on the policymaking process involved. Annexation usually involved an international treaty negotiated under orders from the president or secretary of state, which then had to be ratified by a two-thirds vote in the Senate. If that treaty outlined a purchase, however, it required funding from the House of Representatives. Congress could also authorize annexation by joint resolution, requiring a simple majority vote in both the House and Senate followed by the president's signature. If military action was involved, the president played a central role as commander in chief; Congress was empowered to declare war and fund the military; and military leaders could also affect policy. As a result, the president and the Senate feature prominently in most cases, but other leaders ebb and flow depending on their roles in shaping U.S. policy.

Wherever possible, the case studies rely on primary sources as the most direct evidence of leaders' thinking. They employ personal and official correspondence, congressional records, diaries, memoirs, contextual details, and other sources to assemble as accurately as possible the considerations for and against annexation that arose in each case and to identify which arguments carried the day. They contain more quotations than are typically found in political science research because I believe this best enables readers to judge the theories' persuasiveness for themselves, especially where differing historical interpretations may exist.[72] That said, this book is built on the shoulders of many giants, and the chapters that follow frequently reference excellent histories.

Since this book aims to explain the full pattern of U.S. annexation, readers should base their conclusions on all twenty-three cases rather than on any subset of them. Indeed, the earlier cases examined in chapters 3–6 set expansionist precedents that were defied in the later cases in chapters 5–7. Although similar factors fueled annexation's domestic costs across the cases, their significance varied, with domestic politics playing a central role in chapters 3–6 and xenophobia being especially powerful in chapters 6 and 7. Why did the United States pursue Quebec during the Revolution but reject it later? Why did it take half of Mexico's territory but not the rest? Why did President Jackson try to purchase Texas in 1831 but refuse Texan requests to join the Union five years later? Why did Congress prevent President Grant from annexing the Dominican Republic? Why did U.S. leaders annex Hawaii but not Cuba? Why did the United States expand where it did, and why did it not expand where it didn't?

CHAPTER 3

To the Continent

European Empires and U.S. Annexation

> We were of opinion that the country in contest was
> of great value, both on account of its natural fertility
> and of its position.
>
> John Adams, Benjamin Franklin, and John Jay, 1783

The United States was born into a continent of
European empires, and its first opportunities for territorial expansion came
at their expense. One by one, U.S. leaders relieved Britain of Transappalachia, France of Louisiana, and Spain of Florida, increasing U.S. land area
by roughly 700 percent (about 1.5 million square miles) and transforming
thirteen colonies nestled between the Atlantic Ocean and the Appalachian
Mountains into a continental power.[1] Does profitability theory or domestic
impact theory better explain these early acquisitions?

These three cases are arguably the least puzzling ones in this book, best-
case scenarios in which U.S. territorial expansion was overdetermined. Each
territory offered valuable material benefits: Transappalachia and Louisiana
housed impressive natural resources; Louisiana and Florida provided crucial
security for U.S. exports. The military costs of acquiring them were relatively
minimal: Transappalachia entailed some diplomatic risk but no military
action beyond the sunk costs of the Revolution, France willingly sold Louisiana, and Spanish authority in Florida crumbled under pressure. Since these
cases rank among the most profitable opportunities the United States faced,
profitability theory predicts widespread support for their pursuit among U.S.
leaders.

Domestic impact theory also predicts expansionism in these cases, though
it diverges from profitability theory in predicting varying levels of domestic

political opposition. The pursuit of Transappalachia occurred before the Constitution was ratified, when the United States was not a unified nation-state but an alliance among "free and independent states."[2] Since territorial expansion did not imply annexation in that case, the region's tremendous natural resources could be exploited at no domestic cost. Hence domestic impact theory expects U.S. leaders to broadly support acquiring Transappalachia. In contrast, the pursuits of Louisiana and Florida occurred under the Constitution, when the federal balance of power governed U.S. domestic politics. Those annexations were widely expected to tip that balance toward the South, so domestic impact theory predicts a sectional divide between southern advocates looking to reinforce their domestic support and northern opposition afraid of weakening domestic influence. The Virginia Dynasty's firm grip on the presidency and Congress in both cases implies that the southern preference for expansion should have prevailed, but only over northern objections.

Leaders from both sections had little reason to fear worsening from these acquisitions because of their sparse populations. In 1800 the entirety of the future continental United States was inhabited by 600,000 Native Americans dispersed across hundreds of tribes, and their numbers declined to fewer than 280,000 by 1870.[3] In contrast, the number of Anglo-American settlers in the Mississippi Valley alone reached 377,000 by 1800 and 900,000 thirty years later.[4] Despite decades of Spanish rule, neither Louisiana nor Florida contained many Spaniards beyond civil and military officials. As the historian Karl Schmitt writes, "Americans, British, and blacks (as slaves) predominated among the some 6,000 polyglot Floridians, and the 20,000 inhabitants of Louisiana were almost equally divided between African slaves and French settlers."[5] Many U.S. leaders agreed with former Massachusetts Congressman Fisher Ames that this *"Gallo-Hispano-Indian omnium gatherum* of savages and adventurers" was as worthy of citizenship as "otters in the wilderness," yet their sparse numbers rendered them vulnerable to marginalization via postexpansion policies.[6] Domestic impact theory therefore agrees with profitability theory that the United States should have pursued each of these golden opportunities, though in the later cases over sectional opposition.

Transappalachia

"We do hereby strictly forbid, on pain of our displeasure, all our loving subjects from making any purchases or settlements whatever" west of the Appalachian Mountains.[7] With this royal proclamation, issued on October 7, 1763, King George III attempted to reserve the area between the mountains and the Mississippi River for Native Americans. Disregarding royal preference and Native presence alike, the U.S. leaders who declared independence in 1776 demanded that their new nation include that vast region, called Transappalachia. This demand had no legal or demographic basis. Several of the rebellious colonies' charters granted them territory stretching to the Mississippi and beyond, but the legitimacy of those grants derived from the same British Crown that had set their western boundaries at the Appalachians. Colonial settlers had barely even touched the Ohio River, the Mississippi's main eastward tributary. Still, there was widespread support for expansion into the continent, support which featured prominently both in the Continental Congress's overtures for a Spanish alliance as early as December 1776 and in its instructions to the peace negotiators John Adams, Benjamin Franklin, and John Jay through the war's end.[8] Why did U.S. leaders pursue territorial expansion even before securing their national independence?

Transappalachia's natural resources were a strong lure. As the U.S. negotiators reported to Secretary of Foreign Affairs Robert Livingston in July 1783, "We were of opinion that the country in contest was of great value, both on account of its natural fertility and of its position."[9] Its fertile lands bred visions of rich agriculture easily shipped down the Mississippi to international markets. In October 1780 Franklin wrote to Jay, "Poor as we are, yet as I know we shall be rich, I would rather agree with them to buy at a great price the whole of their right on the Mississippi than sell a drop of its waters. A neighbor might as well ask me to sell my street door."[10] Paired with access to North Atlantic fisheries, Transappalachia guaranteed prosperity for the young United States. In November 1782 Adams recorded in his journal, "Franklin said . . . that the fisheries and the Mississippi could not be given up; that nothing was clearer to him than that the fisheries were essential to the Northern states, and the Mississippi to the Southern, and, indeed, both to all."[11]

If they failed to acquire Transappalachia during the Revolution, U.S. leaders expected that demographic trends would soon make it a cause of war. Fewer than twenty-five thousand colonial settlers lived there in 1782, but their numbers had already exploded from only a few hundred when the Revolution began.[12] Watching this westward movement, U.S. leaders knew that settlers would flood into Transappalachia whether it remained British, passed to Spain, became an independent Native reservation, or any combination of those real possibilities. Expanding into the region later would probably mean another war with whoever controlled it, imposing costs which could be avoided by acquiring it now. As Adams reflected, "From first to last I ever insisted . . . that the fisheries and the Mississippi, if America was not satisfied in those points, would be the sure and certain sources of a future war . . . that the population near the Mississippi would be so rapid, and the necessities of the people for its navigation so pressing, that nothing could restrain them from going down."[13]

Expansion into Transappalachia carried no domestic costs because it did not entail annexation, and in this regard, the case differs from most cases in this book. The United States was not a unified nation-state during the Revolution: the Continental Congress, its first central decision-making institution, functioned as "a diplomatic assembly of sovereign states," a council of ambassadors from the rebellious colonies rather than a national government.[14] As one scholar writes, "It had no authority to pass laws, no powers for enforcing the measures it did take, no means of raising money except printing, begging or borrowing. . . . The Continental Congress, in short, was simply an advisory council which depended for its effectiveness on the good will of thirteen scattered colonies with conflicting interests."[15] In November 1777 the Articles of Confederation formalized this international cooperation by establishing a "firm league of friendship," including a defensive alliance, mutually respected citizenship, and a Congress of representatives to coordinate external relations and resolve interstate disputes. The Articles brought no deeper political integration, however, reserving for each state "its sovereignty, freedom, and independence, and every power, jurisdiction, and right" not "expressly delegated" to Congress.[16] Each state's domestic politics remained independent from the others, leaving their leaders with nothing to fear from expanding their confederation.

The military costs of demanding Transappalachia are difficult to isolate from the broader struggle for independence. The claim clearly antagonized Spain and France, whose aid the United States badly needed during the Revolutionary War, and forgoing Transappalachia might have eased the path to independence by generating more foreign aid sooner. Spain did not hide its ambition to seize the region as spoils of war, offering U.S. leaders a formal alliance if they stopped demanding the western lands, "not having had possession of them before the present war, or not having any foundation for a claim in the right of the sovereignty of Great Britain, whose dominion they have abjured."[17] French leaders also recognized King George III's 1763 proclamation line along the Appalachians as the legitimate border, advising their U.S. counterparts to focus on territories where their population actually resided rather than "run after the shadow and a chimerical object."[18]

Disagreement over Transappalachia did not prevent France and Spain from aiding the U.S. cause, however. Military supplies smuggled through Spanish New Orleans gave a crucial boost to the Continental Army as early as

1776, and these were supplemented by sizable loans in 1777, the U.S.–French alliance in 1778, and the Spanish declaration of war on Britain in 1779.[19] Both France and Spain resented their recent defeats by Britain in the Seven Years' War, and they relished the chance to regain standing in Europe by splintering the British Empire. Knowing this, U.S. leaders played diplomatic hardball to secure independence and expansion simultaneously.

After their victory at Yorktown, Britain's foes strove unsuccessfully to unify their conflicting interests into a final list of demands. In August and September 1782 Jay met repeatedly with the Spanish ambassador to France, Count d'Aranda, rebuffing no fewer than five Spanish boundary proposals calling for a divided Transappalachia.[20] Franklin wrote on August 12, "My conjecture of that court's design to coop us up within the Allegheny Mountains is now manifested. I hope Congress will insist on the Mississippi as the boundary, and the free navigation of the river, from which they could entirely exclude us."[21] The situation grew urgent when Jay discovered that the French foreign minister had secretly dispatched his undersecretary to London in mid-September. Assuming that his mission was to negotiate a separate pro-Spanish settlement, the Americans opened their own bilateral negotiations with Britain to emphasize that if "limiting our western extent . . . east of the Mississippi . . . was insisted upon it was needless to talk of peace, for that we never would yield that point."[22] With British leaders ready to concede independence, the U.S. negotiators went so far as to encourage them to reconquer West Florida from Spain, hoping that "would operate as an additional inducement to their joining with us in agreeing that the navigation of the [Mississippi] river should forever remain open."[23]

Transappalachia's fate ultimately lay in British hands, and it was a stroke of geopolitical fortune that the final peace negotiations coincided with the "Shelburnian moment." Lord Shelburne was British prime minister between July 1782 and February 1783, and during the fall of 1782 he resolved to end the war before Parliament reconvened, even if it meant ceding Transappalachia.[24] The result was a territorial windfall that more than tripled the size of the United States from its birth. As the historian Walter Nugent writes, "Other British politicians, had they been running the government, might have cut some sort of deal with the Americans. But only Shelburne, almost certainly, would have given them so much."[25] Thanks to its diplomats' steadfast insistence and a fortuitous moment of British appeasement, the United States gained Transappalachia alongside independence, a remarkable achievement considering its allies' opposition. Reporting the peace terms from Paris, the negotiators declared, "We knew this court and Spain to be against our claims to the western country, and having no reason to think that lines more favorable could ever have been obtained, we finally agreed to those described in this article; indeed they appear to leave us little to complain of and not much to desire."[26]

The Revolution was unusual among the historical periods examined in this book in that U.S. territorial expansion did not involve annexation. With independence achieved, the Confederation Congress suffered from a "creeping paralysis" as states frequently ignored its requests. In 1782–83 it received less than $1.5 million of its requested $10 million budget, and it failed to defend U.S. sailors from Algerian enslavement in 1785 or effectively manage Shays' Rebellion in 1786.[27] Frustrations boiled at this "anarchy and confusion," a "federalistic saturnalia" during which "Maryland and Delaware fought an undeclared 'oyster war' over fishing rights to the Potomac River; nine states had navies of their own; state militias were separate and distinct armies; seven of the states even printed their own currency; New York placed a tariff on wood from Connecticut and on butter from New Jersey; Boston boycotted grain from Rhode Island."[28] U.S. leaders responded by drafting the Constitution in 1787, binding the states under a unified federal government and giving their leaders a say in each other's affairs.[29] Many chafed against this redistribution of domestic influence, and sectionalism quickly took root as northerners like William Gordon of Massachusetts worried that "the seat of government will be to the southward, and the Northern states be insignificant provinces," while southerners like Virginia's Henry Lee feared living under "the rule of a fixed insolent Northern majority."[30] Moving forward under the Constitution, territorial expansion would imply annexation—incorporating new territories into the Union as states on equal footing with the others. As a result, these sectional concerns began generating formidable domestic costs.

Louisiana

The Louisiana Purchase in 1803 roughly doubled the size of the United States, adding 828,000 square miles to the young republic.[31] This far exceeded U.S. ambitions, which at the time focused on New Orleans and Florida. It also marked the first major episode of territorial expansion under the Constitution, and hence the first case in which U.S. leaders confronted annexation's domestic costs. Why did U.S. leaders target the Gulf Coast, why did they end up purchasing Louisiana, and how did the prospect of annexation affect their approach to territorial expansion?

After the Revolution U.S. leaders coveted one territorial objective above all: controlling the Mississippi River. Transappalachia's swelling settler population depended on the Mississippi to export its agricultural produce, and the river's commerce was loaded onto oceangoing vessels at the Spanish port of New Orleans.[32] As President Thomas Jefferson wrote in 1802, "There is on the globe one single spot, the possessor of which is our natural and habitual enemy. It is New Orleans, through which the produce of three-eighths of our territory must pass to market."[33] The dependence of so much trade on one port represented a critical vulnerability that U.S. leaders hoped to eliminate by annexing it. Secondary avenues for Transappalachia's exports like the Pearl, Mobile, and Apalachicola Rivers opened into the Gulf of Mexico in Spanish Florida, bringing that territory into U.S. crosshairs as well.

U.S.–Spanish relations were rocky after the Revolution. Spanish officials frequently harassed U.S. shipments on the Mississippi, and in October 1802 Spain suspended the U.S. right to deposit merchandise in New Orleans.[34] The resulting crisis saw Secretary of State James Madison threaten military action if the port remained closed, declaring that for "our Western citizens . . . the Mississippi is to them everything."[35] Transappalachia's market access was so important that it generated bipartisan calls for a war of conquest. Alexander Hamilton held that "the best interests of our nation require that we shall annex to the United States all the territory east of the Mississippi, New Orleans included," and he mused that for Jefferson "the great embarrassment must be how to carry on war without taxes."[36] In February 1803 the Federalist senator James Ross of Pennsylvania proposed authorizing the president to call forth fifty thousand troops to seize New Orleans, which he dubbed "the lock and key of the whole western country."[37] The Senate quickly passed a modified resolution sponsored by Democratic-Republican John Breckinridge of Kentucky, raising the number of troops to eighty thousand.[38]

The costs of both action and inaction suddenly increased when Jefferson learned that Spain had agreed to transfer Louisiana to France, a development that, he exclaimed, "completely reverses all the political relations of the U.S."[39] Spanish harassment had been a nuisance, but as Congress's willingness to authorize military force shows, U.S. leaders did not fear the military costs of war with Spain. A new French empire in Louisiana would introduce a far more formidable neighbor capable of squeezing U.S. exports and inciting hostility among Native American tribes. Although he was "not sanguine in obtaining a cession of New Orleans for money," Jefferson approached France with opportunistic diplomacy, offering to purchase the city along with East and West Florida if those had been ceded (they had not) and "putting off the day of contention for it, till we are stronger in ourselves, & stronger in our allies."[40] Fearing that the French acquisition of Louisiana was "the embryo of a tornado which will burst on the countries on both sides of the Atlantic," he told U.S. Minister in Paris Robert Livingston to offer up to $10 million.[41] Although Congress had authorized only $2 million, Livingston used its prior military authorization to underscore the gravity of the situation, threatening that the United States might seize New Orleans if Napoleon refused to sell.[42]

This dread of an imposing French rival in North America proved premature. Napoleon's expeditionary force, sent to fortify Louisiana after subduing a slave rebellion in Haiti, was decimated by yellow fever in the summer of 1802 and failed to accomplish even its initial mission.[43] In response, Napoleon shelved his plans for the Western Hemisphere pending "the unfinished business of smiting Britain," which he assumed would seize Louisiana if he still held it when war resumed in 1803.[44] As he told his treasury director, François Barbé-Marbois, "The conquest of Louisiana would be easy, if they only took the trouble to make a descent there. I have not a moment to lose in putting it out of their reach. . . . I think of ceding it to the United States. . . . They only ask of me one town in Louisiana, but I already consider the colony as entirely lost."[45] Selling Louisiana to the United States would convert Napoleon's lost colony into crucial war funding, give "England a maritime rival, that will sooner or later humble her pride," and foment "rivalries among the members of the Union," which might eventually collapse under its own weight and enable a later French return to North America.[46] Thus motivated, Napoleon answered Livingston's inquiries about New Orleans by offering to sell all of Louisiana.

The territory stretched from the Gulf of Mexico north to modern Canada and from the Mississippi River west to the Rocky Mountains. It was assumed to contain immense natural resources despite being on literally nobody's map in 1803—Lewis and Clark were sent to chart it the following year.[47] The Kentucky traveler Hugh Brackenridge observed in 1814, "From the fatal ravages of the small pox, the present Indian nations of Louisiana, particularly on the Missouri, have not the tenth of the numbers which they had near thirty years ago. . . . [T]hese people are scattered over so wide a country as scarcely to be noticed in it. One may travel for days without meeting a living soul."[48] Only its eastern edge was speckled with fledgling cities, including New Orleans with a population of around eight thousand. By one estimate perhaps one hundred thousand Native Americans spanned the entire territory along with fewer than fifty thousand white settlers, black slaves, free blacks, French, Spanish, and others.[49] Louisiana's small Anglo-American population was growing rapidly as the rising tide of Transappalachian settlement spilled across the Mississippi, however, leading John Jay to speculate that Spain would never have been able to "hold the territory against this human flood."[50]

Nevertheless, the eyes of the new republic initially remained fixed on the Gulf Coast. When the French foreign minister Charles Maurice de Talleyrand-Périgord asked Livingston on April 11, 1803, "whether we wished to have the whole of Louisiana," Livingston protested that the United States desired only New Orleans, prompting Talleyrand to reply "that if they gave New Orleans the rest would be of little value" and to ask "what we would give for the whole."[51] Livingston protested again the following night, this time to Barbé-Marbois, "that we would be perfectly satisfied with New Orleans and the Floridas, and had no disposition to extend across the river," but Barbé-Marbois convinced him that Napoleon was determined to sell all of Louisiana.[52] Despite lacking immediate interest beyond the Gulf Coast, U.S. leaders recognized that the French offer brought control of the Mississippi within reach, while also adding Louisiana's presumably huge resources. Negotiations proceeded quickly. On April 30 Barbé-Marbois, Livingston, and James Monroe—newly arrived in Paris to aid the negotiations—signed a treaty purchasing Louisiana for 68 million francs ($15 million), 18 million of which went toward U.S. claims for ships and cargoes lost during the Quasi-War of 1798–1800.[53]

Louisiana's material benefits and amicable acquisition notwithstanding, the purchase ignited impassioned opposition from northern Federalists who worried about domestic costs rooted in partisanship and sectionalism. Despite Hamilton's insistence that "the acquisition has been solely owing to a fortuitous concurrence of unforeseen and unexpected circumstances, and not to any wise or vigorous measures on the part of the American government," the Louisiana Purchase would be a signature achievement for the Democratic-Republican Jefferson.[54] New states would be carved from it once enough settlers moved westward, and many expected those states to join the southern bloc. Senator Timothy Pickering of Massachusetts bemoaned the Constitution's three-fifths clause, noting that "the Northern states have nothing to countervail the power and influence arising from the negro representation."[55] Connecticut Congressman Roger Griswold feared that "the vast and unmanageable extent which the accession of Louisiana will give to the United States; the consequent dispersion of our population, and the destruction of that balance which it is so important to maintain between the Eastern and Western states, threatens, at no very distant day, the subversion of our Union."[56] The northern Federalists' desperation grew so great that by 1804 several of them plotted to secede from the Union rather than endure southern domination. Senator William Plumer of New Hampshire wrote, "Adopt this western world into the Union, and you destroy at once the weight and importance of the Eastern states, and compel them to establish a separate and independent empire."[57]

Many leaders also complained that the purchase exceeded the president's constitutional powers by granting citizenship to Louisiana's Spanish, French, Creoles, and free black residents, sparse though they were. As the historian Peter Kastor has argued, "It was *demographic* expansion, rather than *geographic* expansion, that was the subject of so much concern."[58] Griswold objected that "the incorporation of a foreign nation into the Union . . . destroys the perfect union contemplated between the original parties, by interposing an alien and a stranger to share the powers of government with them."[59] Fisher Ames grumbled, "The powers that be concern themselves little about the Constitution," while Senator John Quincy Adams thought Louisiana had been purchased "at an immense price, not of money, but of principle."[60] Exceeding his constitutional powers also offended Jefferson's limited-government philosophy, and he fretted to Breckinridge in August 1803 that "the Constitution has made no provision for our holding foreign territory, still less for incorporating foreign nations into our Union. The executive in seizing the fugitive occurrence . . . have done an act beyond the Constitution."[61] Jefferson even went so far as to draft a constitutional amendment to square this worrisome circle, abandoning the amendment only upon realizing it could not be ratified before the treaty's own October 30 ratification deadline.

In the end Jefferson's institutional dominance ensured that neither sectional opposition nor constitutional scruples about alien populations could derail the Louisiana Purchase. His Democratic-Republican Party had routed the Federalists in the 1800 elections and tightened its grip on Congress throughout his presidency. The Senate approved the purchase with only five votes against, and the House followed suit with the required funds, though a potentially troublesome vote requesting documentation of France's title to Louisiana was only narrowly defeated, 59–57.[62] From his firm position atop U.S. domestic politics, Jefferson achieved the *coup de maître* of his presidency: the local French garrison surrendered New Orleans to the United States on December 20, 1803, one month after it had received the city from Spain.

The Louisiana Purchase was the second territorial windfall for the United States. Unlike with Transappalachia, however, U.S. leaders had not pursued the majority of the territory, and many of them did not want it. Securing U.S. control of the Mississippi represented "a great stride to real and substantial independence," but the vast expanse that came with it posed new challenges to leaders' domestic politics and visions.[63] As a result, Congress admitted the state of Louisiana nine years later, but most of the purchased territory remained without congressional representation for decades as uncertainties over alien populations drove a "process of constructing the legal, political, administrative, racial, and military structures of racial supremacy."[64]

Florida

Strained by the Revolutionary War and Napoleonic Wars, respectively, Britain and France proved willing accomplices to U.S. territorial expansion in Transappalachia and Louisiana. In contrast, Spain resisted U.S. efforts to annex East and West Florida for nearly two decades. Why did U.S. leaders continue pressing until Spain finally capitulated?

The Floridas housed a meager population and fewer natural resources than the two previous acquisitions, and their climate was relatively inhospitable to settlers.[65] Barely more than three thousand non-Natives lived in East Florida in 1814 with perhaps another ten thousand in West Florida, and their combined Native population dropped below six thousand after the Creek War.[66] In contrast, the population of neighboring Georgia surpassed a quarter million by the 1810 census.[67] Rather than resources or population, two geopolitical benefits drove U.S. interest in the Floridas. First, with New Orleans in hand, securing other avenues for Transappalachia's trade became a top priority, and the Floridas spanned the entire Gulf Coast east of Louisiana, including the mouths of the Pearl, Mobile, and Apalachicola Rivers.[68] Second, the Mississippi trade remained vulnerable in wartime. As Senator John Pope of Kentucky observed in December 1810, "An enemy in possession of West Florida can with great facility cut off New Orleans from the upper country."[69] That fear was soon realized when Britain assaulted New Orleans in the closing days of the War of 1812. Annexing the Floridas would reduce this vulnerability by denying enemies a proximate landing area.

The crumbling Spanish empire undercut annexation's military costs. As Nugent writes, "The United States benefited greatly from Spain's weakness—in fact, prostration—during the Napoleonic Wars, and did not hesitate to kick the other fellow when he was down."[70] U.S. leaders had been willing to conquer New Orleans from Spain in early 1803, and their contempt for Spanish power only grew over the ensuing years. Unlike the crisis over New Orleans, however, there was little urgency to annex the Floridas, and Spanish authority there was so brittle that leaders preferred to erode it by using less expensive methods than a war that was winnable but still costly.

The first of those methods entailed "unilateralism and fact denial."[71] Secretary of State Madison recognized shortly after the Louisiana Purchase that "the Floridas are not included in the treaty," and he instructed Monroe that "the acquisition of the Floridas is still to be pursued."[72] Capitalizing on a self-contradictory clause in the purchase treaty, however, Livingston convinced first Monroe and then Madison and Jefferson to insist that West Florida actually had been included in the Louisiana Purchase.[73] Though groundless, the expanded claim was immediately popular in the United States, and in February 1804 Congress passed the Mobile Act annexing Florida west of the Perdido River.[74] Spanish protests and French efforts to clear up the "misunderstanding" fell on deaf ears as Jefferson and Madison followed Livingston's advice to "act as if no doubt could be entertained of our title."[75] That April they instructed Monroe to negotiate, "1st, an acknowledgement by Spain that Louisiana, as ceded to the United States, extends to the river Perdido; 2nd, a cession of all her remaining territory eastward of that river, including East Florida."[76] Recognizing Napoleon's influence over Spanish foreign policy, Monroe sought his support, essentially trying to convince the French government "that it had indeed, though without its knowledge, received West Florida in addition to Louisiana from Spain by the Treaty of St. Ildefonso in 1800, and that it had sold West Florida, though equally without its knowledge, to the United States along with Louisiana."[77] France refused to play along, and Spain rebuffed Monroe's offer to drop U.S. claims against Spain and adjust the western border in exchange for the Floridas.[78] A second U.S. effort in 1806 "to secure West Florida which is essential to their interests and to obtain East Florida which is important to them" was similarly rejected.[79]

In the face of Spain's intransigence, Jefferson again considered conquering the Floridas. Anticipating a profitable conquest as long as Napoleon stayed out of the conflict, he plotted to deter France from intervening by gaining a powerful ally of his own. He wrote to Madison in August 1805, "We should lose no time in securing something more than a mutual friendship with England."[80] On October 21 the British navy cast a stone in Jefferson's favor when it destroyed the Spanish fleet as well as the French one at the Battle of Trafalgar, crippling Spain's ability to project power into the Western Hemisphere.[81] Contrary to Jefferson's wishes, though, Britain followed this victory by intensifying its maritime restrictions on U.S. trade in the context of the Napoleonic Wars.[82] Jefferson reacted with his infamous embargo, hoping to compel a quick rapprochement that might yet open the door to alliance and conquest. As he told his secretary of war in August 1808, "Should England make up with us, while Bonaparte continues at war with Spain, a moment may occur when we may without danger of commitment with either France or England seize to our own limits of Louisiana as of right, and the residue of the Floridas as reprisal for spoliations."[83] Alas, Jefferson's embargo proved to be in vain, as did his hope that Napoleon might barter Spanish colonies for U.S. support against Britain.[84]

Madison abandoned visions of conquest after assuming the presidency in 1809, preferring to exploit Spanish weakness by using less expensive forms of coercion, including unilateral claims, local insurgencies, and plausibly deniable military interventions. In the summer of 1810 Madison sent Colonel William Wykoff to incite popular uprisings in West Florida.[85] He simultaneously ordered David Holmes, the governor of Mississippi Territory, to prepare his militia to occupy the area "in the event of either foreign power interference with West Florida, or of internal convulsions."[86] After a series of local conventions demanded self-government, rebels seized the Spanish fort at Baton Rouge on September 23 and requested annexation to the United States, prompting Holmes to write, "The views of our government have been in great measure realized."[87] Madison agreed, proclaiming on October 27, "Whereas the territory . . . has, at all times, as is well known, been considered and claimed by them, as being within the colony of Louisiana . . . and whereas a crisis has at length arrived subversive of the order of things under the Spanish authorities . . . [n]ow be it known, that I, James Madison, President of the United States of America . . . have deemed it right and requisite that possession should be taken of the said territory, in the name and behalf of the United States."[88] With a stroke of his pen Madison reasserted West Florida's inclusion in the Louisiana Purchase, justified the insurgency against Spanish rule in Baton Rouge, and unilaterally annexed Spanish territory.

With Baton Rouge now under U.S. control, events spread east during the winter of 1810–11 as private filibusters schemed to take the Spanish fort at Mobile.[89] Madison sent General George Mathews and Judge Harry Toulmin to urge Mobile's residents to overthrow Spanish rule, declaring that "in the event of a separation from the parent country, their incorporation into our Union would coincide with the sentiments and policy of the United States."[90] Fearing unrest, the Spanish governor of West Florida temporarily offered to transfer his territory to the United States, and Congress in secret session authorized Madison to occupy the Floridas "in case an arrangement has been, or shall be, made with the local authority of the said territory . . . or in the event of an attempt to occupy the said territory, or any part thereof, by any foreign government."[91]

Madison sent Mathews and Colonel John McKee to accept the Floridas from any willing "local authority," but the governor withdrew his offer after receiving aid from Cuba and Mexico.[92] Mathews requested authorization to sponsor a revolution in East Florida, and, hearing no response from Washington, in March 1812 he gathered seventy Georgians and nine Floridians

who branded themselves "Patriots" and seized the border town of Fernan-
dina and Amelia Island.[93] To avoid provoking war Madison formally disavowed Mathews and sent Governor David Mitchell of Georgia to withdraw
the invaders, but he told Mitchell to "delay" and not "to compel the patriots
to surrender the country or any part of it to the Spanish authorities," leaving open the possibility of seizing East Florida amidst the approaching War
of 1812.[94]

The domestic costs of annexing the Floridas were limited by their sparse
population, but the expectation that they would be carved into southern
states drove many northern leaders to fear that the acquisition would weaken
their domestic political positions. As in the case of Louisiana, though, their
opposition had little effect given the Virginia Dynasty's firm grip on the federal government. When the Senate reconvened after Madison's 1810 proclamation annexing West Florida, for example, northern Federalists launched
into heated debate over the limits of presidential authority and the demerits
of the U.S. claim, but they were overwhelmed by the administration's supporters. Even Pickering's revelation of the French letter denying that West
Florida was part of Louisiana, which Jefferson and Madison had kept secret,
provoked only a resolution censuring Pickering's public disclosure of a clas-
sified document.[95]

Only during the War of 1812, when elevated military costs combined with
domestic ones, did sectional opposition break partisan lines to briefly derail
the U.S. acquisition of Florida. Despite the fact that the Floridas were Spanish territory, not British, southern leaders hoped to seize them during the
war. The day after declaring war on Britain, Congressman George Troup of
Georgia proposed authorizing Madison "to occupy East and West Florida,
without delay."[96] Treasury Secretary Albert Gallatin wrote that Madison's
preoccupation with the Floridas was a "Southern one, and will, if it should
involve us in a war with Spain, disgust every man north of Washington,"
and northern Democratic-Republicans joined Federalists to defeat the bill in
the Senate, 16–14.[97] Madison again sought authorization for "an immediate
occupancy" of the Floridas the following March, when a new congressional
session included two sympathetic senators from Louisiana (admitted the previous year), but again a sectional vote blocked Madison's plans.[98]

A rump bill passed this time, authorizing him to occupy the remainder
of West Florida, and the undermanned Spanish fort at Mobile surrendered
without a fight in April 1813.[99] Despite lacking congressional authorization,
Madison ordered General Thomas Pinckney to ready a force "for offensive
operations, preparation to the entire possession of the province of East
Florida" in response to Spain's mobilization of Seminoles and former slaves

against the "Patriots," but the invasion never occurred as U.S. forces strug-gled against Britain.[100] Madison tried to get British leaders to accept U.S. claims to the Floridas during peace negotiations, but they had little reason to do so, especially given the underwhelming U.S. military performance.[101]

The war's end brought a fresh round of U.S.–Spanish negotiations, and in light of Spain's rapidly deteriorating position in the Western Hemisphere Madison knew its leaders would eventually accept any deal allowing them to save face.[102] He offered a firm western boundary between the United States and Spanish Mexico, giving "to the Spanish all the territory that we have, or claim, west of the Sabine [River in Texas], in consideration of East Florida being granted to us," but Spanish hopes to retain Florida lingered through the end of his administration.[103] When Monroe assumed the presi-dency in March 1817, he and Secretary of State John Quincy Adams looked to pressure Spain into making a deal via a twofold strategy: "first, isolating Spain from the other European powers (especially Great Britain), and sec-ond, applying steadily increasing military pressure on the poorly defended Spanish North American possessions."[104] In essence, they sought to maneu-ver the United States into the position of having won a war without having to fight one.

The first goal, denying foreign aid to Spain, undercut Spanish hopes of salvaging its colonial empire, which had recently been fractured by rebel victories in Buenos Aires, New Granada, Venezuela, and Chile.[105] It also coin-cided with a widespread European desire for peace after the carnage of the Napoleonic Wars. Britain's naval power gave it a decisive voice within the Concert of Europe on overseas issues like the Spanish colonial rebellions, and British leaders preferred pressing Spain for trade concessions rather than helping recover its empire. Under their influence, the Concert refused to invite King Ferdinand VII of Spain to its 1818 conference at Aix-la-Chapelle, where its members effectively dashed Spanish hopes by refusing to furnish any military aid toward recovering its lost colonies.[106]

With European politics playing into their hands, Monroe and Adams focused on their second goal, showing Spain that the Floridas were already lost. When filibusters and pirates seized Amelia Island in the summer of 1817, Adams convinced Monroe to launch a military intervention to expel "the marauding parties," illustrating with one swift stroke that Spain was incapable of controlling East Florida, that the resulting anarchy threatened the United States, and that U.S. forces might conquer it if Spain remained unwilling to negotiate a cession.[107] Monroe announced the island's occupa-tion that December along with his decision to retain "possession of it for the present," which Adams translated directly into diplomatic leverage by warning the Spanish minister to the United States Luis de Onís y González-Vara that "if we should not come to an early conclusion of the Florida negotiation, Spain would not have the possession of Florida to give us."[108] In January 1818 Monroe openly labeled Spanish Florida a failed state, declaring, "To a country over which she fails to maintain her authority, and which she permits to be converted to the annoyance of her neighbors, her jurisdiction for the time necessarily ceases to exist."[109]

Monroe doubled down on destabilizing the Floridas by ordering General Andrew Jackson to pursue marauding Seminoles into Spanish territory, ambiguously instructing him that "movement . . . against the Seminoles . . . will bring you on a theatre where you may possibly have other services to perform. Great interests are at issue. . . . This is not a time for repose."[110] After driving the Seminoles into the swamp, Jackson turned on the local Spanish forts. He seized St. Marks that April and Pensacola in May, after which he ordered an assault on the Spanish capital, St. Augustine, and proclaimed a new government for East Florida.[111] This "obvious act of war" risked undermining the negotiations, however, forcing Monroe to recall Jackson.[112] Nevertheless, once Onís accepted that Jackson had acted on his own initiative, Adams defended his actions and accused Spanish commanders of aiding the Seminoles.[113] Monroe used his second annual message in December 1818 to declare Spanish authority in the Floridas "completely extinct," and he justified Jackson's invasion by "right of self-defense."[114] From this position of strength, Adams played his diplomatic trump card by threatening to recognize the independence of Spain's Latin American colonies.[115] When asked if a Florida treaty might persuade the United States to withhold recognition, he made no guarantees but replied that "if Spain had taken the pains to adjust her differences with us, there would probably be much less ardor in this country against Spain, and consequently less in favor of the South Americans."[116]

In January 1819 Onís received authorization from Madrid to cede the Floridas on the best terms possible, and he requested of Adams only that the new western border be "natural and clearly defined, and leave no room for dispute to the inhabitants on either side."[117] Negotiations proceeded quickly, and on February 22 Adams and Onís signed the Transcontinental Treaty. Spain formally gave the Floridas to the United States; a firm transcontinental boundary was established following the Sabine River, Red River, Arkansas River, and the 42nd parallel to the Pacific Ocean; and the United States agreed to pay up to $5 million in private claims against the Spanish government.[118] The Senate unanimously ratified the treaty, then re-ratified it in February 1821 after Spain's ratification was delayed.[119] In March 1822, having no further need of a bargaining chip, Monroe asked Congress to recognize the new Latin American republics.[120]

Transappalachia, Louisiana, and Florida were all valuable territories ripe for the taking. In each case European leaders had more pressing concerns than U.S. expansion—escaping the Revolutionary War for Britain; fighting the Napoleonic Wars for France; salvaging its colonial empire for Spain—and in each case U.S. leaders exploited the resulting opportunities. The pursuit of Transappalachia was not compromised by domestic costs because it occurred before the Constitution was ratified, but the other acquisitions did impose varying domestic consequences on U.S. leaders. As domestic impact theory predicts, those who anticipated domestic costs from Louisiana and Florida (northerners and Federalists) opposed annexation, while those who expected domestic benefits (southerners and Democratic-Republicans) supported it. The United States pursued annexation in both cases because a preponderance of U.S. leaders fell into the latter group, including presidents Jefferson, Madison, and Monroe along with healthy congressional majorities.

Is profitability theory sufficient to explain these cases, or does domestic impact theory make a worthwhile contribution? Profitability theory successfully predicts macro-level U.S. behavior in all three of these cases: given the high material benefits and low military costs, all three cases were profitable, and in all three cases the United States pursued territorial expansion. Nonetheless, all three cases also support domestic impact theory's more fine-grained predictions regarding variations in support and opposition among U.S. leaders. Those variations did not prevent U.S. expansionism because sparse target populations minimized fears of worsening and because policy was dictated by the domestic political bloc that stood to gain from annexation. Those conditions would not always be present in the future, however.

After negotiating the Transcontinental Treaty, Onís reflected, "The Americans believe themselves superior to all the nations of Europe, and see their destiny to extend their dominion . . . to all of the New World."[121] Many of his contemporaries shared that view, yet U.S. territorial expansion would not be as boundless as they expected. Annexation's domestic consequences, first evidenced in northern opposition to the Louisiana Purchase and the Florida cession, would increasingly shape U.S. foreign policy.

CHAPTER 4

To the West

Native American Lands and U.S. Annexation

> This [Indian] Territory would possess the right, in
> due time, to come to this House and demand to be
> admitted as an equal and a sovereign member of our
> political confederacy.
>
> It might be because he was a Southron, but he felt
> disposed to dispute this right at the threshold.
>
> It was a right to introduce a foreign nation, uncongenial
> to ourselves, into our political household . . .
>
> If it was in the power of the gentleman from Vermont
> to add to our Union men of blood and color alien to
> the people of the United States, where was that right
> to stop?
>
> Why not introduce our brethren of Cuba and Hayti? . . .
>
> Such a proposal would bring the Union of these states
> to the brink of a precipice.
>
> Congressman William Archer, 1834

In the heat of U.S.–Spanish negotiations over
Transappalachia in August 1782, John Jay declared, "With respect to the Indians we claim the right of pre-emption; with respect to all other nations, we
claim the sovereignty over the territory."[1] Treaties with Britain, France, and
Spain secured European recognition of U.S. sovereignty over Transappalachia,
Louisiana, and Florida, but those treaties marked only the beginning of their
annexations. Preemption, the U.S. annexation of Native American lands before
they could be offered to any foreign power, remained to follow. The tribes
rejected out of hand the notion that Europeans could give their lands away, so
U.S. leaders negotiated separate treaties with them, annexing specific regions
while recognizing that others remained unannexed tribal property.[2] As opponents of Indian Removal frequently observed, later efforts to disregard tribal
sovereignty could not change the text of those treaties, and a full account of
U.S. annexation should explain the U.S. pursuit of Native American lands.[3]

Early U.S. leaders confronted dozens of tribes holding vast, fertile lands with sparse populations. In 1789 Secretary of War Henry Knox estimated that only seventy-six thousand Native Americans lived throughout Transappalachia; by comparison the 1790 census counted more than seventy-three thousand settlers in Kentucky alone.[4] Was the U.S. pursuit of tribal lands during the decades that followed driven primarily by profitability, or was it also shaped by domestic consequences? Profitability theory and domestic impact theory agree that U.S. leaders should have desired annexation's material benefits and that they should have grown increasingly assertive as its military costs declined. The tribes' sparse populations raised the possibility of annexing their lands without their people, though, and the theories disagree regarding how U.S. leaders should have responded, whether by assimilating them or removing them.

Profitability theory predicts that U.S. leaders should have maximized material benefits and minimized military costs, favoring assimilation (which promised to harness tribal production and reduce resistance) over removal (which was costly to enforce and eliminated one of annexation's key benefits—population). In contrast, domestic impact theory predicts that leaders should anticipate their policies' domestic consequences, which varied dramatically depending on their perceptions of the tribes and their constituents' hunger for spoils. Leaders who saw Native Americans as potential citizens and whose constituents were unconcerned with tribal lands had little reason to fear domestic costs and hence should have maximized annexation's profitability by pursuing tribal assimilation. On the other hand, leaders who saw Native Americans as irretrievably alien and whose constituents coveted tribal lands had much to lose by promoting assimilation but much to gain by sponsoring removal. How did the U.S. pursuit of Native American lands change over time, and how did these factors affect that change?

My central argument here is that Indian Removal was the product of domestic concerns, not a rational response to structural constraints. Early U.S. leaders championed assimilation as being not only feasible but preferable to removal. The cultural distance between Native Americans and Anglo-Americans complicated but did not prevent assimilation. George Washington, Henry Knox, and Thomas Jefferson viewed Native Americans as primitive but improvable and anticipated their eventual citizenship. Moreover, twelve of the thirteen original states were relatively unconcerned with tribal lands, freeing the first federal leaders to address the tribes with a profitability mindset.

Their efforts to civilize and assimilate the tribes were undone by the gradual admission of new frontier states into the Union. As more federal leaders represented settlers who disdained the tribes and clamored for their lands, pressure mounted not only for the annexation of tribal lands but also for the removal of the tribes from those lands. Removal formally replaced assimilation as a federal policy goal under President James Monroe, who was more closely linked to frontier constituents than his predecessors. The first president from a frontier state, Andrew Jackson, executed removal by force. In sum, U.S. leaders consistently sought to annex tribal lands, but how they did so varied with their prospective domestic consequences, which drove frontier leaders to pursue Native American lands without Native Americans. As Colin Calloway wrote, "Native Americans in the new republic found that the American Revolution not only had created a new society; it also provided the justification for excluding them from it."[5]

Washington and Adams

The first generation of U.S. leaders faced minimal domestic costs from tribal assimilation. The various states remained institutionally independent until March 1789. Even after the Constitution bound them together, most congressmen remained disinterested in tribal lands because twelve of the thirteen original states had long since marginalized or expelled any tribes once residing within their borders. Eight states claimed parts of Transappalachia via their colonial charters, but between 1782 and 1792 Congress persuaded seven to cede their claims to help pay Revolutionary War debts and maintain sectional balance within the Union. Georgia remained intransigent—most of its nominal land area was held by the Cherokees, Creeks, and other tribes—but alone it held little sway over federal policy.

The Founding Fathers' perceptions of Native Americans further reduced assimilation's domestic costs. Unlike the hostile racism of their successors, early leaders like Washington, Knox, and Jefferson saw Native Americans as primitive rather than alien, undeveloped rather than inherently worse than themselves. Viewing the "tribes of Indians . . . as foreign nations, not as the subjects of any particular state," Knox, who served as secretary of war from 1785 (under the Articles of Confederation) until 1794 (under President Washington), was the focal point of U.S. efforts to annex tribal lands during this early period.[6] He wrote to Washington in 1789 that "the progress of society from the barbarous ages to its present degree of perfection" proved the possibility of human development, and he advocated the transfer of "knowledge of cultivation and the arts to the aboriginals . . . to civilize the Indians of North America."[7] Washington included similar language in his annual messages to Congress, describing the tribes in 1791 as "an unenlightened race of men" and holding that "an intimate intercourse . . . imparting to them the blessings of civilization" would "attach them firmly to the United States."[8]

With little reason to fear weakening or worsening from annexation, Knox and Washington pursued tribal lands with an eye toward profitability. They quickly realized that conquest would be prohibitively costly for the near-bankrupt United States, especially if the tribes made "common cause" in resisting U.S. aggression.[9] When Congress tried raising two thousand soldiers to suppress a hostile confederation of northwestern tribes in 1786, the troops disbanded after only a few months for lack of pay.[10] The following year Knox estimated that security alone required at least fifteen hundred troops but counted only five hundred across the entire frontier, concluding glumly, "It is to be regretted that the depressed state of the finances will not admit of the measure."[11] Facing such an "embarrassed state of public affairs and entire deficiency of funds," the hamstrung secretary was forced to bluff his way toward frontier security by "posting the troops so as to awe the savages and endeavoring by treaties and presents to incline them to peace."[12]

Conquest being impractical, Knox and Washington hoped to purchase tribal lands instead. A widely circulated presumption held that the tribes would willingly sell their lands for pennies on the dollar as expanding settlements scared off the animals they hunted. General Philip Schuyler wrote to Congress in July 1783, "As our settlements approach their country, they must, from the scarcity of game, which that approach will induce to, retire farther back, and dispose of their lands, unless they dwindle comparatively to nothing, as all savages have done, who gain their sustenance by the chase, when compelled to live in the vicinity of civilized people."[13] Two months later Washington wrote that his thinking "coincides precisely" with Schuyler's, reflecting "that policy and economy point very strongly to the expediency of being upon good terms with the Indians, and the propriety of purchasing their lands in preference to attempting to drive them by force of arms out of their country." He advised Revolutionary War veterans to settle on the frontier, predicting that "the gradual extension of our settlements will as certainly cause the savage as the wolf to retire; both being beasts of prey tho' they differ in shape." Washington concluded that "there is nothing to be obtained by an Indian war but the soil they live on and this can be had by purchase at less expense."[14]

Knox echoed this profitability outlook, writing, "As the settlements of the whites shall approach near to the Indian boundaries established by treaties, the game will be diminished, and the lands being valuable to the Indians only as hunting grounds, they will be willing to sell further tracts for small considerations."[15] He therefore saw the treaty policy as "the most rational that can be devised," telling Congress in July 1787 that it was "wise to extinguish with a small sum of money, a claim which otherwise may cost much blood and infinitely more money."[16] Two years later Knox reiterated that when "the expense of such a conciliatory system . . . shall be compared with a system of coercion, it would be found the highest economy to adopt it."[17]

Pragmatism guided not only the means by which early U.S. leaders pursued tribal lands (negotiation over conquest) but also their intentions for the tribes themselves (assimilation over removal). As early as 1783 congressional reports on tribal affairs called for U.S. commissioners to "use such arguments as shall appear to them most likely to prevail with the Indians to enter into the society of the citizens of the United States."[18] Cultural differences were an obstacle, but Washington hoped that "if . . . an eligible plan could be devised for promoting civilization among the friendly tribes . . . its influence in cementing their interest with ours could not but be considerable."[19] Knox believed that teaching the tribes to farm, giving them domestic animals and tools, and sending missionaries to reside among them would "effect the civilization of the Indians" and attach "them to the interest of the United States," even encouraging assimilation by intermarriage.[20]

To Washington and Knox, the advantages of assimilating the tribes were twofold. Teaching Native Americans agriculture and animal husbandry would increase annexation's material benefits by amplifying their production and easing its integration into the U.S. economy, and teaching them how to live on less land would reduce their resistance to further cessions. Accordingly, they implemented this plan through numerous treaties and communications. For example, a 1790 treaty with the Creeks provided domestic animals and tools "that the Creek nation may be led to a greater degree of civilization, and to become herdsmen and cultivators, instead of remaining in a state of hunters."[21] Two years later Knox wrote to the northwestern tribes, "We should be greatly gratified with the opportunity of imparting to you all the blessings of civilized life, of teaching you to cultivate the earth, and raise corn; to raise oxen, sheep, and other domestic animals; to build comfortable houses, and to educate your children, so as ever to dwell upon the land."[22] Washington used both his reputation as father of his country and his position as the first president to support the effort, which became a regular theme of his annual messages.[23]

The military balance between U.S. and tribal forces swung dramatically in 1794, when General Anthony Wayne's Legion of the United States crushed a northwestern tribal confederation led by Blue Jacket of the Shawnees and

Little Turtle of the Miamis. That confederation had decimated two previous expeditions of untrained militia, prompting Congress to create the legion as a professional force combining light and heavy infantry, cavalry, and artillery.[24] Its victory in the Battle of Fallen Timbers demonstrated that a committed U.S. military could overwhelm the tribes, but this new advantage did not change the federal goal of assimilation. President John Adams continued to pursue the "plan of civilization," assigning agents to educate the tribes in spinning, weaving, agriculture, livestock, and other trades.[25] The envisioned synergies between civilization and assimilation began emerging by the turn of the century. When the Choctaws requested tools in 1801, the local U.S. commissioners reported, "These circumstances induce us to cherish the hope that, by the liberal and well directed attention of government, these people may be made happy and useful; and that the United States may be saved the pain and expense of expelling or destroying them."[26]

Congress also promoted the civilization policy with a series of Trade and Intercourse Acts. In 1790 the first act required licenses to trade with tribes and forbade private citizens or state governments from purchasing tribal lands. "In order to promote civilization among the friendly Indian tribes," a second act three years later authorized the president to furnish them "with useful domestic animals, and implements of husbandry" and appoint agents "to reside among the Indians."[27] In 1796 the third act empowered the president to establish trading houses among the tribes to disseminate the tools of civilization more efficiently. Congress took tribal assimilation seriously enough to legislate substantial fines for squatters on tribal lands and agents who took guns, tools, or clothing from the tribes. It specified that any U.S. citizen caught committing crimes against peaceful tribes "shall be subject to the same punishment . . . as if the offense had been committed within the jurisdiction of the state or district to which he or they may belong, against a citizen or white inhabitant thereof."[28]

Nevertheless, frontier authorities routinely declined to enforce these punishments, and federal leaders proved unable to compel settlers to respect their treaties with the tribes.[29] Washington warned that without frontier security "all pacific plans must prove nugatory," remarking that "anything short of a Chinese wall, or a line of troops" would not stop the encroaching settlers.[30] Congress failed to produce either. Georgia, the original frontier state, was on the front lines of this resistance. When Knox negotiated a treaty in 1790 granting interpreters, domestic animals, and tools to help the Creeks within its borders attain "a greater degree of civilization," Georgia's leaders condemned those provisions and encouraged settlers to violate the treaty, even paying state militia with lands it guaranteed to the Creeks.[31]

Knox's final report before resigning in December 1794 observed that during the preceding decade "a constant solicitude appears to have existed in the executive and Congress, not only to form treaties of peace with the Indians, upon principles of justice, but to impart to them all the blessings of civilized life." Yet these good intentions had been undercut by "the desires of too many frontier white people, to seize, by force or fraud, upon the neighboring Indian lands."[32] Congress and the first two administrations worked to maximize annexation's profitability by negotiating land cessions and assimilating Native Americans, but their failure to secure frontier leaders' compliance subverted those efforts. When Knox left government he lamented that "it would afford a conscious pleasure, could the assertion be made on our parts, that we have considered the murder of Indians the same as the murders of whites, and have punished them accordingly. This, however, is not the case."[33]

Jefferson and Madison

The Louisiana Purchase introduced the prospect of removal by giving federal leaders a vast region, one that was far beyond settlers' near-term reach, which could potentially be exchanged for tribal lands east of the Mississippi River. Both theories expect the continued pursuit of Native American lands into the 1800s, but whereas profitability theory predicts a continued preference for assimilation, domestic impact theory predicts a shift toward removal as frontier leaders gained influence over federal Native American policy. President Thomas Jefferson, who shared his predecessors' Enlightenment perspective and was similarly unconstrained by frontier constituents, continued promoting their vision of tribal assimilation, consistent with both theories. As domestic impact theory predicts, however, things began to change under President James Madison, who delegated substantial authority to frontier leaders who disdained the tribes and whose constituents clamored for their lands.

Like Washington and Knox, Jefferson saw the tribes as undeveloped rather than alien, writing, "The proofs of genius given by the Indians of N. America, place them on a level with whites in the same uncultivated state."[34] Jefferson's numerous tribal contacts generated respect for their cultures and achievements, and his belief in their potential assimilation was shared by Secretary of War Henry Dearborn, who wrote, "The progress made in the introduction of the arts of civilization among the Creeks . . . in my opinion is conclusive evidence of the practicability of such improvements upon . . . the several Indian Nations as may ultimately destroy all distinctions between what are called savages and civilized people."[35]

Like his predecessors, Jefferson pursued the annexation of Native American lands with an eye toward profitability, championing civilization and assimilation largely to facilitate that process.[36] He instructed Dearborn in December 1802: "The method by which we may advance towards our object will be, 1, to press the encouragements to agriculture, by which they may see how little land will maintain them much better. . . . 2. To establish among them a factory or factories for furnishing them with all the necessaries and comforts they may wish . . . encouraging these, and especially their leading men, to run in debt for these . . . and whenever in that situation, they will always cede lands to rid themselves of debt. . . . 3. We should continue to increase and nourish their friendship and confidence by every act of justice and of favor which we can possibly render them."[37] Although several tribes had begun "refusing absolutely all further sale," he apprised Congress of his plan "peaceably to counteract this policy of theirs . . . in leading them thus to agriculture, to manufactures, and civilization; in bringing together their and our sentiments, and in preparing them ultimately to participate in the benefits of our government."[38] Jefferson kept both this message and his instructions to Dearborn confidential lest the tribes gain evidence of what many already suspected, namely, that U.S. civilization policies had a dual purpose: assimilating them and annexing their lands.

Jefferson put his plan into action in February 1803 via several frontier agents. He told Andrew Jackson that "leading the Indians to agriculture" would show them "how useless their extensive forests are," declaring, "I am myself alive to the obtaining of lands from the Indians by all *honest* and *peaceable means*, and I believe that the honest and peaceable means adopted by us will obtain them as fast as the expansion of our settlements . . . will require."[39] Similarly, he wrote to Benjamin Hawkins, "While they are learning to do better on less land, our increasing numbers will be calling for more land, and thus a coincidence of interests will be produced. . . . The ultimate point of rest and happiness for them is to let our settlements and theirs meet and blend together, to intermix, and become one people."[40] Jefferson reiterated his strategy to William Henry Harrison, the governor of Indiana Territory: "To promote this disposition to exchange lands . . . we shall push our trading houses, and be glad to see the good and influential individuals among them run in debt, because we observe that when these debts get beyond what the individuals can pay, they become willing to lop them off by a cession of lands. . . . In this way our settlements will gradually circumscribe and approach the Indians, and they will in time either incorporate with us as citizens of the United States, or remove beyond the Mississippi."[41]

For any tribes that failed to assimilate, the Louisiana Purchase provided a backup plan via "the means of tempting all our Indians on the East side of the Mississippi to remove to the West."[42] Drafting a constitutional amendment concerning the purchase, Jefferson stipulated that "the legislature of the Union shall have authority to exchange the right of occupancy in portions where the U.S. have full right for lands possessed by Indians within the U.S. on the east side of the Mississippi."[43] This prospect resurfaced in congressional debate: the Louisiana Territorial Act of 1804 authorized the president "to stipulate with any Indian tribes owning land on the east side of the Mississippi, and residing thereon, for an exchange of lands, the property of the United States, on the west side of the Mississippi, in case the said tribes shall remove and settle thereon."[44]

Although Jefferson continued to favor assimilation over removal, he began delicately raising the possibility of land exchanges with tribes during his second term.[45] Georgia had finally agreed to relinquish its Transappalachian claims in 1802 on the condition that he "extinguish the Indian title to all the other lands within the state of Georgia," and Jefferson hoped to achieve this by persuading the state's remaining tribes to move westward.[46] In 1805 he informed the Chickasaws, "We have lately obtained . . . Louisiana, in which there is a great deal of land unoccupied by any red men. But it is very far off, and we would prefer giving you lands there, or money and goods as you like best, for such parts of your land on this side of the Mississippi as you are disposed to part with."[47] The Choctaws and Cherokees received similar offers in 1808.[48] Jefferson specified that "the act of removal should be the result of their own inclinations without being urged to the measure," and most tribes declined, but roughly one thousand of the thirteen thousand Cherokees in the region emigrated to Arkansas the following year.[49] Jefferson remained committed to assimilation through the end of his presidency, though, telling the Northwest tribes in January 1809, "We wish you to live in peace, to increase in numbers, to learn to labor as we do. . . . In time, you will be as we are; you will become one people with us. Your blood will mix with ours; and will spread, with ours, over this great island."[50]

Madison assumed the presidency two months later, pledging "to carry on the benevolent plans" for "the conversion of our aboriginal neighbors from the degradation and wretchedness of savage life to a participation of the improvements of which the human mind and manners are susceptible in a civilized state."[51] Consumed by deteriorating U.S.–British relations, however, Madison took relatively little interest in the tribes and initially maintained Jefferson's offers of civilization or voluntary removal.[52] Madison's patience wore thin, however, as British agents incited tribal hostility before the War of 1812, and he began loosening the leash on his frontier agents.[53] During the war hostile campaigns in the Northwest by Tecumseh's confederation and in the South by the Red Stick Creeks were crushed by U.S. forces under Harrison and Jackson, respectively, destroying the last formidable tribal militaries east of the Mississippi.[54]

Those victories solidified U.S. military preponderance over the tribes, reducing the costs of conquest thereafter. Yet like Wayne's victory two decades earlier, they did not immediately transform U.S. policy. The War of 1812 opened the door to forcible removal, but it was frontier representation that pushed federal policy through it. Although U.S. negotiators in the Treaty of Ghent agreed to restore all tribal lands lost during the war, Madison refused to enforce that provision. He did so for fear of provoking frontier leaders, who blamed federal civilization policies for denying their constituents the best lands and enabling the tribes "to compete agriculturally with their white neighbors."[55] By March 1816 their voices had grown so loud that Secretary of War William Crawford asked the Senate "if the civilization of the Indian tribes is considered an object of primary importance, and superior to that of rapidly extinguishing their titles and settling their lands by the whites."[56] The Senate responded that land exchanges "can only take place with the voluntary consent of those tribes," yet Madison's hands-off approach allowed frontier governors like Harrison in Indiana, Lewis Cass in Michigan, and Ninian Edwards in Illinois to adopt ever-harsher negotiating postures.[57] As a result, during Madison's administration "the extinguishment of Indian titles became in truth almost a mania in the Northwest," where many smaller tribes proved unable to offer effective resistance.[58]

The larger southern tribes were more difficult to evict, but Jackson took advantage of Madison's loose oversight to threaten them and bribe them. In this way, "From 1816 to 1818 [Jackson] wrested millions of acres in land cessions from the Choctaws, Chickasaws, and Cherokees."[59] As he wrote in 1817, "Money, is the weapon, in the hand of the commissioner, wielded to corrupt a few of their leaders, and induce them to adopt the plans embraced by the views of the government."[60] Embracing the long-standing federal aim of assimilation, the Cherokees declined his removal offer that year, saying, "Our choice is to remain on our lands, and follow the pursuits of agriculture and civilization, as all the presidents, our fathers, have recommended and advised us to do."[61] Enraged, Jackson warned them to "recollect what had happened to their brothers the Creeks" during the war.[62] He eventually bribed enough chiefs to secure a cession, reporting, "We had to promise by a private article that we would pay to individuals of this nation the sum of four thousand two hundred and twenty-five dollars . . . without this we could not have got the national relinquishment."[63] As frontier leaders like Jackson ascended to positions of federal power, U.S. policy came to mirror their radical preferences.

Monroe, Adams, and Jackson

The administration of James Monroe, the last Founding Father to hold the presidency, was a time of great transition in the United States. As Revolutionary War veterans passed the nation's highest offices to a new generation of leaders and the First Party System ended, so too did serious efforts to assimilate Native Americans.[64] Presidents Monroe, John Quincy Adams, and Andrew Jackson pursued tribal lands with a dedication similar to that of their predecessors, but under their leadership the federal government abandoned its prior civilization policies in favor of forcible removal. Was this shift away from assimilation driven more by domestic concerns or profitability?

After the defeats of Tecumseh's confederation and the Red Stick Creeks, reduced costs of conquest opened the door to a more forcible approach. As Secretary of War John Calhoun explained to Congress in 1818, the remaining tribes east of the Mississippi lacked meaningful military power and hence did not warrant the delicate handling they had in the past. They had "ceased to be an object of terror, and have become that of commiseration." As a result, Calhoun recommended that the United States stop treating the tribes as "independent nations" and instead present them with two choices: (1) abandon their tribal governments and subject their people to U.S. laws, parceling collective territory into individual plots and opening the rest to settlers, or (2) emigrate west of the Mississippi.[65] Retaining their tribal lands as guaranteed by previous U.S. treaties was no longer an option.

Yet rising U.S. military power did not dictate which of Calhoun's options U.S. leaders would prioritize; in other words, it was a necessary but not sufficient condition for forcible removal. Indeed, profitability considerations should have driven Monroe and Calhoun to pursue assimilation as Washington and Knox had. In contrast to those earlier administrations, however, several characteristics of Monroe's presidency generated mounting domestic costs from assimilation and steered federal policy irretrievably toward removal. First, Monroe's early tenure coincided with the 1816–19 admissions of Indiana, Mississippi, Illinois, and Alabama, each of which claimed large territories belonging to Native American tribes under federal treaties. Admitting these states in pairs preserved the sectional balance of power between North and South, but all four joined Georgia, Kentucky, Tennessee, Ohio, and Louisiana to form a powerful frontier coalition calling for the seizure of tribal lands and removal of the tribes. It is no coincidence that the Senate Committee on Indian Affairs was created in 1820, nor that it was chaired by proremoval senators like David Holmes of Mississippi, Thomas Hart Benton of Louisiana, and George Troup of Georgia.[66]

Second, these frontier leaders did not share the Enlightenment racism of Washington, Knox, and Jefferson. Instead, they harbored a more intransigent racism that saw the tribes as fundamentally inferior and irreconcilable with U.S. society.[67] As North Carolina Congressman James Graham declared in 1838, "The history and experience of every state in this Union abundantly prove that the white man and the red man *cannot dwell together* in peace, tranquility, and equality. . . . Some wild animals never can be rendered tame. You cannot change the order of nature. You might as well expect the red man to change the color of his skin as his habits and pursuits."[68] The historian Walter McDougall has written that "racial discrimination was a *sine qua non* if expansion was to be reconciled with liberty. Indians had to be understood as not possessing the rights of citizens, or else how could their lands be taken at all?"[69] This statement rings true, but the form of discrimination and expansion makes all the difference: whereas Enlightenment racism fueled a relatively benign expansionism aimed at turning the Native Americans into productive citizens, dehumanizing racism fueled expansionism with ethnic cleansing.

Third, Monroe himself was far closer to frontier leaders than his predecessors in the Virginia Dynasty had been. In one biographer's words, "Until a generation of native western leaders emerged . . . Monroe was looked upon as the only national figure identified with the aims of the West."[70] He enlisted frontier governors like Cass in Michigan, Edwards in Illinois, and William Clark in Missouri to persuade the tribes in their territories to abandon their lands, resulting in treaties with the Delawares, Kickapoos, and Potawatomis in 1818–19.[71] Meanwhile, Monroe looked the other way as thousands of squatters defied federal treaties and invaded tribal lands. As Anthony Wallace writes, "The policy of guaranteeing the Indian boundary against intrusion, genuinely intended in the intercourse acts and particularly in Jefferson's bill of 1802, progressively failed during his administration and was by 1816 a nullity."[72]

Rising U.S. military power was necessary to carry out forcible removal, but rising frontier influence over federal policy was its driving cause. Freed by the former and propelled by the latter, Monroe promoted coercive annexation, telling Jackson as early as October 1817 that although "it has been customary to purchase the title of the Indian tribes . . . a compulsory process seems to be necessary."[73] In 1818 he sent Jackson and the former governor of Kentucky Isaac Shelby to convince the Chickasaws to leave Kentucky and Tennessee, allotting money and goods "to be used at your discretion in bringing about the treaty, by presents to the principal chiefs, or otherwise." He also noted that a long-overdue annuity payment owed to the tribe "might be turned to advantage."[74] Jackson reported that the Chickasaw chiefs "were very much opposed to meet us," but he brought them to the table by postponing the annuity payment and then threatened that if they refused a land exchange "Congress will pass a law, authorizing them to take possession of it" and "the white people would certainly move on their lands by the thousands and all the evils which their father the president was trying to avert would ensue."[75] Once this threat was understood, negotiations focused on details of a new annuity and the size of bribes needed to secure signatures from the chiefs.[76]

Monroe turned to Jackson again in 1820 amid growing clamor from land-hungry Mississippi settlers. Echoing previous threats, Jackson told the Choctaws that "Congress, at their approaching session, will take the business into their own hands," and he used $4,674.50 in bribes to secure a treaty annexing Choctaw lands in Mississippi.[77] The Cherokees responded to U.S. removal demands by protesting that earlier civilization policies had worked, writing to Calhoun, "Your encouragement to our people has not been unavailing in agriculture, and manufacturing clothing, and educating our children; yet we are told by our neighbors that we shall all have to go over to the Arkansas country as hunters, and return to that state again in which our forefathers lived."[78] Calhoun responded bluntly that civilization was not enough: "Your great object ought to be to hold your land separate among yourselves, as your white neighbors; and to live and bring up your children in the same way as they do. . . . Without this, you will find you will have to emigrate, or become extinct."[79]

Removal continued to gain steam during Monroe's second term. In May 1822 Congress formally abolished the factory system of trading houses, which had been undermined by private profiteers and "a mercenary public opinion which insisted, to a shameful degree, upon the prostitution of the Indian service for personal and partisan advantages."[80] In February 1823 the Supreme Court ruled in *Johnson v. McIntosh* that the federal government possessed "the complete ultimate title" to tribal lands, while the tribes themselves enjoyed merely "right of possession," thus offering a legal foundation for coercive annexations.[81] The House Committee on Indian Affairs laid plans in January 1824 to acquire "as much territory [west of the Mississippi] as will be sufficient to give room for those tribes of Indians, within the present states and territories, who may wish to migrate westwardly."[82] Shortly before leaving office in 1825 Monroe told Congress, "The removal of the Indian tribes from the lands which they now occupy within the limits of the several states and territories . . . is of very high importance to our Union."[83]

John Quincy Adams was selected to succeed Monroe two weeks later, and although he personally preferred assimilation domestic political pressures compelled him to follow in Monroe's footsteps and endorse removal.[84] Adams wrote in his diary, "My own opinion is that the most benevolent course towards them would be to give them the rights and subject them to the duties of citizens, as a part of our own people. But even this the people of the states within which they are situated will not permit."[85] When Secretary of War James Barbour proposed in Cabinet an initial plan for "incorporating the Indians within the states of the Union," Secretary of State Henry Clay dismissed it as impracticable because "it was impossible to civilize Indians," a view, Adams reflected, "for which I fear there is too much foundation."[86] Six weeks later Barbour's new plan echoed Monroe's: since the "unabated desire to bereave them of their lands" ensured "every attempt [at assimilation] must fail," Adams's administration would set apart "the country west of the Mississippi . . . for their exclusive abode."[87]

Adams faced mounting pressure from frontier leaders, especially in Georgia, where many were afraid he would jeopardize Jefferson's unfulfilled promise to extinguish all tribal lands.[88] When Adams renegotiated a Creek treaty in 1826 to annex slightly less land, Georgia's legislature declared the move "illegal and unconstitutional," and when he considered deploying federal troops to enforce it, Governor Troup mobilized two divisions of state militia.[89] Fearing a civil war, Adams defused the situation by coercing the Creeks to cede all their remaining lands in Georgia.[90]

A fresh crisis erupted in July 1827 when the Cherokees adopted a written constitution asserting national sovereignty. Georgia's legislature responded by declaring "that the Indians are tenants at her will, and that she may at any time she pleases, determine that tenancy, by taking possession of the premises." The legislators resolved in December 1828 to carve up the Cherokee territory and subject everyone there to Georgian law by June 1, 1830.[91] Senator Theodore Frelinghuysen of New Jersey, one of removal's most outspoken opponents, compared the resolution to the "partition of Poland," declaring, "Sir, here we find a whole people outlawed—laws, customs, rules, government, all, by one short clause, abrogated and declared to be void as if they had never been."[92] What shocked northeastern leaders appealed to their frontier counterparts, however, and two months later

Mississippi's legislature passed a similar resolution extending its laws over the remaining Choctaw and Chickasaw lands within its borders.[93]

By the end of Adams's administration the writing was on the wall, and the outgoing president used his last annual message to lament assimilation's demise, observing, "We have been far more successful in the acquisition of their lands than in imparting to them the principles or inspiring them with the spirit of civilization."[94] Frontier settlers' growing federal representation along with the corresponding lack of Native American representation had thoroughly swung Congress toward removal. Those who benefited from the support of frontier leaders on other priorities had little to gain but much to lose politically by opposing them on this issue about which they cared so much. By the late 1820s Congress was devoting energy to exploring how "all the Indians east of the Mississippi River may be immediately and gradually removed beyond or west of said river."[95]

Into this situation stepped President Andrew Jackson, who had long since committed himself to removal. As early as 1817 he had written to Monroe, "I have long viewed treaties with the Indians an absurdity. . . . This policy grew out of the weakness of the arm of government . . . [and] was adopted from necessity. Circumstances have entirely changed."[96] Jackson saw the Native Americans as unfit to hold the lands his supporters craved, and U.S. military power enabled him to prioritize domestic benefits over profitability. He began working to remove all remaining tribes immediately on assuming office, warning the Creeks and Cherokees in May 1829 that he would not protect them against the state governments even as he requested broader congressional authority to enforce removal.[97]

Jackson's efforts ignited passionate opposition in the Northeast. Frelinghuysen criticized arguments that removal would protect the tribes, asking, "Shall we commit injustice, and put in, as our plea for it, that our intercourse with the Indians has been so demoralizing that we must drive them from it to save them?"[98] He challenged his fellow senators, "Do the obligations of justice change with the color of the skin? Is it one of the prerogatives of the white man, that he may disregard the dictates of moral principles, when an Indian shall be concerned? No, sir."[99] Congressman Henry Storrs of New York condemned the "sheer, open bribery" used to negotiate the cessions, which rewarded chiefs "for treason to their people."[100] He criticized Jackson for elevating state greed over federal law, declaring, "It requires no skill in political science to interpret these treaties. . . . We are to be released from the effect of our treaties by our own act, against the will of the other party, who has faithfully kept them. Is it indeed too late to inquire if this be just?"[101] Congressman Edward Everett of Massachusetts urged his colleagues to soberly reflect on removal's human costs. "Are there two kinds of rights," he asked, "rights of the strong, which you respect because you must; and rights of the weak, on which you trample, because you dare?"[102] He concluded, "It is all unmingled, unmitigated evil . . . this compulsory removal."[103]

Frontier leaders responded by crying hypocrisy: northerners enjoyed the moral high ground only because they had exterminated their own tribes before the Revolution.[104] The debate was won by politics rather than arguments, though, and Jackson had the votes.[105] Both the Senate and House Indian Affairs committees were dominated by Jackson supporters from frontier states, and in February 1830 both committees proposed bills granting the authority he requested.[106] The Indian Removal Act passed the Senate 28–19 in April, and on May 26 it passed the House by a narrower vote in which "the sectional pattern was striking. The Southeast and Southwest voted 61 to 16 for removing the Indians, the rest of the country 82 to 41 against."[107] Adams resigned himself to the unfortunate outcome, writing that "there was nothing left for the minority to do but to record the exposure of perfidy and tyranny of which the Indians are to be made the victims, and to leave the punishment of it to Heaven."[108]

Jackson immediately set about coercing the remaining tribes to abandon their lands east of the Mississippi. He confronted the Chickasaws first: "Reject the opportunity which is now offered . . . then, like other tribes who have gone before you, you must disappear and be forgotten."[109] Their chiefs protested against this "act of usurpation . . . unwarranted by the Constitution of the United States and the treaties that now exist." But having no viable alternative, they signed a removal treaty that August pending satisfactory inspection of their new western lands.[110] Next, Jackson turned to the Choctaws, observing that while they "could raise one warrior to resist, there would be found one hundred or one thousand to one to oppose that resistance." He secured a treaty that September for their emigration over the next three years.[111] The Creeks signed away their remaining lands in Alabama in March 1832, and Jackson instructed his agents to ensure that they left "as early as possible."[112] Two months later the remaining Seminoles agreed to emigrate pending approval of suitable western lands.[113]

Both the Seminole and Chickasaw inspectors were dissatisfied with the territories they were offered, but mounting pressure from squatters forced them to move anyway during the years that followed.[114] The Sac and Fox also disliked their allotted western lands, but when they tried to reoccupy their former homes in Illinois during the summer of 1832 Jackson sent federal troops to force them back west. To demonstrate the hopelessness of further resistance he paraded their chief, Black Hawk, through a series of U.S. cities, telling him, "You will see the strength of the white people. You will see, that our young men are as numerous, as the leaves in the woods. What can you do against us? You may kill a few women and children, but such a force would be soon sent against you, as would destroy your whole tribe."[115] Similarly, Governor George Porter of Michigan secured a treaty with the Chippewas, Ottawas, and Potawatomis in 1833 by threatening that "Jackson was a great war chief who had collected more scalps in his day than any Indian. He would not hesitate to strike his children if they misbehaved."[116] Upon its signing, Secretary of War Lewis Cass told Jackson proudly that "the whole country north of the Ohio and east of the Mississippi . . . has been cleared of the embarrassments of Indian relations."[117]

The Cherokees fought removal all the way up to the Supreme Court, which in 1832 in *Worcester v. Georgia* found that "the Cherokee Nation . . . is a distinct community occupying its own territory, with boundaries accurately described, in which the laws of Georgia can have no force."[118] The ruling offered no salvation. Jackson simply declined to enforce it, confiding to an associate, "The decision of the Supreme Court has fell still born, and they find that it cannot coerce Georgia to yield to its mandate."[119] In March 1835 a tribal council approved a treaty ceding all Cherokee land to the United States and requiring complete removal within two years. However, the vote was 79–7 because nearly the entire tribe had boycotted it, and more than fifteen thousand Cherokees signed letters to the Senate condemning the treaty. As Major William Davis, a U.S. agent tasked with convincing the Cherokees to emigrate, reported to Cass, "That paper . . . called a treaty is no treaty at all. . . . I solemnly declare to you that upon its reference to the Cherokee people it would be instantly rejected by nine-tenths of them and I believe by nineteen-twentieths of them."[120] Nevertheless, the Senate voted 31–15 to ratify the treaty in May 1836.[121]

With removal treaties on record from all the major tribes, Jackson set about forcing them to leave. Escalating conflict in Alabama prompted Cass to dispatch ten thousand soldiers to remove the Creeks, instructing them as follows: "Your efforts will be directed to the unconditional submission of the Indians. As fast as this is effected, and as any parties of them can be collected, they must be disarmed, and sent immediately to their country west of the Mississippi."[122] Jackson "often badgered his officials to cut costs," and thousands of Creeks died during the journey when the privately contracted Alabama Emigrating Company inadequately supplied them against the freezing winter.[123] When the Cherokees' two-year window for removal closed in May 1838, Jackson urged his handpicked successor, Martin Van Buren, to use military force.[124] Federal troops and local militia herded some seventeen thousand Cherokees at bayonet point from their homes into concentration camps, where they were loaded onto boats and trains headed west before being forced to walk the final stretch of what became known as the Trail of Tears.[125] Roughly four thousand died along the way, and "at every step of their long journey to the Indian Territory, the Cherokees were robbed and cheated by contractors, lawyers, agents, speculators, and anyone wielding local police power."[126] General John Wool described the scene as "heartrending," while General Winfield Scott marveled at the settlers' ability to "forget, or, at least, to deny that a Cherokee was a human being."[127]

Amidst these ongoing removals Congress formally organized the tribal areas west of the Mississippi as Indian Territory.[128] This measure proved controversial when Adams suggested it would guarantee the Native Americans a path to eventual statehood and full citizenship, a proposition that drew sharp rebuttals from southern congressmen. George Gilmer of Georgia declared, "The Indians were a people, all whose habits, interests, and opinions, differed so entirely and essentially from those of the people of the United States, that it was impossible for this government to create a code of laws adapted to their notions and their wants."[129] William Archer of Virginia stated that "it might be because he was a Southron, but he felt disposed to dispute this right at the threshold. It was a right to introduce a foreign nation, uncongenial to ourselves, into our political household. Did any gentleman believe the American people would ever consent to admit the Indian tribes as confederate equals with ourselves?" He speculated that if the legislation in question did "add to our Union men of blood and color alien to the people of the United States, where was that right to stop? Why not introduce our brethren of Cuba and Hayti?"[130] Such views contaminated Congress for generations, and not until 1907—after "a surge of white settlers"— would Oklahoma become a state.[131]

In total, Jackson's presidency produced roughly six dozen tribal treaties annexing nearly one hundred million acres east of the Mississippi in exchange for $70 million and about thirty million acres out west; some forty-six thousand Native Americans were forced to remove.[132] The biographer Robert Remini's summary is apt: "The Five Civilized Tribes—that is, the Cherokees, the Creeks, the Choctaws, the Chickasaws, and the Seminoles—had all been effectively removed. But they were not the only ones. During Jackson's administration the Sac and Fox Indians, the Quapaws, the Apalachicolas, the united tribes of Otos and Missouri, the four confederated bands of Pawnees of the Platte, the Senecas of Sandusky River, and the Chippewas, Ottawas, Potawatomis, Winnebagos, Miamis, Caddos, Wyandots, Menominis, Saginaws, Kickapoos, Kaskaskias, Piankishaws, Delawares, Shawnees, Osages,

Iowas, Pinkeshaws, Weas, and Peorias surrendered valuable land in Illinois, Michigan, Iowa, Wisconsin, Louisiana, Kentucky, Indiana, Ohio, Kansas, Minnesota, and Nebraska."[133] Jackson's removal policies were the culmination of a decades-long shift away from assimilation that echoed the westward shift of federal representation. The first seven presidents shared a desire to annex tribal lands, but the rise of frontier leaders allowed their constituents' land hunger and hostile racism to supplant profitability logic, thereby fueling the forcible removal of the Native Americans.

Early U.S. leaders tried to maximize annexation's material benefits and minimize its military costs by assimilating the tribes. Free to chart their own course thanks to domestic political disinterest and seeing Native Americans as potential citizens, leaders like Washington and Knox followed the predictions of both profitability theory and domestic impact theory. Those predictions begin to diverge during the 1810s with growing federal representation of frontier constituencies and attitudes, coupled with an enduring lack of tribal representation. As more federal leaders saw domestic costs in assimilation and domestic benefits in removal, calls for the former were drowned out by calls for the latter. Jackson's successors, including not only his disciples Van Buren and James Polk but also the Whigs William Henry Harrison, John Tyler, Zachary Taylor, and Millard Fillmore, faced similar domestic pressures and followed in his footsteps.[134]

These cases build on those in chapter 3 while adding an additional layer of within-case evidence to support domestic impact theory. As in those previous cases, U.S. leaders who faced minimal domestic costs could afford to follow profitability logic, pursuing annexation with assimilation. In contrast, those who faced substantial domestic pressures prioritized them over national material interests, seen here in the consistent proremoval machinations of frontier leaders beginning in Georgia and extending westward. Unlike the cases in chapter 3, those discussed here involve domestic costs that hinged not on leaders' expectations of the sectional alignment of new territories, but on their constituents' clamoring for spoils and the contrasting prospects of annexation-with-assimilation versus annexation-with-removal to generate those spoils. The sectional distribution of support for removal and frontier leaders' outspoken motivations lend further credence to domestic impact theory.

The idea of removal that emerged with Jefferson and rose to prominence under Monroe metastasized under Jackson into one of the worst human tragedies in U.S. history. As the French observer Alexis de Tocqueville commented, "The Spaniards, by unparalleled atrocities which brand them with indelible shame, did not succeed in exterminating the Indian race and could not even prevent them from sharing their rights; the United States Americans have attained both these results with wonderful ease. . . . It is impossible to destroy men with more respect to the laws of humanity."[135] In September 2000 the Bureau of Indian Affairs apologized for its role in "the ethnic cleansing . . . and destructive efforts to annihilate Indian cultures," accepting both "this legacy of racism and inhumanity" and "the moral responsibility of putting things right."[136]

CHAPTER 5

To the North

Canada and U.S. Annexation

> The Western and Southern gentlemen are alarmed at
> a point very seriously insisted upon by the Northern—
> that in case Canada is conquered it shall be divided into
> states and inalienably incorporated into the Union. You
> will see the great and permanent weight such an event
> would throw into the Northern scale.
>
> Senator James Bayard, 1812

On October 26, 1774, the First Continental Congress unanimously and "with universal pleasure" invited the colony of Quebec to join its ranks.[1] The desire to include Quebec was widespread during the American Revolution but vanished among later generations of U.S. leaders, who declined to renew the invitation despite plenty of pretexts for renewed expansionism. Time after time events plunged U.S.–British relations into crisis, and time after time large swathes of the U.S. public clamored for war: in the 1800s, when the British navy kidnapped U.S. sailors and restricted U.S. trade; in the 1830s, when a Canadian rebellion sparked conflict along the border; and again in the 1860s, when Confederate raiders employed British ships during the Civil War. Yet in each case U.S. leaders preferred maintaining a stable border with Quebec, limiting their territorial ambitions to the sparsely populated expanse of central and western Canada. U.S. interest in northern annexations disappeared entirely by the twentieth century, as the U.S.–Canadian border became the world's longest nonmilitarized international boundary.

In this chapter, I examine why U.S. leaders lost interest in annexing Canada across case studies of the Revolution, the War of 1812, the crises of 1837–42, the Oregon controversy, the Fenian Raids, and the post–Civil War push for the Pacific Northwest. I use the term "Canada" to refer to the entirety of that modern country despite the changing labels given to its regions over time.[2]

Canada's early European settlers were concentrated along the St. Lawrence River Valley, which held the only large population centers within a thousand miles of the thirteen colonies. The population of modern Quebec, Ontario, and the Maritime provinces was only 130,000 during the American Revolution, but it swelled to more than 510,000 by 1812, surpassing 1,600,000 by 1841 and 3,500,000 by 1871. In contrast, fewer than 2,000 settlers lived west of modern Ontario in 1812, their numbers growing to 4,800 by 1841 and 27,800 by 1871.[3] In other words, the case studies considered here saw U.S. leaders confront a sparsely populated western Canada alongside a relatively densely populated, rapidly growing eastern Canada. This contrast sets the stage for a natural experiment observing which territories they targeted as the expansionist (the United States) and defender (Britain) remained constant.

Beyond its population, U.S. leaders recognized a wealth of other material benefits in eastern Canada, including timber, furs, fisheries, and the added security of expelling British forces from North America. Given these benefits, profitability theory predicts that early U.S. leaders should have craved eastern Canada as adamantly as they craved New Orleans and Florida, pursuing it whenever its military costs seemed affordable. They saw less value in western Canada, being mostly unfamiliar with the region beyond having a basic sense of its inhospitable climate, so profitability theory predicts that it should have been only a secondary objective, one worth taking if it could be easily had but not worth substantial costs or risks.

The British military was consistently formidable throughout these cases, but it maintained only a small detachment in Canada and was frequently distracted by the delicate balance of power in Europe and the diverse commitments of a global empire. As a result, U.S. leaders rarely doubted their ability to defeat the British in North America. Especially during peaks of U.S. military confidence in the War of 1812 and the post–Civil War period, profitability theory predicts that U.S. leaders should have worked to realize the goal of their revolutionary forebears and seize the most valuable target available: Quebec.

Domestic impact theory predicts different behavior. If U.S. leaders thought that annexation might weaken them politically or worsen their country, they should have pursued only territories minimizing those domestic costs. During the Revolution the United States was not a unified nation-state, and Quebec's participation in the rebellion against Britain would have strengthened the rebel cause without generating domestic repercussions. By 1812, in contrast, the potential addition of northern states worried southerners in Congress and the Madison administration, and some saw Quebec's French and Loyalist populations as being too monarchical to participate in democratic governance. Despite its perceived lack of natural resources, sparsely populated western Canada posed no such domestic costs. As a result, domestic impact theory predicts that U.S. leaders under the Constitution should have rejected the annexation of Quebec while remaining open to affordable opportunities to annex western Canada.

My central argument here is that material benefits, military costs, and domestic costs all mattered to U.S. leaders considering northern annexations. Of the three, domestic costs played the most prominent role in reversing the early desire for Quebec and enabling the neighborly relationship that endures today. As federal leaders considered whether or not to pursue Quebec, they focused less on economic and military factors than on the colony's impact on the sectional balance of power within the United States, the potential for that impact to spark disunion, and the undesirable alien qualities of its French and Loyalist population. Consequently, the annexation of Quebec was a nonstarter as early as the War of 1812, and in later periods, U.S. leaders did not seriously consider it. Western Canada, on the other hand, remained attractive enough to rouse the interests of the administrations of Madison, James Polk, and Andrew Johnson, though given its perceived lack of resources, none was willing to invest enough in its pursuit to actually acquire it. Once British Columbia joined the Dominion of Canada in 1871, U.S. leaders grew content to renounce northward territorial ambitions and instead cultivate a stable, friendly northern neighbor.

The American Revolution

For seven weeks in the fall of 1774 delegates from the British colonies of New Hampshire, Massachusetts, Rhode Island, Connecticut, New York, New Jersey, Pennsylvania, Delaware, Maryland, Virginia, North Carolina, and South Carolina gathered in Philadelphia for the First Continental Congress.[4] What began as collective bargaining transformed into armed rebellion by the following spring, when they reconvened with the addition of Georgia, and one year later those colonies declared independence from the British Empire.[5] Although Quebec never joined the Revolution, U.S. leaders consistently hoped to convince it to do so. How seriously did the United States pursue Quebec during the Revolution, and what role did material interests, military costs, and domestic costs play in driving that pursuit?

The main benefit Quebec offered the Continental Congress was leverage. Its leaders planned to use economic sanctions to coerce the British Parliament into repealing the Intolerable Acts. These acts, passed in reaction to the Boston Tea Party, revoked Massachusetts's charter, closed Boston's port, tried accused officials in Britain, and quartered soldiers in private buildings. Realizing that their bargaining position would be stronger if more colonies participated, the Congress formally invited Quebec, St. John's Island, Nova Scotia, Georgia, East Florida, and West Florida to participate in October 1774. Quebec's population made it easily the most important of these—its 130,000 inhabitants more than doubled Georgia's 56,000—so Congress issued a letter appealing directly to its citizens.[6] Labeling "the violation of your rights . . . a violation of our own," it invited them to join "our confederation, which has no other objects than the perfect security of the natural and civil rights of all the constituent members . . . and the preservation of a happy and lasting connection with Great Britain."[7] When the Second Continental Congress convened the following spring and Quebec's representatives remained absent, it sent additional letters lobbying the people of Quebec to join their cause.[8]

The United States was a confederation of "free and independent states" during the Revolution and not a unified nation-state, as noted above, so Quebec's participation would not have entailed annexation.[9] It would have been more analogous to NATO expansion than to German reunification, strengthening the states' collective bargaining leverage while preserving their domestic autonomy. Congress emphasized this as a selling point in its second letter to the residents of Quebec, urging them to join the struggle for self-determination and renounce their subjection to Parliament, "a legislature in which you have no share, and over which you have no control."[10] The Continental Congress was not immune to politics; mutual suspicions ran rampant among the delegates, many of whom were experiencing their first sustained interaction with the other colonies. Yet its loose institutional structure ensured that adding Quebec would fortify the states' independent sovereignties rather than compromise them.[11] As John Adams declared, "The unanimous voice of the continent is Canada must be ours; Quebec must be taken."[12]

For similar reasons, U.S. leaders during the Revolution were also less worried than their successors about the alien characteristics of Quebec's population, chief among them their Catholicism, a "religion, fraught with sanguinary and impious tenets," as John Jay wrote in a letter approved by the First Continental Congress.[13] Many U.S. leaders worried that "Catholic emigrants from Europe" would "reduce the ancient free Protestant colonies to the same state of slavery with themselves," but they were willing to paper over these religious differences along with linguistic and cultural ones.[14] Greeting Quebec's residents as "friends and fellow country-men," they emphasized their common identity as "English subjects" and cited the Swiss cantons, which were independent sovereign states with their own armies and currencies until 1848, as "furnishing proof that men of different faiths may live in concord and peace together."[15] Since membership in the Continental Congress required no domestic political integration, U.S. leaders could fear the spread of Catholicism yet also pursue Quebec's participation.

With no domestic costs to fear, Congress strove ardently to add Quebec. In the summer of 1775 Congress authorized a military invasion of the province after learning that its British governor, Guy Carleton, was recruiting militia, building new ships on Lake Champlain, and inciting the Iroquois against the rebellious colonies. General Philip Schuyler mustered U.S. militia to march north, sending Ethan Allen and John Brown ahead "with letters to the Canadians . . . to let them know, that the design of the army was only against the English garrisons, and not the country, their liberties, or religion."[16] Richard Montgomery assumed command after Schuyler fell ill, taking Fort St. Johns and Montreal by early November and continuing diplomatic outreach efforts among local residents.[17] Montgomery's force merged with another under Benedict Arnold in early December, and their combined army of nine hundred men laid siege to Quebec City, where Carleton was fortified with eighteen hundred defenders. Because many soldiers' enlistments were about to expire, the pair launched a disastrous assault on December 31 in a heavy snowstorm. It was a debacle, as Montgomery was killed and their forces were decimated.[18]

The invasion sparked resentment among Quebec's people, prompting a fresh diplomatic initiative from Congress to convince them that it wanted only "to adopt them into our union as a sister colony" and allow them to establish "such a form of government as will be most likely, in their judgment, to produce their happiness."[19] Within two weeks of arriving in Montreal Benjamin Franklin became convinced that this mission was hopeless: "The priests, who monopolized all the learning and most of the intelligence of the French population, had been prudently conciliated . . . by the British government," and propaganda attempts ran aground on the reality that "not one in five hundred" Canadians could read.[20] Most French Canadians preferred to stay neutral, just as suspicious of their rebellious neighbors as they were of the British. In the historian George Wrong's words, "Quebec remained British because it was French."[21] Congress remained "fully convinced of the absolute necessity of keeping possession of that country," commanding its forces in May 1776 to "contest every foot of ground." By then, however, British reinforcements had driven out Arnold's remaining soldiers, many of whom were suffering from smallpox.[22] On May 17 George Washington wrote to Schuyler lamenting "the melancholy situation of our affairs in Canada" and observing that "the prospect we had of possessing that country, of so much importance in the present controversy, is almost over."[23]

The signing of the Declaration of Independence on July 4 transformed Quebec's appeal from bargaining leverage to geopolitical security and economic gain. If Britain retained Quebec, it would hold a dangerous platform for future invasions. Washington expected it would "be at least a troublesome if not a dangerous neighbor to us," while Franklin declared, "It is absolutely necessary for us to have them for our own security."[24] Driving Britain from North America would leave only the ailing Spanish Empire as competition for regional dominance, virtually ensuring eventual U.S. domination of North America. The Revolution also accentuated Quebec's economic advantages: controlling the St. Lawrence River (the second-largest waterway into the continent after the Mississippi) would boost the emerging economies around the Great Lakes, and fisheries off the coast of Nova Scotia offered prosperity for the Northeast. With these benefits in view, Congress included in the Articles of Confederation a specific allowance that "Canada, acceding to this confederation, and joining in the measures of the United States, shall be admitted into, and entitled to, all the advantages of this union."[25] Since the Confederation preserved the states' domestic autonomy, Franklin proposed leaving the door open not just to Quebec but also to the West Indies, St. Johns, Nova Scotia, Bermuda, the Floridas, and even Ireland.[26]

U.S. leaders remained focused on obtaining Quebec throughout the Revolutionary War, periodically planning fresh northward invasions but unable to launch them as the Continental Army struggled desperately to secure the rebellious colonies themselves. While Britain reinforced its 8,000 pre-war colonial troops to a wartime high of 56,000, colonial enlistments averaged around 20,000 and fluctuated wildly throughout the war, dipping below 2,200 in March 1777 and to roughly 6,000 in 1781.[27] The Continental Army not only lacked soldiers; it struggled to adequately supply those it had. Arnold's Canadian invasion forces so nearly starved that they ate their dogs and leather accessories, begging Congress, "For God's sake send us pork."[28] During the critical winter of 1777–78 at Valley Forge, Washington wrote to Congress, "We have . . . no less than 2,898 men now in camp unfit for duty because they are bare foot and otherwise naked."[29] The Marquis de Lafayette described how "the unfortunate soldiers were in want of everything; they had neither coats, nor hats, nor shirts, nor shoes; their feet and legs froze till they grew black, and it was often necessary to amputate them."[30] Meanwhile, hyperinflation gutted the value of Continental paper dollars, making it that much harder for Congress to finance military supplies. Many soldiers grew mutinous for lack of pay.[31]

Barely able to field his own army, Washington could spare no troops to conquer Canada. In late 1777 he dubbed a planned northward invasion "the child of folly . . . circumstanced as our affairs are at present," and the following year he ruled out a proposed three-pronged invasion supported by a French fleet as "not eligible" because all available forces were still needed further south.[32] Nevertheless, Congress continued to discuss taking Quebec, as did military leaders like Washington and Lafayette.[33] The French alliance raised the prospect of a joint invasion, but it also raised U.S. fears that France would try to keep the province or control its fisheries and fur trade.[34] Despite viewing "the emancipation of Canada as an object very interesting to the future prosperity and tranquility of these states," Washington wrote to Congress in November 1778 that "a co-operation by the French would in my opinion, be as delicate and precarious an enterprise, as can be imagined."[35] For their part, French leaders preferred that Canada remain a geopolitical liability ensuring U.S. suspicion of Britain and amiability toward France, so when Washington proposed a joint northward campaign in late 1781 the French minister reiterated his support for U.S. independence but not for U.S. conquests.[36] Washington continued planning new invasions of Quebec until Cornwallis's surrender at Yorktown brought the war to an end.

Where invitations and invasions had failed, peace negotiations offered one last chance to gain Quebec. Franklin had included the remaining British colonies in North America among his potential demands as early as 1776, and three years later Congress told the U.S. negotiators to claim all territory east of a line connecting the Mississippi River and Lake Nipissing in present-day Ontario.[37] Their instructions emphasized that "it is of the utmost importance to the peace and commerce of the United States that Canada and Nova Scotia should be ceded," but they left no doubt that independence took priority over expansion, specifying that "a desire of terminating the war hath induced us not to make the acquisition of these objects an ultimatum."[38] Those priorities persisted throughout the negotiations. When Franklin distinguished the *necessary* and *desirable* terms of peace to the British negotiator Richard Oswald in 1782, Canada's cession fell into the latter category. Although Oswald was willing to cede Canada, since "Franklin from the first had prepared him for that as the simplest way of settling the whole business," Prime Minister Shelburne preferred ceding Transappalachia instead, so the Treaty of Paris left Quebec in British hands.[39]

U.S. leaders persistently targeted Quebec during the Revolution, limited though they were by military deficiencies and the priority of achieving independence. The precedent set during this formative period of U.S. foreign policy should inform the future course of events, implying that overwhelming military or domestic costs should have been necessary to convince later generations of U.S. leaders to abandon their predecessors' ambitions. As the following cases show, domestic costs did increase under the Constitution, which notably lacked any invitation to Quebec in the manner of the Articles of Confederation. Future debates over annexation took on overtly sectional and racial tenors as U.S. leaders weighed its domestic consequences. As a result, the widespread desire for Quebec during the Revolution dissipated entirely by the War of 1812.

The War of 1812

The United States invaded Canada for a second time after declaring war on Britain in June 1812. Profitability theory strongly predicts that U.S. leaders should have pursued annexation in this case: the decades since the Revolution had only enhanced Quebec's material benefits, and U.S. leaders widely assumed it could be easily conquered given that Britain was distracted by the Napoleonic Wars. This should be a particularly easy case for profitability theory because U.S. leaders initiated the war and because the precedent set during the Revolution works in its favor. In contrast, domestic impact theory predicts that U.S. leaders under the Constitution should have been concerned with the identity of Quebec's population and its likely domestic political impact, rejecting even profitable annexation if they feared its domestic costs.

The War of 1812 was a far more important event in U.S. foreign policy history than most people realize. For the first time U.S. leaders consciously declined a profitable opportunity for annexation due to its domestic costs, establishing a precedent that would echo throughout subsequent U.S. policy toward Canada, Mexico, and countries overseas. Unfortunately, its significance is often overlooked due to the stubborn myth that the United States launched the war to annex Canada. As I have previously detailed in the pages of *Diplomatic History*, this notion is false: U.S. leaders did not declare war in 1812 hoping to achieve their predecessors' goal of securing Quebec's representation in Congress. They declared war in the hope it would force Britain to remove its restrictions on U.S. maritime trade.[40] The War of 1812 was not a land grab; it was an attempt at coercive bargaining, Carl von Clausewitz's "politics by other means."[41]

During Jefferson's presidency U.S.–British relations suffered under Britain's policy of impressment—searching U.S. merchant vessels for suspected British subjects and, when discovered, forcing them to serve in its navy.[42] Yet few saw war on the horizon. Jefferson's territorial ambitions aimed not northward but southward, and as late as the summer of 1805 he plotted to ally with Britain against Spain to conquer the Floridas.[43] Unfortunately for Jefferson, Britain's campaign against Napoleon focused on strangling his seaborne trade, including trade with the United States. As the naval historian Alfred Mahan wrote, "While Great Britain ruled the sea, the neutral was the ally of her enemy."[44] In November 1807 Britain banned all foreign trade with France in its most notorious Orders in Council.[45] The Orders in Council sparked a furious backlash among the U.S. public, which clamored for war in the name of "free trade and sailors' rights."[46] Senator John Quincy Adams of Massachusetts howled that "the Orders of Council . . . strike at the root of our independence."[47] Kentucky's Henry Clay condemned "British slavery upon the water."[48] Congressman John Calhoun of South Carolina protested, "If we submit to the pretensions of England, now openly avowed, the independence of this nation is lost—we will be, as to our commerce, recolonized."[49] This outrage resounded across the Atlantic but had little effect there since "the British government preferred to risk war with the United States than to risk defeat by Napoleon."[50]

With the public demanding war and Napoleon occupying the British military, the Orders in Council offered a ripe opportunity for the United States to renew its former pursuit of Quebec. Instead, Jefferson and congressional leaders tried to coerce Britain to repeal its maritime restrictions by using economic sanctions. After an 1806 Non-Importation Act proved ineffectual, the Embargo Act of December 1807 forbade all U.S.–British trade. This "act of self-immolation" failed to coerce Britain but ravaged the U.S. economy, slashing imports by 60 percent (from $144,740,000 to $58,101,000) and exports by 80 percent (from $103,343,000 to $22,431,000) the following year.[51] After losing ground to the opposition Federalists in the 1808 elections, the Democratic-Republican majority in Congress replaced the embargo with various lesser sanctions over the ensuing years until all hope they might prove effective had evaporated. Secretary of State James Monroe wrote, "We have been so long dealing in the small way of embargoes, non-intercourse, and non-importation, with menaces of war, &c., that the British government has not believed us. . . . We must actually get to war before the intention to make it will be credited either here or abroad."[52] After five years of failed sanctions, Congress declared war on June 18, 1812.

The war was a diplomatic gamble, "a desperate act on the part of U.S. leaders brought to their wits' end by British maritime restrictions, which were themselves desperate acts by a British government fighting for its life against Napoleon."[53] President Madison condemned British leaders for "trampling on rights which no independent nation can relinquish," noting that submission "would recolonize our commerce by subjecting it to a foreign authority; with the sole difference that the regulations of it formerly were made by acts of Parliament and now, by Orders in Council."[54] Yet Madison did not want war.[55] He hoped that the declaration of war would serve as an effective bluff and finally convince Britain to come to terms. From the moment he signed it he actively sought a peace agreement.[56]

On June 26 Monroe informed the U.S. chargé d'affaires in London, Jonathan Russell, that Congress had declared war because "it was impossible for the United States to surrender their rights . . . [or] to rely longer on measures which had failed to accomplish their objects." Nevertheless, he wrote, "this . . . is the most favorable moment for an accommodation with England." He instructed Russell to tell his British counterparts that "this government looks forward to the restoration of peace" and that it was "in the power of Great Britain to terminate the war." He suggested two arguments that might drive home the benefits of an early peace for Britain: (1) that U.S. leaders might choose to annex Canada if their forces occupied it, and (2) that a long war would increase the chances of a formal U.S.–French alliance being forged. The former argument—that it might be "difficult to relinquish territory which had been conquered"—is frequently referenced as evidence of U.S. expansionism, but its context as an argument for avoiding war reveals its true nature as precisely the opposite.[57] The question of whether the United States should pursue territory in Canada—and, if so, which territory—arose as a result of the war rather than as a driving cause.

Profitability theory predicts that U.S. leaders should reject annexation when they fear its military costs: was this the case in the War of 1812? U.S. military deficiencies are glaring in hindsight. "The Royal Navy possessed three warships for every U.S. cannon," and historians agree that "no nation could have been less fitted to wage war than America in 1811."[58] The antiwar congressman John Randolph complained that his colleagues were "outquixoting Quixote himself" by plotting to coerce mighty Britain, crying out, "Go to war, without money, without men, without a navy! . . . The people will not believe it."[59] The U.S. army numbered a mere 6,000 soldiers in 1812 and peaked at 30,000 during the war. Its officer corps of 191 under Jefferson ballooned to 3,495 by 1814, many "utterly unfit for any military purpose whatever" in the eyes of General Winfield Scott.[60] This woeful unpreparedness reflected Jefferson's and Madison's lack of interest in a northern war of conquest, which could have been feasible with greater planning given Canada's equally meager defenses (5,000–10,000 troops).[61]

Yet despite the sorry state of their military, most U.S. leaders were "supremely confident of success."[62] Jefferson boasted, "The acquisition of Canada this year, as far as the neighborhood of Quebec, will be a mere matter of marching," maintaining further that "upon the whole, I have known no war entered into under more favorable auspices."[63] Monroe forecast that "we shall experience little annoyance or embarrassment in the effort."[64] Congressmen outbid each other in predicting how quickly U.S. forces would occupy Canada and how small a force could accomplish the task. Calhoun expected that within "four weeks . . . the whole of Upper and a part of Lower Canada will be in our possession."[65] Jacob Crowninshield of Massachusetts insisted, "Vermont and Massachusetts will ask no other assistance than their own militia to take Canada and Nova Scotia," and Clay proclaimed, "I verily believe that the militia of Kentucky are alone competent to place Montreal and Upper Canada at your feet."[66] Randolph scoffed, "It seems this is to be a holiday campaign. . . . Canada is to conquer herself."[67] In light of this widespread overconfidence, profitability theory cannot explain why U.S. leaders declined to pursue Quebec.

After all, the colony's material benefits had increased since the Revolution. The population of eastern Canada had grown to roughly 510,000 by 1812, and Jefferson's embargo catalyzed a dramatic transformation of its latent natural resources into economic production.[68] As J. C. A. Stagg describes, the region experienced "simply astronomical" growth: "Between 1807 and 1811, the volume of Canadian exports of oak and plank timber rose 549%, of great and middling masts 519%, and of fir and pine timber 556%."[69] Madison recognized this change. Before the embargo he had opposed the notion of threatening Quebec as saying, "Do us justice or we will seize on Canada, though the loss will be trifling to you," but after 1808 he "never again made any remarks suggesting that he still felt Canada was of little or no value to the British Empire."[70] By 1812 Canada was producing enough timber to sustain the British navy even if Napoleon's upcoming invasion of Russia shut down its other suppliers on the Baltic Sea.[71] As New York Congressman Peter Porter observed, Canada was "almost indispensable to the existence of Great Britain, cut off as she now in a great measure is from the north of Europe."[72]

Instead of luring U.S. leaders to pursue annexation, however, Quebec's development offered them exactly the bargaining chip they had been seeking in their quest to get Britain's maritime restrictions repealed.[73] Moreover, Quebec was "tangible," lying within range of U.S. forces rather than being insulated by British command of the seas.[74] The fact that U.S. forces invaded Canada may seem expansionist at first glance, but if one recognizes their strategy it becomes easy to understand why leaders with no desire to annex Quebec still chose to invade it. As Henry Clay explained in 1813, "Canada was not the end but the means; the object of the war being the redress of injuries, and Canada being the instrument by which that redress was to be obtained."[75] Monroe supported the invasion of Canada "not as an object of the war but as a means to bring it to a satisfactory conclusion."[76] Madison himself later reflected, "Had the French Emperor not been broken down, as he was, to a degree at variance with all probability, and which no human sagacity could anticipate, can it be doubted that G. Britain would have been constrained, by her own situation and the demands of her allies, to listen to our reasonable terms of reconciliation?"[77]

Although they did not fear the military costs of annexing Quebec, southern leaders like Jefferson and Madison had good reason to fear its domestic costs since one or more new Canadian states joining the northern bloc would have weakened their dominant political position. Senator James Bayard of Delaware described how "the Western and Southern gentlemen are alarmed at a point very seriously insisted upon by the Northern—that in case Canada is conquered it shall be divided into states and inalienably incorporated into the Union. You will see the great and permanent weight such an event would throw into the Northern scale."[78] Virginia Congressman Hugh Nelson feared that even sparsely populated areas north of the border would be filled by northern settlers and hence believed that "the New Yorkers and Vermonters are very well inclined to have Upper Canada united with them, by way of increasing their influence in the Union."[79] Annexing new territories meant granting federal representation to their inhabitants, a threatening prospect for those who saw the interests of those inhabitants as conflicting with their own.

If the United States did annex Canada and create "a prepondering northern influence," it was widely feared that southern leaders would secede from the Union to preserve their political control.[80] Postmaster General Gideon Granger asked, "But will not the addition of these territories accelerate a dissolution of the Union? Or can it spread securely over the continent? I fear, I doubt."[81] Randolph also feared that his colleagues would "take Canada, at the risk of the Constitution," declaring, "You are laying the foundation for a secession . . . by the possession of Canada."[82] Foreign leaders expected as much: Napoleon had foreseen U.S. dissolution since 1803, and the British colonial secretary Liverpool wrote in 1810, "If some material change should not occur in the system of the government, the result will probably be, the separation of the Eastern from the Southern states. . . . [I]t will take place at no very distant period."[83] Neither Jefferson nor Madison had any interest in annexing a territory that threatened to strengthen their domestic political rivals or disintegrate the Union, especially with their Democratic-Republicans firmly in control of the federal government and the opposition Federalists on the verge of collapse.

Indeed, the Virginia Dynasty's dominance of the federal government was so extensive that it survived not only self-flagellating economic sanctions but also the War of 1812 itself. Although both involved tremendous costs, both aimed to defend the interests of producers in the South, West, and Central states.[84] In contrast, the Northeast reacted to Jefferson's embargo with smuggling so rampant that he thought it "amounted almost to rebellion and treason."[85] When Congress declared war, New Englanders refused to acknowledge it.[86] Connecticut's General Assembly denied that it was constitutionally obligated to participate, declaring itself "a free sovereign and independent state" and the United States "a confederated and not a consolidated republic." The governor of Massachusetts secretly offered Britain part of Maine to end the war.[87] In December 1814 New England Federalist leaders at the Hartford Convention composed a list of constitutional amendments to safeguard their states' influence within a federal government controlled by the South and turning toward the West: removing the three-fifths clause that boosted southern representation, prohibiting successive presidents from the same state, and requiring a two-thirds majority for declaring war or admitting new states (affording New England a veto).[88] Some spoke of northern secession, a prospect that drove U.S. peace negotiators to press claims to northern fisheries, though not to press the annexation of Quebec.[89]

Beyond sectional political concerns, the identity of Quebec's population also deterred U.S. leaders from pursuing annexation. The majority of its inhabitants were French Catholics, whom many Americans "deemed unfit by faith, language, and illiteracy for republican citizenship."[90] Congressman Josiah Quincy of Massachusetts worried that annexing Quebec without granting representation to the French Canadians, which he was unwilling to do, would corrupt American democracy by creating a "dynasty by the sword."[91] Many also viewed British Loyalists with suspicion, regarding their devotion to the British Crown as a sign of the same monarchical spirit associated with Catholicism. They too were concentrated in the east, about 70 percent of the fifty thousand who fled to Canada after the Revolution having settled in its Maritime provinces.[92] As Randolph declared, "I have no desire to see the senators and representatives of the Canadian French, or of the tories and refugees of Nova Scotia, sitting on this floor or that of the other House— to see them becoming members of the Union, and participating equally in our political rights."[93] These prejudices caused operational problems for the U.S. military when soldiers who shared them refused commands to advance across the border lest their efforts be utilized to conquer Canada.[94]

Upper Canada (modern Ontario) remained sparsely populated enough, having only sixty thousand residents in 1811, that future settlers could determine its political destiny.[95] This attracted a small cadre of frontier expansionists in Congress led by John Harper of New Hampshire and Peter Porter of

New York.⁹⁶ Consistent with domestic impact theory, they specifically targeted that low-population region, against the wishes of other War Hawks who valued it only as a bargaining chip. Porter's blueprints for a hypothetical postwar North America featured "a separate French-speaking state" in Quebec that would remain independent. As he declared, "I would content myself with the possession of the *open country*."⁹⁷ These few expansionists failed to achieve much support: the House pledged only to protect Canadians' "lives, liberty, property, and religion," and the Senate rejected even that limited measure.⁹⁸ Most saw any gestures toward annexation as counterproductive: they had voted for war hoping that a credible threat to Canada would finally compel Britain to repeal its maritime restrictions. Why sacrifice their last best hope to achieve what they really wanted? As the historian Roger Brown writes, "Once a pledge had rendered Canada non-negotiable, its diplomatic value was at an end," so "Congress never came close to voting the measure that Harper labored to obtain. In point of fact there had been strong opposition to annexation of Canada from the very beginning."⁹⁹

The Madison administration continued to demonstrate its lack of interest in annexing Canada as the war progressed, suppressing expansionism and jumping at any chance to restore peace. The administration refused to endorse the efforts of certain U.S. military officers to curry local support by promising liberation to the Canadians.¹⁰⁰ When Russia offered to mediate peace negotiations in early 1813, Madison issued a "hasty" acceptance "without waiting to learn whether England would agree to negotiate" (it did not).¹⁰¹ He optimistically instructed his peace commissioners to offer to exchange any areas currently occupied by U.S. forces in return for political concessions: "A reciprocal stipulation will be entered into for the restoration of any territory which either party may have acquired by the war. The probable state of the war at the date of the treaty will render this stipulation favorable to G. Britain."¹⁰² Publicly, Madison insisted that "conquest, with a view of extending our territory, and enlarging our dominion, was not the wish of this government."¹⁰³ His lack of enthusiasm for expansion was so evident that Harper complained, "The executive are not disposed to prosecute the war with vigor, provided they can find any *hole* through which they can creep out and avoid the contest."¹⁰⁴ Congressman Cyrus King of Massachusetts put it plainly: "This administration never intended to conquer Canada."¹⁰⁵

As domestic impact theory predicts, when Madison did entertain the possibility of territorial gains, he too had eyes only for sparsely populated Upper Canada. In June 1813 Jefferson advised him to acquire "all westward of the meridian of Lake Huron, or of Ontario, or of Montreal . . . as an indemnification for the past and security for the future."[106] Accordingly, Monroe told the U.S. peace commissioners to request "a transfer of the upper parts" or "at least of that portion lying between the western end of Lake Ontario and the Eastern end of Lake Huron."[107] This untenable claim was probably another bargaining ploy to be traded away rather than a serious demand, given that U.S. forces had failed to occupy any substantial stretch of Canadian territory during the war. Even had Britain accepted it, though, Upper Canada would have threatened minimal domestic costs as a sparsely populated extension of the Louisiana Territory that could be settled and divided into several new states. Britain finally agreed to negotiate in 1814 after Napoleon's defeat, and that December the Treaty of Ghent restored the status quo ante bellum.

The historian Jon Latimer claimed that "if the war had one concrete result, it was the guarantee of Canada's existence as a separate nation."[108] His assessment was based on a fundamental misreading of U.S. intentions: the War of 1812 was not "a failed war of conquest" proving that Canada could defend itself; it was a failed war of coercion proving that the United States could not threaten Britain more gravely than Napoleon. Nevertheless, Latimer's conclusion rings true: the War of 1812 guaranteed Canada's independence not because the United States failed to conquer it but because U.S. leaders decided they didn't want to conquer it. After all, Canada's military is not what prevents the United States from conquering it today. Confronted with the domestic consequences of absorbing a populous neighboring society, as Bradford Perkins writes, "the United States did not go to war to add new states to the Union."[109] In the War of 1812 U.S. leaders defied the Revolution's precedent and initiated a new pattern (interest in sparsely populated western Canada but not in populous eastern Canada) that would echo through the decades that followed.

The Crises of 1837–42

Rarely in history have two countries endured as many crises in as short a time without descending into war as the United States and Britain did between 1837 and 1842. Rebellions, border raids, military standoffs, territorial disputes, international trials, and yet none led to full-scale war. Why did this rash of crises, any of which offered a credible pretext for expansionism, end in stabilized relations rather than the U.S. annexation of eastern Canada? By the late 1830s the population of modern Ontario, Quebec, and the Maritime provinces had swelled to 1.5 million, and their economy (focused on staple products like furs, timber, fish, and wheat) had grown apace.[110] These increasing material benefits combined with faltering British control to open the door for U.S. leaders to pursue as much or as little of Canada as they pleased.

Profitability theory predicts that U.S. leaders should have desired eastern Canada and so should have exploited these crises to pursue it. But the Canadian rebellion caught U.S. leaders by surprise, as most of their military was deployed against the Seminoles in Florida, making sudden war with Britain a costly prospect. Therefore, profitability theory expects them to have rectified their military deficiencies, employing subtler means of expansionism until they were ready for a more vigorous northward push. Conversely, domestic impact theory predicts that most U.S. leaders should have seen eastern Canada's booming population as a deterrent and hence lacked any interest in annexing it. Why didn't the United States annex eastern Canada during this period?

The rebellion began in November 1837 with Lower Canadians led by reformers like Louis-Joseph Papineau and was joined the next month by Upper Canadians led by William Lyon Mackenzie. Unlike the two previous cases in this chapter, when most Canadians had little desire to break with Britain, this rebellion offered U.S. leaders their first major opportunity to harness a wave of local anti-British sentiment.[111] Had they been interested in annexing eastern Canada, the fruit finally would have appeared ripe. Several private organizations south of the border saw it that way, including the Hunter's Lodge, which claimed fifty thousand members at its peak and recruited forces to invade Canada.[112] Yet instead of pursuing annexation "Washington carefully avoided any involvement" with the rebellion.[113] President Martin Van Buren displayed a "profound commitment to neutrality," ordering governors and district attorneys in Michigan, New York, and Vermont to prevent U.S. citizens from interfering.[114] Instead of using private citizens to fan the flames of rebellion, as Madison had in the Floridas, Van Buren prevented them from doing so despite its popularity, complaining, "It is utterly impossible to prevent the young . . . from embarking in those enterprises, so long as their conduct is indirectly applauded by public expressions of sympathy."[115]

British soldiers escalated the crisis on December 29 by sneaking across the Niagara River and storming the *Caroline*, a steamboat used to supply Mackenzie's rebels. They set the boat ablaze and cast it over Niagara Falls, killing a U.S. citizen in the process and provoking a storm of anti-British fury throughout the United States (the number of casualties rapidly inflated as rumors of the incident spread). Henry Clay described the assault as an "unparalleled outrage."[116] The Pennsylvania senator James Buchanan protested, "The sovereignty and jurisdiction of the United States over our own territory have been grossly violated."[117] Van Buren himself described the incident to Congress as "a hostile though temporary invasion of our territory."[118] War fever spread with the news. Former president John Quincy Adams and Congressman Millard Fillmore of New York both sensed "imminent danger," and the *New York Herald* wrote, "Surely war with England was unavoidable."[119]

Yet despite American blood shed on American soil, the same pretext President Polk would use to launch the Mexican–American War eight years later, Van Buren responded to the *Caroline* incident by aggressively pursuing peace. Upon learning of the raid on January 4 he immediately sent General Winfield Scott to the border to dissuade local Americans from retaliating. The next day he issued a neutrality proclamation warning that any U.S. citizens who interfered would be prosecuted and promising "no aid or countenance" for anyone arrested in Canada.[120] Van Buren asked a receptive Congress to revise existing neutrality laws to be preventive rather than merely punitive, and it did so, authorizing $625,000 for frontier defense and empowering the government "to seize and detain any vessel or any arms . . . provided or prepared for any military expedition . . . against . . . any colony, district or people conterminous with the United States."[121] Dismissing rumors of a warlike mood in Washington as "wholly unfounded," Van Buren insisted that peace "would be the case if the wishes of the men in power in both countries were alone to be consulted."[122]

British leaders recognized the absence of U.S. territorial ambitions. The British minister to the United States, Henry Fox, observed that "the president's government is sincerely striving, as far as so weak and feeble a government can be said to strive at anything,—to fulfill its natural duties."[123] In fact, Van Buren cooperated to an unprecedented extent, allowing Britain to march troops from Halifax to Quebec across territory claimed by Maine in its ongoing boundary dispute with New Brunswick and to temporarily increase its naval forces on the Great Lakes in violation of the Rush-Bagot Agreement. Van Buren, Scott, and Secretary of State John Forsyth repeatedly shared information with the British regarding the activities of private interventionist organizations. Van Buren even sent his son to London in March 1838 to personally appeal to Foreign Secretary Palmerston for peace.[124]

Was this restraint driven by fear of annexation's military costs? Britain maintained only about five thousand troops in Canada in 1837, but U.S. leaders entertained no delusions of grandeur with regard to their own armed forces, as they had in 1812.[125] When the rebellion began virtually all able-bodied U.S. soldiers were fighting the Second Seminole War in Florida, leaving northern garrisons staffed with "the aged and infirm."[126] The situation left congressmen like Joseph Tillinghast of Rhode Island to marvel at "the upper coasts left entirely unprotected."[127] Regretting the "defenseless state of the northern frontier, owing to the military troops having been drawn away for . . . the war in Florida," Isaac Bronson of New York observed, "The [war] department was now unable to send troops to the North, for the simple reason that there were none to send."[128] Fully aware of their military unpreparedness, U.S. leaders dreaded the costs of a sudden northern war. Massachusetts Senator John Davis declared, "Of all the evils that could now befall this nation, the most deplorable in its effects would be a war with Great Britain. We all well know the strength and power of that country."[129] Congressman Waddy Thompson of South Carolina feared the "tremendous consequences," and John Calhoun the "terrible consequences of a war with Great Britain at the present time."[130]

In the late 1830s, unlike in 1812, military costs did constrain U.S. decision-making. Yet if that were the whole story, the historical record should be filled with frustrated leaders complaining that military weakness had prevented them from seizing such a fine opportunity for annexation, and they should have moved quickly to redress the problem and achieve any gains still available. Such sentiments were absent from congressional deliberations, which instead reflected a genuine desire to maintain neutrality in the Canadian rebellion. When the *London Times* speculated about potential U.S. expansionism in Canada, Buchanan objected, "We are accused of a disposition to wrest it from Great Britain, and annex it to the United States. Here, we all know these accusations to be unjust and unfounded."[131] Henry Clay, often considered to be among the most expansionist leaders of his generation, emphasized how little he thought of northward expansion in 1839: "So far from conveying the idea that the U.S. would, at a suitable time, interfere on the question of that [British–Canadian] relation, I took pains to inculcate that they would not interfere, on Canadian account."[132]

Domestic costs affected U.S. decision-making alongside military costs during the late 1830s, making the annexation of eastern Canada undesirable regardless of its profitability. Largely Catholic and French-speaking, the people of Lower Canada were seen as foreigners of questionable merit by many Americans (who were overwhelmingly Protestant), especially after their failure to support the United States in two previous wars. Catholicism remained inherently linked to monarchy and despotism in U.S. domestic political discourse at the time, and political mudslinging frequently saw rivals accuse each other of having Catholic sympathies. Van Buren himself had been targeted. As the biographer Ted Widmer writes, "Because of the letter he had written to the pope in 1829 assuring that Catholics were treated decently in the United States, Whigs accused him of being secretly pro-Catholic" and involved in a "popish plot." [133] In this environment, absorbing a large Catholic population was an unappealing prospect. Upper Canadians, though mostly Protestant, were also problematic due to their willing submission to the British Crown. The *Detroit Advertiser* drove this point home by juxtaposing them with the settlers in Texas, who had recently declared independence and requested annexation, advising its readers to "remember that Upper Canada is not Texas; that Canadians are not Texans; and that Great Britain is not Mexico." [134] Senator John Norvell of Michigan explained his opposition to intervening in the Canadian rebellion by declaring, "Our own rights and liberties were too precious to be jeoparded in those premature and badly digested civil broils between different portions of the same foreign people." [135]

Despite both Van Buren and Congress working to ensure U.S. neutrality, the crisis worsened in late 1838 with the Aroostook War. This militarized dispute, in which no battles were fought, concerned the border between Maine and New Brunswick, which had remained ill-defined since the Revolution. Commissions established by the Jay Treaty and the Treaty of Ghent had failed to resolve the issue, as had several attempted negotiations and a Dutch arbitration effort. The government of Maine, a state since 1820, proved to be a particular obstacle: unwilling to surrender any of its claimed territory, Maine's legislature resolved that no federal treaty on the issue was binding unless a majority of its own people approved in town meetings. [136] The federal government backed Maine until January 1839, when Governor John Fairfield dispatched a posse to expel Canadian timber poachers from the disputed area. When the posse's leader was captured and New Brunswick's governor claimed the right to repel the invasion by force, an outraged Maine legislature approved $800,000 in emergency funds and called forth ten thousand militia. Fairfield sent them north in late February, only then notifying Van Buren of his fait accompli and demanding federal support.

An expansionist president might have leapt to Maine's defense and seized the opportunity to broaden U.S. territorial claims. Instead, Van Buren immediately denounced Fairfield. In a special message to Congress he supported Maine's claim but condemned its military action, pledging not to defend it in any self-initiated conflict. Leaders from the other states, continually jealous of each other's domestic influence under the Constitution, condemned Maine for trying to co-opt their foreign policy by unilaterally attacking Canada. Clay declared that he "could not consent . . . that the will of one of the twenty-six members of the confederacy should control the entire Union, or that one should draw the entire Union, without their consent, into a war with a foreign power."[137] The Senate Foreign Relations Committee introduced resolutions supporting Maine's territorial claim but vowing that if Britain acted peacefully and Maine determined "to settle the controversy for herself by force . . . there will be no obligation imposed on that [federal] government to sustain her by military aid." Senator Daniel Webster of Massachusetts supported these resolutions by arguing, "We could have no war by states any more than by counties or by multitudes of armed persons, acting without any authority at all," to which Calhoun replied, "Certainly not."[138] In early March Congress empowered Van Buren to spend up to $10 million and call out fifty thousand militia, enough to overwhelm both Maine's force and any Canadian adversaries. In doing so, congressmen demonstrated that they were willing to fund an army to rebuke one of their own states but not to pursue conquest. Van Buren proceeded to negotiate a joint memorandum with Fox calling for the withdrawal of all forces from the Aroostook Valley and the prevention of trespassing, to which both governors agreed by the end of March.

Fresh incidents continued to strain U.S.–British relations, however. In November 1840 a British Canadian named Alexander McLeod was arrested in New York for the murder of Amos Durfee during the *Caroline* affair. When an angry mob prevented McLeod's release on bail and pushed for a speedy trial, Palmerston ordered Fox to return to Britain if he was found guilty (the crucial diplomatic step preceding a declaration of war). McLeod was acquitted in October 1841, but the previous month a group of British soldiers crossed into Vermont to beat and abduct James Grogan, a U.S. citizen who had seen his family's farms in Lower Canada burned during the rebellion and had burned several nearby farms in revenge.[139] British leaders released Grogan in October hoping to soothe the outrage his abduction had fanned along the border, but in November slaves on the U.S. ship *Creole* revolted and reached the Bahamas, where they were declared free because slavery had been outlawed in British territories. The local U.S. consul's attempt to retake the ship failed, and among the ship's passengers only the mutineers were briefly detained by British authorities. Despite crisis upon crisis, President John Tyler maintained Van Buren's peaceful course after ascending to office in early 1841 when William Henry Harrison died after scarcely one month in the White House. Tyler sent Secretary of State Daniel Webster to negotiate a final settlement on the northeastern border, which resulted in the Webster–Ashburton Treaty, an agreement that restored cordiality to U.S.–British relations. Tyler wrote, "The peace of the country when I reached Washington . . . was suspended by a thread, but we converted that thread into a chain cable of sufficient strength to render that peace secure."[140]

U.S. leaders during this period feared the military costs of war with Britain, but that fact alone cannot explain why they rejected a prime opportunity for expansion. Contrary to profitability theory, the historical record indicates that they genuinely prioritized neutrality in the rebellions in Canada instead of exploiting them for territorial gain, as they had in the Floridas. Although military unpreparedness was a factor, it cannot explain why Congress proved willing to field a large army to rebuke Maine but not to pursue Canadian territory. Domestic concerns are a more compelling explanation of why U.S. leaders lacked interest in annexing eastern Canada and of why their behavior toward it in this period contrasted so starkly with their approach to Oregon.

Oregon

Though they declined to pursue eastern Canada in the late 1830s, U.S. leaders aggressively targeted western Canada in the mid-1840s. The Oregon Country, stretching from the Pacific Ocean to the Rocky Mountains and from Mexico's northern border at 42° to Russian Alaska's southern border at 54°40', had been left open to joint U.S.–British occupation since 1818, when the U.S.–Canadian border east of the Rocky Mountains was set at latitude 49° north. Daniel Webster and Alexander Baring, 1st Baron Ashburton considered addressing the Oregon boundary in 1842, but their negotiations were cut short by that summer's oppressive heat and humidity. Secretary of State John Calhoun resumed Oregon talks in 1844 with the new British minister to Washington, Richard Pakenham, but he rejected Pakenham's suggestion that they submit to international arbitration. Calhoun was content with a "masterly inactivity," at least until U.S. settlers venturing there forced the issue.[141]

Oregon's status remained unresolved for decades because it lacked substantial consequences for either side. British leaders saw little value in the area, Foreign Secretary Aberdeen referring to it as merely "a few miles of pine swamp."[142] Its primary export, furs, had dwindled by the 1840s, and the Hudson's Bay Company abandoned the Columbia River in favor of more northern regions still suitable for trapping.[143] Congressman Thomas Bayly of Virginia saw Oregon as a generally "inhospitable territory" in which "only a very small portion of the land is capable of cultivation." He said of the upper Columbia River, "There is no freshness in the little vegetation on its borders; the sterile sands reach to its very brink."[144] Its greatest economic appeal was as a conduit for Asian commerce via a port on the Puget Sound, widely seen as the economic key to the entire region.[145] The most enthusiastic description of its resources had been composed by the United States Exploring Expedition, which charted eight hundred miles of Oregon while exploring the Pacific Ocean, but President Tyler had suppressed its 1842 report to avoid jeopardizing the Webster-Ashburton negotiations.[146]

If most U.S. leaders saw Oregon as relatively valueless, why did they pursue it so soon after declining to seek more valuable territory in the Northeast? Unlike eastern Canada, Oregon would bring minimal domestic costs because it had few people and was rapidly attracting U.S. settlers by the mid-1840s. Oregon had virtually no European inhabitants beyond several hundred employees of the Hudson's Bay Company (the Vancouver area didn't attract substantial settlement until the 1858 gold rush), and European diseases had devastated its Native American tribes. A U.S. visitor in 1844 reported that perhaps 150,000 Native Americans had inhabited Oregon fifty years earlier "but a small remnant now remain . . . not more than 18,000," with two-thirds of its former tribes "utterly extinct."[147] The early 1840s also saw U.S. settlers begin following the Oregon Trail, their numbers growing from 1,000 in 1843 to about 6,000 by 1845.[148] As the British foreign minister Castlereagh reportedly told a U.S. diplomat, "You need not trouble yourselves about Oregon, you will conquer Oregon in your bedchambers."[149]

President James Polk declared in his inaugural address that the U.S. claim to Oregon was "clear and unquestionable," and in December 1845 he called for Congress to abrogate the joint occupation agreement.[150] Asserting that "our title to the whole Oregon Territory" was "maintained by irrefragable facts and arguments," Polk adopted a strategy of diplomatic brinksmanship.[151] He broke off negotiations on August 30 when Pakenham rejected a proposed border at 49° without British navigation rights on the Columbia River, a deal Tyler had previously offered. Throughout the fall Polk continued "to assert our extreme right to the whole country," remarking that this was "the decision to which I have irrevocably come in the Oregon question" and leaving "the British minister to take his own course."[152]

Many in Congress supported Polk's bold approach.[153] Congressman Andrew Kennedy of Indiana vowed, "Oregon is ours. This no man, friend or foe, can gainsay or dispute."[154] David Reid of North Carolina agreed: "I believe the country is ours to 54°40'."[155] David Starkweather of Ohio insisted, "Our title to Oregon is perfect."[156] Many newspapers supported Polk's stand as well, encouraging him to claim the entire Oregon Country with slogans like "The Whole of Oregon or None!" and "Fifty-Four Forty or Fight!" As the journalist John O'Sullivan wrote, the United States should demand all of Oregon "by the right of our manifest destiny to overspread and to possess the entire continent."[157]

Few U.S. leaders wanted to fight for Oregon, but most supported Polk's bluster because they assumed that Britain had even more to lose and less to gain from a war. In Cabinet meetings, Polk dismissed Secretary of State James Buchanan's fears that his approach might lead to war, maintaining that "if we do have war it will not be our fault."[158] Even as he called for "vigorous preparations for defense," Polk remained confident in his brinksmanship, telling Calhoun that "Lord Aberdeen and Sir Robert Peel would be averse to going to war . . . and that until . . . the American government boldly faced the British power & asserted their rights, that the latter would yield nothing of her pretensions."[159] Certain that British leaders would rather negotiate than fight over Oregon, he considered offering a tariff reduction as a bargaining chip for which "that government might be willing to surrender her claim to the whole Oregon territory."[160]

Polk's confidence was echoed in Congress, where John Wentworth of Illinois argued that the northeastern crises would pay off out west: "No, no; much as this nation of hypocrites wants Oregon, she would not go to war with us for it. She knows us too well. She knows the soreness of feeling along our whole frontier engendered, during the late Canadian troubles, by the burning of the *Caroline*, the murder of Durfee, and the capture of Grogan."[161] Georgia Congressman Robert Toombs maintained that "England will not fight for that which does not belong to her. She has something to risk by war as well as ourselves."[162] Samuel Gordon of New York agreed, saying, "War with the United States would be the most suicidal policy she could pursue; and she is not so blind as not to see it. The whole of Oregon is of vastly less importance to her than a year's supply of raw cotton. . . . Hence there will be no war declared by Great Britain for this territory."[163] When James Black of South Carolina expressed doubt, Polk reassured him: "The only way to treat John Bull was to look him straight in the eye."[164]

By June 1846 Polk abandoned his claim to all of Oregon and signed the Oregon Treaty, extending the U.S.–Canadian border at 49° to the Pacific. Why did Polk curtail his territorial ambitions so soon after championing U.S. claims to the entire Pacific Northwest? Several events early that year dramatically increased the perceived military costs of maintaining the all-Oregon claim. First, Polk received reports in February of British military "preparations which might be deemed necessary not only for the defense and protection of the Canadas, but for offensive operations," including "the immediate equipment of thirty sail of the line beside steamers and other vessels of war," which called into question Britain's presumed unwillingness to fight.[165] Second, Congress declared war on Mexico in May, raising the prospect of simultaneous wars against Britain and Mexico. Third, Pakenham proposed a new draft treaty in early June, and "all [in the Cabinet] agreed that if the proposition was rejected without submitting it to the Senate . . . war was almost inevitable."[166] As the military risks of pursuing all Oregon increased dramatically, Polk submitted the treaty to the Senate and signed it on June 15. Pakenham reported, "The positive impatience shown by Mr. Buchanan, to sign and conclude, convinces me that the fear lest any complication should arise out of the Mexican war has done a great deal in inducing the American government to accept Your Lordship's proposal without alteration."[167]

Despite their low esteem for its material value, U.S. leaders pursued all Oregon aggressively in 1845 because its demographic future was malleable, and they assumed Britain would rather cede its claim than fight for it. They curbed that ambition in 1846 once the outbreak of war with Mexico and new evidence of British willingness to fight increased the perceived military costs of further expansionism. Although this behavior is consistent with the predictions of both profitability and domestic impact theories, it differs markedly from U.S. leaders' nonpursuit of eastern Canada in the late 1830s—a contradiction best explained by eastern Canada's domestic costs and Oregon's lack thereof. Furthermore, in contrast to the emerging stability of the northeastern border, U.S. ambitions to annex western Canada did not evaporate with the Oregon Treaty; they were merely placed on hold.

The Fenian Raids

Eastern and western Canada grew even more different from each other by the late 1860s. Eastern Canada's population approached 3,500,000, yet fewer than 28,000 had settled west of Ontario.[168] Western Canada also remained almost entirely undeveloped while the eastern economy boomed, especially after Canadian Confederation in 1867: its exports increased from $58 million to $89 million, and its imports rose from $73 million to $128 million between 1868 and 1874.[169] Like their predecessors in the 1830s and 1840s, post–Civil War leaders faced a natural experiment north of the border: a populous, productive society in the east and an untamed wilderness in the west. Moreover, U.S. leaders enjoyed their greatest military advantage to date during this period. As a result, profitability theory strongly predicts that U.S. leaders should have pursued the annexation of eastern Canada after the Civil War, while domestic impact theory predicts that they should have continued to reject populous eastern Canada in favor of sparsely populated western Canada.

Pretexts for expansionism were once again plentiful: crises ignited public opinion, internal rebellions rocked Canada, and U.S. citizens launched private raids across the border. The preference of many British leaders for a Confederate victory was among the worst-kept secrets of the Civil War, whipping public opinion throughout the Union into a fury that left U.S.–British relations perilously low in the war's aftermath.[170] Although Britain had not overtly aided the rebels, it had sold them several warships—including the *Alabama*, which inflicted substantial damage on Union shipping—and Confederate raiders had used Canada as a staging area for incursions into the Northern states. As Secretary of State William Henry Seward wrote, the U.S. public held "a profound sense that it sustained great injury from the sympathy extended in Great Britain to rebels during our civil war."[171] British leaders feared that this resentment would fuel an attempt to seize Canada. Prime Minister Palmerston warned Queen Victoria in January 1865 of "the very hostile spirit towards England which pervades all classes in the Federal States" and noted further that "the probability that, whenever the Civil War in America shall be ended, the Northern states will . . . either make war against England or make inroads into your Majesty's North American possessions."[172]

Had Seward and President Johnson wanted to annex eastern Canada, they had not only the public furor to sustain such a venture but also the military might to make it happen. For the first time in its history the United States enjoyed a military advantage over Britain in North America, having emerged from the Civil War with the most powerful military in the world.[173] Its use of mass armies, mobilized industry, rifles, mines, railroads, steamships, telegraph communications, and other innovations heralded a new age of warfare and marked the United States as the most experienced operator with these tools of the future.[174] Millions of Americans gained military experience during the Civil War. The Union army alone employed more than 1 million members in 1865, and in July 1866 Congress authorized a peacetime military strength of 54,302 soldiers, significantly higher than antebellum levels.[175] In contrast, Britain maintained only about 15,000 troops in Canada during this period.[176] Had U.S. leaders wanted to conquer eastern Canada, they had both the opportunity and the means to do so.

They also had a remarkable opportunity to outsource the military costs of a northward invasion to the Fenians, Irish-Americans looking to undermine British rule in Ireland. The Fenian Brotherhood was established in 1858 as the U.S. branch of the Irish Republican Brotherhood, a precursor to the twentieth-century Irish Republican Army. Over 140,000 Irish-Americans fought in the Civil War, during which the Fenians developed their own government and military units.[177] When the war ended, they set about obtaining surplus arms at low cost while making no secret of their intended target: Canada.[178] Fenian leaders hoped to accomplish three goals by invading Canada: to distract Britain from reinforcing its garrisons in Ireland, thus enabling a general uprising there; to establish an Irish republic-in-exile on Canadian territory, thereby gaining belligerent status with its associated legal and diplomatic benefits; and to obtain a bargaining chip that could be exchanged for Irish independence.[179] Since Canada's defenses relied heavily on inexperienced militia, this plan seemed feasible. The British commander there estimated that "no more than five thousand Fenians could wreak considerable damage if they advanced simultaneously at several points along the colony's defenseless frontier."[180] Given an anti-British public, overwhelming military might, and a ready vanguard for a northward invasion, U.S. leaders arguably enjoyed no better opportunity to conquer Canada.

Moreover, the Fenians were popular. The British consul in New York expected their planned invasion to receive "the undisguised approbation of a large portion of the American people."[181] A vengeful *New York Tribune* wrote in 1865, "Our Canadian neighbors have an opportunity of appreciating the conditions of America a year or two ago, when they permitted bands of Rebel robbers to ride across the border and sack American towns."[182] More than 1.3 million Irish immigrants fleeing the potato famine during the 1840s and 1850s had created an important Irish-American vote, and the surest way to court that vote was "unscrupulous abuse of England."[183] Johnson himself admitted in an interview with the *London Times* that he was "desirous of avoiding, if possible, any collision with the popular sentiments of the Irish masses."[184] The British ambassador Frederick Bruce called on Seward after hearing of a prospective Fenian invasion of Canada in August 1865 but left disappointed, reporting, "The Secretary did not hesitate to make it quite clear that the administration had no intention of jeopardizing its domestic position by opposing an organization that appealed to a significant band of Irish sympathizers and tapped the widespread hostility toward Britain."[185] Irish-American influence was so great that Bruce feared that if the Fenians gave up their "piratical raids" and instead made "the adhesion of the Irish vote contingent on the adoption by some party of a war policy towards Great Britain, the maintenance of friendly relations between the two countries will become very difficult."[186] Johnson was particularly dependent on the Irish-American vote after his 1866 split from the Republican Party, and observers expected equally strong support from Seward, who had openly favored the Irish-American cause.[187]

Though many U.S. leaders resented Britain for favoring the Confederacy, only a few Radical Republicans voiced the territorial ambitions British leaders feared.[188] Congressman Nathaniel Banks of Massachusetts proposed a bill offering annexation to the Canadian provinces, but it was referred to the House Committee on Foreign Affairs and never resurfaced.[189] Others preached annexation, including Senator Zachariah Chandler of Michigan, Congressman Henry Davis of Maryland, and the *Chicago Tribune* editor Joseph Medill, but their motives were "purely political and sectional," Medill pointing out that "the admission of British American territory to the American Union as states would give the northern section of the United States a political predominance which the Southern states when readmitted to the Union, would never be able to overcome."[190] Their schemes failed to infiltrate federal policy, as Johnson and Seward displayed no interest in annexing eastern Canada.[191]

Instead, the Johnson administration materially and diplomatically undercut the Fenian raids, carefully masking its anti-Fenian policies to avoid alienating Irish-American voters.[192] As Johnson reassured Bruce, the Fenians "met with no sympathy on the part of the government, which on the contrary was anxious to discourage it."[193] At Seward's suggestion, U.S. and British diplomats kept the Fenians out of official diplomatic correspondence, enabling the administration to covertly suppress them without sparking an electoral showdown.[194] This secrecy was perhaps too successful: the uninformed Canadian administration repeatedly demanded a formal U.S. anti-Fenian declaration, and the Fenians themselves were emboldened by its absence.[195] Yet Seward worked quietly to undermine the Fenians' public relations, defusing the naturalization controversy that had reemerged as Britain denied consul access to Irish-Americans arrested for fomenting dissent in Ireland. Negotiating a compromise in 1866, Seward advocated a comprehensive naturalization treaty on the grounds that it "would tend considerably to weaken the hold which Fenianism has upon the minds of a part of the population of this country."[196] Ironically, British confidence in "the American government's unavowed determination to prevent a raid" undermined Seward's attempts to use the Fenian threat as diplomatic leverage, but nevertheless a naturalization treaty was signed in May 1870.[197]

Lacking any ambition to annex eastern Canada, the Johnson administration treated the Fenians with increasing firmness as they began launching raids across the border. When roughly one thousand Fenians assembled to invade Campobello Island in New Brunswick in April 1866, Treasury Secretary Hugh McCullough ordered customs officers to seize the *Ocean Spray*, a ship bearing 129 cases of Fenian arms, and Attorney General James Speed prepared the courts for action.[198] Lacking weapons and opposed by U.S. agents as well as British-Canadian defenders, the Fenians resigned themselves to demonstrations and acts of mischief in the area. Two months later one thousand armed Fenians launched another raid across the Niagara River from Buffalo, New York, defeating Canadian militia at the Battle of Ridgeway before they withdrew.[199] Again, U.S. authorities disrupted the invasion, closing the port of Buffalo and alerting the U.S.S. *Michigan*, a reaction which, according to the local British consul, "effectively cut off the Fenian reinforcements and operated powerfully in frustrating their plans."[200] In the days that followed, Johnson issued a fresh neutrality proclamation, dispatched Generals Ulysses Grant and George Meade to Buffalo, and instructed U.S. forces to seize Fenian arms and arrest suspected Fenians.[201] A third Fenian raid launched from Vermont on June 7 proved abortive.[202] Although thousands more Fenians had gathered in towns along the border, Johnson's active opposition and neutrality proclamation convinced most to abandon the invasion. When many of them proved too poor to afford the trip home, some seven thousand were transported at public expense, "having first given their parole to desist from further adventures in Canada."[203]

The Grant administration that took office in March 1869 maintained these anti-Fenian policies and grew increasingly open about them as public support for the Fenians waned even among Irish-Americans. President Grant moved U.S. troops near the Canadian border "on the pretext of giving them the advantage of a cooler climate during the summer, but really that they might be ready to prevent, if necessary, any hostile expedition which may be attempted by the Fenians against Canada."[204] In August he rejected a Fenian appeal to tolerate the group's Canadian ambitions.[205] When plans for a four-pronged invasion of Canada were discovered, Secretary of State Hamilton Fish "requested his colleagues at the Treasury, Navy, and War Departments to instruct commanders of vessels on the Great Lakes and officers commanding military posts close to the frontier to protect the territorial integrity of Canada."[206] The last major Fenian raid, launched from Vermont in May 1870, was a fiasco. Grant had dispatched troops to the border, and, after a brief skirmish, the Fenian leader John O'Neil was arrested by a federal marshal. A second force of some fifteen hundred Fenians crossed the border from New York but retreated before British-Canadian defenders and disbanded within days.[207] Grant publicly condemned their "sundry illegal military enterprises," even asking Attorney General Ebenezer Hoar if he could prosecute the railroads that had transported the Fenians to the border.[208]

Anti-British public opinion and impressive military power notwithstanding, U.S. leaders preferred not to take advantage of the Fenian raids to target eastern Canada. Instead, they consistently undermined the Fenians and defended Canada's territorial integrity. Beyond a few radicals in Congress, no U.S. leaders seriously considered using the raids to pursue annexation. As Fish candidly told the British ambassador Edward Thornton in June 1870, prior public appeasement of the Fenians had been purely for domestic political benefit.[209] Ironically, given the lack of U.S. interest in annexing eastern Canada, the Fenian raids jump-started the unification of Canada by sparking urgent security fears north of the border. As one newspaper wrote, "Nothing could have been done equal to it to carry [Canadian] Confederation."[210]

The Pacific Northwest

The same U.S. leaders who showed no desire to annex eastern Canada after the Civil War did pursue the vast territories to its west, including Russian Alaska, British Columbia, Rupert's Land, and the North-Western Territories overseen by the Hudson's Bay Company. Those regions spanned more than three million square miles but contained fewer than 150,000 Native Americans, no more than 40,000 of whom lived in the Pacific Northwest. As for Europeans, there were virtually none outside of the settlements at Sitka (home to as few as 900), Vancouver (with fewer than 10,000), and Winnipeg (with perhaps 13,000).[211] In light of such sparse populations and with the pre–Civil War sectional balance overturned, annexing these territories posed minimal domestic costs. As a result, both domestic impact theory and profitability theory predict that U.S. leaders should have seized any affordable opportunities to pursue these western territories. The Arctic climate of these areas severely limited prospects for settlement and hence their material value, however, so neither theory expects U.S. leaders to have been willing to pay much for them. How did U.S. leaders approach western Canada after the Civil War?

Russian leaders had wanted to sell their unprofitable and vulnerable colony of Alaska as far back as the mid-1850s, but exploratory talks with the Buchanan administration fell apart as the country descended into civil war.[212] When the Russian ambassador Edouard de Stoeckl approached Seward in March 1867 with a new offer for the purchase of Alaska, Seward quickly accepted. On March 30 they signed a treaty exchanging Alaska for $7.2 million.[213] Russian leaders feared losing Alaska in a future war and preferred to sell to the United States rather than to any of their European rivals, so Seward's main task in the negotiations was determining a suitable price: roughly two cents per acre. As the historian Frederick Merk wrote of Seward, "The province was thrown at him, much as Louisiana had been at Jefferson."[214]

Critics lampooned Alaska as "Seward's icebox" and "Seward's folly," skeptical that any price was low enough for a territory known for nothing but its unfitness for settlement. Seward himself knew little about Alaska, but he was content to purchase it first and explore it later, as Jefferson had done with Louisiana.[215] Senator Charles Sumner of Massachusetts admitted in his influential speech supporting the purchase that "perhaps no region of equal extent on the globe, unless we except the interior of Africa or possibly Greenland, is as little known."[216] Its population of perhaps fifty thousand Natives and fewer than twenty-five hundred Russians was neither a lure nor a deterrent. Sumner observed, "The population . . . may be considered in its numbers and in its character. In neither respect, perhaps, can it add much to the value of the country."[217] Nor was Alaska valued for prospective settlement; after surveying the territory in 1869, General George Thomas reported: "I see no immediate prospect of the country being settled up. The climate is too rigid; there is too much rain and too little sun for agricultural purposes."[218] Indeed, there was little immediate prospect of Alaska's becoming a state. It would be administered in turn by the U.S. Army, Treasury, and Navy until 1884 and not given the status of a U.S. Territory, the precursor to statehood, until 1912.

Nevertheless, the Alaska purchase did offer two attractive benefits: natural resources and Russian friendship. Sumner praised its reserves of timber, coal, copper, ice, furs, and fisheries, "which, in waters superabundant with animal life beyond any of the globe, seem to promise a new commerce to the country."[219] Thomas's report vindicated this praise, noting Alaska's rich supplies of timber, fish, and coal as well as iron ore and gold.[220] Both Sumner and Seward looked to Alaska as a conduit for future trade with Japan and China.[221] Its advocates further pointed to Russian support for the Union during the Civil War, arguing that the purchase would solidify Russian friendship in the future. Seward told the U.S. commissioner who formally accepted the territory that to Emperor Alexander II of Russia it was "a signal proof of that friendship for the United States which has characterized his own reign and that of his illustrious predecessor. It is hoped, therefore, that all your intercourse with the Russian commissioner will be friendly, courteous, and frank."[222] U.S. Minister to Russia Cassius Clay wrote to Seward that "England and France are no match now for the United States and Russia, and the weight of power with the coming years will be still more on our side."[223]

The public came to favor the purchase not only for these reasons but also because Alaska was seen as a stepping-stone to further northwestern expansion.[224] Editors at the *New York Herald*, *New York Tribune*, and *The Nation* initially panned the acquisition, calling Alaska "utterly worthless and good for nothing," branding its purchase a "Quixotic land hunt" and declaring, "We do not want far-distant, detached colonies, nor ice and snow territories, nor Esquimaux fellow citizens."[225] Yet they changed their tune once they came to see the purchase as "a flank movement" on British Columbia.[226] Russian leaders expected as much: Stoeckl assumed it would be "followed sooner or later by the annexation to the country of the immediate coast of the Pacific Ocean now forming a part of the British possessions."[227]

British Columbia's material benefits to the United States were marginal. Its port at Vancouver was largely redundant with Seattle (incorporated in 1865), its climate nearly as inhospitable as Alaska's, its natural resources nearly as uncharted, and sea travel to Alaska was much more efficient than any possible land route. Nevertheless, annexing the colony offered the prospect of uncontested dominance of the northern Pacific Ocean. At the time, British Columbia was isolated from eastern Canada and economically dependent on San Francisco, and its residents craved tighter integration. Seward thus hoped to swing public opinion in favor of U.S. annexation, setting his sights on it as early as January 1866.[228] That July he told U.S. Minister to Britain Charles Adams that the post–Civil War period offered a "peculiarly convenient" time to negotiate a laundry list of issues from the *Alabama* claims to "the North West Boundary."[229] Since British leaders seemed open to arbitrating the *Alabama* claims, Seward "hoped to raise the claims high enough to convince British officials to agree to a *quid pro quo* settlement, ceding British Columbia in exchange."[230]

By the following year news of the Alaska purchase combined with rumors of Seward's interest to drive public sentiment in British Columbia to favor U.S. annexation.[231] In April 1867 the U.S. consul in Victoria reported that "the people . . . are now urging with great unanimity annexation to the United States," and a petition circulated that July asking Queen Victoria for a lengthy set of concessions or, failing that, "the speedy transfer of this colony . . . to the United States."[232] Seward delayed claims negotiations to allow pro-U.S. sentiment to grow, telling Adams's son that the *Alabama* claims "would soon be settled, but *now* they could be settled in one way, by such acquisition from England as would enable us to round off our North-Western territory."[233] When instructed to combine all outstanding issues into one negotiation, Adams confided to his diary, "I saw very clearly the drift of this to be a bargain for the British territory in the northwest."[234] The following month Seward told Senator Orville Browning that "we would pay for British Columbia with the *Alabama* claims."[235]

Meanwhile, the formerly separate colonies of Ontario, Quebec, New Brunswick, and Nova Scotia joined to form the Dominion of Canada, and their leaders began lobbying for British Columbia to join as well. By the winter of 1867–68 talk of annexation had faded from local newspapers. Attendees at a public meeting in Victoria that January favored confederation with Canada over annexation to the United States if certain conditions were met, chief among them the construction of a transcontinental railroad linking British Columbia with eastern Canada.[236] Seward tried to counter by promoting construction of a U.S. railroad to the colony and urging U.S. capitalists "to organize a company for the purpose of buying up the rights of the Hudson's Bay Company" in Rupert's Land—de facto separating British Columbia from the Dominion—but both efforts fell through.[237] Britain's Parliament decided to build the transcontinental railroad that summer, and the following year it purchased the Hudson's Bay Company charter to Rupert's Land and the North-West Territories, paving the way for their integration into Canada.[238]

Still, Seward's ambitions lingered. He noted during a trip to the Northwest in 1869, "British Columbia—We do not need it now, but we shall—we shall have it. G.B. . . . she doesn't need it." Given the region's limited material value, he had no desire to fight for it, instead wondering "how to get it properly as we got Alaska."[239] Prioritizing U.S.–British relations, Seward put off any further expansionist attempts during his last year in office and instead oversaw negotiation of the Johnson-Clarendon Convention settling U.S. claims against Britain. Calls for western Canada continued to echo from Sumner and others in Congress. In January 1870 Senator Henry Corbett of Oregon proposed including British Columbia in any claims settlement, arguing that "a great proportion of the people of British Columbia are emigrants from the United States" and "if it were annexed to the United States it would be rapidly settled."[240] Corbett's proposal proved fruitless, but Senator Jacob Howard of Michigan used it to draw attention to another opportunity for northward expansion: the "insurrection" in "the Red River country, lying directly north of the state of Minnesota."[241]

The Red River Rebellion broke out in October 1869 when Métis protesters disrupted a British Canadian survey intended to prepare Rupert's Land for integration into Canada. The Métis, of mixed Native and French ancestry, made up roughly half of Winnipeg's twelve thousand inhabitants; another 35 percent were of mixed Native and English ancestry while fewer than 15 percent were solely European.[242] Led by Louis Riel, the Métis feared Canadian integration would threaten their way of life, and in early November they seized Fort Garry.[243] Like British Columbia, Winnipeg was geographically isolated from eastern Canada in the late 1860s, with most of its trade, mail, and visitors arriving by horse from the end of rail lines in Minnesota.[244] That state's rapid growth, from under 5,000 in 1849 to more than 172,000 by 1860, put pressure on Canadian leaders to integrate Winnipeg into the Dominion quickly. As the historian George Stanley wrote, "Peaceable American penetration had been the preliminary step to the annexation of Oregon and Texas, and it was not beyond the bounds of possibility that Rupert's Land and the North-West might go the same way."[245] Minnesota's state legislature, for its part, passed a resolution saying that it would "rejoice" at "the cession of North-West British America to the United States."[246]

During the winter of 1869–70 U.S. leaders looked to take advantage of the Red River Rebellion and annex Winnipeg. The U.S. consul there described local popular opinion as being opposed to Canadian integration, emphasizing that the settlement was "unconnected" from eastern Canada due to "natural obstacles" and suggesting that Riel's rebellion opened the door to annexation.[247] That December Secretary of State Hamilton Fish sent former Treasury agent James Taylor to report confidentially on the rebellion as well as on the settlement's geography and demography, "the political relations of the several British possessions between Minnesota and Alaska," and the internal politics of the Dominion of Canada.[248] As far back as 1861, when the Royal Canadian Regiment withdrew leaving Winnipeg without any established defensive force, Taylor had speculated to Treasury Secretary Salmon Chase that "the Americanization of this important section of British America is rapidly progressing," and "in case of a collision with England, Minnesota is competent to 'hold, occupy, and possess' the valley of Red River to Lake Winnipeg."[249] Taylor had also pursued the Hudson's Bay Company's charter before the British government purchased it, telling a company man in St. Paul, "I know that President Grant is most anxious for a treaty with England, which shall transfer the country between Minnesota and Alaska, in settlement of the *Alabama* controversy. . . . I have no doubt that a clause could be inserted in such a treaty giving $5,000,000 to the Hudson's Bay Company in satisfaction of the title to one twentieth of the land in Central British America."[250]

The Grant administration monitored events north of the border with anticipation, poised to annex western Canada if a suitable opportunity arose but unwilling to take any step that would undermine U.S.–British relations. Upon receiving an annexation request from British Columbian residents in November 1869, Fish advised Grant "to keep our eyes fixedly on the movement, & to keep our hands off," which the president considered "precisely" the right approach.[251] In January 1870 Fish thought the movement in British Columbia, "together with the troubles in the Red River settlement, and the opposition to the union with the Dominion" would result in "the separation of the connection between Great Britain and the colonies," concluding, "I think it must come before very long."[252] He instructed the U.S. minister to Britain to pursue the subject diplomatically, stating, "Should you find any

inclination of opinion or of interest toward the annexation of these possessions to this country, you will discreetly encourage it . . . availing yourself
of every opportunity to obtain information as to the sentiments of the British government on the question of the separation of the colonies from the
Mother Country and when opportunity offers, indicating the facts which
seem to make such separation a necessity."[253] In view of the importance of
upholding good U.S.–British relations and the limited material value of the
colonies, though, Grant and Fish were unwilling to move beyond quiet diplomacy, rejecting a suggestion by Senator Alexander Ramsey of Minnesota
that "if about $25,000 could be sent to the insurgents they would be able to
maintain themselves."[254]

The early months of 1870 saw Métis leaders negotiate with Canadian
representatives regarding the list of rights needing protection in order for
them to join the Dominion. Fish continued his gentle diplomacy, repeatedly suggesting to Thornton that the province become independent and
cautioning him against military intervention.[255] Congress proved equally
unwilling to force the issue. Senator Zachariah Chandler of Michigan, one
of Congress's few remaining expansionists, observed in April, "The United
States today have more men that have actually been in battle under fire
than all the rest of the world put together, more experienced soldiers and
more experienced officers. We are today the strongest military power on
earth." He urged his colleagues to "open negotiations with Winnipeg with
a view to its annexation . . . and my word for it, you will have no fighting.
There is no desire on the part of any nation on the earth to fight with us on
the land."[256] Although Chandler harnessed profitability logic, his colleagues
roundly rejected his ambitions and merely ridiculed him for "riding a favor-
ite hobbyhorse."[257]

When British Canadian leaders organized a military expedition under
Colonel Garnet Wolseley to suppress the rebellion in May, Grant bought
time for the rebellion by denying Wolseley transit across U.S. territory.[258]
This move held the door to annexation open a bit longer, but in vain. That
same month Queen Victoria assented to an act of Canadian Parliament creating the province of Manitoba, including a list of protections based on the
Métis demands.[259] The province came into being in July 1870, when Canada
officially absorbed Rupert's Land and the North-Western Territory. Even as
Treasury Secretary George Boutwell told Grant of his enduring hope for
"arrangements with England by which she may be relieved from the *Alabama*
claims and the transfer of the Canadas to the United States accomplished,"
the writing was on the wall.[260] Wolseley's expedition reached Fort Garry in
August to find that Riel's forces had fled, and Manitoba became part of the

Dominion of Canada. With central Canada integrated, British Columbia negotiated its own deal for debt relief and a transcontinental railroad, joining the Dominion in July 1871.[261]

That year, the Grant administration moved to resolve all major outstanding issues with Britain. The resulting Treaty of Washington provided for arbitration of the *Alabama* claims, addressed disputes regarding northeastern fishing rights, stipulated free navigation of border waterways, and arranged for international arbitration to settle a northwest boundary dispute involving the San Juan Islands, which dated back to an imprecision of the Oregon Treaty and had become militarized in 1859 during the so-called Pig War.[262] That treaty set U.S.–British relations on the stable footing that would facilitate their peaceful power transition over the decades to come, and it also signaled the formal end of U.S. northward expansion in favor of a stable, demilitarized northern border.[263] As the biographer Allan Nevins writes, Fish (who led the negotiations on the U.S. side) prioritized U.S.–British relations over Canadian territory: "Fish would have been quite as glad as Sumner to see it, or at least its Western half, attached to the republic . . . [but] whatever Canada's destiny, they were intent upon restoring cordial Anglo-American relations."[264]

When Riel launched a second Métis rebellion in March 1885, again protesting Canadian surveys to establish a new district (this time in Saskatchewan), it generated relatively little interest in the United States. Secretary of State Thomas Bayard reiterated U.S. neutrality policies toward the internal British conflict, telling his British counterpart that the United States "will take all available precautions to prevent the dispatch of hostile expeditions, or of arms and munitions of war, from within the jurisdiction of the United States to aid the insurgents in the North-West provinces."[265] The rebellion was short-lived: Canadian forces defeated the rebels by mid-May, and Riel was found guilty of treason and hanged later that year. The early 1890s saw calls for a voluntary annexation of Canada from some prominent voices such as Secretary of State James Blaine (who came from Maine) and the National Continental Union League (which included Charles Dana, Theodore Roosevelt, John Hay, and Henry Cabot Lodge). Most of these proponents, however, were businessmen from border states with material interests involved, and proposals by Congressman Amos Cummings of New York and Senator Jacob Gallinger of Vermont failed to gain any traction.[266] By the beginning of the twentieth century congressional debates over a U.S.–Canadian reciprocity treaty saw annexation mentioned only by its opponents as a boogeyman to scare Canada into rejecting the treaty. Congress itself was "singularly lacking in the usual annexationist effusions," as the historian Donald Warner writes, since "few Americans now wanted to acquire any more territory or population."[267]

Why did the United States stop trying to annex Canada? The case studies examined here indicate that U.S. territorial ambitions north of the border excluded Quebec as early as the War of 1812 and continued shifting westward over time to avoid most of Canada's population. U.S. leaders pursued Quebec only during the Revolution, when the United States was an international organization and its potential membership would have given Quebec no influence over their domestic affairs. That episode stands in marked contrast to the War of 1812, when U.S. leaders fretted over the sectional and normative consequences of annexing Quebec and entertained only sparsely populated Ontario despite initiating the war, recognizing Quebec's material value, and expecting an easy victory.

As Ontario's population grew in later decades, U.S. leaders prioritized border stability east of the Great Lakes and limited their ambitions to Canada's sparsely populated western reaches. Numerous crises failed to kindle a pursuit of eastern Canada during the late 1830s or the late 1860s, despite federal leaders' willingness to forcibly rebuke Maine during the former and their recognition of U.S. military power during the latter. Rather than take advantage of those crises to pursue annexation, Van Buren, Johnson, and Grant all dispatched U.S. forces to thwart private border raids and reiterated U.S. neutrality toward the Canadian rebellions.

In contrast, U.S. leaders actively pursued the sparsely populated Pacific Northwest: Polk threatened war over Oregon, Seward purchased Alaska, and both he and Fish pursued western Canada from Manitoba to British Columbia. Holding the material benefits of those territories in relatively low esteem, though, Polk compromised on British Columbia to ensure success in the far more valuable California, and post–Civil War U.S. leaders utilized only diplomatic means and ultimately conceded their territorial ambitions to ensure lasting amicable U.S.–British relations.

These findings are consistent with domestic impact theory. Quebec's domestic political and normative implications explain why its annexation became a nonstarter among U.S. foreign policymakers as well as why Ontario joined it on the list of regions U.S. leaders were disinterested in between 1812 and the 1830s. In contrast, U.S. leaders' behavior in these case studies repeatedly contradicted profitability theory. First, they consistently rejected the annexation of the territory they considered most valuable (eastern Canada) while pursuing areas they saw as far less valuable (western Canada). Second, their choice of targets was not driven by U.S. military strength, which was at its lowest during the Revolution (when they targeted Quebec) and at its highest after the Civil War (when they did not). Third, federal leaders were willing to use military force to bargain over maritime policies during the War of 1812, to pursue sparsely populated Oregon in the 1840s, and to prevent subfederal actors like Maine and the Fenians from invading eastern Canada, but not to annex their most valuable neighbor (Quebec). Finally, as domestic impact theory predicts but profitability theory does not, U.S. leaders saw the growing population of eastern Canada as a cost of annexation rather than a benefit, basing that assessment on their perceptions of its identity rather than materialistic assessments of its productivity and propensity for resistance. U.S. leaders' reluctance to annex Canadian territory was driven by sectionalism and xenophobia, domestic concerns that ballooned as their eyes turned to the south.

CHAPTER 6

To the South

Mexico and U.S. Annexation

> We do not want the people of Mexico, either as citizens or subjects. All we want is a portion of territory, which they nominally hold, generally uninhabited, or, where inhabited at all, sparsely so, and with a population, which would soon recede, or identify itself with ours.
>
> Senator Lewis Cass, 1847

Mexico achieved independence from Spain in September 1821 and immediately found itself in U.S. crosshairs. The United States enjoyed a power advantage over its southern neighbor that grew more extreme over time, and since European great powers were reluctant to intervene there was little standing between the young republic and Mexico's agricultural and mineral resources, geopolitical ascendancy on the Gulf of Mexico and the Pacific Ocean, and the largest external population on the continent. Despite annexation's material benefits, however, the U.S. pursuit of Mexican territory was domestically contentious, its targets were expressly circumscribed, and it ultimately stopped well short of absorbing all Mexico. Reprising their approach in Canada, U.S. leaders pursued Mexico's sparsely populated lands while rejecting any large-scale assimilation of Mexican population.

My central argument in this chapter is that domestic concerns were the primary constraint on U.S. territorial ambitions in Mexico and the main reason those ambitions rapidly dwindled after the 1840s. I examine six major U.S. opportunities to annex Mexican territory: the Texas Revolution, the annexation of Texas, the Mexican–American War, the prospect of taking all Mexico introduced by that war, the antebellum period, and the Maximilian affair. Both Texas and California were widely prized for their natural resources and geopolitical position, and since they had small populations U.S. leaders were able to overcome sectional strife and annex both. When U.S. military success raised the possibility of annexing populous southern Mexico, however, differences of race, culture, language, religion, and political history fueled xenophobia that drove northern and southern leaders alike to reject any large-scale assimilation of Mexican population. As a result, the all-Mexico movement was short-lived. U.S. leaders repeatedly tried to purchase the few remaining sparsely populated borderlands during the decade that followed but renounced any further territorial ambitions in Mexico after the Civil War.

At first glance, this behavior seems to fit profitability theory well: the United States took advantage of a weak neighbor and seized resource-rich regions with relatively little military difficulty. Yet closer examination raises numerous problems inherent in that account, and ultimately it falls short of explaining much U.S. behavior toward Mexico. Why did U.S. leaders rebuff a decade of Texan requests to voluntarily join the Union before finally changing course and annexing Texas? Why were U.S. war aims against Mexico consistently limited to its lightly peopled northern lands despite military success and the material value of populous southern Mexico? Why did U.S. leaders offer to purchase only narrow border territories after the war, and why did they decline several offers of Mexican territory after the Civil War? Domestic impact theory has ready answers for these questions: sectional and racial differences sparked passionate resistance to annexation among leaders worried about its domestic costs. The case studies bear out the theory's predictions. Annexation's domestic impact helps us understand why, contrary to popular thinking at the time, the United States did not "manifest [a] destiny to overspread the continent."[1]

The Texas Revolution

Anglo-American settlers migrated to Texas steadily beginning with Moses Austin's land deal in 1821, and by 1829 they outnumbered the few Mexicans living there. When Mexico belatedly tried to assert authority over the largely autonomous settlers, they revolted, establishing the independent Republic of Texas in March 1836. After defeating a Mexican invasion and capturing the Mexican leader Antonio López de Santa Anna in the process, the Texans requested annexation to the United States. President Andrew Jackson declined the Texan invitation, as did his successors Martin Van Buren, William Henry Harrison, and John Tyler. Profitability theory predicts that U.S. leaders should decline annexation opportunities that they judge unprofitable, while domestic impact theory expects them to also decline profitable opportunities that threaten prohibitive domestic costs. Why did U.S. leaders decline Texan requests for annexation?

Texas's material benefits were widely recognized in the United States, including natural resources as well as other economic and geopolitical benefits. Jackson sent Henry Morfit on a fact-finding mission to Texas shortly after it gained independence from Mexico, and he reported that the new republic spanned 104.5 million acres of fertile land while also claiming an additional 60 million acres between the Nueces River and the Rio Grande. Those lands fed a growing production of cotton, corn, and cattle, and Morfit predicted that, once properly settled, they could support an economy as strong "as any state in our Union."[2] Estimating the population of Texas at 30,000 Anglo-Americans, 3,500 Hispanic Tejanos, 12,000 Natives, and 5,000 slaves, Morfit recognized that it was ripe for growth: a flood of American settlers would swell its population to 213,000 by 1850.[3]

The annexation of Texas also offered sizable economic benefits to the United States. Mexico's economy declined by more than 10 percent overall between 1800 and 1860, but its northern provinces thrived thanks to growing connections with their prosperous northern neighbor.[4] New Orleans emerged as the focal point of Texan trade, which rarely reached southern Mexico, and trade along the Santa Fe Trail connecting New Mexico and St. Louis grew thirtyfold between 1822 and 1843.[5] Moreover, Texas was the only major non-U.S. cotton-growing region in North America, offering the prospect of a regional monopoly that would reduce domestic prices and make U.S. cotton more influential in international markets.[6]

Yet the most important benefits of annexing Texas were geopolitical, chief among them preventing the rise of a regional rival. Mexico's long-term power trajectory would be substantially greater if it managed to effectively integrate Texas, and Texan leaders might harbor their own ambitions for regional influence if they remained independent and continued siphoning off industrious settlers from the United States. As the Texan president Sam Houston wrote, "All the powers, which either envy or fear the U States, would . . . build us up, as the only rival power which can ever exist on this continent, to that of the U States."[7] Most Texans had been born in the United States, but Houston warned that "a common origin has its influence, so long as a common *interest* exists, and no longer."[8] Annexing the new republic before it found its legs would prevent Texas from turning into a threat later. Doing so would also increase U.S. influence over the Gulf of Mexico (the crucial outlet for Mississippi River exports), pave the way to California for future settlers, and head off the threat (real or imagined) of Britain seizing Texas. Given these impressive material benefits, it is unlikely U.S. leaders declined Texan requests for annexation because they did not value the territory.

In fact, U.S. interest in Texas's material benefits was long-standing. Although the United States had renounced any claims it might have had there in the Adams–Onís Treaty, many U.S. leaders coveted the province nonetheless, and when Mexico became independent they set about trying to persuade the new government to sell it. In March 1825 President John Quincy Adams had U.S. Minister to Mexico Joel Poinsett approach Mexican leaders about pushing the border beyond the Sabine River to the Brazos, Colorado, or Rio Grande. Secretary of State Henry Clay reiterated these instructions in March 1827, offering $1 million for a Rio Grande boundary, but Poinsett anticipated a Mexican rejection and never submitted the offer. In 1829 President Jackson ordered him to reopen negotiations, now offering up to $5 million, and after recalling Poinsett he assigned Anthony Butler to continue the effort, reaffirming "the great importance of the cession of Texas to us" and threatening to seize it if Mexico refused to sell, "being well aware that Mexico cannot prevent Texas from becoming independent of her."[9] Mexican leaders consistently rebuffed the U.S. offers, and Jackson abandoned the official pursuit of Texas in 1835 amidst worsening U.S.–Mexican relations.

If Jackson valued Texas's material benefits, having tried to purchase it for years, did he abandon his pursuit of it because he thought annexation would require a costly fight? Military costs could have come from three sources: Texas, Mexico, or Europe. In Texas, resistance to annexation was nonexistent. Texan leaders pushed for annexation immediately after achieving independence, and Texan citizens strongly favored it even as U.S. leaders declined their requests. Seeing themselves as Americans, they were "eager for reunion with the homeland," and their leaders made no secret of that fact.[10] In April 1838 the Texan Committee on Foreign Relations announced, "Texas, deriving her origin from the United States of North America, and allied to her by the strong ties of consanguinity, common origin, similar government, and language, feels for that nation a deep and filial regard. So powerful has been this feeling, and so intimate has been the connection and the intercourse between them and us, that we have still thought and felt as if we were yet a part and portion of them."[11] Far from fueling resistance, Texan nationalism was U.S. nationalism. Morfit reported, "The desire of the people to be admitted into our confederacy is so prevailing, that any conditions will be acceptable which will include the guaranty of a republican form of government."[12]

The local residents may have been unlikely to resist, but what about the neighboring claimant? Mexican leaders denied Texan independence, disowned Santa Anna after his defeat, and plotted to reestablish control over their wayward province. As Jackson told Congress, there remained, "in appearance at least, an immense disparity of physical force on the side of Mexico," leaving Texan security, in Morfit's words, dependent "more upon the weakness and imbecility of her enemy than upon her own strength."[13] Yet Mexico was weak—in fact, it was so wracked by political instability and so thinly stretched in its northern provinces that *Texan* leaders plotted a campaign of conquest across northern Mexico to the Pacific.[14] An associate wrote to the Texan secretary of state, Anson Jones, that potential immigrants feared instability not from Mexican aggression against Texas but from Texan aggression against Mexico, which would disturb the calm of Mexico's being "utterly powerless."[15]

Even Mexico's raw numbers advantage over Texas was dwarfed by its weakness compared to the United States, which had far outpaced its southern neighbor over the preceding decades and was more than ten times stronger by the 1830s.[16] Comparing U.S. policy toward Canada and Mexico, Senator Thomas Hart Benton of Missouri declared, "Would we take 2,000 miles of the Canadas in the same way? I presume not. And why not? Because Great Britain is powerful and Mexico weak."[17] Many Americans came to view Mexican instability as evidence of an inherent racial weakness. Pennsylvania Senator James Buchanan proclaimed, "The Anglo-Saxon blood could never be subdued by anything that claimed Mexican origin."[18] Some may have expected Mexico to fight a U.S. annexation of Texas, but few expected it to be much of a fight.

Unlike Mexico, the European great powers were capable of making life very difficult for the United States. France was significantly stronger than the United States throughout this period, Britain was roughly twice as strong as France, and both remained interested in North America.[19] Britain ran a profitable trade through Canada and the West Indies, while France fought a brief war with Mexico in the winter of 1838–39 over unpaid debts. It was also widely known in Texas and the United States that both European powers preferred that Texas remain independent as a bulwark against further U.S. expansion. The Texan minister Ashbel Smith reported of British Foreign Secretary Aberdeen, "The purpose of his government is, if possible, to prevent our annexation to the American Union."[20]

Yet both countries' leaders recognized that fighting the United States over Texas would be expensive and would siphon resources away from their primary area of concern: the balance of power in Europe. In September 1844 Aberdeen warned Santa Anna in no uncertain terms that "if he tried to reconquer Texas and got into trouble, Britain would not help him."[21]

Three months later he ordered the British consul in Texas to avoid overtly opposing U.S. interests, writing, "You should in no way commit your government to any line of active policy with regard to that country."[22] Smith read British policy accurately, reporting that Aberdeen "will do nothing that can justly give offense to the United States."[23] When a scandal threatened to see U.S. Consul Duff Green expelled from Galveston, British Prime Minister Robert Peel feared that it offered a "pretext with the U.S. for direct hostility against Texas—and annexation by that means," which he would not forcibly oppose.[24] Smith also reported that French Foreign Minister François Guizot "seemed less ready than formerly to take any decisive course in relation to our affairs, being impressed, as I believe, by Mr. King, American minister at Paris, with the apprehension that such a course would give umbrage to the American government."[25] In light of Mexico's inability and the Europeans' unwillingness to offer much resistance, military costs cannot explain why U.S. leaders rejected the voluntary annexation of Texas for eight years.

Jackson declined to annex Texas in 1836, despite having pursued its purchase for years, because he feared the associated domestic costs. Unlike later cases in this chapter, xenophobia played little role here because Texas was dominated by Anglo-Americans in the late 1830s.[26] Many Tejanos had supported the revolution against Mexico only to see Anglo-American settlers wrest away their ranches and livestock in its aftermath.[27] As a result, "the Tejanos, who could claim Texas in 1820, had lost that claim by 1836."[28] Without more migration from southern Mexico, the once and future Americans dominated Texan politics, basing their constitution and laws on the U.S. model to smooth the way for annexation.

U.S. leaders saw the Texans as Americans as well. Congressman Alexander Stephens of Georgia declared, "They are of the Americo-Anglo-Saxon race. They are from us, and of us; bone of our bone, and flesh of our flesh."[29] Senator Levi Woodbury of New Hampshire noted that Texas had "a body of intelligent and talented men of the true Saxon race. And if all these do not constitute a state, what does?"[30] Mississippi Senator Robert Walker similarly saw the Texans as "our kindred race," and New York Congressman David Seymour looked forward to "the easy and natural union of two contiguous nations, both founded by the Anglo-Saxon race, both organized upon the same basis of popular rights and republican equality."[31] Even John Quincy Adams, who opposed annexing Texas, recognized the Texans as American "progeny," though he thought them "misbegotten and illegitimate."[32] Most did not consider the few remaining Tejanos a problem because they agreed with Sam Houston that "they will, like the Indian race, yield to the advance of the North American population."[33]

Where a shared sense of kindred identity opened the door to annexation, however, sectional political strife slammed it shut. Had Jackson accepted the Texan offer, his best-case scenario was that the Senate would reject the resulting annexation treaty, and his worst-case scenario was that the issue would spark a civil war. The decade leading up to Texan independence saw heightened sectional polarization as the northern states' industrialization and urbanization drove their preferences increasingly apart from those of their agricultural southern neighbors, igniting a series of crises in the late 1820s and early 1830s.[34] When Congress passed tariffs protecting northern industry in 1828 and 1832, South Carolina declared them null and void within its borders, prompting Congress to authorize Jackson to use military force against the defiant state. Although South Carolina repealed its Nullification Ordinance the following year, sectional pressures continued to mount as growing numbers of northern abolitionists attacked slavery on moral grounds. Seeing abolition as a threat to their society's socioeconomic foundations, southern leaders grew so desperate that they instituted a series of gag rules that kept the issue off the congressional agenda from 1836 to 1844. As one congressman described, "The whole nation was in a state of agitation, working like a troubled sea."[35] In the context of this sectional crisis, northern and southern leaders alike saw the future of their nation as being dependent on the sectional balance of power, with Texas as its fulcrum.

When Texas revolted in 1835, the Union contained an even balance of twelve free and twelve slave states that had been carefully maintained over the preceding decades. Indiana and Mississippi balanced each other's admission in 1816–17, followed by Illinois and Alabama in 1818–19. When Missouri's admission threatened to disrupt the sectional equilibrium, Maine was split from Massachusetts to maintain the balance rule. Missouri's southern border of 36°30' was set as the northern boundary of slavery in the remaining Louisiana territory as part of the Missouri Compromise, but since almost all of the remaining territory lay north of that line the compromise effectively guaranteed that most future states would join the northern bloc.[36]

As the last few slave territories became states, southern leaders realized that maintaining their federal influence required new annexations, and Texas was their primary target.[37] As Virginia Congressman Henry Wise explained, "Let one more Northern state be admitted and the equilibrium was gone—not for a few years, but forever. . . . This must be the inevitable result, unless, by a treaty with Mexico, the South could add more weight to her end of the lever. Let the South stop at the Sabine, while the North might spread unchecked beyond the Rocky Mountains, and the Southern scale must kick the beam."[38] In 1837 the Mississippi legislature hoped that through "the annexation of Texas, an equipoise of influence in the halls of Congress will be secured, which will furnish us a permanent guaranty of protection."[39] When the Senate rejected President Tyler's annexation treaty in June 1844, a former senator offered the most concise expression of why it had happened: "Because Texas was not represented."[40] Had Texas been represented in the Senate, the South would have had the influence necessary to ratify treaties favorable to southern interests, like the one annexing Texas.

Whereas southern leaders saw the annexation of Texas as critical to preserving their domestic influence, northern ones saw it as a threat to their own. As far back as 1819 northern opposition had caused President Monroe to back away from plans to seize Texas (along with Florida) if the Adams–Onís Treaty fell through. "I have been decidedly of the opinion," he noted, "that we ought to be content with Florida for the present, and until the public opinion in that quarter [New England] shall be reconciled to any further change."[41] When the Texas Revolution generated invitations for annexation, northern opinions hardened further. In an open letter to Henry Clay, the influential preacher William Channing wrote, "We cannot consent, that the South should extend its already disproportionate power by an indefinite extension of territory."[42] John Quincy Adams and eleven other congressmen published their own open letter, declaring that "the particular objects of this new acquisition of slave territory were the perpetuation of slavery and the continued ascendancy of the slave power."[43] It was hardly a foregone conclusion that Texas would enter the Union as only one state—dividing it into three or more new states was equally feasible and especially worrying.[44] Memucan Hunt, the first Texan minister to the United States, complained in 1838 that annexation was "utterly impracticable under existing circumstances" even though President Van Buren, Secretary of State John Forsyth, and U.S. Minister to Mexico Poinsett all favored it because "hampered as they are . . . by the furious opposition of all the free states[,] . . . they dare not and will not come out openly for the measure."[45]

Sectional strife drove many to fear that any executive push to annex Texas would irreparably fracture the United States. As Hunt reported, "Many of our friends as well as enemies in Congress dread the coming of the question at this time, on account of the desperate death-struggle, which they foresee, will inevitably ensue between the North and the South;—a struggle involving the probability of a dissolution of this Union."[46] William Henry Seward was afraid that slavery's expansion would become "the ground for secession, nullification, and disunion."[47] Adams and his coauthors believed that if Texas was annexed, the northern states might secede rather than face domination by the South, writing, "We hesitate not to say that annexation . . . would be identical with dissolution."[48] If annexation was rejected, on the other hand, some expected the southern states to secede rather than face domination by the growing North. Benton, who believed this to be the goal of some proponents, declared, "Disunion is at the bottom of this long-concealed Texas machination. . . . Under the pretext of getting Texas into the Union, the scheme is to get the South out of it. A separate confederacy, stretching from the Atlantic to California . . . is the cherished vision of disappointed ambition."[49]

Amidst such extreme sectional polarization, Jackson treaded carefully when the initial Texan request for annexation arrived. He personally disapproved of the Texans' revolution, preferring to purchase Texas and the San Francisco Bay area from Mexico directly rather than to annex an independent state and be accused of fomenting the revolt.[50] Since Mexico refused to sell, though, he searched for ways to make Texas more appealing to northern leaders, advising a Texan agent in 1836 "to claim territory to the Pacific Ocean in order to arouse support from powerful United States shipping interests in the north and east for annexation."[51] Yet northern opposition remained virulent, driving Jackson to advise against annexation in two messages to Congress that December, referencing "the known desire of the Texans to become a part of our system, although its gratification depends upon the reconcilement of various and conflicting interests."[52] As the historian Frederick Merk observes, "Jackson even then was eager for Texas but was aware of a sectional storm that would arise if even recognition of Texas came prematurely."[53]

Prominent in influencing Jackson's opinion were Secretary Forsyth and then-Vice President Van Buren, "who were concerned over rising Northern opposition to annexation."[54] Prioritizing Van Buren's succession to the presidency, Jackson was careful not to rock the boat, refusing to recognize Texan independence until the final days of his administration.[55] Even this Van Buren resisted because any widespread annexation debate would mean "the Democrats would divide sectionally upon it in the approaching elections, and their leader . . . would find his friends a minority in the next Congress."[56] As president, Van Buren maintained Jackson's nonannexation policy for "fear of a clash between the sections of the Union over the issue of the extension of slavery," which, "resurgent in American politics, had been the most potent among the forces producing caution on the annexation issue."[57]

The Annexation of Texas

President John Tyler reversed course in 1843 and publicly championed annexation. By February 1845 he secured a congressional joint resolution, and Texas formally joined the United States that December. Profitability theory predicts expansionism here, as in the previous case, given Texas's high material benefits and low military costs. Domestic impact theory predicts that after declining Texan annexation because of its domestic political implications, U.S. leaders should have embraced annexation only if those implications changed. After years of refusing to do so, why did U.S. leaders annex Texas?

Federal leaders' domestic political incentives did change by Tyler's administration. The sectionalist fires of the preceding decade burned relatively low by the 1840s, allowing southern leaders to reintroduce the prospect of annexation to the public by focusing on its economic benefits. Despite having allied with the Whigs to oppose Jackson during the Nullification Crisis and having been elected on the Whig ticket alongside William Henry Harrison, Tyler was a Virginia Democrat, and he was committed to expanding southern influence via annexation if possible. As he wrote to Secretary of State Daniel Webster, "Could the North be reconciled to it, would anything throw so bright a lustre around us?"[58] Tyler's presidency hung by a thread after he vetoed Henry Clay's National Bank legislation in September 1841, however. The Whig Party expelled him and his entire Cabinet resigned with the lone exception of Webster. As a result, Tyler depended on Webster as a crucial ally, and the Massachusetts man's opposition to the annexation of Texas on slavery grounds forced Tyler to put the issue on hold until Webster's own resignation in May 1843.[59]

Once given the opportunity, Tyler appointed a more like-minded secretary, Abel Upshur. Texan Ambassador Isaac Van Zandt greeted Upshur's appointment with glee, writing, "His whole soul is with us."[60] A Virginian like Tyler and a well-known expansionist, Upshur wrote in October that "the annexation of Texas to the Union . . . is the great object of my ambition."[61] He set to work laying a foundation of propaganda tailored to appeal to the different sectional audiences. Southern journals spoke of defending slavery and securing the southern way of life, while northern ones ran enticing descriptions of Texas's economic prospects and emphasized how its cotton production would lower prices for northern textile manufacturers. As another proponent told Anson Jones, "Mr. Upshur is a great advocate for this measure, and as he is the first one occupying the position he does that has had the boldness to make it a leading measure of his policy, I consider our prospects at present more flattering for accomplishing the object than they have ever been."[62] Together, Tyler and Upshur worked tirelessly to move public opinion toward annexation. As Van Zandt reported, "The president said to me the other day in a private interview, 'Encourage your people to be quiet, and to not grow impatient. We are doing all we can to annex you to us, but we must have time.' . . . The opposition is so great, that he moves very cautiously indeed, and I think very properly, too."[63]

When Upshur died suddenly in a warship party accident in February 1844, Tyler replaced him with perhaps the only man even more "eager to expand Southern influence in national affairs," John Calhoun.[64] The South Carolina politician continued his predecessor's work, telling the U.S. minister to France in August that annexation was inevitable. He spoke of the destiny of the United States to bring "within the pale of cultivation, improvement, and civilization, that large portion of the continent lying between Mexico on one side, and the British possessions on the other, which is now, with little exception, a wilderness with a sparse population, consisting, for the most part, of wandering Indian tribes." Calhoun neatly summarized the U.S. approach to expansion by concluding, "It is our policy to increase, by growing and spreading out into unoccupied regions, assimilating all we incorporate."[65]

The primary obstacle to annexing Texas remained Whigs and northerners in the Senate.[66] When they rejected two of his appointments in April 1843, Tyler told Van Zandt, "Sir, I wish you to be assured that I feel the deepest interest in the affairs of your country, and wish . . . if possible to annex you to us; but you see how I am situated."[67] That August Van Zandt reported back to Texas that "unfortunately for us, the other branches of the government, especially the Senate, are not disposed to aid Mr. Tyler."[68] Tyler signed an annexation treaty in April 1844, but the Senate struck it down by a vote of 16–35, with twenty-eight of the twenty-nine Whigs joining northern Democrats to doom the treaty.[69] In response, the administration and Texan agents redoubled their public relations efforts, hoping to compel senators to support annexation by influencing their constituents.

Building on Upshur's work, Tyler and Calhoun shaped public discussion with propaganda highlighting the most powerful arguments for annexation in the contrasting sections: "To the South, it is a question of safety; to the North, it is one of interest."[70] The administration used British calls for the abolition of slavery to incite dread over an existential threat to the South's way of life, solidifying that region's support for annexation even among Whigs. The abolition of slavery throughout the British Empire had given U.S. slaveholders a substantial economic advantage over their competitors, and southern leaders suspected British plots to eliminate that advantage by destroying slavery in North America. As Calhoun wrote, "In order to regain her superiority, she not only seeks to revive and increase her own capacity to produce tropical productions, but to diminish and destroy the capacity of those who have so far outstripped her in consequence of her error." The first step was pressuring Texas to abolish slavery, which required preventing its annexation to the United States: "It is unquestionable, that she regards the abolition of slavery in Texas as a most important step towards this great object of policy . . . and the defeat of the annexation of Texas to our Union as indispensable to the abolition of slavery there."[71] Meanwhile, proponents lobbied northern support by arguing that Texas would draw slaves from the eastern states—thereby facilitating "peaceful and gradual emancipation," in the words of Congressman Robert Owen of Indiana—and also that it would be an outlet for the emigration of free blacks, preventing them from moving north in increasing numbers (which many northerners opposed).[72]

Annexation became the focus of the 1844 elections, with pressure from southern Whigs forcing even Tyler's adversaries like Henry Clay to reverse course and support it.[73] Tyler himself did not prove competitive as an independent candidate for a second presidential term, but James Polk's election on an expansionist platform allowed Tyler to claim a public mandate for annexation. Tyler managed to secure the annexation of Texas just days before the end of his term via congressional joint resolution, a procedure of questionable constitutional validity.[74] The Senate vote this time was 27–25 in favor, with the Texans' kindred identity contributing substantially to the result. Senator James Doolittle of Wisconsin explained, "I went for the annexation of Texas . . . because its people went out from among us, and were of us, and desired with one voice to be re-annexed to the Union."[75]

The annexation of Texas was delayed by a decade because northern leaders anticipated its domestic costs. Only after the sectional crises of the 1830s had somewhat faded—and with great effort—were Tyler, Upshur, and Calhoun able to galvanize enough support for annexation to pass. Even then, the United States absorbed Texas only barely, by a narrow Senate vote on a joint resolution. Military costs did not play a major role in U.S. decision-making, as the Texan population remained eager to join the United States, Mexico threatened retaliation but was ill-equipped to exact it, and the European great powers were able but unwilling to forcibly oppose annexation. Most great powers in history would have immediately seized such an easy opportunity by accepting the first Texan request, assuming they had not conquered Texas from Mexico even earlier. In contrast, annexation's contentious domestic political implications drove three U.S. administrations to decline Texan invitations. Even when Tyler finally pursued annexation its success was far from assured, and the United States came very close to leaving Texas independent.

The Mexican–American War

The United States declared war on Mexico in 1846 and proceeded to conquer the northern half of its territory. Profitability theory strongly predicts expansionism here given California's natural resources and geopolitical advantages, U.S. military power, and Mexico's weak northern defenses. Since California and New Mexico were sparsely populated, domestic impact theory also predicts expansionism sensitive to the likely sectional allegiances of those territories. Why did the United States go to war with Mexico, and what role did material benefits, military costs, and domestic costs play in the decision to target those territories?

Unlike the War of 1812, the Mexican–American War was a land grab, plain and simple. Annexing Texas created a multilayered territorial dispute as Mexico continued to claim that province, while Texan leaders claimed lands stretching beyond the Nueces River (Texas's southern intra-Mexican border) to the Rio Grande. President Polk took advantage of that dispute to pursue further territorial gains at Mexico's expense, sending John Slidell to offer $25 million for a new border following the Rio Grande to El Paso and thence west to the Pacific.[76] Mexican President José Herrera was deposed when he considered even receiving Slidell, who returned to the United States empty-handed.[77] Polk proposed "a cession of New Mexico & California" to the new Mexican president, Mariano Paredes, but knowing that Paredes was unlikely to accept, he also moved U.S. forces under General Zachary Taylor into the disputed area between the Nueces and the Rio Grande, to a spot overlooking the town of Matamoros, where they were likely to be attacked by nearby Mexican forces.[78] The attack came on April 25, 1846, and when news of it reached Washington two weeks later, Polk used it as a pretext to rally the United States to war. Announcing that war existed "by the act of Mexico herself"—which he claimed had "invaded our territory and shed the blood of our fellow-citizens on our own soil"—he convinced the House to declare war after only two hours' debate and the Senate followed suit within days.[79]

There is ample evidence that Polk maneuvered the United States into war with Mexico for the explicit purpose of annexing California and New Mexico. His intention to foment hostility along the border is visible in his prewar instructions directing U.S. Minister to Texas Andrew Donelson and U.S. Army Captain Robert Stockton to encourage Texans to attack Mexican forces in the disputed area north of the Rio Grande.[80] That spring he marched Taylor's force into the disputed area fully aware of "the possibility of a collision between the American & Mexican forces."[81] Predicting an "imminent" Mexican attack during a Cabinet meeting on May 9, Polk wrote in his diary, "All agreed that if the Mexican forces at Matamoras committed any act of hostility on Gen'l Taylor's forces I should immediately send a message to Congress recommending an immediate declaration of war."[82] That very evening word arrived that two companies of dragoons from Taylor's army had been ambushed while scouting, and the Cabinet set to work preparing Polk's war message to Congress.

Polk made no secret of his territorial objectives. When Secretary of State James Buchanan prepared a dispatch notifying foreign governments of the war but including the disclaimer "that our object was not to dismember Mexico or to make conquests," Polk struck the passage, arguing "that though we had not gone to war for conquest, yet it was clear that in making peace we would if practicable obtain California and such other portion of the Mexican territory as would be sufficient to indemnify our claimants on Mexico, and to defray the expenses of the war."[83] Although his attempts to purchase California and New Mexico had failed, Polk reasoned, "Now that we were at war the prospect of acquiring them was much better, and to secure that object military possession should with as little delay as possible be taken of all these provinces."[84]

Drawing up his initial war plans, Polk insisted that "the first movement should be to march a competent force into the Northern Provinces and seize and hold them until peace was made."[85] Two weeks later he detailed his rationale in Cabinet: "I stated that if the war should be protracted for any considerable time, it would in my judgment be very important that the U.S. should hold military possession of California at the time peace was made, and I declared my purpose to be to acquire for the U.S. California, New Mexico, and perhaps some others of the Northern Provinces of Mexico."[86] That June he reiterated that "in any event we must obtain Upper California and New Mexico in any treaty of peace we would make."[87] Polk moved U.S. military forces to quickly achieve these ambitions, capturing New Mexico without a shot that August and defeating Mexican forces in California the following January. Given the unambiguous evidence that Polk sought to purchase California and New Mexico prior to the war, deliberately provoked the war itself, and focused U.S. military maneuvers on seizing Mexican territory, the Mexican–American War stands as the lone U.S. war that can legitimately be labeled a land grab. How did profitability and domestic concerns factor into the decision to go to war?

California and New Mexico offered impressive natural resources and geopolitical benefits. In his 1847 message to Congress Polk highlighted "their resources—mineral, agricultural, manufacturing, and commercial," praising California's harbors as future naval bases and economic centers that "would in a short period become the marts of an extensive and profitable commerce with China and other countries of the East."[88] The former U.S. minister to Mexico Waddy Thompson concurred: "As to Texas I regard it as of very little value compared with California, the richest, the most beautiful and the healthiest country in the world," and he looked forward to U.S. "ascendency on the Pacific."[89] If Mexico ever harnessed California's potential, it might emerge as a regional rival to the United States even without Texas. For this reason, scholars often point to the Mexican–American War as the event that cemented U.S. regional hegemony.[90] As Polk told his Cabinet in September 1845, these material benefits were so great that to acquire them "the amt. of pecuniary consideration to be paid would be of small importance."[91]

Mexico's political disarray compounded a considerable U.S. military advantage, and neither Polk nor most other U.S. leaders feared the costs of war with that "feeble power."[92] Mexico had seventy-three presidents in its first forty years of independence; 1846 alone saw four presidents, six war ministers, and sixteen finance ministers.[93] As Senator Lewis Cass of Michigan remarked, "Her government is ephemeral. Its members are born in the morning and die in the evening."[94] Beyond this, "the Mexican army was poorly armed and supplied, and affected by the unpopularity of military service, and by flaws in command and equipment."[95]

On the other hand, the U.S. military had undergone substantial professionalization since the War of 1812. Whereas 14.8 percent of officers had been West Point graduates in 1817, that number had risen to 63.8 percent by 1830.[96] Training practices were imported from the French Napoleonic model that had set a new standard in Europe. The United States enjoyed naval superiority over Mexico and had better artillery, and its forces were led by experienced veterans.[97] These advantages made Slidell optimistic as he embarked on his prewar purchase mission: "The truth is that although I have no very exalted idea of the calibre of Mexican intellect, yet I cannot imagine that anyone who could by possibility be elected president, could have so small a modicum of sense as to think seriously of going to war with [the] United States."[98]

What of potential European intervention? British ambitions in California were common knowledge in the United States (though not so well-known in Britain), and the ongoing Oregon dispute offered British leaders a ready pretext for inserting their formidable military into the Mexican conflict.[99] Although Polk saw a potential war with Britain as a subject of "grave" concern and was "not without some apprehension that there may be some European interference on behalf of Mexico," he dismissed that apprehension after the Oregon Treaty was signed.[100] His confidence was justified, as by the 1840s no European great power was willing to fight the United States over territory peripheral to its own interests. In August 1845 British Foreign Secretary Aberdeen refused Mexican requests for aid and advised Mexican leaders to avoid war. The same year, Mexico's minister to Spain reported that although the Spanish government had noticed the "ambitious tendencies" and "dishonorable conduct" of the United States, it would not fight to prevent the "usurpation which is projected."[101] In 1847 British leaders told the French ambassador "that Great Britain was too wise a country to interfere in such a cause; that Mexico in the hands of the people of the United States would be to England of far more value than she ever was before in respect to commerce and security of property invested there."[102]

In both the United States and Europe "the general assumption was that a weak and degraded Mexico could offer no real resistance to the United States forces."[103] The course of the war proved that prediction accurate, as up to 50,000 Mexicans were killed in action compared to 1,733 U.S. soldiers, though some 13,000 more died of disease. The total cost of the war to the United States was approximately $58 million plus the treaty terms, a substantial investment but hardly out of line with other expansionist wars in history.[104] Highlighting the mismatch, Ulysses Grant labeled the war "one of the most unjust ever waged by a stronger against a weaker nation . . . an instance of a republic following the bad example of European monarchies, in not considering justice in their desire to acquire additional territory."[105]

Like its military costs, the domestic costs of annexing northern Mexico were limited due to its sparse population. New Mexico held roughly 65,000 people in 1846, including 10,000 Pueblo Natives, and it marked "the largest concentration to be found anywhere in the immense arch of frontier territories dwarfing California and Texas."[106] California was home to about 7,300 Mexicans and 100,000 Native Americans in the mid-1840s, and the following decade saw its Native population cut by two-thirds through violence, disease, and starvation associated with the California Gold Rush.[107] Mexican efforts to encourage northward migration had been stymied by the threat of Native violence, the expense of moving, and the availability of land further south, but U.S. settlers started to move to California in increasing numbers. At least 680 were already there and 500 more on the way when the war broke out.[108] As one newspaper put it, "Let the tide of emigration flow toward California and the American population will soon be sufficiently numerous to play the Texas game."[109]

Even as these territories' sparse populations made them appealing targets, sectionalism continued to fuel domestic political debate over annexation. Many southern leaders cheered the declaration of war, anticipating that a sizable cession below the Missouri Compromise line would breed new slave states to bolster their influence in the federal government. Senator Albert Brown of Mississippi declared, "I want Tamaulipas, Potosi, and one or two other Mexican states; and I want them all for the same reason—for the planting or spreading of slavery."[110] The *Federal Union* asked how any southerner could oppose a war which promised to "secure to the South the balance of power in the Confederacy, and, for all coming time, to give to her the control in the operations of the government?"[111] Northern leaders opposed Polk's war for the same reason southerners favored it. Congressman Robert Winthrop appealed to his constituents during the 1846 election by saying, "I believe I speak the sentiments of the whole people of Massachusetts— I know I speak my own, in saying we want no more territorial possessions to become nurseries of new slave states."[112]

Revealingly, opinions changed as people learned more about California and realized that its climate was not actually conducive to the slave economy.[113] John Quincy Adams, a vocal critic of Texas annexation on slavery grounds, supported the Mexican cession once he was persuaded it would produce free states.[114] Thompson, on the other hand, grew convinced that expansion into Mexico would deal "a fatal blow to the institution of slavery," declaring, "Woe to the Southern man who lends his aid to doing that."[115] Similarly, Calhoun accused northern politicians of spending southern "blood & treasure . . . freely in the war to acquire territory, not for the common good, but as a means of . . . ruling us. We are to be made to dig our own grave."[116]

Polk recognized this domestic political minefield and maneuvered his territorial ambitions through it. He "deprecated the agitation of the slavery question in Congress," which had become a "fire-brand" for politicians looking to rally sectional support.[117] He told Senator John Crittenden of Kentucky, "I did not desire to acquire a more Southern territory than that which I had indicated, because I did not desire by doing so to give occasion for the agitation of a question which might sever and endanger the Union itself."[118] When controversy arose over the Wilmot Proviso banning slavery in the Mexican cession, Polk carefully navigated meetings with Pennsylvania Congressman David Wilmot and Calhoun, among others, in order to maintain support for the cession.[119] As he wrote in his diary, "There is no probability that any territory will ever be acquired from Mexico in which slavery could ever exist. New Mexico and California is all that can ever probably be acquired by treaty, and indeed all that I think it important to acquire."[120] Polk's pursuit of these territories accords well with both profitability theory and domestic impact theory, but U.S. military success during the Mexican–American War also opened the door to a larger opportunity that would see their predictions diverge.

All Mexico

With northern Mexico in hand by early 1847 U.S. forces closed on southern Mexico from all sides: the navy blockaded its southwestern coast, occupying

Baja California and coastal cities like Guaymas and Mazatlán; land forces invaded from Texas and New Mexico; and an amphibious army led by Winfield Scott landed near Veracruz and captured Mexico City. Yet despite continued military success U.S. war aims barely expanded during the war and never approached all Mexico. Why did U.S. leaders limit their southward ambitions, even amidst the brash self-confidence of the Manifest Destiny era? Profitability theory predicts that U.S. leaders should keep their ambitions in lockstep with affordable opportunities, refusing further conquests only if the remaining targets would be more trouble than they were worth. In contrast, domestic impact theory predicts that U.S. leaders who saw Mexicans as alien and inferior should have expected their assimilation in large numbers to generate profound domestic costs, making southern Mexico's dense population a powerful deterrent against annexation. Why did the United States annex far less territory than its military occupied?

Polk wanted the war to end as soon as he had achieved his core objective: the cession of California and New Mexico. As U.S. forces approached Santa Fe and Los Angeles in August 1846, he requested a congressional appropriation of $2 million to capitalize on disorder in the Mexican government by bribing whichever officials might assent to peace on those terms. As he wrote in his diary, "Whatever party can keep the army in its support can hold the power" in Mexico, and had his appropriations bill passed he "should have made an honorable peace by which we should have acquired California, & such other territory as we desired, before the end of October."[121] When that effort fell through, he dispatched Scott with twelve thousand soldiers to capture Mexico City, hoping to deal a quick knockout blow that would enable his agent Nicholas Trist to negotiate peace on his terms.

Yet even as Scott occupied Mexico City and other U.S. forces marched south, Polk's initial war aims expanded only to include Baja (Lower) California, which he thought had "but little value," and his instructions to Trist demanded only the cession of "the Californias & New Mexico."[122] Those territories "constituted an ultimatum" to Mexico, but Polk specified in his third annual message that he did not want the "many of her principal towns and cities, which we had conquered and held in our military occupation." [123] On the contrary, he expressly rejected the annexation of all Mexico, declaring, "It has never been contemplated by me, as an object of the war, to make a permanent conquest of the Republic of Mexico or to annihilate her separate existence as an independent nation."[124] Most great powers in history would have regarded conquering the capital and most of the territory of a neighboring country as heralding its total annexation. Why didn't the United States annex all Mexico?

Southern Mexico offered natural resources and geopolitical implications arguably even more impressive than California's. Like many journals of the time, the *Democratic Review* praised "the admirable climate, fertile fields, and boundless mineral resources of Mexico."[125] Stabilizing its local politics and developing its economy would require substantial investments, but given its population of nearly 7,500,000, Mexico's returns for U.S. power could dwarf California's.[126] Seizing California ensured U.S. regional hegemony by preventing Mexico from ever approaching its power, but it could still become a thorn in U.S. leaders' side as a platform for foreign interventions (as France attempted during the Civil War) and a potential ally of hostile powers (as Germany attempted during World War I). Annexing all Mexico would have traded those vulnerabilities for a huge increase in resources and population, and even if maximizing those gains would have demanded substantial investment, so did developing California, which lacked a preexisting labor base.

The military costs of annexing all Mexico are more difficult to estimate. Depending on the form of assimilation U.S. leaders pursued, such a campaign might have elicited far greater local resistance than the war, which saw an "absence of large-scale guerilla warfare."[127] The French intervention in Mexico during the 1860s offers a useful counterfactual. Forty thousand French troops were not enough to maintain order throughout the country in that instance, though the anti-French resistance under Benito Juárez received substantial covert support from the United States.[128] It stands to reason that a carefully engineered U.S. partnership with local elites could have suppressed much of that resistance, especially if the Mexican people were granted citizenship and representation in an enlarged United States. The European powers, for their part, remained unwilling to intervene no matter how much territory the United States conquered. In May 1847 U.S. Minister to Britain George Bancroft reported, "England is even preparing to hear of our negotiating for half, or two thirds, or even the whole of Mexico. . . . They see our growth to be certain; & they like publicly & officially to take as little note of it as possible."[129] Annexing all Mexico would certainly have inflicted greater military costs than the war, as it happened, but with the Mexican army already defeated and Mexico City captured, additional costs would likely have remained well within the means of the prosperous United States and perhaps even beneath the Treaty of Guadalupe Hidalgo's $18.25 million price tag.

Military costs did play a role in ending the war—Congress's reluctance to fund a prolonged campaign influenced Polk's decision to submit Trist's treaty to the Senate—but only due to widespread agreement that the United States had already achieved everything worth fighting for.[130] Though they were willing to conquer California and stare down the European great powers in the process, neither Polk nor Congress wanted to annex all Mexico. Most U.S. leaders shared Buchanan's opinion that California made an appealing target because it was "comparatively uninhabited & will therefore be almost exclusively colonized by our own people." In contrast, southern Mexico housed millions of people deemed unfit for U.S. citizenship by the endemic racism of that era. If the United States did annex all Mexico, Buchanan wondered, "how should we govern the mongrel race which inhabits it? Could we admit them to seats in our Senate & House of Representatives? Are they capable of self-government as states of this confederacy?"[131] The former U.S. minister to Texas Andrew Donelson agreed that there was "no danger" in acquiring California "because in five years 4/5 of its population will be emigrants from the Union." But he insisted that "the Mexicans are not fit for incorporation into our Union," telling Polk, "We can no more amalgamate with her people than with negroes."[132] When Polk was accused of wanting all Mexico, he "particularly disclaimed such a scheme" as "annexing the whole of Mexico to the United States, with a population of seven or eight millions of people, who are unfit to participate in the benefits of our free institutions."[133]

The administration's thinking mirrored Congress's fears that annexing all Mexico would force an impossible choice: subvert the self-perceived identity of their nation by granting federal representation to the Mexican people, or subvert their democracy by imposing permanent imperial rule on the Mexican people. Calhoun was among the most outspoken on the subject, arguing that to annex Mexico "would be to overthrow our government, and, to hold it as a province, to corrupt and destroy it."[134] In a widely publicized speech he insisted that "Mexico is to us the forbidden fruit; the penalty of eating it would be to subject our institutions to political death."[135] California, New Mexico, and the area north of the Rio Grande were "almost literally an uninhabited country" and thus compatible with U.S. territorial goals: "What we want is space for our growing population—and what we ought to avoid is, the addition of other population, of a character not suited to our institutions."[136] Objecting that the United States had never "incorporated into the Union any but the Caucasian race," Calhoun declared, "I protest against the incorporation of such a people. Ours is the government of the white man."[137]

Calhoun was by no means alone in holding these sentiments. Florida Congressman Edward Cabell rejected the annexation of all Mexico because "if we annex the land, we must take the population along with it."[138] Jacob Collamer of Vermont forebodingly warned, "We should destroy our own nationality by such an act. We shall cease to be the people that we were; we cease to be the Saxon Americanized. . . . We shall take in seven or eight millions of people in no way homogenous, incapable of being reduced to common feelings, common interests, common desires with us."[139] The U.S. Constitution, according to Connecticut Senator Jabez Huntington, was not "for people of every color, and language, and habits."[140] Congressman William Wick of Indiana stressed, "I do not want mixed races in our Union, nor men of any color except white, unless they be slaves. Certainly not as voters or legislators."[141] Polk sought to assuage these fears in his 1847 annual message, clarifying that "in proposing to acquire New Mexico and the Californias, it was known that but an inconsiderable portion of the Mexican people would be transferred with them, the country embraced within these provinces being chiefly an uninhabited region."[142] As the historian Thomas Hietala writes, "The dilemma was to strike a happy balance between the desire for Mexico's land and resources and the demand that masses of non-white people be excluded from the Union."[143]

This opposition stemmed from racist convictions that Mexicans were inherently unsuited for republican government. Senator Edward Hannegan of Indiana held that "Mexico and the United States are peopled by two distinct and unhomogeneous races. In no reasonable period could we amalgamate . . . [Mexicans being] utterly unfit for the blessings and the restraints of rational liberty."[144] Tennessee Senator John Bell argued that "all history, all experience" showed Mexicans incapable of entering the Union as equal citizens, while New York Congressman Washington Hunt judged the Mexican "medley of mixed races" fit "neither to enjoy nor to administer our free institutions."[145] Congressman James Pollock of Pennsylvania agreed: "The Mexican provinces are filled with a population, not only degraded, but of every possible shade and variety of color and complexion. . . . If we annex these provinces to our Union, will we admit those who are now the free citizens of Mexico to the privileges of American citizenship?"[146] Calhoun wondered, "Can we incorporate a people so dissimilar from us in every respect—so little qualified for free and popular government—without certain destruction to our political institutions?"[147] If the United States did absorb the Mexican population, many predicted a "war between races and creeds" that would tear the Union apart.[148]

These racist views, openly expressed on the floor of Congress, echoed public xenophobia targeting the Mexicans' alien ethnicity and culture, as well as their Spanish language and Catholic religion. The *Charleston Mercury* wondered what the United States would do with millions of Mexicans who were "bigotted, ignorant, idle, lawless, slavish, and yet free?"[149] Pseudoscientists asserted a natural racial superiority, one writing that "everything in the history of the Bee shows a reasoning power little short of that of a Mexican."[150] The *Augusta Chronicle* opined that although the United States could swallow Mexico "as easily as Jonah was by the whale," it would not sit well in "the republican stomach. . . . It would likely prove to be a sickening mixture, consisting of such a conglomeration of Negroes and Rancheros, Mestizoes, and Indians."[151]

Literary figures of the era expressed similar sentiments. Ralph Waldo Emerson predicted in 1846 that "the United States will conquer Mexico, but it will be as the man swallows the arsenic, which brings him down in turn. Mexico will poison us."[152] Walt Whitman asked, "What has miserable, inefficient Mexico . . . to do with the great mission of peopling the New World with a noble race?"[153] As U.S. citizens confronted the prospect of a shared multiracial society through the illusory lens of their own homogeneity—maintained at that time through African American slavery, Native American removal, and geographic isolation from other races—Enlightenment visions of universal liberty increasingly gave way to presumptions of "an unbridgeable gap" between races, thrusting "Anglo-Saxon" as a racial term into the U.S. vocabulary for the first time.[154]

Even all-Mexico proponents argued not that the United States should embrace the Mexican people, but rather that they should be marginalized and exterminated as terribly as the Native Americans had been. Senator Sam Houston of Texas declared, "The Mexicans are no better than Indians, and I see no reason why we should not go in the same course now, and take their land."[155] The *Illinois State Register* labeled Mexicans "reptiles in the path of progressive democracy . . . they must either crawl or be crushed."[156] Many shared the assumption of Senator Daniel Dickinson of New York that this result was inevitable: "Like their doomed brethren, who were once spread over the several states of the Union, they are destined, by laws above human agency, to give way to a stronger race from this continent or another."[157] Waddy Thompson wrote, "That the Indian race of Mexico must recede before us is quite as certain as that that is the destiny of our own Indians."[158] Pollock confronted his fellow congressmen: "Extermination and acquisition must go together. Are we prepared for this? Are we prepared to make the war a war of races, and not stay our hand until every Mexican is driven from the land of his fathers, and the Anglo-Saxon race established in the Halls of the Montezumas?"[159]

Other all-Mexico advocates foresaw a Mexican genocide by sex rather than by violence, positing that the United States could suppress annexation's worsening effect by postponing Mexicans' political representation until they had sufficiently diluted their troublesome DNA by intermarrying with Anglo-Saxons.[160] The *Philadelphia Public Ledger* thought the United States might safely annex all Mexico by allotting it only three or four congressional delegates at first, noting colorfully, "Our Yankee young fellows and the pretty senoritas will do the rest of the annexation, and Mexico will soon be Anglo-Saxonized and prepared for the confederacy."[161] The *New York Herald* agreed that "the admission into the union, on an equality with the other states, of any Mexican state in whose population Mexican blood preponderates, must be after years of patient probation . . . as each qualifies for that privilege by a sufficient admixture of our own blood."[162] The *Louisville Democrat* echoed, "The people of the settled parts of Mexico are a negative quantity. . . . We think all Mexico will fall, piece by piece, into this government; but then it must first be settled by a different population, and the union effected by other means than the sword."[163] The *Democratic Review* likewise called for federal representation to be granted to southern Mexico "piece by piece" as it was "Anglo-Saxonized."[164]

Most U.S. leaders in both Congress and the Polk administration were deeply skeptical that southern Mexico could be Americanized, however, and their xenophobia drove them to reject its annexation. When Buchanan advocated securing "Tamaulipas & all the country east of the Sierra mountains" in January 1848, for example, Polk "expressed a doubt as to the policy or practicability of obtaining a country containing so large a number of the Mexican population."[165] Senator Cass gave this prevailing perspective its most concise summary when he declared in February 1847, "We do not want the people of Mexico, either as citizens or subjects. All we want is a portion of territory, which they nominally hold, generally uninhabited, or, where inhabited at all, sparsely so, and with a population, which would soon recede, or identify itself with ours."[166]

The Treaty of Guadalupe Hidalgo, signed in February 1848, gave the United States some 525,000 square miles of territory stretching from New Mexico to California in return for $15 million and the assumption of $3.25 million of Mexican debt to U.S. citizens.[167] Southern Mexico remained independent—and with it the lion's share of the Mexican population—so the treaty met with general satisfaction from federal leaders and the U.S. public. Since it achieved his prewar territorial ambitions, Polk submitted the treaty to the Senate despite his frustration that Trist had ignored a recall order to negotiate it.[168] The Senate was equally pleased with the scope of the Mexican Cession, ratifying the treaty by a vote of 38–14. As the *Washington Daily Union* remarked, "Fortunately for us, we obtain that very portion of the country which is the sparsest in population. Our own population . . . will so rapidly pour into the new territory, as to control the actual settlers, and overcome their moral degradation."[169] The *Louisville Democrat* described the cession as "not the best boundary, but all the territory of value that we can get without taking the people."[170]

In the Mexican–American War U.S. leaders conquered Mexico's sparsely populated north but declined to pursue its densely populated south because they feared its domestic costs. Judging the Mexican army to be toothless and the prospect of European intervention remote, they were undeterred by military costs. Polk maneuvered the United States into war with Mexico to obtain California, New Mexico, and the Rio Grande boundary, and once U.S. forces had secured those acquisitions, he sent Scott to end the war quickly by capturing Mexico City. Polk expanded his ambitions only slightly to include border areas with small populations like Baja California, but once the Treaty of Guadalupe Hidalgo was signed he left their pursuit to his successors.

The Antebellum Period

Growing U.S. power and ongoing Mexican political disarray notwithstanding, U.S. pursuits of Mexican territory in the decade before the Civil War were relatively meager in both scope and means. Presidents Zachary Taylor and Millard Fillmore requested transit rights across the Isthmus of Tehuantepec, but Mexico refused. President Franklin Pierce achieved the Gadsden Purchase, but both he and his successor, James Buchanan, failed to annex Baja California and other border areas. Mexican leaders finally granted the Tehuantepec transit rights in the 1860 McLane–Ocampo Treaty only for the Senate to vote it down, and further pursuits were cut short by the Civil War. Profitability theory expects U.S. leaders to tailor their efforts to fit affordable opportunities, predicting that U.S. restraint during this period should have been driven by skepticism regarding the material value of further Mexican territory or fear of its acquisition price. Domestic impact theory predicts that xenophobia and sectionalism should have continued to limit U.S. leaders' ambitions, expecting them to target only sparsely populated areas that would strengthen their domestic political influence. Why did the United States annex only the Gadsden Purchase during the 1850s?

U.S. leaders did not forsake further territorial gains because they feared military costs. Since they were willing to fight Mexico in the 1840s, they should have been equally willing to do so in the 1850s. Mexico's military continued to be far outmatched and its government unstable leading up to a civil war in 1857–60 between the rival camps of Benito Juárez and Miguel Miramón. The former Mexican president Manuel Pedraza told U.S. Minister to Mexico Robert Letcher in 1850, "Your government is strong; ours is weak. You have the power to take the whole or any portion of our territory you may think fit."[171] European leaders increasingly considered intervening in Mexico to secure debts as the decade progressed, but they remained unwilling to forcibly oppose further U.S. annexations. As British Prime Minister Palmerston wrote in November 1855, "Britain and France would not fight to prevent the United States from annexing Mexico, 'and would scarcely be able to prevent it if they did go to war.'" He prophesied that the U.S. annexation of Mexico was "written in the Book of Fate."[172] U.S. leaders understood this, Secretary of State Lewis Cass commenting, "I do not think that France or England will pursue such a course of interference as will be in hostility with the American system we have laid down."[173]

Nor did U.S. leaders forsake additional Mexican territory because they thought it worthless. On the contrary, the northern areas they targeted were primarily arid desert (relatively valueless compared to the rich forests further south) and lofty assessments of southern Mexico's natural resources and geopolitical position remained common. In 1859 U.S. Envoy William Churchwell informed Cass that "recent disclosures and the most authoritative accounts respecting its soil and mineral resources represent [Mexico] as being even more valuable than Upper California."[174] The United States launched a war to conquer California, so it stands to reason that on material grounds alone Mexico should have been worth a similar effort. Although its economic development lagged, Mexico represented a large market for northern manufactures; the *New York Times* labeled it the "immense India of the West."[175]

Beyond Mexico's economy and natural resources, U.S. leaders particularly fancied several geographic routes across Mexican territory that could link California with the eastern United States more efficiently than was possible across existing U.S. territory. As Congressman John Quitman of Mississippi put it in 1856, Mexico was valuable not only for "her delightful climate, her fertile soil, her jeweled mountains, and her rich valleys" but also because she held "in her possession the commercial 'philosopher's stone'—the power to tax the commerce of the world by the junction of the two oceans."[176] Three corridors were especially attractive: a railroad route from Texas to California, a railroad route from the new Southwest to the Gulf of California (from which ships could sail east), and a canal or railroad route connecting the Gulf of Mexico to the Pacific Ocean across the Isthmus of Tehuantepec (Mexico's narrowest part). All three offered unique advantages, and all three were pursued by antebellum presidents. Yet while U.S. leaders sought to annex the first two routes (which crossed border regions that had few inhabitants), they requested only transit rights for U.S. citizens across the third (which spanned a populous area of southern Mexico). They declined to pursue any other populous Mexican territories.

Annexation's domestic consequences continued to figure prominently in U.S. leaders' decision-making during the 1850s. The Mexican Cession reanimated the sectional controversy over slavery in federal territories, a dilemma that was settled only uneasily by the Compromise of 1850, which admitted California as a free state and allowed the status of slavery in the remaining federal territories to be decided by popular sovereignty. From that point on, southern leaders bore witness as California's admission left slave states outnumbered in the Senate, and the slave economy of the Southeast proved inefficient in the Southwest.

Terrified of their waning influence over federal policy, southern leaders pushed to create new slave states by annexing further territories in Mexico and the Caribbean.[177] Their list of targets deliberately excluded the free Mexican population, any assimilation of which, the *Augusta Sentinel* noted, "would almost inevitably terminate in a vast increase of the political power of the enemies of our institutions."[178] Northern leaders opposed these southern ambitions for reasons of domestic politics (sectionalism), morality (abolitionism), and economics (prioritizing commerce through transit rights and market access).

With these concerns in mind, the Whig administrations of presidents Taylor and Fillmore rejected further territorial ambitions and instead sought transit rights across the Isthmus of Tehuantepec. In September 1849 Secretary of State John Clayton instructed Letcher to negotiate the transit rights, specifying that Taylor "does not covet, however, and will not stipulate for any rights of sovereignty over the country through which communication may pass."[179] Further underlining Taylor's lack of interest in annexation, Clayton invited other nations to join the proposed transit treaty after learning of British interest, and he proceeded to negotiate the Clayton–Bulwer Treaty pledging U.S.–British cooperation on any Central American canal.[180]

Clayton defended his policies by explicitly wielding the logic of domestic impact theory. When Senator Stephen Douglas of Illinois complained that the Clayton–Bulwer Treaty prevented further southward territorial expansion, Clayton reiterated familiar arguments in one of his most highly praised speeches: "Whenever the day shall come that . . . we set about the business of annexing nine or ten millions of Mexicans to the United States, the days of our republic will be numbered. . . . Could we permit them to take a part in the election of our representatives and senators in Congress? Could we admit them to assist in governing us?" He directly observed how the interaction between democracy and xenophobia made Mexico an undesirable target: "If we could annex other countries as England does, or as Rome did . . . the whole subject might receive another consideration. Whenever we annex, we make citizens of the people whom we unite to us." Hence, he reasoned, "if we annex Mexico, we are compelled, in obedience to the principles of our own Declaration of Independence, to receive her people as citizens. Yes! Aztecs, Creoles, Half-breeds, Quadroons, Samboes, and I know not what else—'ring-streaked and speckled'—all will come in, and, instead of our governing them, they, by their votes, will govern us."[181] With Mexico's annexation off the table for these domestic reasons, Clayton argued that the United States should prioritize border security and economic opportunity by promoting a stable, friendly southern neighbor—an orientation that would command U.S. policy toward Mexico after the Civil War.

Upon succeeding Clayton, Daniel Webster continued working to obtain transit rights with the understanding that any agreement would not "infringe upon the rights of sovereignty which Mexico holds in the territory."[182] Letcher's efforts produced multiple treaties, though each was rejected by a Mexican Congress afraid of enduring U.S. expansionism. Ironically, this led frustrated U.S. leaders to begin wondering whether further annexations were the only way to secure the desired routes. As Webster wrote to Fillmore in May 1852, Mexico's stubbornness might "provoke the United States to take another slice of its territory."[183] The following October Acting Secretary of State Charles Conrad instructed the new minister to Mexico, Alfred Conkling, to inquire about a direct cession of the Tehuantepec route, but the idea came to naught with only months left in Fillmore's administration.[184]

The change to a Democratic president beholden to southern interests brought a full-fledged return to expansionism. Within months of taking office, Franklin Pierce moved to annex both northern transit routes. He instructed James Gadsden to offer up to $50 million for a strip of border territory including all of Baja California.[185] Disclaiming any interest in absorbing Mexican population, Secretary of State William Marcy told the Mexican ambassador that "beyond a feasible route for a railroad the American government wanted no territory except what was incidentally necessary in securing a safe and easily-defended boundary."[186] Santa Anna, having retaken power in Mexico and urgently needing funds to support his regime, agreed to sell but refused to cede more than the minimum sought: the railroad route connecting Texas and California through the Mesilla Valley. Rapid negotiations produced the Gadsden Purchase, which the Senate ratified in April 1854 after lowering the price tag to $10 million and slightly reducing the size of the ceded territory.[187] The purchase transferred roughly thirty thousand square miles of desert to the United States; even by the 1860 census its population barely exceeded twenty-four hundred settlers and four thousand Native Americans.[188]

President Buchanan continued Pierce's pursuit of Mexico's remaining "sparsely settled regions," instructing U.S. Minister to Mexico John Forsyth Jr. to offer $4–5 million for Baja California and $8–10 million for other Mexican lands north of 30° as well as transit rights across any ocean-to-ocean route that might be constructed.[189] When the Mexican government rejected any further cessions, Buchanan proposed establishing a temporary protectorate over northern Chihuahua and Sonora, but northern congressmen overruled his southern supporters and denied his requests.[190] Facing committed northern opposition, Buchanan decided to focus on Baja California, which was sparsely populated but valuable as a Pacific outlet for southwestern U.S. trade. He offered Juárez $10 million for Baja California and transit rights across Tehuantepec, but Juárez was reluctant to consider further cessions and insisted on negotiating only transit rights despite badly needing cash to support his regime. Buchanan attached "the greatest importance to the cession of Lower California," but he authorized Robert McLane to negotiate transit rights separately as a last resort.[191] The resulting McLane–Ocampo Treaty pledged the United States to pay $4 million for perpetual transit rights across Tehuantepec as well as two other routes connecting the U.S. Southwest with the Pacific Ocean: from Arizona across Sonora to Guaymas and from Texas across central Mexico to Mazatlán.

In an age before the transcontinental railroad or the Panama Canal, this treaty achieved the long-standing U.S. foreign policy goal of enabling efficient communication between the Atlantic and Pacific Oceans. Yet upon reaching the Senate the agreement raised suspicions that U.S. responsibility for the transit routes might foreshadow the annexation of Mexican population centers. Senator Louis Wigfall of Texas denounced the treaty because he "did not want Mexico or her mongrel population. Juarez and his Indian crew could not govern themselves, and if brought into contact with our people would contaminate them."[192] James Hammond of South Carolina "could not see how the South was to be benefited by the addition of that mongrel population."[193] McLane himself promoted the treaty as the only way to *prevent* further annexations, asserting that "if it is rejected, anarchy will be the order of the day" in Mexico, forcing the United States to assume "responsibility of . . . a conquest that few would desire to undertake or consummate."[194] The Senate rejected the treaty but voiced willingness to consider an amended version, although the onset of the Civil War prevented that from happening.[195]

His purchase efforts floundering, Buchanan repeatedly requested congressional authorization to use military force in Mexico to head off a potential European intervention (and enable him to seize the border regions he wanted).[196] Britain, France, and Spain all contemplated military interventions in Mexico to recover unpaid debts during the late 1850s, but Congress steadfastly refused Buchanan's requests, its northern members being dead set against further annexations and preoccupied with the deepening sectional schism.[197] Buchanan continued to press the issue, hoping to deter the Europeans by preserving at least the possibility of a U.S. intervention.[198] If the Europeans did intervene to secure debt payments, Cass informed McLane in September 1860, "We insist that such hostilities be fairly prosecuted for that purpose and not converted into the means of acquisition or of political control." He emphasized that any attempt to conquer Mexico "will be met by the armed action of the United States."[199] McLane conveyed the message later that year, telling European ministers in Mexico that if any of their governments compromised Mexican independence the United States would "to the extent of its power defend the nationality and independence of said republic."[200] Lacking congressional support, however, Buchanan remained unable to pursue his own southward ambitions.

Annexation's domestic consequences weighed heavily on the minds of antebellum U.S. leaders, simultaneously fueling southern desires to carve new slave states from Mexico's remaining sparsely populated border territories and northern opposition to their efforts, as well as the widespread refusal to consider annexing more densely populated Mexican regions. As a result, Whig presidents beholden to northern interests limited their ambitions to securing transit rights, while Democratic presidents beholden to southern interests tried to annex border areas over northern opposition in Congress. With the election of Abraham Lincoln and the descent into civil war, the credibility of U.S. threats of deterrence evaporated, opening the door for a French intervention in Mexico.

The Maximilian Affair

When Juárez suspended foreign interest payments in July 1861, France took advantage of U.S. preoccupation with the Civil War and invaded Mexico, installing Austrian Archduke Maximilian as its emperor.[201] Although Secretary of State Seward lodged diplomatic objections, he and President Lincoln recognized that the United States needed to put its own house in order before it could influence events to its south.[202] As the Union army neared victory over the Confederacy, Seward escalated his coercive diplomacy, threatening war with France if it refused to abandon its Mexican venture and with Austria if it intervened to support Maximilian. Rather than pursue further territorial gains at Mexico's expense, he worked to "save Mexico from European re-conquest and subjugation."[203]

Seward not only declined to pursue Mexican territory, he refused offers of Mexican territory from a renegade Mexican military officer, from Juárez looking for help against France, and from France in exchange for recognition of Maximilian's regime. Why didn't the United States take advantage of these opportunities generated by the French intervention to secure further territorial gains for itself? Profitability theory predicts a stark contrast between U.S. behavior during the Civil War, when no potential annexation was worth the risk of losing the Union, and after the Civil War, when the U.S. military had emerged as the strongest in the world. In contrast, domestic impact theory predicts that U.S. leaders' perceptions of the Mexican people as being fundamentally alien should have continued fueling their opinions of Mexico as undesirable. Why didn't the United States pursue further Mexican territory after the Civil War?

Mexico's material resources remained impressive. Its mineral wealth continued to attract foreign investors, and accessing those minerals became a key objective of Seward and his successors. The country's population of roughly 8.5 million remained the largest in North America outside the United States.[204] Mexico's geography had also not changed: it still spanned prime transportation routes between the Atlantic and Pacific Oceans. Moreover, the French intervention underlined a key geopolitical benefit of annexing Mexico: preventing foreign leaders from stirring up trouble for the United States in its neighborhood. In purely material terms, then, Mexico should have remained an enticing target for U.S. leaders.

Yet Lincoln and Seward parted ways with their predecessors by abandoning their quest for Mexican territory. As Seward wrote to U.S. Minister to Mexico Thomas Corwin in April 1861, "The president is fully satisfied that the safety, welfare, and happiness of [the United States] would be more effectually promoted if [Mexico] should retain its complete integrity and independence, than they could be by any dismemberment of Mexico, with a transfer or diminution of its sovereignty, even though thereby a portion or the whole of the country or its sovereignty should be transferred to the United States."[205]

Lincoln and Seward entertained the notion of annexing Mexican territory only twice, both times reluctantly and abortively. First, they tried to head off the French intervention by assuming interest payments on Mexican debt themselves, and when no alternative Mexican collateral for this loan could be found they agreed to assume a lien on public lands and mineral rights in Baja California, Sonora, Sinaloa, and Chihuahua, which would become U.S. property if Mexico failed to repay the loan within six years.[206] A "nearly unanimous" Senate rejected this treaty, however, and beyond a general reluctance to divert Union funds from the war effort, Seward told Corwin that it had faced major opposition from senators who believed "that Mexico ought never, in any contingency whatever, either in whole or in part, to be brought into the Union, and who fear that a loan would result in its annexation."[207] Second, when Seward heard reports early in the war that the Confederacy planned for "expansion" into "the northern parts of Mexico," he wrote to Corwin that "the United States, though she desired no part of Mexico, would buy Lower California to save it from the Confederates, if Mexico would name the price."[208] On learning that Confederate leaders had put their expansion on hold for fear of starting a two-front war with Juárez as well as with the Union, however, Seward returned to his previous position that "the United States were not ambitious of territorial aggrandizement on the south of our present frontiers."[209]

Seward received several noteworthy offers of Mexican territory as the French intervention unfolded, but he refused them all. After French troops entered Mexico City in June 1863, he was approached by a former Mexican military officer, José Cortes, who claimed to represent the northern Mexican provinces of Sonora, Sinaloa, Chihuahua, Durango, and Baja California. Cortes proposed their annexation to the United States to free them from the French, but instead of negotiating Seward reported him to Juárez's ambassador, who disavowed the man as an impostor.[210] Juárez himself was reported to have secretly offered to sell Baja California and part of Sonora to prevent the United States from recognizing Maximilian, but Seward replied "that Maximilian's regime remained counter to the interests of the United States and no offer of Mexican territory need be considered."[211] Explaining the U.S. refusal, the French parliamentarian Charles Corta quoted Winfield Scott as once having said, "Mexico is an old country, having its own religion, its own customs; its population, though thin, is scattered over its whole extent. The United States wants deserts to people and virgin soil to work, upon which their institutions may readily be implanted. Mexico is not to our taste."[212]

Domestic impact theory's dynamics thus continued to operate even as the urgency of winning the Civil War pushed Seward's focus inward. As he wrote to U.S. Minister to Britain Charles Adams in March 1864, "Domestic perils crowd out the consideration of foreign and remote dangers."[213] But this constraint disappeared as the war drew to a close and left the United States with its most powerful military to date. Observers in London called the

Union army "the finest army in the world" as early as 1862; by war's end U.S. power had surpassed that of France, and its advantage over Mexico stretched as high as 50:1.[214] By March 1865 visions of that formidable military turning south were causing "great anxiety" in Paris.[215] Maximilian's sponsors sought to prolong his regime by appeasing the United States. As U.S. Minister to France John Bigelow reported the following month of Emperor Napoleon III, "If we do well by him in Mexico, he will do yet better by us."[216] By October the door was open for U.S. leaders to do as they pleased with Mexico. Bigelow wrote that Napoleon "wished to leave Mexico . . . as soon as he could go safely and honorably," and France "would not attempt to defend Mexico in a war with the United States."[217]

U.S. leaders recognized their military ascendancy, but instead of translating their newfound power into territorial expansion they grew increasingly hostile toward France and defended Mexican independence.[218] In the autumn of 1865 Seward warned Napoleon that with the Civil War over, Congress "will give a very large share of attention to . . . our relations toward France with regard to Mexico." He defined the French occupation as being "in direct antagonism to the policy of this government" as well as "disallowable and impracticable."[219] When Bigelow conveyed this message, French Foreign Minister Édouard Drouyn de Lhuys "derived neither pleasure nor satisfaction from its contents," asking, "If you mean war why not say so frankly?"[220] Andrew Johnson, thrust into the presidency by Lincoln's assassination, included a stern rebuke of France in his December 1865 annual message, followed two weeks later by a warning that failure to withdraw from Mexico would place U.S.–French relations in "imminent jeopardy."[221] General Philip Sheridan mobilized fifty-two thousand U.S. troops to the border "to impress the Imperialists . . . with the idea that we intended hostilities." He also began covertly funneling arms to the Mexican opposition, sending some thirty thousand muskets to Juárez's men during the winter of 1865–66.[222] Lacking any interest in absorbing Mexico's population, however, Seward maintained that sending U.S. forces into Mexico "would increase our debt immeasurably without leading to any clearly defined gain."[223] Instead, he leveraged U.S. military power to expel France from Mexico, sending General John Schofield to Paris "to impress France with the danger of war," reinforce Bigelow's stern diplomacy, and head off the more belligerent impulses of Sheridan, Grant, and others.[224]

As Napoleon grew increasingly disenchanted with his costly Mexican venture, Seward again found himself being offered Mexican territory. Looking to recoup French losses, Drouyn de Lhuys proposed to Bigelow in January 1866 "that France should take Sonora or some portion of Mexican territory that would be of most value to the United States and of least value to Mexico as security for her debt, and . . . that the United States should buy the territory from France at a price as near as might be to the amount due from Mexico to France." The way this offer used legal and economic rationales to paper over naked aggression echoed previous U.S. conduct in pursuing Florida and California and hence might have been expected to appeal to expansionist U.S. leaders. Yet Bigelow rejected it out of hand, telling Drouyn de Lhuys "that while the sovereignty of a weak state like Mexico was in controversy," France and the United States ought not "traffic in her territory."[225] This final effort having failed, Napoleon III declared his intent to recall all French troops from Mexico on February 22. The last French troops withdrew by March 1867, after which Juárez swiftly defeated the remaining Monarchists and executed Maximilian. With France gone and only Juárez to deal with, Seward maintained his policy of nonaggrandizement, deferring even the presentation of U.S. claims against Mexico in order to help Juárez's regime get established.[226]

Why didn't Seward, often remembered as one of the greatest expansionists in U.S. history, jump at the offers of Mexican territory he received during this period? In light of his willingness to wield U.S. military power diplomatically to expel France from Mexico, military considerations can hardly be responsible for the absence of U.S. territorial ambitions in this case. Instead, domestic costs once again proved decisive. The racial stigmas of previous decades endured, and, preoccupied as they were with reassimilating the former Confederate states, Seward and Johnson had little desire to further upset U.S. domestic politics by absorbing a large Mexican population. Seward had a long history of expansionist visions, forecasting as a senator in 1853 that the "borders of the federal republic . . . shall be extended so that it shall greet the sun when he touches the tropic, and when he sends his glancing rays toward the polar circle, and shall include even distant islands in either ocean."[227] Yet even then he had been troubled by the prospect of assimilating large numbers of Mexicans via a Tehuantepec grant, asking his colleagues, "If you bring them in as states, have you settled the question whether you are to govern them, or whether they are to exercise self-government, and so govern you? Have you reached that point in your charity that you will be willing to be governed by five millions of Indians in Mexico?" Like his contemporaries, Seward preferred to annex only sparsely populated territories, observing that "time will speedily fill the regions which you already possess with a homogeneous population and homogeneous states."[228] In the words of Seward's biographer Frederic Bancroft, "He favored expansion, but expansion merely in proportion to our capacity for absorption."[229]

On this foundation of xenophobia so endemic during his time, Seward built a new and enduring orientation toward commercial expansion: opening foreign markets to U.S. exports and investments but rejecting the conquest of foreign societies. As he wrote during the Mexican–American War, "I want no war. I want no enlargement of territory, sooner than it would come if we were contented with a 'masterly inactivity.'"[230] This view had not changed after the Civil War, when Seward made clear that the United States was "not looking for . . . aggrandizement" at Mexico's expense and would entertain only the voluntary assimilation of kindred populations: the "annexation of adjacent peoples . . . through their own consent."[231] If the United States ever did annex more Mexican territory in the future, he expected it would do so only because "the future of Mexico would be largely influenced by a gradual process of Americanization through slow and peaceful emigration of citizens and capital and development of transportation and trade."[232]

By the time he left office, Seward had begun to translate the long-standing U.S. refusal to annex alien populations into a broader doctrine of territorial stability. Having successfully compelled France to leave Mexico, he proclaimed in October 1868 that "the Monroe doctrine, which eight years ago was merely a theory, is now an irreversible fact."[233] After retiring the following year, Seward told an audience in Mexico, "My system is to leave every community on this continent unassailed by threats and without undue solicitation to stay out of the United States as long as they can, and to receive them on the freest + most equal terms when they choose to come in only insisting that they shall not become foreign nations or monarchical states."[234] Expressing his wish "that the several American republics . . . while mutually abstaining from intervention with each other, shall become, more than ever heretofore, political friends," he called for a "mutual moral alliance, to the end that all external aggression may be prevented, and that internal peace, law and order and progress may be secured throughout the whole continent."[235] Recognizing the mutual benefits of territorial integrity—for the powerful United States that no longer desired Mexican territory as well as for its weaker neighbor that valued independence—Seward paved the way for a stable border over the centuries to come.

Early U.S. pursuits of Mexican territory were contentious not because they lacked material benefits or threatened military costs but because of the domestic consequences of annexation. Sectional crises during the 1830s prevented even an expansionist like Jackson from annexing Texas, and Tyler only narrowly overcame northern opposition to achieve that goal a decade later. California offered impressive natural resources and geopolitical benefits, and given the U.S. military advantage over Mexico and the lack of opposition from European great powers, profitability theory can explain relatively well why Polk maneuvered the United States into war to seize it. However, that theory struggles to explain why Polk sought to swiftly end the war with California in hand rather than press for further gains, not to mention why later administrations refused to exploit even greater power imbalances to pursue populous southern Mexico.

Domestic impact theory readily explains these behaviors, offering a better account of the pattern of U.S. territorial expansion at Mexico's expense. Sectional political competition caused the long delay in the U.S. annexation of Texas and fueled both southern interest in sparsely populated Mexican territory and northern opposition to new slave states. Even more powerfully, racist perceptions of Mexicans as being inherently alien and unfit for U.S. citizenship crossed partisan and sectional lines, driving xenophobic U.S. leaders to reject out of hand any annexations in populous southern Mexico. The refusal to annex populous Mexican territories first emerged during the Mexican–American War, was reinforced during the antebellum period, and crystallized in Seward's efforts to support a liberal Mexican regime. As long as a large alien society existed to their south, U.S. leaders preferred a stable border and a friendly neighbor that could provide economic opportunities with minimal foreign policy difficulties. By the 1870s, when U.S. troops revived Mexican fears of northern aggression by pursuing bandits across the Rio Grande, President Rutherford Hayes reassured his southern neighbor that "the United States does not want any more territory in that direction even if offered as a gift."[236]

CHAPTER 7

To the Seas

Islands and U.S. Annexation

Twenty years hence, it may be that you will have a polyglot House and it will be your painful duty to recognize "the gentleman from Patagonia," "the gentleman from Cuba," "the gentleman from Santo Domingo," . . . or, with fear and trembling, "the gentleman from the Cannibal Islands," who will gaze upon you with watering mouth and gleaming teeth. In that stupendous day there will be a new officer within these historic walls, whose title will be "interpreter to the Speaker."

Congressman James Clark, 1898

As their continental borders solidified, those U.S. leaders still interested in annexation turned their gaze overseas. Caribbean islands commanding key waterways made appealing targets, as did Hawaii in the Pacific Ocean. Annexing them would prevent enemies from using those islands as platforms to raid U.S. coasts or harass U.S. shipping, and many U.S. leaders also valued their tropical products. Yet of all the potential targets, they annexed only Hawaii. Cuba (twice), the Dominican Republic, Puerto Rico, the Philippines, and Guam also drew expansionists' gaze in the second half of the nineteenth century, but those territories failed to generate enough interest to launch a genuine annexation attempt. Why did most U.S. leaders shy away from those islands, and what made Hawaii different from the others?

My central argument here is that domestic concerns continued to act as the primary constraint on U.S. territorial ambitions. The first two cases examined below treat failed bids by small cadres of U.S. leaders to annex Cuba before the Civil War and the Dominican Republic after it. Three later cases explore U.S. decision-making during the Spanish–American War, when leaders faced concurrent opportunities to annex Cuba, Hawaii, Puerto Rico, the Philippines, and Guam. As in Mexico, sectionalism was a key driver of southern efforts to annex Cuba before the Civil War as well as northern leaders' successful rallies to defeat those efforts. Beyond sectional or partisan politics, though, the alien character of Cuba's population proved a deal breaker for many in Congress in the 1850s and again in 1898. Xenophobia also undermined the other islands' appeal, especially in the Philippines. Among these island territories Hawaii alone was sparsely populated enough for proponents to argue that it could be Americanized, a line of reasoning that combined with geopolitical incentives to turn the tide in favor of its annexation.

U.S. decisions in these cases are irreconcilable with profitability theory, which predicts that the United States should have annexed all of these territories. The ruling Dominican regime willingly signed over its sovereignty in 1870, and the U.S. military routed Spain's forces in the Caribbean and Pacific in 1898, making these among the easiest opportunities for annexation the United States ever faced, yet still U.S. leaders declined. They did so because they were not thinking in terms of profitability. As they considered whether or not to annex these islands, U.S. leaders were less focused on increasing national power than on avoiding the domestic costs of assimilating their alien populations.

Antebellum Cuba

Southern leaders worked vigorously but unsuccessfully to annex Cuba before the Civil War, seeing in the island a tantalizing combination of natural resources, geopolitical security, and domestic political benefits. Slave-powered sugar plantations had transformed Cuba into "the centre of gravity of the Caribbean in the nineteenth century," and the industrial revolution made the United States its largest customer.[1] In 1859 Congressman Laurence Keitt of South Carolina highlighted its production of "sugar-cane, coffee, tobacco, vegetables, and fruits, together with the breeding of cattle," annual U.S. trade "amounting to $80,000,000," and "almost unlimited" potential for future growth.[2] Georgia Senator Robert Toombs argued that this tropical production would complement the existing U.S. economy: "We have their bread and their clothing. Give us Cuba . . . and we shall command all the other wants of the human race; we shall control their commerce in everything; we shall control their tonnage, and it will be of more value even to the Northern people than to the South."[3] As one southern newspaper argued, "Were Cuba annexed, Havana would speedily become the great *entrepot* of southern commerce, and in a few years be the rival of New York itself . . . and she would be a southern city, a slaveholding city."[4]

Cuba's value was even greater in geopolitical terms. Presidents Jefferson, Madison, and Monroe had pursued Louisiana and Florida to secure access to the Gulf of Mexico for U.S. exports, but ships in the gulf could reach the Atlantic Ocean and hence international markets only by passing Cuba.[5] Its "command of the Gulf of Mexico" made the island critical not only for U.S. exports but also for seaborne domestic trade.[6] In Keitt's words, "It keeps ward and pass over our commerce from New Orleans to New York, and from New York and our other ports, through the Isthmus transits, to our possessions on the Pacific coast."[7] In the hands of relatively weak Spain, the island represented only a latent vulnerability, but as U.S. Minister to Britain Andrew Stevenson wrote, "The possession of Cuba by a great maritime power would be little less than the establishment of a fortification at the mouth of the Mississippi, commanding both the Gulf of Mexico and Florida, and consequently the whole trade of the western states."[8] That prospect drove U.S. leaders to panic whenever they sensed Cuba being targeted by Britain, setting off diplomatic crises in 1810, 1822, 1837, and 1843.[9]

For southern leaders, however, the most important benefit of annexing Cuba was political: the creation of a new slave state to bolster their influence in the federal government.[10] The prospect of Britain abolishing slavery in Cuba was as threatening to them as if it established a military base there.[11] In November 1822 U.S. Minister to Spain John Forsyth wrote to Secretary Adams that "independent of its formidable position, its slave population would make us anxious to keep the island out of the hands of governments which would be compelled by their institutions to make changes in it extremely dangerous to the repose and prosperity of the Southern states."[12] In 1843, amid reports that British agents in Cuba were promoting "a general emancipation of the slaves . . . converting the government into a black military republic, under British protection," President Tyler grew "exceedingly anxious" that Cuban emancipation would "strike a death-blow at the existence of slavery in the United States."[13] Successive U.S. ministers to Spain were told that "the United States will prevent it at all hazards" and instructed to "exercise a sleepless vigilance in watching over Spain in that quarter."[14]

This peculiar mix of material and domestic political benefits drove southern leaders to favor the annexation of Cuba as far back as Jefferson, who openly discussed seizing the island from Spain along with Florida and sent agents to gauge Cuban interest in annexation in 1807–8.[15] In 1810, while inciting rebellion against Spanish rule in West Florida, Madison sent his agent William Shaler "to feel the pulse of Cuba" regarding "incorporation of that island with the United States."[16] Requesting reinforcements for his Florida campaign eight years later, Andrew Jackson wrote to Monroe, "Add another Regt. and one Frigate and I will insure you Cuba in a few days."[17] In 1820 John Calhoun wrote to Jackson that Cuba "is the key stone of our Union. No American statesman ought to ever withdraw his eye from it."[18] In 1823 Jefferson wrote to Monroe, "I candidly confess, that I have ever looked on Cuba as the most interesting addition which could ever be made to our system of states."[19] With the balance rule of state admissions still holding strong, and northern leaders reliably opposed to any Cuban annexation, however, these aspirations went unfulfilled. The geopolitics of northern leaders and the domestic politics of southern ones gave rise to fears that another European power might take over Cuba, and those apprehensions fueled a no-transfer policy that carried bipartisan support between the 1820s and 1840s.[20]

U.S. policy changed in the late 1840s. Growing northern abolitionism combined with the impending extinction of the balance rule to rally southern leaders around a major push for the annexation of Cuba, along with Democrats like Buchanan and Pierce who saw the abolitionist movement as a threat to the Union. Northern states' fast-growing populations had long since given them control of the House of Representatives—they held 142 of its 233 seats by 1850—and the admission of California with no new southern state on the horizon threatened to give them the Senate as well.[21] Hoping to avoid this outcome, Senator David Levy of Florida proposed annexing Cuba in December 1845, but the idea was a nonstarter as long as the Mexican–American War commanded attention.[22] In June 1848, the war now over, President Polk raised the notion in Cabinet and found that only Postmaster General Cave Johnson "did not favor the proposition, chiefly because he was unwilling to incorporate the population of Cuba with the Federal Union."[23] Secretary of State James Buchanan instructed U.S. Minister to Spain Romulus Saunders to offer Spanish leaders up to $100 million for the island. When Saunders did so that August and again the following December, however, he was told that "sooner than see the island transferred to any power, they would prefer seeing it sunk in the ocean."[24]

The Whig presidents Zachary Taylor and Millard Fillmore were more beholden to northern interests and so abandoned Polk's pursuit of Cuba, reviving the no-transfer policy and working to prevent private filibustering expeditions to the island.[25] Secretary of State Edward Everett wrote a lengthy dispatch to his British and French counterparts in December 1852 in which he admitted that "territorially and commercially, it would, in our hands, be an extremely valuable possession. Under certain contingencies, it might be almost essential to our safety. Still, for domestic reasons, on which, in a communication of this kind, it might not be proper to dwell, the president thinks that the incorporation of the island into the Union at the present time, although effected with the consent of Spain, would be a hazardous measure."[26] Fillmore elaborated in his annual message a few days later, "Were this island comparatively destitute of inhabitants or occupied by a kindred race, I should regard it, if voluntarily ceded by Spain, as a most desirable acquisition. But under existing circumstances I should look upon its incorporation into our Union as a very hazardous measure."[27]

President Franklin Pierce resumed the pursuit of Cuba, filling his Cabinet and major diplomatic posts with expansionists.[28] With Britain and France distracted by the Crimean War, he requested congressional authority to seize the island in February 1854 after the U.S. merchant ship *Black Warrior* was held by Spanish authorities in Havana.[29] Suspecting that Britain and Spain were colluding "to Africanize that island," senators Stephen Mallory of Florida and John Slidell of Louisiana grew increasingly desperate to seize the island while it remained "in such a state as to make her valuable to the South," and they proposed resolutions empowering the president to suspend neutrality laws and allow filibustering.[30] At the same time, the controversy over the Kansas–Nebraska Act ignited northern public opinion against any extension of slavery, and their proposals met stiff opposition from New York's William Henry Seward and Delaware's John Clayton, among others.[31] Congressman Joshua Giddings of Ohio objected to Pierce's effort "to maintain slavery, at the point of the bayonet, at the expense of our blood, our treasure, and our honor," proclaiming, "There is a spirit in the North which will set at defiance all the low and unworthy machinations of this executive."[32] In the words of one newspaper, "There was a time when the North would have consented to annex Cuba, but the Nebraska wrong has forever rendered annexation impossible. . . . *No new slave state will ever again be admitted into this Union*, and no slave territory ever again be annexed to it."[33] Secretary of State William Marcy lamented that "the Nebraska question" had shattered the Democratic Party in the northern states "and deprived it of the strength which was needed & could have been much more profitably used for the acquisition of Cuba."[34]

His call for conquest rejected by Congress, Pierce revived Polk's effort to purchase the island. That April Marcy instructed U.S. Minister to Spain Pierre Soulé to offer up to $130 million for Cuba and, if Spain refused, to "direct your efforts to the next most desirable object, which is to detach that island from the Spanish dominion and from all dependence on any European power."[35] Finding Spanish leaders unreceptive yet again, Soulé consulted the opposition Spanish Democratic Party, reporting in July that with $300,000 they could seize power and cede Cuba to the United States.[36] In early August Pierce requested $10 million from Congress for a three-man commission to persuade Spain to sell Cuba, but again the northern-majority Congress refused to play along.[37]

Stymied, Marcy told Soulé to devise a diplomatic plan for Cuba's acquisition with the U.S. ministers to Britain and France, James Buchanan and John Mason.[38] Meeting that October in Ostend, Belgium, the three ministers declared that if Spanish leaders remained unwilling to sell Cuba, "We shall be justified in wresting it from Spain." They asserted, "We should however be recreant to our duty, be unworthy of our gallant forefathers and commit base treason against our posterity, should we permit Cuba to be Africanized and become a second St. Domingo with all its attendant horrors to the white race."[39] Northerners howled against the extension of slavery when the Ostend Manifesto was published, and the resulting scandal, combined with the Democrats' defeat in the 1854 midterm elections, effectively ended Pierce's campaign for Cuba. Secretary of War Jefferson Davis complained that "the administration has done all that was in its power to acquire the island.... It would have been done, if Congress had sustained the president."[40]

His popularity in the South boosted by the Ostend Manifesto, Buchanan rode to the presidency in 1856 on a platform calling for "ascendancy in the Gulf of Mexico."[41] The following year he sent Christopher Fallon to Europe "to ascertain whether Spain is willing to sell, & upon what terms," telling him "that the government of the United States is as willing now to obtain the island by fair purchase as it was in 1848."[42] Spain remained as cold as ever to the prospect. U.S. agents reported that "both the government and the Spanish people concurred . . . all of the treasure of the earth could not purchase Cuba."[43] With Congress unwilling to fund annexation, Buchanan was forced to think outside the box. After entertaining a variety of schemes, he plotted to counter Spanish intransigence by providing his agents in Spain with resources to opportunistically finance any Spanish leader willing to transfer Cuba to the United States.[44] U.S. Minister to Spain William Preston wrote that the volatile nature of Spanish politics ensured such an opportunity would arise: "Before the end of the year some ministerial crisis might, nay would occur, that would cause me to be sought, instead of seeking, and probably thrust an offer on the United States, as when we acquired Louisiana. Statesmen will make great sacrifices to retain power, but still greater to save their lives; and, it is probable or possible that the rulers of Spain may find both in peril before a twelvemonth."[45]

Since the federal power of the purse lies with the House of Representatives, Buchanan decided in his 1858 annual message to "lay the whole subject before Congress." He requested $30 million to facilitate a treaty of annexation, to be used as "an advance to the Spanish government immediately after the signing of the treaty, without awaiting the ratification of it by the Senate."[46] This request ignited the climactic pre–Civil War debate on Cuba. Southern expansionists rallied to Buchanan's cause, Slidell and Congressman Lawrence Branch of North Carolina proposing bills authorizing the appropriation.[47] Discounting any risk of war, they highlighted Cuba's natural resources and geopolitical position, stressing that annexation would maximize U.S. national security by transforming the Gulf of Mexico into "a *mare clausum*" (closed sea).[48] Mississippi Congressman Reuben Davis argued that "as a means of defense from a foreign foe, or for national preservation, it is indispensable. . . . It would become a mighty fortification far out at sea, which, of itself, would give protection to many hundred miles of our coast."[49] William Avery of Tennessee agreed: "Did Cuba bring with her no commerce; had she no resources, no soil, no climate, no productions; were she a wild, barren waste upon the waters, her geographical position would still decree that she should be part and parcel of this government." He drove the point home by considering what other great powers would do in the same situation: "Sir, put any one of the enlightened principalities of Europe—Great Britain, France, Russia, or any of them—in the same relative position towards Cuba which this government sustains, and Cuba would have long since ceased to be a province of Spain."[50]

Northern opposition was swift and unyielding, however, coalescing around three major arguments: (1) the appropriation would de facto cede the Senate's advice-and-consent power to the president; (2) the plot to annex Cuba was aimed at extending slavery; and (3) the population of Cuba would be an undesirable addition to the United States. Seward and Congressman Homer Royce of Vermont were among those who criticized Buchanan's request for usurping the Senate's power to approve foreign treaties. Authorizing an immediate down payment on Cuba of up to $30 million would essentially allow the president to blackmail the Senate into accepting any treaty he might craft with Spain, since its rejection after payment was already made would forfeit that hefty sum.[51]

More prominent among northerners' objections was the recognition that annexing Cuba would add another slave state to the Union, a development they opposed for both moral and political reasons.[52] Southern leaders made little secret of slavery's role in motivating their territorial ambitions; as Senator Albert Brown of Mississippi told his constituents in September 1858, "It is against our interest to have an anti-slave state . . . come into the Union, and help to swell that hostile power at the North. . . . I want Cuba . . . I want

Tamaulipas, Potosi, and one or two other Mexican states; and I want them all for the same reason—for the planting or spreading of slavery."[53] Northern leaders responded fiercely. Royce declared, "There is today a large majority of the people of this country who are solemnly pledged to resist, by all constitutional means, the further extension of slavery . . . and those who think that the acquisition of Cuba will add to the political strength of the South, are laboring under a great delusion."[54] Jacob Collamer of Vermont asked, "Will the people of the free states contribute their substance to enter upon this policy for the purpose of aiding the South in obtaining power to govern the North in the Union?"[55] New Hampshire's John Hale mused, "If slavery were to be abolished in Cuba . . . I believe the same administration which today seeks Cuba at an expense of $100,000,000, would give $100,000,000 rather than take it."[56] Even northern Democrats who had initially backed Buchanan for partisan reasons stayed largely silent during this debate, turning against annexation whenever it became identified with extending slavery.[57]

As powerful as such arguments were amidst the sectional tensions of the late 1850s, Cuba's opponents focused even more sharply on the character of its roughly one million inhabitants.[58] Seward described Cuba as "a foreign country" containing "a population different entirely from the citizens of the United States; different in language, different in race, different in habits, different in manners, different in customs, and radically different in religion; a population that will, practically, forever hold the power to exclude all American immigration, at least to exclude it as effectually as the old states of Europe exclude our migration there."[59] Royce followed his other arguments by declaring, "The objection with me to the acquisition of Cuba, which is paramount to all others, is the character of its people. . . . The people of Cuba are wholly unfitted to share in the benefits of our government, or to participate in its administration; and the introduction of such a population must weaken instead of adding strength to the republic."[60] Hale proclaimed, "The genius of a free government requires the genius of a Protestant religion. I am willing that the Cubans shall have any faith they please . . . but when the proposition is made to annex them . . . I do not consider the acquisition of Cuba desirable."[61]

Senator John Crittenden of Kentucky summarized his own concerns with an analogy: "We do not want the trouble and expense of governing other people; much less do we want to bring into the bosom of our republic people who, like the Asiatics that came to Rome, governed Rome. . . . I do not want to see our Anglo-Saxon race; I do not want to see our American tribe, mingled up with that sort of evil communication. I mean evil in a political sense. They do not understand our rights; they do not think as we think; they do not speak as we do."[62] Collamer challenged his expansionist colleagues: "Well, now, what are the people of Cuba? . . . They are undrilled, unintelligent, speaking the Spanish language, unacquainted with ours. How are you going to make such a people as that become a part of a society like ours, with our schools, our churches, our institutions of learning, our notions of popular self-government? What are we to take them in for? To help us administer our own government? To assist us, by their enlightenment and power, to select a president? To aid us here in shaping the institutions of our own country?"[63] Connecticut Senator James Dixon added to the earlier arguments on slavery "another objection which, it seems to me, may be made with great force to the present acquisition of Cuba. . . . I allude to the character, the habits, and the peculiarities of the people inhabiting that island. . . . Are these people fit to come into our government as equals?" He explained, "The difficulty is in the race. All southern senators claim that the black portion of that population are unfit for self-government, and they constitute a large proportion. How is it with the whites? They are not of our race. They are of a race which has never yet succeeded with self-government. . . . They are totally unfit to come into the Union today as citizens of a republican government. . . . I doubt whether the race is capable of self-government."[64]

Expansionists countered not by championing Cuban assimilation but by maintaining there was nothing to worry about because Cuba would be Americanized. As secretary of state in 1848, Buchanan had written that U.S. territorial expansion "is always subject to the qualification that the mass of the population must be of our own race. . . . It is true that of the 418,291 white inhabitants which Cuba contained in 1841, a very large proportion is of the Spanish race; still, many of our citizens have settled on the island, and some of them are large holders of property. Under our government it would speedily be Americanized, as Louisiana has been."[65] Keitt expected Cuba to be flooded with Anglo-American settlers, saying, *"Take it, I care not in what manner*—and then we will roll into it a Gulf Stream of Southern population that will make it truly the gem of the Antilles."[66] Congressman Augustus Wright of Georgia was similarly confident that "our element of population will naturally soon predominate."[67] Georgia Senator Robert Toombs replied to Seward by referencing previous U.S. annexations: "As to the diversities of population, which the senator urges as an objection, we have had them at all our acquisitions. We had diversities of language and race when we acquired Louisiana, when we acquired Florida, when we acquired Texas, and when we acquired California . . . but we have molded them into one American people. . . . We shall get Spaniards, Englishmen, free negroes, slaves, and coolies, when we acquire Cuba. . . . We can Americanize them."[68]

Anti-expansionists rebutted these counterarguments by noting that such analogies were misplaced: previous acquisitions had been sparsely populated, and the relatively dense population of Cuba was a much more serious deterrent. Dixon observed, "In Louisiana there were scarcely any people; in Florida there were not many; and at this very day, they send no Spaniards here to represent them in the Senate. They send men with good Anglo-Saxon names, and with good Saxon blood running in their veins. Those people never were a foreign people. That was not the annexation of a foreign country. . . . It was the annexation, for the most part, of virgin soil, not peopled."[69] Collamer observed that Louisiana was "almost utterly uninhabited, with only a French settlement down at the mouth of the Mississippi, and here and there a scattered Indian post. . . . It was clearly seen that when that country was settled up to any considerable extent, it would be Americanized." Similarly, "Florida, a large country, with a small, scattered Spanish population . . . was a country which we could assimilate to our own. . . . Texas . . . was very sparsely peopled, and therefore furnished the opportunity for our people to Americanize that too. . . . [T]he people who were there were ours; there was a comparatively small number of Mexicans." In contrast, he objected that Cuba "is thickly populated, for the number of people in proportion to the square mile is as large as it is in Virginia or in Tennessee. It is a well-inhabited country; comparatively, a populous country."[70]

Slidell withdrew his bill once it became clear that northern senators would block it from ever coming to a vote.[71] Although he pledged to reintroduce it in the next session, the Democrats lost control of the House heading into the 36th Congress, guaranteeing that the venture would be denied funding even if a Cuba bill did somehow pass the Senate.[72] Calls for Cuban annexation continued emanating from the South in the lead-up to the 1860 presidential election, featuring prominently in the platforms of both Democratic candidates, while the Republican platform openly opposed the spread of slavery.[73]

Abraham Lincoln's election confirmed to southern leaders that they had lost any hope of controlling the federal government. On December 20, 1860, South Carolina seceded from the Union, followed quickly by Mississippi, Florida, Alabama, Georgia, and Louisiana; Texas, Virginia, Arkansas, Tennessee, and North Carolina followed suit by May 1861. Crittenden led one final effort to avoid civil war by restoring the Missouri Compromise, which allowed slavery south of Missouri, but Northern Republicans refused to go along for fear that the compromise "would be holding out a premium for filibustering against Mexico & Cuba, in order to make new slave states."[74] President-elect Lincoln rejected the compromise because acceding to the secessionists' demands would trap the federal government in a cycle of extortion: "A year will not pass, till we shall have to take Cuba as a condition upon which they will stay in the Union. . . . There is, in my judgment, but one compromise which would really settle the slavery question, and that would be a prohibition against acquiring any more territory."[75] By the end of the Civil War the sectional balance that was tipped by California had been destroyed by the admissions of Minnesota in 1858, Oregon in 1859, Kansas in 1861, West Virginia in 1863, and Nevada in 1864. Calls for the annexation of Cuba disappeared after the war.

Cuba would have given the United States natural resources, population, and the gates to the Gulf of Mexico. U.S. leaders recognized these material benefits, yet expansionists in positions of power consistently failed to mobilize enough support to annex Cuba. Contrary to profitability theory, their failure was not caused by annexation's military costs. Several presidents considered conquering the island from a Spanish military they had disparaged as far back as the 1810s. Instead, as domestic impact theory predicts, northerners in Congress consistently denied southern ambitions because they feared annexation's domestic consequences.

The Dominican Republic

Fifty miles east of Cuba lies Hispaniola, an island divided into French and Spanish colonies for more than a century before its unification in 1821 under independent Haiti. In 1844 an uprising in the formerly Spanish eastern portion of the island brought tenuous independence to the Dominican Republic, also known as Santo Domingo. Dominican leaders repeatedly invited the United States to annex their country during the decades that followed, but U.S. leaders rejected their offers. Profitability theory predicts that their refusals should have been spurred by low opinions of its material benefits or a reluctance to incur high military costs, while domestic impact theory predicts the blame should fall with its domestic consequences. Why didn't the United States annex the Dominican Republic?

The same southern-oriented administrations that pursued Cuba before the Civil War also considered the Dominican Republic, but they shied away from it because under Haitian rule slavery had been abolished throughout Hispaniola.[76] Haiti tried to reconquer its neighbor in the decade after Dominican independence, prompting the terrified Dominican dictator, Pedro Santana, to approach any great power willing to listen with proposals for an alliance, protectorate, or annexation.[77] President Polk responded to one such entreaty in 1846, sending naval officer David Porter to report on the island's abundant natural resources and its excellent site for a naval base at Samaná Bay. Further action was delayed by the Mexican–American War and then deferred in favor of pursuing Cuba.[78] In 1854 President Pierce sent Texas businessman William Cazneau to negotiate the creation of a coaling station at Samaná Bay, but the talks fell apart over the Dominicans' misgivings regarding racial discrimination against local inhabitants, doubts encouraged by European agents.[79] President Buchanan renewed Cazneau's mission in 1859, again to no avail.[80] As the United States headed toward civil war, Spain accepted Santana's invitation and resumed colonial rule in March 1861, but it withdrew again four years later amidst a bloody insurrection.

As the dominant regional power after the Civil War, the United States faced a prime opportunity to expand. Secretary of State William Henry Seward toured the Caribbean during the winter of 1865–66 and, impressed by the naval potential of Samaná Bay, sent his son Frederick with Porter to negotiate its purchase or lease.[81] The Dominican president, José María Cabral, agreed to lease the bay in return for cash and weapons, but he was overthrown before the deal could be implemented. Buenaventura Báez assumed power in May 1868 and renewed the lease offer, but with his own regime faltering, Báez offered to sell the bay that July for a price to be named later if the United States would send immediate support. By October he invited the United States to annex the Dominican Republic altogether.[82] A willing local leader, an overwhelming military advantage over neighboring Haiti, and disinterested European powers made the military costs of annexation as low as ever.

Seward correctly anticipated that domestic politics would stand in the way, however, observing that it was "unlikely . . . that Congress would entertain . . . the annexation of Dominica."[83] Tension was high between the executive and legislative branches, Republicans in Congress frequently passing legislation over Johnson's veto and falling only one vote short of removing him in 1868. Many in Congress were disinclined to support his foreign policy initiatives.[84] The only island acquisition Congress approved in the 1860s, Midway, was uninhabited, so "there was nothing offensive morally or financially in the acquisition and no politics in opposing it."[85] In January 1869 Congressman Nathaniel Banks of Massachusetts proposed a protectorate over Hispaniola, which, though underdeveloped, was seen as offering attractive opportunities for American investment.[86] The effort failed by a vote of 126–36, opponents branding it a plot for annexation "by indirection," recognizing "a speculation in it," and marveling at the notion of wanting "more negroes brought within our limits" amidst Reconstruction.[87] A fresh

Dominican annexation offer two weeks later prompted Indiana Congressman Godlove Orth to propose admitting the Dominican Republic "as a territory of the United States . . . with a view to an ultimate establishment of a state government," but that too was quickly defeated, 110–63.[88]

The most meaningful push for annexation came from President Grant. Soon after his March 1869 inauguration, he met Joseph Fabens, a partner of Cazneau with financial interests in the Dominican Republic, who convinced him of its material benefits. Grant composed a private memorandum titled "Reasons Why San Domingo Should Be Annexed to the United States," outlining arguments that would feature prominently in his public speeches over the ensuing months. Touting the Dominican Republic's "unequaled fertility" and geographic position, he observed that "it has but a sparse population and that in entire sympathy with our institutions," and he saw the island as "capable of supporting the entire colored population of the United States, should it choose to emigrate."[89] Grant looked forward to breaking the British "cordon of islands . . . commanding the entrance to the Gulf of Mexico," and he worried that Dominican leaders might look to Europe for security again if the United States passed up this opportunity.[90] Applauding Dominican timber, coffee, sugar, tobacco, tropical fruits, dyes, and chocolate, he concluded, "Can anyone favor rejecting so valuable a gift who voted $7,200,000 for the icebergs of Alaska?"[91]

Grant sent General Orville Babcock to meet with Báez in July, telling him to report on Dominican natural resources and economic production as well as the racial composition of the local population.[92] Babcock returned the following winter, reporting that the population of roughly 150,000 was composed in equal parts of white, black, and mixed races.[93] He also brought a signed treaty of annexation, much to the surprise of the Cabinet members, who assumed that Babcock had exceeded his authority.[94] Yet the treaty delighted Grant, who quickly submitted it to the Senate for ratification.[95]

Grant's enthusiasm notwithstanding, the treaty was tepidly received by both the Senate and the public, owing in large part to xenophobic attitudes toward the Dominican population.[96] Secretary of State Hamilton Fish had been less than enthusiastic from the start, telling British Ambassador Edward Thornton in May 1869 that "however possible it might be for the United States to annex countries inhabited by the Anglo-Saxon race and accustomed to self-government, the incorporation of these people by the Latin race would be but the beginning of years of conflict and anarchy."[97] By February 1870 Fish grew openly skeptical of the treaty's prospects, citing "doubts honestly entertained by many of the policy of acquiring insular possessions, and of the effect of the tropical climate upon the race who inhabit them" as well as the Senate's "habit of criticism, if not of opposition" to initiatives emanating from the executive branch, especially under secretive, potentially corrupt conditions.[98]

While the Senate Foreign Relations Committee studied the treaty, its advocates sought to strengthen their hand. Hoping that a strong sign of Dominican support would catalyze action in the Senate, Báez staged a referendum producing 15,169 votes for annexation and only 11 opposed. Such skewed results betrayed rampant election fraud, including announcement of the vote only four days earlier, misrepresenting the question, recording nonvotes as positive votes, and threatening opponents with lost jobs, imprisonment, exile, or execution. Even the 11 no votes were cast "at the suggestion of Báez to preserve appearances."[99] Meanwhile, Grant dispatched U.S. warships to support Báez, instructing Rear Admiral Charles Poor to "inform the present Haitian authorities that this government is determined to protect the present Dominican government with all its powers."[100]

The gambit failed. The committee's chairman, Charles Sumner, reported the treaty on March 15 with a scathing condemnation that ranked among the most powerful speeches of his career.[101] Although it was delivered in executive session, newspapers reported that his primary argument centered on the Dominican population, including remarks that "the character of the people would render acquisition of their country undesirable" and that "the negro and foreign populations there would not be desirable citizens."[102] Proclaiming that the United States was "an Anglo-Saxon republic, and would ever remain so by the preponderance of that race," he declared, "To the African belongs the equatorial belt and he should enjoy it undisturbed."[103] Sumner also questioned the purported European interest in the island and highlighted its civil unrest and considerable debt, problems widely assumed to be inherent to supposed inferior races.[104] In the days that followed word spread that the House Appropriations Committee "appeared to be unanimous in opposition to recommending an appropriation for the purchase should the Senate ratify the treaty."[105]

Advocates of annexation tried to rally in the wake of Sumner's speech, and as in previous cases they fought Sumner's live-and-let-live brand of xenophobia with visions of Americanization. Describing the Dominican Republic as worth "ten Alaskas," Indiana Senator Oliver Morton countered Sumner's race-based portrayal of debt and unrest by asserting that the island's chronic violence had actually served U.S. interests by depleting the local population, which he agreed was the main impediment to annexation. He concluded, "The question in this light presents a vast territory open to the hand of art and science and industry, and almost without inhabitants."[106]

Others shared Grant's hope that Dominican annexation would be an outlet for black migration from the continent. As the historian Nicholas Guyatt has observed, "Most Republicans thought deeply about the effects of annexation on Reconstruction," but even its advocates were deeply divided over whether a Dominican U.S. state would relieve racial tensions or serve as a laboratory for racial mixing.[107] With concerns over the demographic future of the United States undercutting annexation's prospects, the treaty's ratification window lapsed at the end of March without a vote.

Undeterred, Fabens returned from the Dominican Republic on April 27 with an extension of the treaty deadline. Grant pulled out all the stops in his final push, lobbying senators directly at the Capitol (an unheard-of measure) and offering appointments to their friends in return for votes.[108] In the most egregious example of his dealing, he was accused of dismissing Attorney General Ebenezer Hoar because "a concession to the Southern states seemed necessary & that for that purpose the Judge would have to make way for a Southern man."[109] Grant wrote a fresh appeal to the Senate on May 31, describing the Dominican Republic as "one of the richest territories under the sun," warning that a European power stood poised to seize it, and observing that it "commands the entrance to the Caribbean Sea and the Isthmus transit of commerce."[110] Practically begging at this point, he invited the Senate to append whatever "amendments as may suggest themselves to the minds of senators to carry out, in good faith, the treaty."[111]

Grant's appeals stood little chance of success, especially when early June produced damning public revelations: the financial interests of Fabens, Cazneau, Báez, and others in annexation; the fact that Báez and Babcock had deliberately prolonged the imprisonment of Davis Hatch, an American salt trader, because they feared his release would undermine Báez's public image; diplomatic improprieties, including Babcock's circumventing of Fish; and Grant's deployment of U.S. naval forces to support Báez's regime.[112] This growing list of malfeasances combined with "the danger of annexing an alien tropical people" to turn public opinion "decidedly against the treaty," and the Senate formally rejected it on June 30 by a vote of 28–28, far short of the two-thirds majority required.[113]

Still, Grant persevered, writing to Báez the following October, "My interest in extending the authority of the United States over the territory, and people of San Domingo is unabated."[114] In his annual message two months later Grant reiterated his arguments for annexation and urged Congress to authorize a commission for that purpose.[115] Morton proposed Grant's commission to the Senate, sparking a series of vitriolic opposition speeches.[116] Sumner condemned the proposition as aiming "to commit Congress to the policy of annexation," which he denounced as menacing to Haiti and likely to result in a "bloody dance" like Spain experienced in the 1860s. He declared the "conclusive" argument to be the fact that "the island of San Domingo, situated in tropical waters and occupied by another race, never can become a permanent possession of the United States."[117] Senator Thomas Bayard of Delaware objected to transforming the United States "into an imperial government of outlying and distant dependencies with a foreign population, strangers to us in race, in blood, in customs, in all their systems, political, social, moral, and religious." He warned that "such a scheme of empire, if indulged in, will destroy our republican system of government. The population of this island . . . can never be governed by a constitutional government like ours. They are utterly unfitted for it, permanently, naturally disqualified for it."[118] Although he had "no objection to expansion in the direction of the people . . . who are, by race, habits, and education, homogeneous with ourselves," Congressman John Farnsworth of Illinois reminded his colleagues that "the moment we annex San Domingo its people become citizens of the United States and voters . . . a motley mixture of French, Spanish, and other Europeans, with Indians, savages, and negroes from every part of western Africa. . . . If any man wants such people as these incorporated as fellow-citizens of the United States he must be a man of an 'unbounded stomach.'"[119]

The most eloquent opposition in this instance came from Missouri's Carl Schurz, who declared, "If you incorporate those tropical countries with the republic of the United States, you will have to incorporate their people too. . . . You cannot exterminate them all; you must try to incorporate them with our political system."[120] Schurz saw only two possible outcomes, both abhorrent to his mind. The first, permanent imperialism, would produce "satrapies . . . nurseries of rapacity, extortion, plunder, oppression and tyranny, which will, with the certainty of fate, demoralize and corrupt our political life beyond any degree yet conceived of, and impart to our government a military character most destructive of its republican attributes." The second option involved granting a large alien population representation in the federal government, a prospect he considered equally undesirable: "Fancy the senators and representatives of ten or twelve millions of tropical people . . . people who . . . have neither language nor traditions nor habits nor political institutions nor morals in common with us; fancy them sitting in the halls of Congress, throwing the weight of their intelligence, their morality, their political notions and habits, their prejudices and passions, into the scale of the destinies of this republic . . . fancy this, and then tell me, does not your imagination recoil from the picture?"[121]

As Tanisha Fazal notes, "The main reasons for senatorial opposition were related more to domestic than to international politics."[122] Rather than endanger U.S. democracy or absorb a large alien population, Congress rejected the annexation of the Dominican Republic. It eventually approved Grant's commission as a face-saving allowance for the president and the Republican Party, but only with the strict amendment "that nothing in these resolutions contained shall be held, understood, or construed as committing Congress to the policy of annexing the territory of said republic of Dominica."[123] Grant submitted the commission's report to Congress in April 1871 along with a vindictive letter justifying expansionism, condemning its opponents and expressing his hope that the public might yet rally behind him. It did not, and there the issue lay. With his legacy in mind, Grant felt compelled to offer one more defense of his ambitions in his final annual message of 1876, but the speech came and went without any renewed expansionism.[124]

Cuba and the Spanish–American War

The Spanish–American War is frequently identified as a watershed moment in U.S. expansionism. For the first time, the United States soundly defeated a European military and embarked on decades of overseas imperialism. Yet the Spanish–American War was a humanitarian intervention, not a land grab. Had U.S. leaders desired Cuba, there could have been no better opportunity to annex it, yet they explicitly rejected Cuban annexation before, during, and after the war. Why?

Profitability theory predicts that U.S. leaders should decline to annex territories they see as unaffordable, but there is no evidence of such views playing a major role in this case. Cuba's natural resources and geopolitical position remained desirable, and U.S. military forces won the war convincingly. Most U.S. leaders headed into the war sharing Grover Cleveland's expectation that "we shall find Spain so weak and inefficient that the war will be short."[125] Senator William Chandler of New Hampshire predicted that the war would last "from fifteen minutes to ninety days," while New York Congressman William Sulzer predicted that "Spain will be humiliated in the dust" and "compelled to get out of Cuba in twenty-four hours."[126] As it happened, U.S. forces suffered 345 battle deaths in driving Spain from Cuba.[127] The island was an easy target, yet U.S. leaders preferred to fight for its independence rather than its annexation because, as domestic impact theory predicts, they feared the domestic consequences of absorbing its 1.6 million inhabitants.[128]

Southern motives to annex Cuba vanished after the Civil War overturned the sectional balance of power and abolished slavery, and decades passed without any renewed pursuit. When Cuban revolutionaries launched a bid to overthrow Spanish rule in the Ten Years' War of 1868–78, calls for action among the U.S. public tended to favor Cuban independence rather than annexation, and even as they pursued the Dominican Republic, Grant and Fish prioritized only the protection of U.S. interests in Cuba.[129] Fish even offered to help Cuba purchase its independence by acting as a mediator, convincing British leaders that the United States held no hidden expansionist motives because it "could not undertake to manage so alien a population."[130] His views had evidently not changed since 1855, when he had visited Cuba and reflected, "With its present population, the island of Cuba is anything other than a desirable acquisition to the United States, and I can see no means of getting rid of a population of some 450,000 called white but really every shade and mixture of color."[131] Even the 1873 *Virginius* Affair, which saw the Spanish navy seize a U.S. ship for aiding the rebels and execute dozens of its crew, was defused through diplomacy rather than used as a pretext for conquest.[132] Looking back two decades later, President Grover Cleveland reflected that "no other great power, it may safely be said, under circumstances of similar perplexity, would have manifested the same restraint and the same patient endurance."[133]

U.S. leaders spent the late 1870s and 1880s focused not on annexation but on preventing Germany and France from establishing colonies in the Caribbean.[134] In December 1881 Secretary of State James Blaine wrote to the U.S. minister to Hawaii that "if ever ceasing to be Spanish, Cuba must necessarily become American," a comment frequently interpreted as evidence of enduring U.S. expansionism. Yet Blaine referenced an "American" Cuba not as a state of the Union but as an independent country in the American hemisphere. "Cuba must necessarily become American," he wrote, "and not fall under any other European domination. . . . The material possession of Hawaii is not desired by the United States any more than was that of Cuba. But under no circumstances can the United States permit any change in the territorial control of either which would cut it adrift from the American system, whereto they both indispensably belong."[135] Far from advocating the annexation of either island, Blaine was restating the long-standing U.S. desire to pursue its commercial interests in a Western Hemisphere free of European influence. Moreover, like Fish, Blaine shared his contemporaries' view that the "'mixed and mongrel people' of the island of Cuba would be too difficult for the United States to digest and assimilate."[136]

By 1894 reciprocal tariff reductions had turned the Cuban economy heavily toward the United States, which accounted for 90 percent of Cuba's exports and 40 percent of its imports. Instead of using this economic dependence to pursue annexation, however, Congress passed the Wilson–Gorman Tariff reinstituting a massive tax on Cuban sugar.[137] Combined with retaliatory Spanish policies and a sudden drop in global sugar prices, the tariff devastated Cuba's economy. Sugar production fell by more than three-quarters over the next two years, local prices for basic foodstuffs like wheat and corn rose tenfold, and thousands of plantation laborers found themselves out of work.[138] In response, the surviving leaders of the Ten Years' War renewed their struggle against Spanish rule.

Whereas expansionist U.S. leaders might have used the rebellion as a pretext, President Cleveland observed that "many of the fairest talkers in favor of intervening . . . are opposed to incorporating the country into the United States system."[139] Instead, Cleveland looked to protect U.S. commerce, citizens, and property on the island.[140] Judging them safer under Spanish rule than a potentially independent Cuban regime, he issued a neutrality proclamation to dissuade U.S. citizens from aiding the rebels, resolving minor crises diplomatically rather than using them to justify intervention.[141] As Britain's minister to Spain reported, Cleveland "disliked the insurrection altogether and was opposed either to the annexation or the independence of Cuba."[142] By 1896 he grew increasingly concerned about the rebels' scorched-earth strategy.[143] That April Secretary of State Richard Olney complained to Spanish Ambassador Enrique Dupuy de Lôme that "outside of the towns still under Spanish rule, anarchy, lawlessness, and terrorism are rampant. The insurgents realize that the wholesale destruction of crops, factories, and machinery . . . drives into their ranks the laborers who are thus thrown out of employment. The result is a systematic war upon the industries of the island."[144] Still, Cleveland backed Spain and shunned talk of an intervention, though U.S. peace proposals based on local autonomy were rejected by both the Spanish (who demanded the rebels lay down their arms) and the Cuban rebels (who demanded independence).[145]

Meanwhile, Congress called for a military intervention.[146] Republicans had controlled both the Senate and the House since the Panic of 1893 undercut the Democratic president's support, and they saw Cleveland's deference to Spain as an opportunity to score further political points heading into the 1896 presidential election. Yet although modern accounts often label them "expansionist," these Republicans championed Cuban independence, not annexation.[147] Their 1896 platform praised "the heroic battle of the Cuban patriots against cruelty and oppression" and declared that "the United States should actively use its influence and good offices to restore peace and give independence to the island."[148]

The Republicans succeeded in electing William McKinley as the next president, but in a turn that revealed the partisan nature of their previous calls for an intervention, McKinley maintained Cleveland's quest for a negotiated peace in Cuba, proclaiming in his first inaugural address, "We want no wars of conquest; we must avoid the temptation of territorial aggression."[149] With McKinley embracing diplomacy, Democrats launched their own partisan attacks calling for an intervention. As George Auxier wrote of newspapers at the time, "Immediately after the election in November, Republican editors reversed themselves and advised a Cuban policy equally as cautious as that which the Democrats had pursued under Cleveland . . . [whereupon] Democratic editors . . . pointed out the inconsistencies of their political foes and sought to embarrass them precisely as they had been embarrassed by the Republicans during Cleveland's regime."[150] This partisan flip-flop stood out to some observers. As a friend reflected to Massachusetts Senator Henry Cabot Lodge, "A war is a damned sight too big a chip to play party poker with."[151] Nevertheless, public pressure on McKinley regarding Cuba stayed relatively low through the end of 1897, prompting Cleveland to complain, "How differently the present administration is treated though pursuing the same policy as the last."[152]

McKinley used this relative calm to assess his options, sending William Calhoun to gather firsthand intelligence on the situation in Cuba. Calhoun's June 1897 report described a nightmare: "The country outside the military posts was practically depopulated. Every house had been burned, banana trees cut down, cane fields swept with fire, and everything in the shape of food destroyed. . . . I did not see a sign of life, except an occasional vulture or buzzard sailing through the air. The country was wrapped in the stillness of death and the silence of desolation."[153] Since February 1896 General Valeriano Weyler had led a Spanish campaign to fight the insurgency by laying waste to the countryside, the rebels' main source of support, and herding rural Cubans into concentration camps where hundreds of thousands died of starvation and disease.[154] As Secretary of State John Sherman remarked, the Spanish strategy "attempts to make Cuba worthless to the Cubans."[155] By October U.S. consuls at Matanzas and Havana were reporting dozens of deaths from starvation every day, describing the situation as "beyond belief" and "simply indescribable" and observing that "in some towns one-third to one-half the population has disappeared."[156] Newspapers such as Joseph Pulitzer's *New York World* and William Randolph Hearst's *New York Journal* had spent the previous years sensationalizing events in Cuba to generate higher circulation (earning their nickname "yellow press" in the process), but mounting evidence from Cuba left little room for embellishment. As

Senator Shelby Cullom of Illinois observed, "The press did not create the facts. . . . [T]he situation is so full of horrors it cannot be overstated, cannot, indeed, be adequately stated in all the length and breadth of its appalling horribleness."[157]

The news that Spain had matched the rebels' scorched-earth policy with a de facto genocide crystallized McKinley's belief that more assertive diplomacy was needed, but not war. He lodged repeated protests that summer through Sherman and U.S. Minister to Spain Stewart Woodford, who told his British counterpart, "The island is being literally destroyed. . . . [T]he policy now pursued by the Spanish government can only restore peace by producing a graveyard that shall be as large as Cuba herself."[158] Spain removed Weyler and reformed its approach to Cuba during the months that followed, prompting McKinley to urge patience in his first annual message that December. Insisting that Spain "should be given a reasonable chance" to resolve the crisis, he supported its effort "to give full autonomy to the colony . . . yet conserve and affirm the sovereignty of Spain." He went on to declare, "I speak not of forcible annexation, for that cannot be thought of. That, by our code of morality, would be criminal aggression."[159] Even two major crises in February 1898, the publication of an insulting letter by De Lôme and the explosion of the U.S.S. *Maine* in Havana harbor, failed to turn McKinley away from diplomacy. In the end, De Lôme resigned and Spain agreed to arbitrate the *Maine* claims.[160]

The key turn on the road to war came in March, when U.S. leaders realized how ineffective the Spanish reforms had been.[161] For many in Congress the tipping point was a March 17 speech by Senator Redfield Proctor of Vermont, a moderate Republican who had visited Cuba skeptical of the yellow press and wishing to assess the situation for himself. Proctor reported, "It is desolation and distress, misery and starvation. . . . [T]here is no human life or habitation" outside the concentration camps. He stressed that "what I saw . . . [i]t must be seen with one's own eyes to be realized." Confirming that Spain's reforms had achieved "little or no practical benefit," he declared, "To me the strongest appeal is not the barbarity practiced by Weyler nor the loss of the *Maine* . . . but the spectacle of a million and a half of people, the entire native population of Cuba, struggling for freedom and deliverance from the worst misgovernment of which I ever had knowledge."[162]

Proctor's account was soon bolstered by testimonials from other senators who had also visited the island. John Thurston of Nebraska professed, "I went to Cuba firmly believing that the condition of affairs there had been greatly exaggerated by the press. . . . There has been no exaggeration, because exaggeration has been impossible." Accusing even Proctor of understatement, he described the plight of those in the concentration camps: "Their only hope is to remain where they are, to live as long as they can on an insufficient charity, and then die."[163] Jacob Gallinger of New Hampshire labeled the conflict "a war of starvation and extermination—a war more cruel than any the world has ever known." He recalled, "The scenes in the streets of Havana are harrowing beyond description. People in want and suffering are everywhere seen and walking skeletons meet one on every hand. Naked children, emaciated and ragged women, and diseased and starving men throng the streets. . . . What a chapter of horrors and death is that! And still the tragedy goes on."[164] Hernando Money of Mississippi observed that even if the camps were closed and the Cubans were permitted to return home, "most of the men have died; they have neither homes to go to, oxen to plow, implements to use, seeds to sow, nor have they the strength in their starved bodies to use them if they had them."[165] All agreed that any prospect of a resolution based on Cuban autonomy under the Spanish Crown had long since disappeared.[166]

McKinley reacted to these reports by threatening intervention if Spain did not immediately close the concentration camps, impose an armistice, and allow U.S. humanitarian aid. "We do not want Cuba," he stressed, "[but] we do wish immediate peace in Cuba."[167] Spanish leaders accepted most of his demands, but they refused to extend an armistice, as did the rebels unless independence was attached.[168] Meanwhile, calls for action in the Senate were growing so loud that McKinley complained, "Congress is trying to drive us into war with Spain."[169] Congress's fervor stemmed from two main motivations. The first was genuine horror at the atrocities being committed in Cuba and a sense of responsibility to do something about mass suffering so near U.S. borders. Congressman William Harris of Kansas was among the many who voiced frustration at McKinley's slow diplomacy, saying, "The Spaniard has planned and carried on the destruction by starvation of a whole race. If blood and tears and death are the price of liberty, the Cubans have earned it, and more dearly than any nation of earth. . . . All over this land there is the cry 'Why do you wait?'"[170] Senator George Perkins of California agreed, noting that "a little more delay, and we should become accessories to the greatest crime of modern times."[171] When the Senate Foreign Relations Committee finally issued its report calling for U.S. intervention in Cuba, it presaged the twenty-first-century doctrine known as the Responsibility to Protect, proclaiming that "the state which thus perverts and abuses its power thereby forfeits its sovereignty. . . . Justification for intervention is strengthened in such cases as the present, where the oppressions by a state of its subjects have been so inveterate, atrocious, and sanguinary as to require intervention by other nations in the interests of humanity and the peace of the world."[172] Several senators branded the Spanish concentration camps a "crime against humanity."[173]

The second reason Congress demanded war was rooted in domestic politics. Republican leaders knew that U.S. voters cared about the Cubans' plight, and though they supported McKinley many were growing uneasy that his diplomatic ineffectiveness would leave them vulnerable in the upcoming midterm elections. Lodge warned the president, "If the war in Cuba drags on through the summer with nothing done we should go down in the greatest defeat ever known before the cry 'Why have you not settled the Cuban question?'"[174] Vice President Garret Hobart told McKinley that pressure in the Senate was growing so great that it might soon declare war on its own authority: "They will act without you if you do not act at once."[175] Prominent histories of the war have concluded that "it was those political considerations, the erosion of support within his own party and the fear of electoral losses that led McKinley finally to acquiesce to the demands for intervention" and that "Republican legislators made war on Spain not to obtain control of Cuba but to retain control of Washington."[176] McKinley himself later reflected that "but for the inflamed state of public opinion and the fact that Congress could no longer be held in check, a peaceful solution might have been had."[177]

McKinley's war message, submitted to Congress on April 11, met wide approbation in the House, which two days later voted 325–19 to authorize him "to intervene at once to stop the war in Cuba, to the end and with the purpose of securing permanent peace and order there and establishing by the free action of the people thereof a stable and independent government of their own in the island of Cuba."[178] In the Senate, McKinley's war message set off an intense debate that saw a fifteen-minute time limit imposed on speeches because so many senators wanted to be heard. The debate was not about whether the United States should go to war, though: a strong majority supported the intervention. Nor was it about whether to annex Cuba, which senators opposed almost unanimously. Rather, the debate revolved around the question of whether the Senate resolution should immediately recognize Cuban independence.[179]

A careful reading of the documents reveals that no fewer than thirty senators used the occasion to publicly declare their opposition to annexation, while only one offered a timid expression in its favor.[180] The consensus was so broad that Massachusetts Senator George Hoar asked whether there was "any person, in the Congress or out of it, representing any considerable American sentiment, who desires either to conquer Cuba or annex

Cuba. . . . It is disclaimed by the president, disclaimed by the committee, disclaimed by everybody, so far as I am aware."[181] Many who disavowed annexation in this case did so succinctly, but those who explained their motivations echoed their predecessors' xenophobia. Proctor announced during his influential report on conditions in Cuba, "I am not in favor of annexation . . . because it is not wise policy to take in any people of foreign tongue and training, and without any strong guiding American element."[182] Thurston exclaimed during his own report, "God forbid! I would oppose annexation with my latest breath. The people of Cuba are not our people; they cannot assimilate with us."[183] These views accorded with McKinley's own position, expressed to Archbishop John Ireland on March 10, that his administration "did not wish to annex the island because it did not want two Cubans voting in the Senate."[184]

Even those who thought Cuba would eventually join the United States foresaw annexation only after the island had been Americanized. Donelson Caffery of Louisiana predicted that Cuba's "heterogeneous population" would succumb to periodic revolutions once independent and gradually give way to Anglo-American immigration: "I do not say . . . that I desire to see Cuba a state in the American Union. Certainly not until after a long tutelage of the population under Federal guardianship. That tutelage will be found necessary to fit the mass of the inhabitants there for the duties of citizenship as we understand them."[185] Even as he rejected the absorption of its current population, Proctor looked forward to U.S. commercial penetration of Cuba: "Americans will furnish them lines of transportation by land and water, will sell them their food and wares and merchandise, will rebuild their mills, restore and people the solitude Spain has made and called peace. In short, full commercial annexation will come quickly. If political annexation ever comes, it should not be until the island is sufficiently Americanized to fully warrant it."[186]

Though they agreed on rejecting annexation, the senators bitterly debated whether to recognize Cuban independence immediately or withhold recognition until the rebels had formed a stable government.[187] Illustrating yet again their lack of territorial ambitions, one of the strongest arguments in favor of recognition was that it would dispel international misperceptions of a U.S. desire to annex Cuba. Florida Senator Samuel Pasco was among those who insisted, "Such a recognition will relieve us of any well-founded charge of aggression or self-aggrandizement if we thus make it clear that we propose to claim no power, when the victory has been won, to force upon an unwilling people unwelcome rulers."[188]

Toward that end Henry Teller of Colorado proposed an amendment "disclaiming any disposition or intention to exercise jurisdiction or control over said island except for the pacification thereof and a determination when that is accomplished to leave the government and control of the island to the people thereof."[189] Since the Teller Amendment publicly disavowed annexation while sidestepping recognition, it won broad approval and was enshrined in the joint resolution McKinley ultimately signed. McKinley's biographer Margaret Leech attributes the amendment's success to a "general repugnance to the idea of admitting to the Union an alien and insubordinate people, Roman Catholic in faith, with a large admixture of Negro blood. The advocacy of recognition of the insurgent republic had been partly motivated, in all sincerity, by the apprehension that neutral intervention savored of a desire for conquest."[190] The documents reveal little reason to question her assessment.

Military operations proceeded swiftly after McKinley signed the joint resolution on April 20, and in early July a decisive U.S. naval victory outside Santiago Bay drove Spain to sue for peace.[191] The two sides signed an armistice on August 12, Spain pledging to relinquish sovereignty over Cuba and evacuate the island.[192] Had U.S. leaders wanted to annex Cuba they had one more chance to do so when the commissioners met that October to negotiate a peace treaty, yet McKinley's instructions to them remained consistent with his previous statements. He explained, "We had no design of aggrandizement and no ambition of conquest" when intervening in Cuba. "This country was impelled solely by the purpose of relieving grievous wrongs and removing long-existing conditions which disturbed its tranquility, which shocked the moral sense of mankind, and which could no longer be endured."[193]

Spain repeatedly offered up Cuba during the negotiations, hoping to foist its debt, rumored to be several hundred million dollars, on the United States. Had U.S. leaders accepted it, this debt would have been a substantial cost, and hence it represents the most viable possible deterrent for profitability theory. Although it arose occasionally during the debate, no senators invoked Cuba's debt as something that regretfully precluded its annexation. Rather, they invoked the debt to advocate recognizing Cuban independence immediately, lest international law see the United States as assuming responsibility for the debt by conquest.[194] The point was moot anyway since U.S. leaders had no interest in annexing Cuba. The U.S. negotiators consistently rebuffed Spain's offers, signing a treaty on December 10 that guaranteed Cuban independence.[195] Although the United States would practice informal imperialism in Cuba in the future, calls to transform this emergent influence into formal annexation continued falling on deaf ears in Congress. When former

Secretary of State Richard Olney advocated annexation in 1900, citing familiar arguments that "its command of the Gulf of Mexico" made Cuba "essential to our security against foreign aggression," former President Cleveland aptly summarized prevailing opinion in replying, "I am afraid Cuba ought to be submerged for a while before it will make an American State or Territory of which we will be particularly proud."[196]

The Annexation of Hawaii

U.S. leaders may have refused to annex Cuba in 1898, but they did annex Hawaii. Their interest in Hawaii was long-standing: various administrations had opposed foreign interventions there since the 1840s, signed a reciprocity treaty in 1875 to undercut growing Hawaiian–British trade, and acquired Pearl Harbor as a coaling station in 1887 to ensure "paramount influence" there.[197] Calls for annexation ebbed and flowed throughout those decades.[198] Why did the United States annex Hawaii in 1898? Given its geopolitical importance, ease of acquisition, and limited population, both profitability theory and domestic impact theory correctly predict that U.S. leaders should have pursued annexation in this case. The theories diverge in their predictions for U.S. decision-making, though, especially regarding how Hawaii's population factored into U.S. leaders' discussions of annexation. Profitability theory expects U.S. leaders to have considered Hawaii's population primarily in terms of its economic value and potential resistance, while domestic impact theory expects them to have emphasized its normative fitness to join U.S. society. What arguments featured most prominently in the U.S. decision to annex Hawaii?

The military costs of annexation were relatively minimal. The U.S. military had a long presence in the islands, which had been governed since 1893 by a cadre of Anglo-American planters who had overthrown Queen Liliuokalani and wanted to join the United States.[199] Meanwhile, annexation's urgency was heightened by fears that U.S. influence over the islands—and hence over the Pacific Ocean—was slipping. A recent wave of Japanese immigration threatened to erode the planters' authority by sheer demographic weight, and when they denied entry to hundreds of new immigrants in 1897 Japanese leaders deployed a warship to Honolulu.[200]

This assertiveness alarmed McKinley, who feared that Japan might seize Hawaii if the United States did not annex it. He responded by requesting anti-Japanese war plans, fresh naval deployments to deter further escalation, and the negotiation of an annexation treaty as a clear "hands off" signal.[201] He told Massachusetts Senator George Hoar, "We cannot let those islands go to Japan. . . . Her people are crowding in there. . . . If something be not done, there will be before long another revolution, and Japan will get control."[202] Sensitive to annexation's potential domestic costs, however, McKinley left it to "the wisdom of Congress" to figure out how to ratify the treaty while "avoiding abrupt assimilation of elements perhaps hardly yet fitted to share in the highest franchises of citizenship."[203]

When the House of Representatives took up the issue, its members widely praised Hawaii's material benefits. Many echoed the esteem of Nevada's Francis Newlands for its "soil of great fertility, unsurpassed climate, and an incomparable harbor," with Charles Henry of Indiana calling it "an earthly paradise."[204] Joseph Graff of Illinois anticipated that "it will aid in our commercial expansion," and others joined John Lacey of Iowa in labeling Hawaii "the key to the trade of the Pacific Ocean."[205]

Far and away the most widely discussed benefit was the security Hawaii would afford. In the age of steamships, a midocean coaling station was a virtual necessity for any Asia-based navy to attack the U.S. Pacific coast, and congressmen quoted a wide array of naval strategists to argue that Hawaii's annexation would secure that coast for the foreseeable future. Freeman Knowles of South Dakota called it "as necessary to our defense as is the picket line of an army."[206] James Mann labeled Hawaii "the fort which protects the Pacific coast," and his fellow Illinoisan Robert Hitt noted that annexing that "strategic point" would "paralyze any fleet, however strong . . . before it can attack our coast."[207] To Michigan's Edward Hamilton, the fact that it would "preempt . . . the only coaling station and base of supplies from which a hostile fleet could make descent upon our western coast" was "the most powerful argument in favor of annexation."[208] As the Senate Foreign Relations Committee later summarized, "The Hawaiian treaty was negotiated for the purpose of . . . preventing any other great power from acquiring a foothold there, which might be adverse to the welfare and safety of our Pacific coast in time of war."[209]

Many congressmen shared McKinley's fear that a U.S. failure to act would hand the islands to Japan, given its recent immigration and increasing assertiveness. De Alva Alexander of New York quoted naval historian Alfred Mahan in remarking that "the people of Hawaii are in danger of passing under the domination of Japan 'by a peaceful process . . . of overrunning and assimilation.'"[210] The islands were widely expected to be a focal point of future conflict if they were not annexed.[211] Nevertheless, proponents struggled to find the two-thirds majority needed to ratify the treaty throughout 1897 and early 1898. Tariff policy and the Cuban crisis monopolized attention, and promoters faced vocal opposition from anti-imperialists who feared that subjecting the Hawaiian population would weaken U.S. democracy, sugar interests worried about competition from Hawaiian planters, and labor organizations afraid of Asian immigrants taking American jobs.[212] George Dewey's victory in the Battle of Manila Bay in May 1898 not only earned him a promotion from commodore to rear admiral, it rejuvenated annexation's advocates by adding the need to support his fleet during the ongoing war with Spain. As Samuel Barrows of Massachusetts observed, "Admiral Dewey has taught us some lessons in geography and as to the necessities of modern naval warfare. They clinch the argument for the annexation of Hawaii."[213]

Opponents largely accepted Hawaii's economic and geopolitical benefits, though some protested that it was too far away. William Bate of Tennessee exclaimed, "We might as well contemplate a part of the moon as a point of defense as look to Hawaii."[214] Advocates countered by noting that steamships made travel to Hawaii faster than travel to New Orleans or Alaska had been when those territories were annexed. Instead of disputing its material benefits, opponents overwhelmingly rejected annexation based on the character of its inhabitants.[215] James Richardson of Tennessee labeled its "population of about 109,000 . . . about fifteen-sixteenths, or nearly 16 to 1, being Japanese, Chinese, Portuguese, and natives of the Sandwich Islands, wholly unfit for free representative or local self-government." Reflecting the views of many of his colleagues, he gasped, "Is it to become a state of the American Union? Heaven forbid!"[216]

The Native Hawaiians drew criticism from congressmen like Kentucky's John Rhea, who deemed them "wholly undesirable . . . moral vipers and physical lepers," and Missouri's James Clark, who considered them "not fit to vote" and hence thought the islands as attractive as "a dog with the rabies."[217] Henry Johnson of Indiana protested, "Why, sir, these mongrel denizens of the Tropics are utterly incapable of self-control, to say nothing of self-government. What, pray, do they know about free institutions, and what can they be taught concerning them, for that matter? Confer statehood and suffrage upon them, and they will not only be in confusion themselves, but they will also work irreparable injury to the whole Union."[218] William Howard of Georgia seconded those thoughts, saying, "I am opposed to it because I believe that the introduction of that heterogeneous population is not a desirable addition to our population."[219]

Beyond disparaging the Native Hawaiians, opponents objected to Hawaii's many Japanese and Chinese laborers, who, they speculated, would use annexation as a stepping-stone to circumvent U.S. immigration laws and lower wages in the continental United States. Marcus Smith of Arizona called Hawaii a "virus," reminding his colleagues, "We have passed laws against Chinese immigration to this country . . . yet in this one act you make

American citizens, or at least American residents, of 25,000 Chinese."[220] North Carolina's Romulus Linney warned that "the hordes from which they come are inexhaustible," while John Fitzgerald of Massachusetts asked, "Are we to have a Mongolian state in this Union?"[221] Clark insisted that "a Chinaman never can be fit for American citizenship. His color, his diet, his mental conformation, his habits of thought, his methods of conduct, his style of living, his ideas of government, his theory of the domestic relations, his code of morals, his religion, his passiveness in servitude, his ultra conservatism, his manners, his amusements, the very fashion of his dress, are radically un-American."[222] Arguing that to accept Chinese immigration "is surely to write the epitaph of free government on this continent," he asked his colleagues, "How does the prospect of heathen-Chinese domination suit you?"[223]

Many also feared that Hawaii would lead to further annexations of objectionable peoples. John Bell of Colorado warned, "If you annex Hawaii, I expect to see you hold the Philippines, I expect to see you hold Puerto Rico, and you will find that they will never be Americanized."[224] Clark beseeched his colleagues, "If we annex Hawaii . . . twenty years hence, it may be that you will have a polyglot House and it will be your painful duty to recognize 'the gentleman from Patagonia,' 'the gentleman from Cuba,' 'the gentleman from Santo Domingo,' . . . or, with fear and trembling, 'the gentleman from the Cannibal Islands,' who will gaze upon you with watering mouth and gleaming teeth. In that stupendous day there will be a new officer within these historic walls, whose title will be 'interpreter to the Speaker.'"[225] He reminded them that "the way to remain sober is to resolutely refuse the first drink."[226]

Judging its people unfit for U.S. citizenship and its tropical climate unfit for Anglo-American settlement, some observed that ruling Hawaii would require an imperial regime corrosive to American democracy.[227] Johnson warned that imperialism "would establish in this great republic by legal enactment the hateful rule of caste, and create an oligarchy under the American flag as tyrannical and brutal as any that ever flourished in the despotisms of the Old World. . . . We cannot remain a republic and at the same time practice the methods of a despotism."[228] Bell cautioned his colleagues, "It will require a government by the bayonet rather than the ballot to make this heterogeneous people harmonize with our institutions."[229]

Advocates responded effectively to this vocal opposition by contending that annexation's domestic costs were being oversold. Their arguments coalesced around two points: (1) some of Hawaii's population was actually desirable, and (2) the objectionable groups would rapidly disappear after annexation. First, they emphasized that Americans already controlled both Hawaii's government and the vast majority of its property. Hamilton affirmed that "the controlling intelligent forces of Hawaii are bone of our bone and flesh of our flesh. In the annexation of Hawaii we merge no alien nationality. We annex American institutions, American holidays, American courts, and American laws."[230] Amos Cummings of New York echoed these observations in saying, "The ferry is longer, but the business and government of the island are essentially American. . . . The islands have been civilized by Americans. They are governed by Americans, men of our kith and kin, anxious for the union."[231]

The Native Hawaiians were essentially American as well, proponents maintained, since American missionaries had been educating them for decades.[232] Alexander recounted that "for seventy years they have been living under the influences of American civilization. They speak and study our language; the Stars and Stripes are as familiar as their own flag; their laws are copied from those of the United States."[233] Given that history, Charles Grosvenor of Ohio insisted, "It is a mistake to let it be understood that we are trying to annex a barbarian population."[234] Albert Berry of Kentucky noted the Hawaiian literacy rate, which exceeded 85 percent, as evidence that "education is more universal in the Hawaiian Islands than it is in the state of Georgia. They are not the savages which some of our friends here would have us believe."[235] Pennsylvania's Horace Packer pointed to previous acquisitions, asking, "Have any of our people residing in territories heretofore annexed had such a training and preparation for American citizenship as have the people of Hawaii?"[236]

Whether or not the Native Hawaiians were desirable additions to the United States, annexation's supporters emphasized that they were too few in number to impose formidable domestic costs and that they would not be a long-term problem because they were disappearing anyway. Albert Todd of Michigan observed that only thirty-one thousand Hawaiian aborigines remained of the four hundred thousand that the British explorer James Cook had found on the islands in 1778, noting that just like the tribes of North America, "all authorities agree that in but a few years a once happy people of trustful and confiding 'children of nature' will be extinct."[237] Hitt observed that Hawaii's population was "not equal in people to a congressional district represented on this floor," and Lacey agreed: "Fortunately the population is not large enough to involve us in any difficult social problems."[238] Unlike the Filipinos, Newlands observed, the Native Hawaiians were "inconsiderable" and "gradually becoming extinct."[239]

Advocates told their colleagues not to fret over Hawaii's forty-six thousand Japanese and Chinese laborers because they would be forced to emigrate once U.S. laws banning immigration from Asia had been extended to cover the islands. Edwin Ridgely of Kansas was one of many who insisted that "when we have taken political control we will at once apply our national policy by shutting the gates against a further influx of the Asiatic races."[240] Todd announced, "Objection is made that Asiatics will be thus allowed citizenship. . . . If this were true, I should oppose the measure with all my power. Happily both the facts and effects are the opposite."[241] Alexander anticipated that "within ten years after the sources of supply are cut off as effectually as in the United States the Orientals of Hawaii will be found infrequently, and then only washing the dirty linen of a superior and more prosperous people."[242]

In place of the Native Hawaiians and East Asian laborers residing there, advocates expected Hawaii to quickly fill with Anglo-American settlers. Newlands predicted that "by the peaceful processes of emigration from our own country the entire character of the population will be changed."[243] Linney agreed, declaring, "American immigration would quickly make them truly American. . . . I wish no possession that we cannot Americanize. I wish nothing where the population is so large that a final difference must be made between the colonist and the homeborn."[244] Packer thought that "the danger consequent upon a mixture of the races and blending of foreign customs and habits is more fancied than real," not because such blending would be beneficial but because he expected Anglo-American settlers to quickly descend on Hawaii and believed that "the stronger races always have and always will dominate the weaker."[245]

Finally, many champions of annexation observed that they could easily manage its domestic costs by delaying statehood for Hawaii until they judged it ready. As William Smith of Michigan noted, "It has been said by some opposed to annexation that the population is undesirable; possibly that may be so, but the same argument was used against the admission of California and Texas into the Union, but the undesirable element in both states was soon lost sight of in the sturdy immigration that stable government attracted, and so it will be with these islands."[246] Iowa's William Hepburn reminded his colleagues that Montana was held as a territory "for eighty-six years before it was given statehood" and that nothing required that Hawaii be admitted any sooner if they deemed it unworthy.[247] Some shared the "doubt" of Massachusetts' Frederick Gillett that Hawaii would "ever attain a population or importance entitling it to statehood."[248]

Most congressmen joined Lacey in "conceding the disadvantages involved in taking nearly a hundred thousand people of an alien race into our population" but considered those people "a small incumbrance when compared with the great importance that these islands must be to our commerce on the one hand and to the defense of our Pacific coast on the other."[249] The House voted 209–91 for annexation on June 15, 1898.[250] The arena of debate then shifted to the Senate, where proponents had already made their case during an executive session and opponents now used the public spotlight to make familiar arguments in one final effort to defeat the measure.

Warning his colleagues that Hawaii would eventually become a state, William Bate of Tennessee remarked, "I do not, for one, desire to see here the character of representatives that would come from there. . . . In Hawaii there can be no popular will, no people's consent. The Asiatics must be denied participation in consent, the natives are too ignorant of all governmental responsibility."[251] South Carolina's Benjamin Tillman agreed: "We are to annex under this resolution one group of these islands with only 6,700 white men, women, and children on them and 103,000 . . . aliens in blood, aliens in language, aliens in thought and feeling."[252] He concluded, "I will vote for the annexation of Hawaii upon one condition . . . that the government there shall be extended only to and participated in by those with white blood in their veins."[253] Donelson Caffery of Louisiana, William Allen of Nebraska, and Richard Pettigrew of South Dakota all complained about the Chinese and Japanese workers in Hawaii and despaired that its tropical climate made Anglo-American resettlement impossible.[254] They expected annexation to produce "a quasi-military government," a "naked despotism" that would transform the United States into "an oligarchy, if not into absolute monarchy itself."[255] Assuming that Hawaii would lead to the annexation of the Philippines, Cuba, and other islands, Allen complained that "they will come to reduce the standard of civilization in all the occupations in this country among our legitimate population. . . . [O]ur society cannot carry the load; civilization will stagger under it."[256]

Confident of their majority, annexation's sponsors in the Senate pressed for a vote after George Hoar of Massachusetts stood forth to offer the familiar counterarguments. Hoar sympathized with the logic that was motivating opposition to the measure, declaring, "If we are ourselves to be governed in part by peoples to whom the Declaration of Independence is a stranger; or, worse still, if we are to govern subject and vassal states, trampling as we do it on our own great charter which recognizes alike the liberty and the dignity of individual manhood, then let us resist this thing in the beginning, and let us resist it to the death."[257] But it was not so in Hawaii, he insisted. The Native Hawaiians were "a perishing people," the Chinese and Japanese laborers "will get out when we get proper American labor laws," and the Hawaiian Islands "will not come in as a state unless they are fit to be a state. If they have got hereafter a population of a million or fifteen hundred thousand of

American lineage and American character and American ideals . . . they will come in and we shall welcome them. But if they are unfit, they will not come in; we never have been in a hurry about this thing."[258] Well versed in Hawaii's geopolitical benefits and the Japanese threat there, the Senate approved the joint resolution for annexation 42–21 on July 6, and McKinley signed it the next day.[259]

The annexation of Hawaii fits the expectations of both profitability theory and domestic impact theory given its high material benefits, low military costs, and low domestic costs. Nevertheless, the contents of these congressional debates provide overwhelming evidence that U.S. leaders were thinking just as domestic impact theory predicts and that profitability theory is insufficient to understand their decision-making. The major counterarguments focused not on questions of affordability but on the character of Hawaii's people and the domestic political and normative implications of assimilating them. Accordingly, a strong argument can be made that U.S. leaders would not have annexed Hawaii had its population been comparable in size to the other islands discussed in this chapter.

Imperialism in Puerto Rico, the Philippines, and Beyond

If U.S. leaders raised their eyebrows at Hawaii's 100,000 mixed-race inhabitants, they found the prospect of absorbing 7.6 million Filipinos downright terrifying, driving them to embrace overseas imperialism as an alternative to annexation. Wars often outpace their original motives, and the Spanish–American War (undertaken to free Cuba from Spanish tyranny) led to the U.S. conquest of Puerto Rico, the Philippines, and Guam. Unlike previous acquisitions, though, U.S. leaders chose not to annex these islands and instead created a new designation for them: unincorporated territories—areas falling under U.S. sovereignty but outside the United States. The twentieth century saw that designation extended to American Samoa, the Panama Canal Zone, the U.S. Virgin Islands, the Northern Mariana Islands, and more than a dozen other islands, reefs, and atolls.

Why did U.S. leaders choose imperialism instead of annexing those island territories or leaving them independent? Profitability theory predicts that this decision should have been based on a material cost-benefit analysis: U.S. leaders should have pursued imperialism because they judged it the most profitable option. In contrast, domestic impact theory predicts that leaders should have weighed the domestic consequences of each approach, including the identities of the islands' populations. Does accounting for annexation's domestic impact help explain the U.S. turn to imperialism?

Puerto Rico, the Philippines, and Guam were all secondary targets, featured in U.S. war plans only to impair Spanish reinforcements or "injure Spain at little cost to the United States."[260] U.S. leaders knew little about them when the war began. Commodore George Dewey found the most recent naval intelligence report on the Philippines to be more than twenty years old, later remarking, "The Philippines were to us a *terra incognita*."[261] Dewey's victory over the Spanish fleet at Manila Bay on May 1, 1898, only one week into the war, caught President McKinley without a follow-up plan, and only after British leaders inquired about U.S. intentions there did his Cabinet discuss what to do with the archipelago.[262] A small U.S. fleet captured Guam in June on its way to reinforce Dewey, and a late-July invasion of Puerto Rico, launched after the Spanish fleet at Santiago had already been destroyed, was cut short by the war's end.[263] Heading into the peace negotiations, McKinley instructed his commissioners to demand U.S. sovereignty over Puerto Rico and Guam, but he left the Philippines' status undetermined for four weeks until finally deciding to take them on October 26.[264]

All three territories occupied strategically valuable geographic positions and offered economic benefits. Puerto Rico flanked a gateway to the Caribbean Sea that would be useful for securing the Central American canal envisioned by expansionists like Lodge and Theodore Roosevelt.[265] After leading McKinley's fact-finding commission there in 1899, Henry Carroll reported that it exported more than $12 million of coffee, $4 million of sugar, and lesser amounts of tobacco, molasses, and hides.[266] That tropical produce appealed to congressional leaders interested in reducing U.S. dependence on imports, and it offered opportunities for investors ready to provide the island with sorely needed capital and production technologies.[267] Senator Chauncey Depew of New York described the island as "one of the most fertile territories on earth. From seashore to mountain top it can be cultivated. With capital, enterprise, and modern machinery the possibilities of increase in its productiveness cannot be calculated."[268]

In the Pacific, Guam offered a useful coaling station and the Philippines a local gateway to Asia's lucrative markets. Depew underscored "the tremendous advantages of position from Manila for reaching the limitless markets of the Orient," while Lodge praised its "enormous material benefits to our trade, our industries, and our labor," declaring further that the Philippines' "value to this country is almost beyond imagination."[269] Amid growing European efforts to control the China market, the *Wall Street Journal* noted that the Philippines would allow the United States "to protect, not only the existing trade with the Far East, but the enormously greater trade likely to be developed in the next 25 years."[270] Given these material benefits and the fact that U.S. forces had already seized these islands from Spain, profitability theory predicts relatively straightforward annexations after the war.

Yet McKinley agonized for months over what to do with the Philippines, ultimately backing into his decision mainly for fear of provoking war between Germany and Japan.[271] German leaders sent an outsized force of five warships to Manila after Dewey's victory, positioning to assume control if McKinley did not, and German newspapers clamored for the Philippines throughout the summer.[272] Meanwhile, Japanese leaders made no secret of their own ambitions, volunteering "to join with the United States" in governing the archipelago.[273] U.S. Minister to Japan Alfred Buck reported in July, "It is well understood that Japan would like to have the Philippine Islands added to her possessions, and high officials of the government do not disguise their desire in that direction."[274] After consulting with recently returned military officers in late September and early October, McKinley concluded that "we could not give them . . . to any European power for we should have a war on our hands in fifteen minutes," that independence would produce the same result, and that keeping anything short of the whole archipelago would leave "hostile territory" within a "stone's throw."[275] He finally informed his peace commissioners that "the cession must be of the whole archipelago or none. The latter is wholly inadmissible and the former must therefore be required . . . believing that this course will entail less trouble than any other."[276]

There is thus a good argument to be made that apprehension over military costs drove McKinley's decision to take the Philippines rather than leave them independent, but it is far more difficult to argue that profitability logic drove U.S. leaders to choose imperialism over annexation. Imposing the U.S. imperial regime required a three-year war that killed more than sixteen thousand Filipino insurgents and four thousand U.S. soldiers.[277] Neither McKinley nor Congress justified that war on the grounds that it was more efficient than placing the Philippines on a path to statehood. Logic suggests the opposite: cooperating with the local resistance against Spain to establish local political representation may have undercut their opposition to U.S. efforts. Yet McKinley had little sympathy for Emilio Aguinaldo's rebels, considering them "unfit for self-government" and liable to produce "anarchy and misrule over there worse than Spain's was."[278] He instructed U.S. forces in August 1898 that "there must be no joint occupation with the insurgents," authorizing them to "use whatever means in your judgment are necessary to this end."[279] Congress was similarly unconcerned with avoiding military costs, as reports of Filipino insurgents attacking U.S. forces in early February 1899 galvanized the peace treaty's ratification by the Senate.[280]

If military costs did not drive U.S. leaders to reject annexation, what about domestic costs? With a population of only nine thousand, Guam was too small to be a realistic candidate for statehood, but Puerto Rico's roughly nine hundred thousand inhabitants were a central focus of congressional debate.[281] Unlike other island populations, Puerto Ricans were regarded by many U.S. leaders as promising future citizens. Carroll's fact-finding report labeled 64 percent of Puerto Rico's population "whites," 27 percent "mixed," and 9 percent "blacks," emphasizing that "the colored classes are decreasing."[282] He described them as "a kindly, hospitable, polite people" who welcomed U.S. sovereignty and "knew pretty well what the rights and privileges of American citizenship were."[283] Declaring them "capable of self-government," Carroll judged that "the people as a whole are a moral, law-abiding class, mild in disposition, easy to govern, and possess the possibilities of developing a high type of citizenship."[284]

Many in Congress echoed that assessment during debate over the Organic Act establishing Puerto Rico's civilian government. Senator Henry Teller of Colorado declared, "The people of Porto Rico are fit for self-government to-day."[285] Mississippi Congressman Thomas Spight saw Puerto Rico as "contiguous territory," its people "of Caucasian blood, knowing and appreciating the benefits of civilization" and "desirous of casting their lot with us. They know much of our system of government, the beneficence of our institutions and the blessings of civil and religious liberty."[286] Congressman William Lorimer of Illinois observed that Puerto Ricans had "embraced the civilizing Christian religion many years ago," while Senator Alexander Clay of Georgia saw "830,000 of them belonging to the Caucasian race" as evidence that "the people of Porto Rico will become valuable and useful citizens of the United States and will at no distant day in the future ask and receive the privileges of statehood."[287] Congressman John Gaines of Tennessee emphasized that the islanders "came willingly under our flag," while Maryland Senator George Wellington emphasized that "the Porto Rican is an American laborer; he now belongs to the American family."[288]

Not all U.S. leaders saw the Puerto Ricans as a kindred people. Some criticized the island's 85 percent illiteracy rate and lack of previous experience with representative government; others questioned their racial whiteness or objected to their Catholicism.[289] Yet many critics remained optimistic that Puerto Rico was small enough and close enough to be sufficiently Americanized over time. Desiring "above all things . . . that the Union shall be limited to states composed of our own people," Senator John Spooner of Wisconsin maintained that most Puerto Ricans had "not the intelligence which would fit them for citizenship" and "know nothing of our ways . . .

nothing of our institutions," yet he allowed that "there is no haste about it" and "someday conditions may be changed."[290] California Senator George Perkins complained that "more than one-third of the entire population is of the negro or mixed race; the balance are mostly of Spanish origin. . . . [T]heir beliefs and customs are not those of the Anglo-Saxon," yet even as he labeled the Puerto Ricans "foreign to our institutions and our civilization," he anticipated future statehood "when the island, through education and experience, becomes American."[291] After assuring his colleagues, "I do not believe that we will incorporate the alien races, and civilized, semicivilized, barbarous, and savage peoples of these islands into our body politic as states of our Union," Depew predicted that "order, law, justice, and liberty will stimulate and develop our new possessions. Their inhabitants will grow . . . beyond their wildest dreams of the results of that self-government they now so vaguely understand."[292]

Had it been the only island acquired from Spain in 1898, Puerto Rico may well have been incorporated into the United States like previous annexations. After all, the weight of precedent was on its side, and Congress was in no rush to turn territories into states. New Mexico and Arizona had been waiting half a century by then and Oklahoma almost a full century to be deemed worthy.[293] Consistent with their relatively positive views of Puerto Rico's inhabitants, Senator Joseph Foraker of Ohio and Congressman Sereno Payne of New York initially drafted bills granting them U.S. citizenship and free trade.[294] But Puerto Rico was not the only new acquisition, and its chances for quick incorporation were doomed by the emerging view that Congress's treatment of it would establish a precedent for the Philippines.[295] As Tennessee Senator William Bate remarked, "There is something behind Porto Rico . . . a political dagger in shape of the Philippines. . . . That is the real question. Porto Rico is but its front shadow."[296]

If Puerto Ricans' fitness for U.S. citizenship was debatable to turn-of-the-century U.S. leaders, the prospect of assimilating 7.6 million Filipinos was a complete nonstarter.[297] Former senator Carl Schurz urged McKinley not to absorb "a large mass of more or less barbarous Asiatics," saying, "I suppose no sane American thinks of taking them into the Union as states to help govern us," a prospect "too monstrous to be seriously thought of even by the wildest imperialist."[298] Bate propagated ugly stereotypes in his attack: "The Philippines . . . is like Pandora's box, full of ills. . . . Let us beware of those mongrels of the East, with breath of pestilence and touch of leprosy. Do not let them become a part of us with their idolatry, polygamous creeds, and harem habits."[299] Senator Stephen White of California disparaged the Philippines' "heterogeneous compound of inefficient Oriental humanity," while Missouri Congressman James Clark vowed, "no matter whether they are fit to govern themselves or not, they are not fit to govern us."[300] Nebraska Senator William Allen announced, "I am not willing to incorporate in our population, as citizens of the United States, 15,000,000 people belonging to alien races, the most of them ignorant, brutal, hostile, and savage, and reduce the standard of our home civilization to that of a low and brutal Asiatic population."[301] Senator Hoar similarly cautioned, "We must change all our constitutional methods of procedure before we can undertake the government of millions of people at a distance who cannot be admitted to our self-government."[302]

Unlike those of Puerto Rico, Guam, and Hawaii, the acquisition of the Philippines represented a paradigm shift, forcing U.S. leaders to reevaluate their historical approach to territorial expansion. As Spooner reasoned, "It has been hitherto for a great many years a matter of comparatively trifling importance what constitutional relation the territories sustain to the United States, because our territories have been peopled by those of our own blood and kindred." In contrast, "the Spanish war . . . has placed under our control . . . territory containing eleven or more millions of people, a sixth of the population of this country, strangers to us, strangers to our language, strangers to our institutions, strangers to our aspirations and to our race. And that control . . . brings with it responsibility of the gravest sort."[303] Senator Albert Beveridge of Indiana concurred: "This question is deeper than any question of party politics; deeper than any question of the isolated policy of our country even; deeper even than any question of constitutional power. It is elemental. It is racial."[304] Xenophobia thus emerged once again as "a formidable obstacle to expansion," so formidable, in fact, that "not a single expansionist proposed that the privileges of citizenship be extended to the Philippines."[305]

Since imperialists and anti-imperialists agreed that annexing the Philippines was not an option, the congressional debate was not annexation versus imperialism but rather imperialism versus independence, and both sides focused primarily on assessing imperialism's domestic consequences rather than its profitability.[306] Anti-imperialists stressed that an empire abroad would undermine American democracy at home, reviving arguments from the 1840s all-Mexico debate. Senator George Vest of Missouri insisted that "under the Constitution of the United States no power is given to the federal government to acquire territory to be held and governed permanently as colonies."[307] Lorimer wondered "whether or not it is best for the nation to remain true to its republican principles or abandon them for the policy of empire."[308] Virginia Congressman James Hay protested that "the bill violates every principle of our form of government. It sets up an oligarchy, a form of government in no sense republican . . . which denies the right of self-government to a portion of the people of the United States."[309] Spight objected that the Filipinos "are of wholly different races of people from ours—Asiatics, Malays, negroes, and mixed blood. They have nothing in common with us and centuries cannot assimilate them. . . . They can never be clothed with the rights of American citizenship nor their territory admitted as a state of the American Union, nor can we hold and govern the islands as colonies nor their people as vassals without the utmost violence to the basic principles upon which our system of government is founded."[310]

Those who rejected imperialism tried to outlaw it by proposing that "all territory acquired by the government . . . must be acquired and governed with the purpose of ultimately organizing such territory into states suitable for admission into the Union," a resolution which would have limited U.S. options to independence or annexation (with the deck stacked heavily against the latter).[311] Their efforts failed, however, as imperialists like Senator Orville Platt of Connecticut denied that "there is any constitutional or moral obligation to fit the territory for statehood or to ever admit it as a state."[312] Michigan Congressman Edward Hamilton responded to anti-imperialist claims that "the Constitution follows the flag" by retorting, "That is not true. The Constitution follows the flag or not as we please and when we please."[313] Foraker agreed: "The mere acquisition of territory by the United States does not make the Constitution applicable to it, but that it is a question for the Congress."[314] Acquisition could not be synonymous with annexation, Perkins argued, for "suppose the Chinese Empire should fall to us as a war indemnity. We would have acquired a territory with 400,000,000 population, of a class that we have spurned from our shores as we would a pestilence. Should those unassimilative people be permitted to overrun us and affect the body politic and our institutions with a leprosy worse than death itself?"[315] As Spooner summarized the emerging distinction, "Territory belonging to the United States, as I think Puerto Rico and the Philippine Archipelago do, become a part of the United States in the *international sense*, while not being at all a part of the United States in the *constitutional sense*."[316]

The imperialists argued that imperialism was the best of both worlds. Unlike independence, it furthered U.S. commercial and geopolitical interests abroad, and unlike annexation, it preserved democracy at home. Senator Jonathan Ross of Vermont claimed that denying representation to island populations undermined democracy no more than having a minimum voting age: "In a representative government the right to govern is not derived from the consent of the governed until they arrive at a stage of advancement which will render them capable of giving an intelligent consent. . . . Doubtless the boys of fifteen in this country are better prepared to give an intelligent consent than are the inhabitants of those islands."[317] Moreover, the new empire would be explicitly temporary and good for the Filipinos, Platt argued, providing "the most liberal, just, and beneficent government which they may be capable of enjoying . . . in the hope that they may be finally fitted for independent self-government."[318]

The treaty that ended the Spanish–American War made no mention of territorial status or citizenship rights for the islands' populations, specifying only that "the civil and political status of the native inhabitants of the territories hereby ceded to the United States shall be determined by Congress."[319] Republican leaders, who controlled both houses of Congress as well as the presidency, thus felt empowered to remove the assimilating measures from early drafts of Puerto Rico's Organic Act and impose overtly imperial rule on all of the islands acquired from Spain. The version that passed in April 1900 created a distinct Puerto Rican citizenship, applied a temporary tariff, and empowered the president to appoint the island's governor and executive council (which held veto power over legislation passed by a popularly elected lower house). Congress replicated these measures in the Philippine Organic Act two years later, while Guam was ruled by the United States Navy until receiving its own Organic Act in 1950.[320]

Failing to stop their imperialist colleagues in Congress, the anti-imperialists went to court, where they were defeated again in the Insular Cases, a series of Supreme Court rulings underscoring the fact that acquisition need not equal annexation.[321] As Justice Henry Brown argued in *Downes v. Bidwell*, the United States might acquire territory for numerous reasons, and "if those possessions are inhabited by alien races, differing from us in religion, customs, laws, methods of taxation, and modes of thought, the administration of government and justice according to Anglo-Saxon principles may for a time be impossible."[322] A 5–4 majority in that case decided that Puerto Rico was "belonging to the United States, but not a part of the United States," or, as Justice Edward White wrote in his concurring opinion, "foreign to the United States in a domestic sense . . . not . . . incorporated . . . but . . . merely . . . a possession."[323] In contrast, the Supreme Court decided in *Hawaii v. Mankichi* and *Rassmussen v. United States* that Congress had incorporated Hawaii and Alaska by granting citizenship to their Anglo-Saxon/European residents, paving the way for their eventual statehood.[324]

The Supreme Court's decisions in the 1901 Insular Cases applied arguments made two years earlier by Abbott Lowell of Harvard University, who wrote in the *Harvard Law Review* that "territory may be so annexed as to make it a part of the United States . . . but that possessions may also be so acquired as not to form part of the United States," within which "constitutional limitations . . . do not apply." Which form should any particular acquisition take? Lowell concluded that many "rights guaranteed to the citizens . . . are inapplicable except among a people whose social and political evolution has been consonant with our own."[325] This conviction was at the core of his *Atlantic Monthly* article nine months earlier, in which he asserted among other things that New Mexico's inhabitants "of Spanish race" were "not sufficiently trained in habits of self-government," that "Indians . . . in the tribal state . . . are not men," and that "the argument that the Chinese could never be assimilated . . . was sound."[326] Whereas "the application of . . . equal political rights" in previous acquisitions was "justified by the fact that the population of states and territories has been substantially homogeneous," Lowell claimed that "to let the Filipinos rule themselves would be sheer cruelty," that "even in case of the people of Porto Rico, who stand on an entirely different footing, self-government must be gradual and tentative," and that Hawaii's "Anglo-Saxon" leaders deserved representation but "it would be a gross blunder to attempt to extend the franchise to" its "Japanese . . . Chinese . . . Kanakas and Portuguese."[327]

As recent scholars have observed, the distinction between incorporated and unincorporated territories that U.S. leaders made after the 1898 acquisitions (and that remains in use today) was "transparently an invention" to legitimize imperialism over territories populated by people they considered not "racially qualified to be equal citizens."[328] As in other cases, U.S. leaders' decisions not to annex these territories was driven by their fear of annexation's domestic consequences. Congress's subsequent restrictions on corporate exploitation of the Philippines' natural resources reinforce the fact that U.S. imperialism was driven by more than profitability, as do successive presidents' calls to keep the archipelago's future independence in view.[329] The 1916 Philippine Autonomy Act established "a more autonomous government," Congress reinforcing that "it is, as it has always been, the purpose of the people of the United States to withdraw their sovereignty over the Philippine Islands and to recognize their independence as soon as a stable government can be established therein."[330] After the 1934 Philippine Independence Act started a countdown to independence, Congress granted the Philippines independence in 1946. As for Puerto Rico and Guam, Congress recognized their smaller, more kindred populations, gradually extending local governance and U.S. citizenship as the twentieth century progressed, but it continued to withhold the prospect of statehood and firmly maintained its final say on their status.[331]

The cases explored here vividly illustrate how U.S. leaders' approach to annexation continued to be colored by its domestic costs as their gaze turned overseas. Cuba's implications for the sectional balance of power put it on the agenda for southern leaders before the Civil War, and those same implications drove northern leaders to block its annexation. When the Civil War shattered the sectional balance, it didn't open the door to a campaign of conquest; instead, the xenophobia that had driven their predecessors to avoid southern Mexico was magnified among U.S. leaders during the late nineteenth century. Their low esteem for the populations of the Dominican Republic, Cuba, and the Philippines—a judgment rooted in normative, not material, concerns—effectively deterred the United States from annexing any of those territories. Xenophobia failed to prevent annexation only in Hawaii, where there were few enough people to justify visions of its Americanization.

These case studies confirm the expectations of domestic impact theory. U.S. leaders regularly evaluated the domestic consequences of annexation alongside its material benefits and military costs, and domestic costs overwhelmed material incentives in all four cases where they were significant. This history defies profitability theory, which predicts that the United States should have seized all of these opportunities. It can account reasonably well for the annexation of Hawaii given the high material benefits and low military costs involved, but it cannot explain either the substance of the congressional debates or why a century's worth of will-they-or-won't-they speculation produced no annexation of Cuba despite its arguably greater material benefits.

As the nineteenth century gave way to the twentieth, U.S. leaders increasingly pursued informal imperialism to prevent European powers from interfering in their neighborhood, yet repeated military interventions into various island neighbors produced no further annexations. The 1901 Platt Amendment authorized the United States to intervene in Cuba, but subsequent calls for annexation from Cubans who were disenchanted with their own government fell on deaf ears in the United States.[332] President Theodore Roosevelt similarly "rebuffed Haitians and Dominicans who dropped proannexation hints" despite claiming the right to intervene in any Latin American country under his corollary to the Monroe Doctrine.[333]

Temporary military interventions became standard U.S. practice when nearby countries fell into trouble, as did accompanying disclaimers of any long-term territorial ambitions. The Dominican experience alone provides abundant examples. Seizing control of Dominican customs to prevent a European intervention in 1905, Roosevelt told the Senate, "It cannot be too often and too emphatically asserted that the United States has not the slightest desire for territorial aggrandizement. . . . We do not propose to take any part of Santo Domingo."[334] President Woodrow Wilson accompanied his own 1916 Dominican intervention (intended to head off a potential German one) with the vow, "The United States will never again seek one additional foot of territory by conquest," and the commander of the intervening force, Admiral William Caperton, reassured the Dominicans that "it is not the intention of the United States Government to acquire by conquest any territory in the Dominican Republic."[335] President Lyndon Johnson repeatedly proclaimed, "We covet no territory" amidst his Dominican intervention in 1965.[336] There is plenty of room to debate the merits and demerits of these interventions, but in each case the disclaimer proved accurate: U.S. forces came and went, leaving the Dominican Republic independent.

Rather than describe U.S. imperialism in 1898 as coming late to the European game, it may be viewed more usefully as the country's first experience with temporary stewardship over foreign territory, a formal experiment with the informal imperialism that would come to characterize much of U.S. foreign policy moving forward. The interim nature of later U.S. military interventions helps square the circle of "Americans' understanding of the United States not only as a nonempire, but as an antiempire."[337] Had their calculations been rooted primarily in profitability, it is hard to imagine that U.S. leaders would not have found other appealing targets for annexation during the twentieth century. Instead, their refusal to consider annexing the Philippines spurred U.S. leaders' embrace of imperialism, the rise of military interventions and overseas bases as instruments of U.S. foreign policy, and their renunciation of annexation as a foreign policy goal.

CHAPTER 8

The International Implications of U.S. Annexation

> If Americans believed that other peoples would not disappear before the American advance, if they also thought that colonialism would corrupt the nation, and if they believed that other races were incapable of participating in a free government, then opposition to a further extension of territory became their only hope of preserving a free American Anglo-Saxon republic.
>
> Reginald Horsman, 1981

Annexation's domestic costs made U.S. leaders consistently picky in their territorial pursuits. Contrary to common accounts of the history of U.S. expansionism, leaders' territorial ambitions did not evaporate once an economic or military transformation undercut the value of additional territory; nor were their decisions to reject specific opportunities for annexation usually driven by its profitability. Instead, they ruled out the desirability of annexing their remaining neighbors episodically, largely for fear of their domestic costs. Politically vulnerable to demographic changes thanks to their democratic institutions and looking down on alien peoples through xenophobic eyes, U.S. leaders frequently feared that annexation would weaken their domestic influence and worsen their state. These domestic costs drove them to reject even profitable opportunities for annexation, especially where they faced the unthinkable choice between compromising their democratic institutions or allowing people they considered inferior to participate in governing their state. By transforming alien societies into a powerful deterrent, democracy and xenophobia effectively limited the course of U.S. territorial expansion.

This book's case studies have shown the conventional wisdom to be useful but inadequate. Its core premise—that states try to conquer each other when it pays—explains much of the history of great power politics, but it struggles to explain much of U.S. foreign policy history. Profitability theory accurately predicts U.S. behavior in thirteen of the twenty-three cases explored here (table 8.1).

Table 8.1 Summary of case study findings

CASE STUDY	MATERIAL BENEFITS[a]	MILITARY COSTS[a]	DOMESTIC COSTS[a]	ANNEXATION PURSUED?	CORRELATION FAVORS	WITHIN-CASE EVIDENCE FAVORS
Transappalachia	High	Low	Low	Yes	Both	Both
Louisiana	High	Low	Low	Yes	Both	DIT
Florida	High	Low	Low	Yes	Both	DIT
Native American Lands						
Washington-Adams	High	Low	Low	Yes	Both	Both
Jefferson-Madison	High	Low	Low	Yes	Both	DIT
Monroe-Jackson	High	Low	Low w/removal	Yes w/removal	Both	DIT
Canada						
American Revolution	High	Low Early, High Late	Low	Yes Early, No Late	Both	Both
War of 1812	High	Low	Low West, High East	Yes West, No East	DIT	DIT
Crises of 1837–42	High	High	High	No	Both	Both
Oregon	Low	Low	Low	Yes	Both	Both
Fenian Raids	High	Low	High	No	DIT	DIT
Pacific Northwest	Low	Low	Low	Yes	Both	Both

Mexico

Texas Revolution	High	Low	High	No	DIT	DIT
Annexation of Texas	High	Low	Low	Yes	Both	Both
Mexican–American War	High	Low	Low	Yes	Both	Both
All Mexico	High	Low	High	No	DIT	DIT
Antebellum	High	Low	Low North, High South	Yes North, No South	DIT	DIT
Maximilian Affair	High	Low	High	No	DIT	DIT
Cuba: Pre–Civil War	High	Low	High	No	DIT	DIT
Dominican Republic	High	Low	High	No	DIT	DIT
Cuba: Span.–Am. War	High	Low	High	No	DIT	DIT
Hawaii	High	Low	Low	Yes	Both	DIT
Puerto Rico/Philippines	High	Low	High	No	DIT	DIT

[a] Material benefits, military costs, and domestic costs as perceived by U.S. leaders.

It does well with the positive cases, accounting for every U.S. pursuit of annexation, but it cannot account for the negative cases, correctly predicting only two out of twelve nonpursuits. As the case studies reveal, U.S. leaders rarely pursued annexations they expected to be unprofitable, but they frequently rejected annexations they expected to be profitable. In other words, profitability theory may tell us why U.S. leaders annexed the territories they did, but it cannot tell us why U.S. leaders didn't annex the territories they didn't.

Domestic impact theory builds on the strengths of profitability theory while remedying this weakness, offering a more comprehensive account that explains positive and negative cases alike. U.S. leaders feared domestic costs every time they rejected a profitable opportunity for annexation. The case studies reinforce this broad correlation with more fine-grained evidence, particularly regarding who the opponents of annexation were and what arguments they levied against it. Taking such within-case evidence into account, domestic impact theory offers a better explanation than profitability theory in fifteen of the twenty-three cases, while also accounting for the remaining eight (see the rightmost column of table 8.1).

Domestic impact theory gains further support from specific comparisons within and across cases. For example, the 1812 Canada and antebellum Mexico cases saw leaders face vast neighboring territories yet specifically target only the sparsely populated regions where they foresaw low domestic costs, rejecting more populous and materially beneficial regions where they anticipated high domestic costs. U.S. policies toward Native American tribes changed from assimilation to exclusion as earlier leaders who were less subject to assimilation's domestic costs gave way to a new generation of leaders who were more so. U.S. leaders distinguished between desirable and undesirable targets similarly in 1848 and 1898, annexing territories with populations small enough to be Americanized but rejecting the assimilation of large alien societies.

Table 8.1 is a summary, intended not as a scoreboard between the two theories but a means to refresh our memories of the quoted documents, contextual evidence, and other factors discussed in the case studies themselves. Those case studies provide compelling and often unquantifiable evidence of a connection between U.S. leaders' fears of domestic costs and their decisions to reject profitable opportunities for annexation. For example, when Vermont Senator Redfield Proctor—whose influential report on his visit to Cuba turned many of his colleagues toward intervention in 1898—declared, "I am not in favor of annexation . . . because it is not wise policy to take in any people of foreign tongue and training, and without any strong guiding American element," he corroborated domestic impact theory's predictions regarding U.S. decision-making in that case.[1] Based on the available evidence, we can conclude that domestic costs powerfully limited the pattern of U.S. territorial expansion.

How should these findings influence the way we view the world? This chapter explores several implications of domestic impact theory, identifying fruitful pathways for future research. The first section focuses on its implications for U.S. foreign policy, exploring the relationship between systemic and domestic factors and probing what that means for such phenomena as American exceptionalism, benign hegemony, and informal imperialism. The second section addresses its implications for international relations more broadly, considering whether the logic of domestic impact theory generalizes to other countries and underscoring its contributions to how we understand the roots of international territorial ambitions, the democratic peace, and the norm against conquest.

U.S. Foreign Policy

By exploring how democracy and xenophobia worked together to limit U.S. territorial ambitions, this book adds to a rich literature dealing with how domestic political factors interact with international systemic factors to drive U.S. foreign policy.[2] Starting in the late 1970s with insights about domestic political sources of foreign economic policy,[3] scholars have produced impressive studies of how domestic politics shape U.S. grand strategy,[4] military spending,[5] military deployments,[6] war financing,[7] internationalism,[8] and foreign aid,[9] among other subjects. In doing so, they have identified a range of domestic factors that bear on leaders' foreign policy decisions, including democratic institutions,[10] partisanship,[11] sectionalism,[12] business interests,[13] ideological traditions,[14] and ethnic politics.[15] This diverse literature understands that foreign policy is domestically contentious, promising to create winners and losers economically, socially, and politically in ways that push leaders toward some policy options and away from others. In Robert Putnam's words, it recognizes the "inevitability of domestic conflict about what the 'national interest' requires."[16]

This book joins that literature in focusing on how domestic forces shape leaders' reactions to international incentives. Lacking any guarantee of their nation's survival more reliable than its own relative power, U.S. leaders throughout the case studies faced international incentives to reinforce it by pursuing profitable annexations. Instead of robotically following those incentives, they anticipated the domestic consequences of annexing each potential target through the lenses of their democratic institutions and xenophobic biases. When annexation threatened to tip the domestic balance of power against them or force them to share their self-government with large groups they considered unfit, U.S. leaders proved quite willing to defy their international incentives and reject it for domestic reasons.

This argument has important consequences for our understanding of U.S. foreign policy. First, it confirms that there is a profound difference between the United States and most other great powers in history, especially those that have risen to positions of military primacy. Where most great powers regularly sought to convert rising power into territorial expansion, the United States gradually rejected the prospect of annexing its remaining neighbors because its leaders wanted no part of their domestic costs. The eventual end of U.S. interest in annexation had an important side effect: no matter how powerful the United States became, its foreign policy did not generally threaten the survival of most other states.

As David Lake writes, U.S. leaders spent the twentieth century "supporting anticolonialism and accepting the principle of juridical sovereignty," policies which were "self-abnegating" and hence "puzzling" to traditional theories of international relations.[17] This self-abnegation greased the wheels for the acquisition of client states under hierarchical economic and security relationships. Other governments were willing to trade some authority in those areas to the United States for help in ensuring their security, relatively confident that it had no interest in fully extinguishing their sovereignty.[18] In essence, U.S. leaders encouraged cooperation by reducing the "special peril of defection" in international security agreements.[19] This was a symptom rather than a cause, however. U.S. leaders championed juridical sovereignty not because they sought to extend their influence over other countries but because they had long since lost interest in annexing them. Even as the United States ascended to a position of unipolarity after the Cold War, its foreign policy remained more focused on preserving international stability than on exerting offensive dominance.[20]

Second, the case studies in this book show that U.S. leaders rejected annexation for selfish reasons, not through any sense of international altruism. Although the result marked a meaningful departure from typical great-power aggression, these case studies go a long way toward correcting myths of American exceptionalism.[21] No illusion of U.S. leaders as being uniquely noble or compassionate can survive the litany of selfish and racist quotations cited here, nor should it if we value an accurate reading of U.S. history. Therefore, one implication of this book is to suggest that greater attention should be paid to the role of race in U.S. foreign policy.[22] U.S. leaders were not imbued with special respect for international law or compassion for foreign peoples; they simply feared how absorbing those peoples would change their country. If the decline of U.S. territorial ambitions set U.S. foreign policy on an exceptional path, it was driven by unusual domestic politics rather than by moral superiority.

Many Americans like to imagine the U.S.-led international order as a "benevolent hegemony" protecting U.S. and global interests simultaneously.[23] Yet no hegemon genuinely has other states' interests at heart. How could it? Hegemons are states, too, run by leaders subject to their own domestic institutions and incentives, and divergences in relative power often amplify divergences of interest.[24] In Samuel Huntington's words, U.S. illusions of benevolent hegemony assume "that a natural congruity exists between their interests and values and those of the rest of the world. It does not."[25] Although such illusions endure partly because U.S. leaders like to depict their policies as being "consistent with the common good," they also endure partly because U.S. foreign policy does look different from that of the empires of old.[26] Its unexceptional origins do not change the fact that "contemporary U.S. grand strategy, despite widespread criticism, poses a threat to only a very limited number of regimes and terrorist groups."[27] The United States may not be a benevolent hegemon, but it is an unusually benign one (at least in the pathological sense).[28]

Third, domestic impact theory can help us understand why informal imperialism remains a common feature of U.S. foreign policy even though annexation does not. As U.S. leaders rejected annexation in favor of stable borders with their remaining neighbors, imperialism remained their most direct avenue for controlling areas beyond those borders. Formal imperialism in the Philippines dodged annexation's domestic costs, but it also spawned a costly insurrection and rapid disenchantment with the idea of taking responsibility for the governance of foreign nations. That experience informed a long-term preference for informal imperialism and a perspective on military occupations as periods of tutelage in democracy for once and future independent nations.[29]

Accordingly, twentieth-century U.S. leaders increasingly turned to diplomatic and economic coercion backed by military force to shape events in the Western Hemisphere and deter European leaders from interfering in their neighborhood.[30] In 1904 President Theodore Roosevelt could declare in one breath, "It is not true that the United States feels any land hunger," yet in the next assert "an international police power" to intervene in any state not "making good use" of its independence.[31] His successors extended this practice worldwide during the Cold War, establishing a vast network of overseas military bases. These bases, in turn, undergirded economic and security relationships that allowed them to steer the foreign policies of friendly nations while continuing to avoid annexation's domestic costs.[32] In return for participation in their preferred international order, U.S. leaders promised strategic restraint and championed other states' territorial integrity.[33]

Even as they rejected annexation, U.S. leaders found offensive military operations increasingly useful as informal imperialism became their modus operandi, especially for regime change. Without domestic impact theory, it is difficult to comprehend why a powerful state would so thoroughly prefer regime change over annexation when the latter yields greater material benefits at an often-comparable military cost. European great powers utilized regime change amidst ideological conflicts to avoid upsetting their delicate balance of power and provoking balancing coalitions, yet most remained interested in pursuing profitable annexations.[34] With the United States atop a thoroughly skewed regional distribution of power, why has it favored regime change over annexation in Latin America?[35] Locked in the rigidly balanced Cold War, why did it launch dozens of regime change operations without annexing any more territory?[36] Enjoying global unipolarity, why did it change regimes in countries like Afghanistan, Iraq, and Libya but not seize more territory for itself?[37] This book provides a compelling answer: regime change offers a direct method for dealing with hostility abroad while avoiding the domestic costs of annexation.

Fourth, domestic impact theory helps resolve the apparent contradiction between U.S. liberal ideals and illiberal foreign policy behavior. As Michael Desch observes, "Abroad, the United States has pursued a strategy of hegemony, verging on empire, and almost unilaterally launched a preventive war in Iraq in a fashion inconsistent with its Liberal values."[38] Indeed, illiberal U.S. foreign policy is as old as the United States itself, producing what Walter LaFeber calls "the continuing contradiction . . . between the principle of self-determination, whose value has been self-evident to the U.S. mind, and the expansion of their own nation's power, whose value has also been self-evident."[39]

Philosophers and leaders alike have typically sought to resolve this contradiction by arguing that liberal ideology motivates illiberal foreign policies only within strict boundaries and with good long-term intentions. Following Immanuel Kant, liberals see the spread of liberalism as the surest path to perpetual peace, justifying the overthrow of "barbarous governments" and "outlaw states" to achieve it.[40] Yet liberalism also mandates that such violations of sovereignty be temporary: as Kant writes in his second preliminary article for perpetual peace, "A state is not, like the ground which it occupies, a piece of property. . . . [T]o incorporate it into another state, like a graft, is to destroy its existence as a moral person."[41] To the liberal eye, regime change looks very different from annexation even if both are forcibly achieved. As Woodrow Wilson stated, "Territorial integrity is not destroyed by armed intervention; it is destroyed by the retention of territory."[42] Accordingly, both annexation and imperialism defy liberal ideals, forcing liberal theorists in nineteenth-century Britain and France to justify their empires by turning to social norms or civilizing missions and ultimately making those empires "self-liquidating."[43]

If U.S. foreign policy seems largely consistent with this liberal vision from a twenty-first-century perspective, the case studies indicate that this congruity is due more to coincidence than to causality. Democratic institutions helped steer U.S. foreign policy away from annexation not by fostering respect for foreign peoples but by making their assimilation incompatible with U.S. leaders' xenophobia. Liberalism's saturation of U.S. political thought notwithstanding, nineteenth-century U.S. foreign policy was decidedly illiberal. From Franklin to Jefferson to Jackson to Polk, U.S. leaders eagerly despoiled neighbors of their lands with little regard to international or local wishes, and they oversaw an extensive campaign of ethnic cleansing to remove Native American tribes from desirable frontier lands.[44]

Domestic impact theory helps us understand why a liberal democracy would do something so completely antithetical to its core values of life, liberty, and the pursuit of happiness. As Michael Mann observes, "Democracy has always carried with it the possibility that the majority might tyrannize minorities, and this possibility carries more ominous consequences in certain types of multiethnic environments."[45] Fearful of domestic costs, xenophobic democratic leaders face institutional incentives to marginalize alien inhabitants of territories they annex. They promote resettlement by existing constituents to reinforce their domestic political influence and mold their growing nation to match their normative vision. U.S. leaders did exactly that, using federal land policy coupled with military force to reshape the demographics of western territories along their preferred racial and domestic political lines.[46]

This book suggests that even the most fundamentally liberal element of modern U.S. foreign policy, respecting international borders, owes its origins to a fundamentally illiberal process. U.S. leaders genuinely lack interest in annexing other countries, justifying the view that U.S. hegemony is more benign than others in history. But the reason for such disinterest has less to do with liberalism than with their domestic political incentives and normative biases. Recognizing this can help resolve the apparent contradiction between U.S. liberal ideals and illiberal foreign policy behavior by lowering our expectations of those ideals and revealing the relatively modest limits of U.S. benignity.

Can a book focused on such ancient history speak to modern U.S. foreign policy? Even if the case studies accurately depict U.S. leaders' preoccupations in the nineteenth century, skeptics may argue that the United States has matured since then and question whether the factors that influenced those cases remain relevant today. For example, several cases saw leaders' decision-making slanted by sectionalism: with U.S. domestic politics polarized between North and South, the sectional alignment of each new state presaged meaningful domestic costs for those on the other side. Even if sectionalism hamstrung U.S. efforts in the War of 1812 and nearly prevented the annexation of Texas, does it still matter this long after the Civil War? Many cases also saw leaders' decision-making colored by xenophobia. As Thomas Hietala writes, "American feelings of superiority over other peoples provided a self-serving sanction for taking territory from them, but these same feelings also inhibited expansion by making areas more densely populated by non-white peoples less attractive."[47] Perhaps "race placed hard limits on American expansion" when it came to Cuba and southern Mexico, but hasn't the virulent racism that fueled slavery before the Civil War given way to a more inclusive American melting pot?[48]

Neither sectionalism nor racism vanished after the Civil War. U.S. economic policies continue to differently affect the industrial and agrarian sections of the country, which continue to organize coalitions representing their interests within the U.S. government. As Richard Bensel concludes in his seminal study of American political development, "Sectional competition . . . has been and remains the dominant influence on the American political system."[49] Sectionalism also continues to influence U.S. foreign policy, as Peter Trubowitz writes: "The domestic costs and benefits of decisions about the national interest are never distributed evenly across the country," and therefore "conflicts over American foreign policy have consistently divided the nation along sectional lines."[50] Sectional concerns notably fueled "*domestic* geopolitical alliances" that debated expanding U.S. interests overseas in the 1890s, 1930s, and 1980s.[51]

Similarly, there is a sizable dose of wishful thinking in the notion that U.S. leaders have shed the ethnic nationalism of their forebears—most of whom championed a nation governed by white, Anglo-Saxon, Protestant men—and replaced it with a more inclusive civic nationalism.[52] Scholars have increasingly criticized the concept of a purely civic nationalism divorced from cultural and ethnic characteristics, observing their constant tension even in modern liberal societies.[53] Rogers Smith has demonstrated that "through most of U.S. history, lawmakers pervasively and unapologetically structured U.S. citizenship in terms of illiberal and undemocratic racial, ethnic, and gender hierarchies, for reasons rooted in basic, enduring imperatives of political life."[54] Especially in times of crisis—for example, amidst waves of immigration, wars, or terrorist attacks—ethnic markers tend to dominate civic ones when it comes to identity formation.[55] Despite much progress, recent years have thoroughly undermined the notion that we have moved to a "post-racial" society. One need look no further than post-9/11 discrimination against American Muslims and immigration anxieties to see that the United States remains an imperfect melting pot.[56]

Moreover, sectionalism and racism are not the only fissures capable of raising annexation's domestic costs. Although sectionalism proved to be the most salient divide between U.S. leaders in several cases, the key to generating domestic costs was not sectionalism itself but the fact that annexed populations would gain democratic representation, thereby throwing a wrench into domestic political rivalries regardless of how their lines were drawn. Similarly, xenophobia need not be explicitly racist in order for leaders to label people as too alien to share in governing their state. Differences in language, religion, culture, or historical experience may also suffice. Even principles at the heart of modern international law like nationalism and self-determination are rooted in the notion that diverse groups of people deserve their own states because they are too different to share mutual self-government. As long as these ideas and institutions continue to shape U.S. leaders' perspectives and incentives, domestic impact theory will remain relevant.

International Relations

I have focused on explaining the end of U.S. annexation, but the logic of domestic impact theory is not uniquely American. On the contrary, all leaders whose political authority depends on democratic institutions and who share xenophobic perspectives toward their neighbors should be prone to annexation's domestic costs. Therefore, one intriguing avenue for further research centers on the extent to which domestic impact theory generalizes beyond the United States. If its logic travels, domestic impact theory should deepen our understanding of international territorial ambitions writ large, implying that domestic costs have become a powerful deterrent against annexation in much of the modern world.

Autocratic backsliding notwithstanding, the number of democracies rose from only a dozen in 1900 to nearly one hundred by 2015.[57] Domestic impact theory sees democratic leaders as especially vulnerable to annexation's domestic costs, implying that the spread of democracy may have undercut international territorial ambitions. The democratization of the former Axis powers after World War II may hold particular significance given their previous campaigns of conquest. Indeed, since powerful states can feasibly consider pursuing annexation more frequently than weaker ones, the fact that a preponderant majority of powerful states have been democracies since World War II likely helped fortify the norm against conquest.

Nationalism has also recently spread throughout the world, fueling the belief that foreign peoples belong in foreign states.[58] As Ernest Gellner has described it, nationalism is "inherently xenophobic," fostering favoritism for the in-group and contempt for out-groups.[59] As leaders have cultivated nationalist mythologies and distinct national identities have deepened over time, perceptions of foreign populations as kindred have become limited to special cases like divided nations or large-scale migrations. Despite decades of economic integration and the efforts of ideational entrepreneurs to forge a common European identity, even Europe has fallen back on nationalism and xenophobia in recent years.[60]

Although the topic is beyond the scope of this book, domestic impact theory may thus help us understand why interest in annexation has faded in other countries, as democracy and xenophobia have raised the prospect of its domestic costs for increasing numbers of leaders around the world. Globalization, escalating costs of major war, and other recent developments may be pushing in the same direction, but this book gives us reason to suspect that those modern economic and military transformations may be reinforcing a trend that was already under way for political reasons.[61] In contrast to the brazen rhetoric on display in some of the above case studies, though, domestic costs are more likely to operate in the shadows today. After all, leaders who are uninterested in annexing a neighboring country have little reason to harm relations with that neighbor by broaching the subject. Domestic impact theory may therefore help us understand why annexation has so completely disappeared from the foreign policy conversation in many countries today.

The case studies in this book also have implications for our understanding of the democratic peace. Numerous statistical analyses have found that pairs of democracies have gone to war less frequently than other pairs of states, yet scholars have struggled to uncover why this relationship exists because most potential explanations are belied by other aspects of democracies' foreign policy behavior.[62] Democracies neither externalize norms of nonviolent conflict resolution nor reliably respect other democracies, nor are democratic leaders consistently restrained by public or institutional checks and balances.[63] International conflicts shape leaders' perceptions of how democratic other states are, and democracies have avoided war in several near-miss cases not because of their shared democracy but because one side expected it would lose.[64] Although the democratic peace retains its proponents, others have sought to explain the rarity of war among democracies by turning to their economic characteristics instead.[65]

This book makes no direct claim regarding the relative propensity of democracies to wage war. Nor does it imply that democracies are less prone to international conflicts of interest or more likely to enjoy harmonious relations with each other than other states. On the contrary, domestic impact theory is built on the explicit assumption that leaders often have goals that conflict with those of other domestic and international actors. Yet its findings bear on the democratic peace through the relationship between territorial conflict and war. Numerous studies have found that territorial disputes are more likely to escalate to war than other conflicts of interest and that states are more likely to go to war when engaged in territorial disputes.[66] If democratic leaders are more limited in their territorial ambitions than autocratic leaders, as domestic impact theory predicts, they may be less likely to have territorial conflicts than autocrats (especially with other democracies) and hence may be less likely to end up at war with each other.

Douglas Gibler explains the democratic peace in exactly this way, finding that democracies are less likely to experience territorial conflicts than other states and arguing that this absence of territorial conflict is responsible for their shared peace.[67] The causal arrow in Gibler's territorial peace theory reverses that of domestic impact theory, however, arguing not that democracies are less likely to get into territorial disputes but that states with territorial disputes are less likely to become democracies. In his words, states involved in territorial disputes become increasingly autocratic because "territorial threats lead to centralized public opinion, a centralized party system, centralized institutions, and . . . an increasingly repressive state."[68] Since his argument hinges on the public salience of territorial threats, it is less applicable to expansionist campaigns in which the aggressor's existing territory remains unthreatened, as in most case studies here, nor does it explain why democratic leaders are less likely to desire annexation. There may well be reciprocal causation at work as democratic leaders decline to initiate some potential territorial conflicts, and the absence of territorial threats helps their democratic institutions endure. Further research integrating these theories and examining the roots of international peace is an exciting prospect.

Finally, this book sheds light on the origins and sustainability of the international norm against conquest.[69] With the most powerful states embracing the illegitimacy of forcible annexation, "wars of outright territorial aggrandizement have been rare since 1945," transforming the international system from a battleground into a playing field of "bounded competition."[70] The reduced threat of conquest has enabled many states to enjoy sovereignty despite lacking the institutional strength to survive in more merciless international systems.[71] As I discussed in chapter 1, this norm owes its existence to U.S. leaders, who embedded it firmly at the heart of the United Nations.[72] In Tanisha Fazal's words, "The norm against conquest emerged and became consequential because it was sponsored by the most powerful state in the system."[73]

Why did the most powerful state in the system choose to prohibit international conquest? After all, U.S. leaders have had little reason to fear being conquered in recent decades. In historical perspective, the creation of the norm against conquest seems like a momentous sacrifice: the strongest state voluntarily refraining from using its power to directly rule others. Domestic impact theory makes this otherwise perplexing decision seem obvious: U.S. leaders had long since lost interest in annexing their remaining neighbors for domestic reasons, so the norm against conquest offered a major bargaining chip to other countries (security reassurance) at no cost to themselves (eliminating a foreign policy option they had rejected anyway). In this way, U.S. domestic politics profoundly shaped the course of international relations.

How long will the norm against conquest last? Although it may seem firmly rooted, the norm continues to depend on powerful states' willingness to abide by it, implying several ways it might decay. A revival of U.S. territorial expansion could quickly dissolve the norm by undercutting its enforcement and spurring others to associate expansion with survival. Such a development seems unlikely, however, as it would require an American metamorphosis that undercuts the fundamental roles of democracy and xenophobia in U.S. domestic politics. More likely is a scenario in which the norm is battered by increasing violations from powerful autocracies confident that their nuclear weapons and sizable militaries will deter its sponsors from responding with more than economic retaliation. Russia's annexation of Crimea in 2014 is an example. This dynamic may be exacerbated if U.S. and European leaders stop punishing future violations of the norm, if efforts to reshape international law degrade the norm's moral clarity (by linking self-determination with irredentism), or if a wave of autocratization dilutes annexation's domestic costs for more countries.[74]

Long-term stability is impossible among expansionist states, which manage orderly relations only through mutual deterrence. In the past that deterrence was achieved through shifting alliances, as in balance-of-power Europe, and mutual assured destruction during the Cold War, but stability becomes sustainable only when enough great powers reject annexation and can deter others from pursuing it. North America was profoundly unstable in the early nineteenth century but became the most stable continent in the world as U.S. leaders began promoting firm borders, first with Quebec and later with the rest of Canada and Mexico. If demographic and economic trends support continued U.S. military primacy in the decades to come, U.S. leaders will remain capable of extending their own rejection of annexation to the international system.[75] But erosion of that primacy may hollow out the enforcement of the norm against conquest. Just as domestic factors drove U.S. leaders to abandon annexation, moreover, we should expect them to continue shaping debate about U.S. foreign policy in the future.[76]

Upon winning the 1949 Nobel Peace Prize, the British scientist John Boyd Orr reflected on how "empires one after another have arisen, waxed powerful by wars of conquest, and fallen by internal revolution or attack from without. . . . The increase of territory . . . by force of arms has been the policy of all great powers."[77] Orr's words may have described the past, but they did not define the future. The United States emerged from World War II with the world's strongest economy and a powerful military featuring the newly invented atomic bomb, yet its leaders chose not to translate this advantageous position into territorial gains. After all, it had been generations since annexation's domestic costs, heightened by democracy and xenophobia, had driven U.S. leaders to rule out the annexation of their remaining neighbors. Their enduring lack of interest in annexation despite their unprecedented military power is exceptional when viewed in historical context. But sometimes exceptional results emerge from the basest of causes, and U.S. territorial ambitions were selective from the start.

NOTES

1. The Limits of U.S. Territorial Expansion

Epigraph: Mark Twain, *Following the Equator: A Journey Around the World* (Hartford, CT: American Publishing Co., 1897), 623.

1. Throughout this book, the term "leaders" refers to those individuals who directly shaped U.S. foreign policy. This group varies from case to case but usually includes the president and secretaries of state or war or both, who conduct diplomacy and order military operations; members of the Senate, who ratify treaties; and the House of Representatives, who control the budget available for purchases and wars.

2. Robert Gilpin, *War and Change in World Politics* (New York: Cambridge University Press, 1981); Jack Snyder, *Myths of Empire: Domestic Politics and International Ambition* (Ithaca, NY: Cornell University Press, 1991); Fareed Zakaria, *From Wealth to Power: The Unusual Origins of America's World Role* (Princeton: Princeton University Press, 1998); Jeffrey W. Meiser, *Power and Restraint: The Rise of the United States, 1898–1941* (Washington, DC: Georgetown University Press, 2015).

3. Stephen D. Krasner, *Sovereignty: Organized Hypocrisy* (Princeton: Princeton University Press, 1999), 20–25.

4. Hans J. Morgenthau, *Politics among Nations: The Struggle for Power and Peace* (New York: McGraw Hill, 1993), 124–43; John J. Mearsheimer, *The Tragedy of Great Power Politics* (New York: W. W. Norton 2001), 55–82.

5. Max Weber, "Politics as a Vocation," in *From Max Weber: Essays in Sociology*, ed. H. H. Gerth and C. Wright Mills (New York: Routledge, 2005), 78; Alexander Wendt, *Social Theory of International Politics* (New York: Cambridge University Press, 1999), 201–14.

6. Thomas M. Wilson and Hastings Donnan, eds., *Border Identities: Nation and State at International Frontiers* (New York: Cambridge University Press, 1998); Juliet J. Fall, "Artificial States? On the Enduring Geographical Myth of Natural Borders," *Political Geography* 29, no. 3 (2010): 140–47; James D. Fearon, "Signaling Foreign Policy Interests: Tying Hands versus Sinking Costs," *Journal of Conflict Resolution* 41, no. 1 (1997): 68–90.

7. Michael W. Doyle, *Empires* (Ithaca, NY: Cornell University Press, 1986), 35.

8. Kenneth N. Waltz, *Theory of International Politics* (New York: McGraw-Hill, 1979), 71–72, 121–28; Colin Elman, "Horses for Courses: Why Not Neorealist Theories of Foreign Policy?" *Security Studies* 6, no. 1 (1996): 12–17.

9. Marc Trachtenberg, *A Constructed Peace: The Making of the European Settlement, 1945–1963* (Princeton: Princeton University Press, 1999), 36.

10. Geoffrey Blainey, *The Causes of War* (New York: Free Press, 1988), 59.

11. Paul Kennedy, *The Rise and Fall of the Great Powers: Economic Change and Military Conflict from 1500 to 2000* (New York: Vintage Books, 1987); Stuart J. Kaufman, Richard Little, and William C. Wohlforth, eds., *The Balance of Power in World History* (New York: Palgrave Macmillan, 2007).

12. David Day, *Conquest: How Societies Overwhelm Others* (New York: Oxford University Press, 2008), 3.

13. Charles Tilly, *Coercion, Capital, and European States, AD 990–1990* (Cambridge, MA: Basil Blackwell, 1990), 28.

14. Gilpin, *War and Change*, 106.

15. Zakaria, *From Wealth to Power*.

16. On race's significance in American political development: Desmond King and Rogers M. Smith, "Racial Orders in American Political Development," *American Political Science Review* 99, no. 1 (2005): 75–92; Joseph Lowndes, Julie Novkov, and Dorian T. Warren, eds., *Race and American Political Development* (New York: Routledge, 2008); Mini symposium "American Political Development through the Lens of Race," *Political Research Quarterly* 61, no. 4 (2008): 649–718.

17. Paul Frymer, *Building an American Empire: The Era of Territorial and Political Expansion* (Princeton: Princeton University Press, 2017); Kevin Bruyneel, "Hierarchy and Hybridity: The Internal Postcolonialism of Mid-Nineteenth-Century American Expansionism," in Lowndes, Novkov, and Warren, *Race and American Political Development*, 106–24.

18. Julie Novkov, *Racial Union: Law, Intimacy, and the White State in Alabama, 1865–1954* (Ann Arbor: University of Michigan Press, 2008); Moon-Ho Jung, *Coolies and Cane: Race, Labor, and Sugar in the Age of Emancipation* (Baltimore: Johns Hopkins University Press, 2006); Stephen Skowronek, "The Reassociation of Ideas and Purposes: Racism, Liberalism, and the American Political Tradition," *American Political Science Review* 100, no. 3 (2006): 385–401; Nikhil P. Singh, *Black Is a Country: Race and the Unfinished Struggle for Democracy* (Cambridge: Harvard University Press, 2004); Richard F. Bensel, *Yankee Leviathan: The Origins of Central State Authority in America, 1859–1877* (New York: Cambridge University Press, 1990).

19. See chapters 3, 6, 7; Stephen Skowronek, *Building a New American State: The Expansion of National Administrative Capacities, 1877–1920* (New York: Cambridge University Press, 1982).

20. Hilde E. Restad, *American Exceptionalism: An Idea that Made a Nation and Remade the World* (New York: Routledge, 2015); Godfrey Hodgson, *The Myth of American Exceptionalism* (New Haven: Yale University Press, 2009); Seymour M. Lipset, *American Exceptionalism: A Double-Edged Sword* (New York: W. W. Norton, 1996).

21. UN Charter art. 2, para. 4; cf. G. John Ikenberry, *After Victory: Institutions, Strategic Restraint, and the Rebuilding of Order after Major Wars* (Princeton: Princeton University Press, 2001), chaps. 5–7; Oona A. Hathaway and Scott J. Shapiro, *The Internationalists: How a Radical Plan to Outlaw War Remade the World* (New York: Simon and Schuster, 2017).

22. Ray S. Baker and William E. Dodd, eds., *The Public Papers of Woodrow Wilson*, vol. 2 (New York: Harper, 1925), 407; cf. George W. Egerton, *Great Britain and the Creation of the League of Nations: Strategy, Politics, and International Organization, 1914–1919* (Chapel Hill: University of North Carolina Press, 1978), 131.

23. Stephen C. Schlesinger, *Act of Creation: The Founding of the United Nations* (Boulder, CO: Westview, 2003), 111.

24. Harry S. Truman, *Memoirs*, vol. 2 (Garden City, NY: Doubleday, 1956), 333; George H. W. Bush, "Address on Iraq's Invasion of Kuwait" (speech, Washington, DC, August 8, 1990), Miller Center, https://millercenter.org/the-presidency/presidential-speeches/august-8-1990-address-iraqs-invasion-kuwait.

25. Charles Tilly, "Reflections on the History of European State-Making," in *The Formation of National States in Western Europe*, ed. Charles Tilly (Princeton: Princeton University Press, 1975), 24.

26. Richard N. Rosecrance, *The Rise of the Trading State: Commerce and Conquest in the Modern World* (New York: Basic Books, 1986); cf. Robert O. Keohane and Joseph S. Nye, *Power and Interdependence: World Politics in Transition* (Boston: Little, Brown, 1977).

27. Robert H. Jackson, *Quasi-States: Sovereignty, International Relations and the Third World* (New York: Cambridge University Press, 1993); Jeffrey Herbst, "War and the State in Africa," *International Security* 14, no. 4 (1990): 117–39.

28. Alexander Hamilton, "The Federalist No. 7," in *The Federalist: A Commentary on the Constitution of the United States*, ed. Robert Scigliano (New York: Random House, 2001), 34; cf. John A. Vasquez, *The War Puzzle* (New York: Cambridge University Press, 1993), 130; Gary Goertz, Paul F. Diehl, and Alexandru Balas, *The Puzzle of Peace: The Evolution of Peace in the International System* (New York: Oxford University Press, 2016).

29. Robert Jervis, "Theories of War in an Era of Leading-Power Peace," *American Political Science Review* 96, no. 1 (2002): 1–14.

30. Martha Finnemore and Kathryn Sikkink, "International Norm Dynamics and Political Change," *International Organization* 52, no. 4 (1998): 887–917; Tanisha M. Fazal, *State Death: The Politics and Geography of Conquest, Occupation, and Annexation* (Princeton: Princeton University Press, 2007), 47.

31. Nuno P. Monteiro, *Theory of Unipolar Politics* (New York: Cambridge University Press, 2014), 63; cf. Mearsheimer, *Tragedy of Great Power Politics*, 5.

32. Will Dunham, "Kerry Condemns Russia's 'Incredible Act of Aggression' in Ukraine," *Reuters*, March 2, 2014, http://www.reuters.com/article/2014/03/02/us-ukraine-crisis-usa-kerry-idUSBREA210DG20140302.

33. M. Taylor Fravel, "International Relations Theory and China's Rise: Assessing China's Potential for Territorial Expansion," *International Studies Review* 12, no. 4 (2010): 507.

34. Waltz, *Theory of International Politics*; Mearsheimer, *Tragedy of Great Power Politics*.

35. Gilpin, *War and Change*, chap. 5; Kennedy, *Rise and Fall of the Great Powers*; Snyder, *Myths of Empire*.

36. Zakaria, *From Wealth to Power*; Scott A. Silverstone, *Divided Union: The Politics of War in the Early American Republic* (Ithaca, NY: Cornell University Press, 2004); Meiser, *Power and Restraint*.

37. See chapters 3–7; Colin Elman, "Extending Offensive Realism: The Louisiana Purchase and America's Rise to Regional Hegemony," *American Political Science Review* 98, no. 4 (2004): 563–76.

38. Blainey, *Causes of War*, 59.

39. Silverstone, *Divided Union*, 59–62.

40. Zakaria, *From Wealth to Power*, 11.

41. Meiser, *Power and Restraint*, xvi, 12.

42. Snyder, *Myths of Empire*, 49, 257.

43. Arthur M. Schlesinger, *The Imperial Presidency* (New York: Houghton Mifflin, 2004).

44. Sean Lynn-Jones, "Realism and America's Rise: A Review Essay," *International Security* 23, no. 2 (1998): 170.

45. Waltz, *Theory of International Politics*; Jeffrey W. Taliaferro, "Security Seeking under Anarchy: Defensive Realism Revisited," *International Security* 25, no. 3 (2000/01): 128–61.

46. Mearsheimer, *Tragedy of Great Power Politics*, 238; cf. Elman, "Extending Offensive Realism"; Christopher Layne, "The 'Poster Child for Offensive Realism': America as a Global Hegemon," *Security Studies* 12, no. 2 (2002): 120–64.

47. Carl Kaysen, "Is War Obsolete? A Review Essay," *International Security* 14, no. 4 (1990): 53–57; Stephen Van Evera, *Causes of War: Power and the Roots of Conflict* (Ithaca, NY: Cornell University Press, 1999), chap. 5.

48. Stephen G. Brooks, *Producing Security: Multinational Corporations, Globalization, and the Changing Calculus of Conflict* (Princeton: Princeton University Press, 2005), 61.

49. Stephen Van Evera, "Why Europe Matters, Why the Third World Doesn't: American Grand Strategy after the Cold War," *Journal of Strategic Studies* 13, no. 2 (1990): 5.

50. Stephen G. Brooks, "The Globalization of Production and the Changing Benefits of Conquest," *Journal of Conflict Resolution* 43, no. 5 (1999): 655–66.

51. Richard Cobden, *The Political Writings of Richard Cobden* (London: Unwin, 1903), 225; Norman Angell, *The Great Illusion* (New York: G. P. Putnam's Sons, 1933); Dale C. Copeland, *Economic Interdependence and War* (Princeton: Princeton University Press, 2015), 18–20.

52. Erik Gartzke, "The Capitalist Peace," *American Journal of Political Science* 51, no. 1 (2007): 172; cf. Patrick J. McDonald, *The Invisible Hand of Peace: Capitalism, the War Machine, and International Relations Theory* (New York: Cambridge University Press, 2009).

53. Lars-Erik Cederman, T. Camber Warren, and Didier Sornette, "Testing Clausewitz: Nationalism, Mass Mobilization, and the Severity of War," *International Organization* 65, no. 4 (2011): 605–38; Mike Bourne, *Arming Conflict: The Proliferation of Small Arms* (New York: Palgrave Macmillan, 2007).

54. John Mueller, *Retreat from Doomsday: The Obsolescence of Major War* (New York: Basic Books, 1989).

55. Kenneth N. Waltz, "Nuclear Myths and Political Realities," *American Political Science Review* 84, no. 3 (1990): 730–45.

56. William C. Wohlforth, "The Stability of a Unipolar World," *International Security* 24, no. 1 (1999): 5–41.

57. Western Europe's GDP was roughly $160 billion in 1820 versus $7.5 trillion in 2001, while China's was roughly $230 billion in 1820 versus $4.5 trillion in 2001: Angus Maddison, *The World Economy: Historical Statistics* (Paris: OECD, 2003), 249.

58. Peter Liberman, *Does Conquest Pay?* (Princeton: Princeton University Press, 1996), 4.

59. Paul K. MacDonald, "Is Imperial Rule Obsolete?: Assessing the Barriers to Overseas Adventurism," *Security Studies* 18, no. 1 (2009): 79–114.

60. Richard W. Maass, "Salami Tactics: Faits Accompli and the Future of U.S.–Russian Relations," paper presented at the International Studies Association Annual Convention, Baltimore, February 22–25, 2017; Glenn Snyder, "The Balance of Power and the Balance of Terror," in Paul Seabury, ed., *The Balance of Power* (San Francisco: Chandler, 1965), 184–201.

61. Liberman, *Does Conquest Pay?*, chap. 3; Stephen Van Evera, "Hypotheses on Nationalism and War," *International Security* 18, no. 4 (1994): 5–39. Mearsheimer ultimately explains U.S. reluctance to annex Canada and Mexico by claiming that "because of the power of nationalism, subduing the people in those countries and turning them into Americans would have been a difficult if not impossible task": Mearsheimer, *Tragedy of Great Power Politics*, 488, n. 18. Yet Canadian and Mexican nationalism did not develop on a sufficient scale until well after U.S. leaders resolved not to pursue those territories, and U.S. decisions not to pursue them had little to do with the potential difficulty of subduing their populations (see chapters 5 and 6).

62. Robert Jervis, *Perception and Misperception in International Politics* (Princeton: Princeton University Press, 1976); Jack S. Levy, "Misperception and the Causes of War: Theoretical Linkages and Analytical Problems," *World Politics* 36, no. 1 (1983): 76–99.

63. Randall L. Schweller, "Managing the Rise of Great Powers: History and Theory," in *Engaging China: The Management of an Emerging Power*, ed. Alastair I. Johnston and Robert S. Ross (London: Routledge, 1999), 3.

64. William A. Williams, *The Tragedy of American Diplomacy* (New York: W. W. Norton, 1972), 20, critiquing Samuel F. Bemis, *A Diplomatic History of the United States*, 5th ed. (New York: Holt, Rinehart and Winston, 1965), 463–75.

65. Walter LaFeber, *The New Empire: An Interpretation of American Expansion, 1860–1898* (Ithaca, NY: Cornell University Press, 1963), 1; cf. Charles S. Campbell, *The Transformation of American Foreign Relations, 1865–1900* (New York: Harper and Row, 1976); Lloyd C. Gardner, Walter F. LaFeber, and Thomas J. McCormick, *Creation of the American Empire*, vol. 1 (Chicago: Rand McNally, 1973); Ernest N. Paolino, *The Foundations of the American Empire: William Henry Seward and U.S. Foreign Policy* (Ithaca, NY: Cornell University Press, 1973); William A. Williams, *The Roots of the Modern American Empire: A Study of the Growth and Shaping of Social Consciousness in a Marketplace Society* (New York: Random House, 1969); LaFeber, *New Empire*; R. W. Van Alstyne, *The Rising American Empire* (Oxford: Basil Blackwell, 1960).

66. Stuart C. Miller, *Benevolent Assimilation: The American Conquest of the Philippines, 1899–1903* (New Haven: Yale University Press, 1982), 4.

67. A. G. Hopkins, *American Empire: A Global History* (Princeton: Princeton University Press, 2018); Adam Burns, *American Imperialism: The Territorial Expansion of the United States, 1783–2013* (Edinburgh: Edinburgh University Press, 2017); Richard H. Immerman, *Empire for Liberty: A History of American Imperialism from Benjamin Franklin to Paul Wolfowitz* (Princeton: Princeton University Press, 2010); Walter Nugent, *Habits of Empire: A History of American Expansion* (New York: Alfred A. Knopf, 2008); Niall Ferguson, *Colossus: The Rise and Fall of the American Empire* (New York: Penguin Books, 2004); Andrew J. Bacevich, *American Empire: The Realities and Consequences of U.S. Diplomacy* (Cambridge: Harvard University Press, 2002); cf. Walter L. Hixson, *The Myth of American Diplomacy: National Identity and U.S. Foreign Policy* (New Haven: Yale

University Press, 2008), 13; Ian Tyrrell, *Transnational Nation: United States History in Global Perspective since 1789* (New York: Palgrave Macmillan, 2007), chap. 10; Thomas Bender, *A Nation among Nations: America's Place in World History* (New York: Hill and Wang, 2006), chap. 4.

68. For a related critique: Paul K. MacDonald, "Those Who Forget Historiography Are Doomed to Republish It: Empire, Imperialism and Contemporary Debates about American Power," *Review of International Studies* 35, no. 1 (2009): 45–67. Even U.S. foreign policy in the 1920s and 1930s is better described using neutrality than isolationism: Brooke L. Blower, "From Isolationism to Neutrality: A New Framework for Understanding American Political Culture, 1919–1941," *Diplomatic History* 38, no. 2 (2014): 345–76.

69. Cf. Victor Bulmer-Thomas, *Empire in Retreat: The Past, Present, and Future of the United States* (New Haven: Yale University Press, 2018), 129–30; Charles S. Maier, *Among Empires: American Ascendancy and Its Predecessors* (Cambridge: Harvard University Press, 2007), 143–44.

70. William A. Williams, *Empire as a Way of Life* (New York: Oxford University Press, 1980), 96; cf. 100–102; William A. Williams, *The Roots of the Modern American Empire: A Study of the Growth and Shaping of Social Consciousness in a Marketplace Society* (New York: Random House, 1969).

71. Walter LaFeber, *The American Age: United States Foreign Policy at Home and Abroad*, 2nd ed. (New York: W. W. Norton, 1994), 171; cf. 157; LaFeber, *New Empire*.

72. Walter A. McDougall, *Promised Land, Crusader State: The American Encounter with the World since 1776* (New York: Houghton Mifflin, 1997), 215–16; Frank Ninkovich, *The Global Republic: America's Inadvertent Rise to World Power* (Chicago: University of Chicago Press, 2014), chap. 2. Suggestions that prohibitive military costs prevented further U.S. annexations have been understandably rarer; an exception is Ferguson, *Colossus*, 40, 60.

73. Frederick Merk, *Manifest Destiny and Mission in American History* (New York: Alfred A. Knopf, 1963), 215.

74. Reginald Horsman, *Race and Manifest Destiny: The Origins of American Racial Anglo-Saxonism* (Cambridge: Harvard University Press, 1981), 245.

75. Thomas R. Hietala, *Manifest Design: American Exceptionalism and Empire* (Ithaca, NY: Cornell University Press, 2003), xvii, 134; cf. 158–66.

76. Cf. Michael H. Hunt, *Ideology and U.S. Foreign Policy* (New Haven: Yale University Press, 1987), chap. 3; D. W. Meinig, *The Shaping of America: A Geographical Perspective on 500 Years of History*, vol. 2 (New Haven: Yale University Press, 1993), 188–96; Walter L. Hixson, *The Myth of American Diplomacy: National Identity and U.S. Foreign Policy* (New Haven: Yale University Press, 2008), chaps. 1–4.

77. Eric T. L. Love, *Race over Empire: Racism and U.S. Imperialism, 1865–1900* (Chapel Hill: University of North Carolina Press, 2004), 199.

78. David C. Hendrickson, *Union, Nation, or Empire: The American Debate over International Relations, 1789–1941* (Lawrence: University Press of Kansas, 2009), 60–62, 113–14, 177, 181–84.

79. Frymer, *Building an American Empire*, 17, 15; cf. 175–76.

80. For a similar argument on U.S. anticolonialism and imperialism: Jay Sexton, *The Monroe Doctrine: Empire and Nation in Nineteenth-Century America* (New York: Hill and Wang, 2011), 5.

81. Nugent, *Habits of Empire*, chaps. 1–4; George C. Herring, *From Colony to Superpower: U.S. Foreign Relations since 1776* (New York: Oxford University Press, 2008), 26–34; David Mayers, *Dissenting Voices in America's Rise to Power* (New York: Cambridge University Press, 2007), chap. 1; Hendrickson, *Union, Nation, or Empire*, 47–53.

82. E.g., Frymer, *Building an American Empire*.

83. E.g., Nugent, *Habits of Empire*.

84. David Narrett, *Adventurism and Empire: The Struggle for Mastery in the Louisiana–Florida Borderlands, 1762–1803* (Chapel Hill: University of North Carolina Press, 2015), chaps. 8–10; William C. Davis, *The Rogue Republic: How Would-Be Patriots Waged the Shortest Revolution in American History* (Boston: Houghton Mifflin Harcourt, 2011); James G. Cusick, *The Other War of 1812: The Patriot War and the American Invasion of Spanish East Florida* (Gainesville: University Press of Florida, 2003); James E. Lewis Jr., *The American Union and the Problem of Neighborhood: The United States and the Collapse of the Spanish Empire, 1783–1829* (Chapel Hill: University of North Carolina Press, 1998); Joseph B. Smith, *The Plot to Steal Florida: James Madison's Phony War* (New York: Arbor House, 1983); Isaac J. Cox, *The West Florida Controversy, 1798–1813* (Gloucester, MA: Peter Smith, 1967); Rembert W. Patrick, *Florida Fiasco: Rampant Rebels on the Georgia–Florida Border, 1810–1815* (Athens: University of Georgia Press, 1954).

85. Recent contributions include John P. Bowes, *Land Too Good for Indians: Northern Indian Removal* (Norman: University of Oklahoma Press, 2016); Blake A. Watson, *Buying America from the Indians: "Johnson v. McIntosh" and the History of Native Land Rights* (Norman: University of Oklahoma Press, 2012); Lindsay G. Robertson, *Conquest by Law: How the Discovery of America Dispossessed Indigenous Peoples of Their Lands* (New York: Oxford University Press, 2005); Frederick E. Hoxie, Ronald Hoffman, and Peter J. Albert, eds., *Native Americans in the Early Republic* (Charlottesville: University of Virginia Press, 1999); R. Douglas Hurt, *The Ohio Frontier: Crucible of the Old Northwest, 1720–1830* (Bloomington: Indiana University Press, 1998).

86. On Jackson: Robert V. Remini, *Andrew Jackson and His Indian Wars* (New York: Viking, 2001); Anthony F. C. Wallace, *The Long, Bitter Trail: Andrew Jackson and the Indians* (New York: Hill and Wang, 1993); Ronald Satz, *American Indian Policy in the Jacksonian Era* (Lincoln: University of Nebraska Press, 1975). On a longer view of removal: Anthony F. C. Wallace, *Jefferson and the Indians: The Tragic Fate of the First Americans* (Cambridge: Harvard University Press, 1999); Francis P. Prucha, *American Indian Treaties: The History of a Political Anomaly* (Berkeley: University of California Press, 1997); Francis P. Prucha, *The Great Father: The United States Government and the American Indians* (Lincoln: University of Nebraska Press, 1984).

87. Cf. Tyrrell, *Transnational Nation*, 78; Remini, *Andrew Jackson and His Indian Wars*, 278–79; Michael D. Green, *The Politics of Indian Removal* (Lincoln: University of Nebraska Press, 1982), 45–46.

88. The best recent account is John Ferling, *Almost a Miracle: The American Victory in the War of Independence* (New York: Oxford University Press, 2007); cf. Gustave Lanctot, *Canada and the American Revolution, 1774–1783* (Cambridge: Harvard University Press, 1967). Mark R. Anderson, *The Battle for the Fourteenth Colony: America's War of Liberation in Canada, 1774–1776* (Lebanon, NH: University Press of New England, 2013) focuses on the 1775 invasion of Quebec; cf. William Duane, *Canada and the Continental Congress* (Philadelphia: Edward Gaskill, 1850); George M. Wrong, *Canada and the American Revolution: The Disruption of the First British Empire* (New York: Macmillan,

1935); James M. Callahan, *American Foreign Policy in Canadian Relations* (New York: Macmillan, 1937).

89. Richard W. Maass, "'Difficult to Relinquish Territory Which Had Been Conquered': Expansionism and the War of 1812," *Diplomatic History* 39, no. 1 (2015): 70–97, dismantles the myth of an expansionist War of 1812, building on many strong histories, including Troy Bickham, *The Weight of Vengeance: The United States, the British Empire, and the War of 1812* (New York: Oxford University Press, 2012); Donald R. Hickey, *The War of 1812: A Forgotten Conflict* (Chicago: University of Illinois Press, 2012); Alan Taylor, *The Civil War of 1812: American Citizens, British Subjects, Irish Rebels, and Indian Allies* (New York: Alfred A. Knopf, 2010); J. C. A. Stagg, *Mr. Madison's War: Politics, Diplomacy, and Warfare in the Early American Republic, 1783–1830* (Princeton: Princeton University Press, 1983); Roger H. Brown, *Republic in Peril: 1812* (New York: W. W. Norton, 1971); Reginald Horsman, *The Causes of the War of 1812* (Philadelphia: University of Pennsylvania Press, 1962); Bradford Perkins, *Prologue to War: England and the United States, 1805–1812* (Los Angeles: University of California Press, 1961).

90. The best studies of U.S. northward ambitions in this period include Francis M. Carroll, *A Good and Wise Measure: The Search for the Canadian–American Boundary, 1783–1842* (Toronto: University of Toronto Press, 2003); Reginald C. Stuart, *United States Expansionism and British North America, 1775–1871* (Chapel Hill: University of North Carolina Press, 1988); Howard Jones, *To the Webster–Ashburton Treaty: A Study in Anglo-American Relations, 1783–1843* (Chapel Hill: University of North Carolina Press, 1977). On Oregon: Walter R. Borneman, *Polk: The Man Who Transformed the Presidency and America* (New York: Random House, 2009), 150–70, 216–24; Robert W. Merry, *A Country of Vast Designs: James K. Polk, the Mexican War and the Conquest of the American Continent* (New York: Simon and Schuster, 2009); Nugent, *Habits of Empire*, chap. 6; David M. Pletcher, *The Diplomacy of Annexation: Texas, Oregon, and the Mexican War* (Columbia: University of Missouri Press, 1973).

91. The most notable work here is still David E. Shi, "Seward's Attempt to Annex British Columbia, 1865–1869," *Pacific Historical Review* 47, no. 2 (1978): 217–38. On the Fenian raids: Brian Jenkins, *Fenians and Anglo-American Relations during Reconstruction* (Ithaca, NY: Cornell University Press, 1969); Hereward Senior, *The Last Invasion of Canada: The Fenian Raids, 1866–1870* (Toronto: Dundurn Press, 1991); Peter Vronsky, *Ridgeway: The American Fenian Invasion and the 1866 Battle that Made Canada* (Toronto: Allen Lane, 2011). On the Red River rebellion: J. M. Bumsted, *The Red River Rebellion* (Winnipeg: Watson and Dwyer, 1996); J. M. Bumsted, *Reporting the Resistance: Alexander Begg and Joseph Hargrave on the Red River Resistance* (Winnipeg: University of Manitoba Press, 2003). For contemporary public opinion on annexation north and south of the border: Donald F. Warner, *The Idea of Continental Union: Agitation for the Annexation of Canada to the United States, 1849–1893* (Lexington: University of Kentucky Press, 1960).

92. Matthew Karp, *This Vast Southern Empire: Slaveholders at the Helm of American Foreign Policy* (Cambridge: Harvard University Press, 2016); Amy S. Greenberg, *A Wicked War: Polk, Clay, Lincoln, and the 1846 U.S. Invasion of Mexico* (New York: Alfred A. Knopf, 2012); Mayers, *Dissenting Voices*, chap. 5; Michael A. Morrison, *Slavery and the American West: The Eclipse of Manifest Destiny* (Chapel Hill: University of North Carolina Press, 1997); William E. Weeks, *Building the Continental Empire: American Expansion from the Revolution to the Civil War* (Chicago: Ivan R. Dee, 1996); Karl M. Schmitt,

Mexico and the United States, 1821–1973: Conflict and Coexistence (New York: John Wiley and Sons, 1974); Pletcher, *Diplomacy of Annexation*; Frederick Merk, *Slavery and the Annexation of Texas* (New York: Alfred A. Knopf, 1972); Kinley J. Brauer, *Cotton versus Conscience: Massachusetts Whig Politics and Southwestern Expansion, 1843–1848* (Lexington: University of Kentucky Press, 1967); Justin H. Smith, *The Annexation of Texas* (New York: Barnes and Noble, 1941).

93. Merk, *Manifest Destiny and Mission*, chaps. 5–8; Horsman, *Race and Manifest Destiny*, chaps. 11–13; Hietala, *Manifest Design*.

94. Robert E. May, *Slavery, Race, and Conquest in the Tropics: Lincoln, Douglas, and the Future of Latin America* (New York: Cambridge University Press, 2013); Robert E. May, *Manifest Destiny's Underworld: Filibustering in Antebellum America* (Chapel Hill: University of North Carolina Press, 2002); Robert E. May, *The Southern Dream of a Caribbean Empire, 1854–1861* (Baton Rouge: Louisiana State University Press, 1973); cf. Philip S. Foner, *A History of Cuba and Its Relations with the United States*, 2 vols. (New York: International Publishers, 1962/1963).

95. Love, *Race over Empire*, chap. 2; cf. William J. Nelson, *Almost a Territory: America's Attempt to Annex the Dominican Republic* (Newark: University of Delaware Press, 1990); Luis Martínez-Fernández, "Caudillos, Annexationism, and the Rivalry between Empires in the Dominican Republic, 1844–1874," *Diplomatic History* 17, no. 4 (1993): 571–98; G. Pope Atkins and Larman C. Wilson, *The Dominican Republic and the United States: From Imperialism to Transnationalism* (Athens: University of Georgia Press, 1998), 14–27.

96. Nick Cleaver, *Grover Cleveland's New Foreign Policy: Arbitration, Neutrality, and the Dawn of American Empire* (New York: Palgrave Macmillan, 2014); Richard F. Hamilton, *President McKinley, War and Empire*, 2 vols. (New Brunswick, NJ: Transaction Publishers, 2006/2007); John L. Tone, *War and Genocide in Cuba, 1895–1898* (Chapel Hill: University of North Carolina Press, 2006); David M. Pletcher, *The Diplomacy of Trade and Investment: American Economic Expansion in the Hemisphere, 1865–1900* (Columbia: University of Missouri Press, 1998); John L. Offner, *An Unwanted War: The Diplomacy of the United States and Spain over Cuba, 1895–1898* (Chapel Hill: University of North Carolina Press, 1992); Louis A. Pérez Jr., *Cuba between Empires, 1878–1902* (Pittsburgh: University of Pittsburgh Press, 1983); Lester D. Langley, *Struggle for the American Mediterranean: United States–European Rivalry in the Gulf-Caribbean, 1776–1904* (Athens: University of Georgia Press, 1976); H. Wayne Morgan, *America's Road to Empire: The War with Spain and Overseas Expansion* (New York: John Wiley and Sons, 1965).

97. William M. Morgan, *Pacific Gibraltar: U.S.–Japanese Rivalry over the Annexation of Hawai'i, 1885–1898* (Annapolis: Naval Institute Press, 2011), an excellent reevaluation of Hawaiian annexation, falls into this category; cf. Love, *Race over Empire*, chap. 4; David M. Pletcher, *The Diplomacy of Involvement: American Economic Expansion across the Pacific, 1784–1900* (Columbia: University of Missouri Press, 2001); Thomas J. Osborne, *"Empire Can Wait": American Opposition to Hawaiian Annexation, 1893–1898* (Kent, OH: Kent State University Press, 1981); Merze Tate, *Hawaii: Reciprocity or Annexation* (East Lansing: Michigan State University Press, 1968); Merze Tate, *The United States and the Hawaiian Kingdom: A Political History* (New Haven: Yale University Press, 1965); Sylvester K. Stevens, *American Expansion in Hawaii, 1842–1898* (New York: Russell and Russell, 1945).

98. Susan K. Harris, *God's Arbiters: Americans and the Philippines, 1898–1902* (New York: Oxford University Press, 2011); Paul A. Kramer, *The Blood of Government: Race, Empire, the United States, and the Philippines* (Chapel Hill: University of North Carolina Press, 2006); Sam Erman, *Almost Citizens: Puerto Rico, the U.S. Constitution, and Empire* (New York: Cambridge University Press, 2019); Gerald L. Neuman and Tomiko Brown-Nagin, eds., *Reconsidering the Insular Cases: The Past and Future of the American Empire* (Cambridge: Harvard University Press, 2015); Charles R. Venator-Santiago, *Puerto Rico and the Origins of US Global Empire: The Disembodied Shade* (New York: Routledge, 2015); César J. Ayala and Rafael Bernabe, *Puerto Rico in the American Century: A History since 1898* (Chapel Hill: University of North Carolina Press, 2007); Bartholomew H. Sparrow, *The* Insular Cases *and the Emergence of American Empire* (Lawrence: University Press of Kansas, 2006); Gary Lawson and Guy Seidman, *The Constitution of Empire: Territorial Expansion and American Legal History* (New Haven: Yale University Press, 2004); Christina D. Burnett and Burke Marshall, eds., *Foreign in a Domestic Sense: Puerto Rico, American Expansion, and the Constitution* (Durham: Duke University Press, 2001).

2. Explaining Annexation

1. Theda Skocpol, "Bringing the State Back In: Strategies of Analysis in Current Research," in *Bringing the State Back In*, ed. Peter B. Evans, Dietrich Rueschemeyer, and Theda Skocpol (New York: Cambridge University Press, 1985), 16; cf. Fareed Zakaria, *From Wealth to Power: The Unusual Origins of America's World Role* (Princeton: Princeton University Press, 1998), 38; Robert Kagan, "Power and Weakness," *Policy Review* 113 (2002): 3–28.

2. Geoffrey Blainey, *The Causes of War* (New York: Free Press, 1988), 149.

3. Robert Gilpin, *War and Change in World Politics* (New York: Cambridge University Press, 1981); G. John Ikenberry, *After Victory: Institutions, Strategic Restraint, and the Rebuilding of Order after Major Wars* (Princeton: Princeton University Press, 2001).

4. John J. Mearsheimer, *The Tragedy of Great Power Politics* (New York: W. W. Norton, 2001), 157.

5. Paul Kennedy, *The Rise and Fall of the Great Powers: Economic Change and Military Conflict from 1500 to 2000* (New York: Vintage Books, 1987), 321–23.

6. Brantly Womack, ed., *China's Rise in Historical Perspective* (Lanham, MD: Rowman and Littlefield, 2010).

7. Hans J. Morgenthau, *Politics among Nations: The Struggle for Power and Peace* (New York: McGraw Hill, 1993), 124–43; Mearsheimer, *Tragedy of Great Power Politics*, 55–82.

8. This generalization excepts strategic needs for specific resources; e.g., Rosemary A. Kelanic, "The Petroleum Paradox: Oil, Coercive Vulnerability, and Great Power Behavior," *Security Studies* 25, no. 2 (2016), 181–213; Robert G. Albion, *Forests and Sea Power: The Timber Problem of the Royal Navy 1652–1862* (Annapolis: Naval Institute Press, 1926).

9. Jeffrey Herbst, *States and Power in Africa: Comparative Lessons in Authority and Control* (Princeton: Princeton University Press, 2000), 16, 35–57. Precolonial Africa's population density in 1750 was roughly 2.7 persons/km^2 versus 45 persons/km^2 in modern Iran, 229 persons/km^2 in modern Germany, and 7,148 persons/km^2 in modern Singapore. At the time of their acquisition, territories annexed by the United

States were home to fewer than 0.5 persons/km² on average: B. R. Mitchell, *International Historical Statistics: The Americas, 1750–1993* (London: Macmillan, 1998).

10. Southeast Asia's population density in 1700 was roughly 5 persons/km²: James C. Scott, *Seeing Like a State: How Certain Schemes to Improve the Human Condition Have Failed* (New Haven: Yale University Press, 1998), 185–86.

11. John L. Gaddis, *Strategies of Containment: A Critical Appraisal of Postwar American National Security Policy* (New York: Oxford University Press, 1982), 29, 278.

12. Jack Snyder, *Myths of Empire: Domestic Politics and International Ambition* (Ithaca, NY: Cornell University Press, 1991), 10.

13. Stacie E. Goddard, *Indivisible Territory and the Politics of Legitimacy: Jerusalem and Northern Ireland* (New York: Cambridge University Press, 2009).

14. William C. Wohlforth, *The Elusive Balance: Power and Perceptions during the Cold War* (Ithaca, NY: Cornell University Press, 1993), 1–5; Gabriel A. Almond and Stephen J. Genco, "Clouds, Clocks, and the Study of Politics," *World Politics* 29, no. 4 (1977): 502–4; Mearsheimer, *Tragedy of Great Power Politics*, 55–57.

15. Robert Jervis, "Cooperation under the Security Dilemma," *World Politics* 30, no. 2 (1978): 179. This prospect of successful policies having undesirable side effects distinguishes domestic impact theory from theories of audience costs resulting from failed policies: James D. Fearon, "Domestic Political Audiences and the Escalation of International Disputes," *American Political Science Review* 88, no. 3 (1994): 577–92.

16. Rogers Smith, *Civic Ideals: Conflicting Visions of Citizenship in U.S. History* (New Haven: Yale University Press, 1997), 31. For this reason state admissions remained highly contentious even after the Civil War: Charles Stewart and Barry Weingast, "Stacking the Senate, Changing the Nation: Republican Rotten Boroughs, Statehood Politics, and American Political Development," *Studies in American Political Development* 6, no. 2 (1992): 223–71.

17. Amy Oakes, "Diversionary War and Argentina's Invasion of the Falkland Islands," *Security Studies* 15, no. 3 (2006): 431–63; Jaroslav Tir, "Territorial Diversion: Diversionary Theory of War and Territorial Conflict," *Journal of Politics* 72, no. 2 (2010): 413–25.

18. Dietrich Rueschemeyer and Peter B. Evans, "The State and Economic Transformation: Toward an Analysis of the Conditions Underlying Effective Intervention," in Evans, Rueschemeyer, and Skocpol, *Bringing the State Back In*, 55–56; cf. Zakaria, *From Wealth to Power*, 39; Alberto Alesina and Enrico Spolaore, *The Size of Nations* (Cambridge: MIT Press, 2003), 4–6.

19. "The Sorcerer's Apprentice" (German: *Der Zauberlehrling*) is a poem written by Johann Wolfgang von Goethe in 1797, popularly animated in Walt Disney's 1940 *Fantasia*. Hoping to avoid chores, the apprentice magically animates a broom and commands it to fetch water for the tub. As the tub fills and begins to overflow, the apprentice realizes he does not know how to disenchant the broom. In desperation, he splits the broom with an axe, gasping in horror as the splinters grow into new brooms that continue fetching water until the house is flooded. The apprentice is saved only when the sorcerer returns and undoes his mischief, though here the analogy ends because the anarchic international system lacks such a safety net.

20. For example, Cicero opposed Caesar's undermining of the Roman Republic regardless of its continued rise in power: Richard W. Maass, "Political Society and

Cicero's Ideal State," *Historical Methods: A Journal of Quantitative and Interdisciplinary History* 45, no. 2 (2012): 79–92.

21. Montesquieu, *The Spirit of the Laws*, trans. Anne M. Cohler, Basia C. Miller, and Harold S. Stone (New York: Cambridge University Press, 1989), 124.

22. Barry R. Posen, "Nationalism, the Mass Army, and Military Power," *International Security* 18, no. 2 (1993): 80–124; Deborah Avant, "From Mercenary to Citizen Armies: Explaining Change in the Practice of War," *International Organization* 54, no. 1 (2000): 41–72.

23. Anthony D. Smith, "Culture, Community and Territory: The Politics of Ethnicity and Nationalism," *International Affairs* 72, no. 3 (July 1996): 445–58.

24. Jerry Z. Muller, "Us and Them: The Enduring Power of Ethnic Nationalism," *Foreign Affairs* 87, no. 2 (2008): 18–35; cf. Joseph B. Schechtman, *Postwar Population Transfers in Europe, 1945–1955* (Philadelphia: University of Pennsylvania Press, 1962), vii.

25. Dov H. Levin and Benjamin Miller, "Why Great Powers Expand in Their Own Neighborhood: Explaining the Territorial Expansion of the United States 1819–1848," *International Interactions* 37, no. 3 (2011): 229–62; Stephen M. Saideman and R. William Ayres, *For Kin or Country: Xenophobia, Nationalism, and War* (New York: Columbia University Press, 2008); Stephen Van Evera, "Hypotheses on Nationalism and War," *International Security* 18, no. 4 (1994): 5–39.

26. Steven L. Myers and Ellen Barry, "Putin Reclaims Crimea for Russia and Bitterly Denounces the West," *New York Times*, March 18, 2014, http://www.nytimes.com/2014/03/19/world/europe/ukraine.html?_r=0.

27. Michael W. Doyle, "Liberalism and World Politics," *American Political Science Review* 80, no. 4 (1986): 1151–69; Bruce M. Russett, *Grasping the Democratic Peace: Principles for a Post–Cold War World* (Princeton: Princeton University Press, 1993); Spencer R. Weart, *Never at War: Why Democracies Will Not Fight One Another* (New Haven: Yale University Press, 1998).

28. David A. Lake, "Powerful Pacifists: Democratic States and War," *American Political Science Review* 86, no. 1 (1992): 24–37; Dan Reiter and Allan C. Stam, *Democracies at War* (Princeton: Princeton University Press, 2002); Michael C. Desch, *Power and Military Effectiveness: The Fallacy of Democratic Triumphalism* (Baltimore: Johns Hopkins University Press, 2008).

29. George F. Kennan, *American Diplomacy: Expanded Edition* (Chicago: University of Chicago Press, 1951), 66; cf. Snyder, *Myths of Empire*; Walter R. Mead, *Special Providence: American Foreign Policy and How It Changed the World* (New York: Routledge, 2002).

30. Russett, *Grasping the Democratic Peace*, 14–16; Weart, *Never at War*, 11–12; Bruce Russett and John Oneal, *Triangulating Peace: Democracy, Interdependence, and International Organizations* (New York: W. W. Norton, 2001), 44; Reiter and Stam, *Democracies at War*, 5–7.

31. Bruce Bueno de Mesquita, Alastair Smith, Randolph M. Siverson, and James D. Morrow, *The Logic of Political Survival* (Cambridge: MIT Press, 2005), 417–19.

32. John M. Owen IV, *Liberal Peace, Liberal War* (Ithaca, NY: Cornell University Press, 1997), 32–41; Michael Doyle, "Kant, Liberal Legacies, and Foreign Affairs," part 1, *Philosophy and Public Affairs* 12 (1983): 207.

33. Jessica L. P. Weeks, *Dictators at War and Peace* (Ithaca, NY: Cornell University Press, 2014); Jessica C. Weiss, *Powerful Patriots: Nationalist Protest in China's Foreign Relations* (New York: Oxford University Press, 2014).

34. I thank Bill Wohlforth for this counterargument. Others suggest that democracies should more easily mobilize for easy wars, making them more likely to try to annex weak states: Bruce M. Russett, "Democracy, War and Expansion through Historical Lenses," *European Journal of International Relations* 15, no. 1 (2009): 9–36; Bueno de Mesquita et al., *Logic of Political Survival*, 252.

35. Scott A. Silverstone, *Divided Union: The Politics of War in the Early American Republic* (Ithaca, NY: Cornell University Press, 2004), 40; cf. 15–17, 49; James Madison, "The Federalist No. 10" and "The Federalist No. 51," in *The Federalist: A Commentary on the Constitution of the United States*, ed. Robert Scigliano (New York: Random House, 2001), 53–61, 330–35.

36. Snyder, *Myths of Empire*; Zakaria, *From Wealth to Power*; Silverstone, *Divided Union*; Jeffrey W. Meiser, *Power and Restraint: The Rise of the United States, 1898–1941* (Washington, DC: Georgetown University Press, 2015).

37. Doyle, "Kant, Liberal Legacies, and Foreign Affairs," 206; William J. Dixon, "Democracy and the Peaceful Settlement of International Conflict," *American Political Science Review* 88, no. 1 (1994): 15; John Rawls, *The Law of Peoples* (Cambridge: Harvard University Press, 1999); Russett, *Grasping the Democratic Peace*, 30–37.

38. Sebastian Rosato, "The Flawed Logic of Democratic Peace Theory," *American Political Science Review* 97, no. 4 (2003): 588–91; Lindsey A. O'Rourke, *Covert Regime Change: America's Secret Cold War* (Ithaca, NY: Cornell University Press, 2018); Michael C. Desch, "America's Liberal Illiberalism: The Ideological Origins of Overreaction in U.S. Foreign Policy," *International Security* 32, no. 3 (2007/08): 19.

39. Immanuel Kant, "Perpetual Peace," trans. Lewis W. Beck, in *Kant on History*, ed. Lewis W. Beck (Upper Saddle River, NJ: Prentice Hall, 2001), 86; Rawls, *Law of Peoples*.

40. Alexis de Tocqueville, *Democracy in America*, trans. Harvey C. Mansfield and Delba Winthrop (Chicago: University of Chicago Press, 2000), 235–49; John S. Mill, *On Liberty* (Wheeling, IL: Harlan Davidson, 1947).

41. Arash Abizadeh, "On the Demos and Its Kin: Nationalism, Democracy, and the Boundary Problem," *American Political Science Review* 106, no. 4 (2012): 867–82.

42. I focus on xenophobia rather than racism for two reasons. First, although U.S. leaders' xenophobia was often fueled by racist presumptions that people with darker skin were inherently inferior, it also frequently targeted cultural, religious, linguistic, and educational differences. Second, the causal logic of domestic impact theory functions similarly whether leaders' xenophobia is driven by racial or other differences.

43. Peter Katzenstein, ed., *The Culture of National Security: Norms and Identity in World Politics* (New York: Columbia University Press, 1996); Alexander Wendt, *Social Theory of International Politics* (New York: Cambridge University Press, 1999), 170; Rawi Abdelal, *National Purpose in the World Economy: Post-Soviet States in Comparative Perspective* (Ithaca, NY: Cornell University Press, 2001), 24–31.

44. James G. March and Johan P. Olsen, *The Logic of Appropriateness* (Oslo: University of Oslo Centre for European Studies, 2004); Rawi Abdelal, Yoshiko M. Herrera, Alastair Iain Johnston, and Rose McDermott, "Identity as a Variable," *Perspectives on Politics* 4, no. 4 (2006): 695–711.

45. Deborah Welch Larson and Alexei Shevchenko, "Status Seekers: Chinese and Russian Responses to U.S. Primacy," *International Security* 34, no. 4 (2010): 63–95;

Michelle Murray, "Identity, Insecurity, and Great Power Politics: The Tragedy of German Naval Ambition before the First World War," *Security Studies* 19, no. 4 (2010): 656–88.

46. Henri Tajfel, "Social Psychology of Intergroup Relations," *Annual Review of Psychology* 33 (1982): 1–39; Jonathan Mercer, "Anarchy and Identity," *International Organization* 49, no. 2 (1995): 229–52; Wendt, *Social Theory of International Politics*, 228.

47. Saideman and Ayres, *For Kin or Country*, 2.

48. Alexander DeConde, *Ethnicity, Race, and American Foreign Policy: A History* (Boston: Northeastern University Press, 1992), 12.

49. *CG*, 35th Cong., 1st sess., Appendix, 461.

50. *CG*, 41st Cong., 3rd sess., Appendix, 29; cf. *CS*, 5: 204.

51. *CR*, 55th Cong., 2nd sess., 5903.

52. Terry Martin, "The Origins of Soviet Ethnic Cleansing," *Journal of Modern History* 70, no. 4 (1998): 815.

53. Ian Kershaw, *Hitler, the Germans, and the Final Solution* (New Haven: Yale University Press, 2008), 90.

54. Peter Gourevitch, "The Second Image Reversed: The International Sources of Domestic Politics," *International Organization* 32, no. 4 (1978): 881–912.

55. Gideon Rose, "Neoclassical Realism and Theories of Foreign Policy," *World Politics* 51, no. 1 (1998): 146; cf. Steven E. Lobell, Norrin M. Ripsman, and Jeffrey W. Taliaferro, eds., *Neoclassical Realism, the State, and Foreign Policy* (New York: Cambridge University Press, 2009); Brian Rathbun, "A Rose by Any Other Name: Neoclassical Realism as the Logical and Necessary Extension of Structural Realism," *Security Studies* 17, no. 2 (2008): 294–321.

56. Stephen Van Evera, *Guide to Methods for Students of Political Science* (Ithaca, NY: Cornell University Press, 1997), 19; cf. Harry Eckstein, "Case Study and Theory in Political Science," in *Case Study Method: Key Issues, Key Texts*, ed. Roger Gomm, Martyn Hammersley, and Peter Foster (Thousand Oaks, CA: SAGE, 2000), 126.

57. Wohlforth, *Elusive Balance*, 2.

58. Van Evera, *Guide to Methods*, 30–34.

59. Andrew Bennett, "Stirring the Frequentist Pot with a Dash of Bayes," *Political Analysis* 14, no. 3 (2006): 341.

60. Andrew Bennett and Colin Elman, "Case Study Methods in the International Relations Subfield," *Comparative Political Studies* 40, no. 2 (2007): 172.

61. John Gerring, *Social Science Methodology: A Criterial Framework* (New York: Cambridge University Press, 2001), 192–93; Dan Lindley, *Promoting Peace with Information: Transparency as a Tool of Security Regimes* (Princeton: Princeton University Press, 2007), 51.

62. Jack S. Levy, "Prospect Theory, Rational Choice, and International Relations," *International Studies Quarterly* 41 (1997): 87–112; Richard Maass, "Why Washington and Moscow keep talking past each other," *The Monkey Cage*, March 12, 2014, https://www.washingtonpost.com/news/monkey-cage/wp/2014/03/12/why-washington-and-moscow-keep-talking-past-each-other/?noredirect=on&utm_term=.4a6793948be9.

63. Gary King, Robert O. Keohane, and Sidney Verba, *Designing Social Inquiry: Scientific Inference in Qualitative Research* (Princeton: Princeton University Press, 1994), 129–36.

64. Jason Seawright and John Gerring, "Case Selection Techniques in Case Study Research: A Menu of Qualitative and Quantitative Options," *Political Research Quarterly* 61, no. 2 (2008): 294–308; Bennett and Elman, "Case Study Methods," 174–76.

65. On pretexts: Richard W. Maass and Joshua R. Itzkowitz Shifrinson, "Correspondence: NATO Non-expansion and German Reunification," *International Security* 41, no. 3 (2016/17): 197.

66. James Mahoney and Gary Goertz, "The Possibility Principle: Choosing Negative Cases in Comparative Research," *American Political Science Review* 98, no. 4 (2004): 653–69.

67. Aaron Rapport, "Hard Thinking about Hard and Easy Cases in Security Studies," *Security Studies* 24, no. 3 (2015): 431–65; Henry E. Brady and David Collier, *Rethinking Social Inquiry: Diverse Tools, Shared Standards* (New York: Rowman and Littlefield, 2004), 297.

68. Jack S. Levy, "Qualitative Methods in International Relations," in *Evaluating Methodology in International Studies*, ed. Frank P. Harvey and Michael Brecher (Ann Arbor: University of Michigan Press, 2002), 144.

69. Alexander L. George and Andrew Bennett, *Case Studies and Theory Development in the Social Sciences* (Cambridge, MA: Belfer Center for Science and International Affairs, 2004), 205–32; Andrew Bennett, "Process Tracing: A Bayesian Perspective," in *The Oxford Handbook of Political Methodology*, ed. Janet Box-Steffensmeier, Henry E. Brady, and David Collier (New York: Oxford University Press, 2008), 702–21; James Mahoney, "Process Tracing and Historical Explanation," *Security Studies* 24, no. 2 (2015): 200–218.

70. John Gerring, *Case Study Research: Principles and Practices* (New York: Cambridge University Press, 2007), 173, 180.

71. George and Bennett, *Case Studies and Theory Development*, 86–88; Marc Trachtenberg, *The Craft of International History: A Guide to Method* (Princeton: Princeton University Press, 2006), 140–41.

72. Ian S. Lustick, "History, Historiography, and Political Science: Multiple Historical Records and the Problem of Selection Bias," *American Political Science Review* 90, no. 3 (1996): 605–18.

3. To the Continent

1. This figure does not include 400,000 square miles of Pacific Northwest claims ceded by Spain in 1819 but disputed by Britain, roughly 250,000 of which were incorporated as Oregon Territory in 1848.

2. U.S. Declaration of Independence.

3. Russell Thornton, "Population History of Native North Americans," in *A Population History of North America*, ed. Michael R. Haines and Richard H. Steckel (New York: Cambridge University Press, 2000), 24.

4. Bruce E. Johansen, *The Native Peoples of North America: A History*, vol. 1 (Westport, CT: Praeger, 2005), 182.

5. Karl M. Schmitt, *Mexico and the United States, 1821–1973: Conflict and Coexistence* (New York: John Wiley and Sons, 1974), 16.

6. Fisher Ames to Thomas Dwight, October 31, 1803, in *Works of Fisher Ames*, ed. Seth Ames, vol. 1 (Boston: Little, Brown, 1854), 329.

7. King George III, "Royal Proclamation," October 7, 1763, in *American State Papers: Public Lands* 2: 95.

8. *JCC*, 13: 239–42, 263–65, 329–31, 339–41; *JCC*, 14: 920–26; *JCC*, 16: 115; *RDC*, 3: 300–302. *RDC*, 4: 78–79, 257, 743.

9. Adams, Franklin, and Jay to Livingston, July 18, 1783, *RDC*, 6: 567; cf. 468.

10. Franklin to Jay, October 2, 1780, *RDC*, 4: 75; cf. Jay to Franklin, September 11, 1783, *RDC*, 6: 692.

11. *RDC*, 6: 58.

12. Walter Nugent, *Habits of Empire: A History of American Expansion* (New York: Alfred A. Knopf, 2008), 15.

13. *RDC*, 6: 92.

14. H. James Henderson, *Party Politics in the Continental Congress* (New York: McGraw-Hill, 1974), 2; cf. 1.

15. Lynn Montross, *The Reluctant Rebels: The Story of the Continental Congress, 1774–1789* (New York: Barnes and Noble, 1970), 8; cf. Robert Leckie, *From Sea to Shining Sea: From the War of 1812 to the Mexican War, the Saga of America's Expansion* (New York: HarperCollins, 1993), 8.

16. Articles of Confederation, art. 2; cf. Montross, *Reluctant Rebels*, 12; Alan Taylor, *The Civil War of 1812: American Citizens, British Subjects, Irish Rebels, and Indian Allies* (New York: Alfred A. Knopf, 2010), 120.

17. *JCC*, 16: 114–15; cf. William Carmichael to the Committee of Foreign Affairs, May 28, 1780, *RDC*, 3: 737; *RDC*, 4: 40, 54.

18. François Barbé-Marbois, October 1780, "Observations on the Boundary between the Spanish Settlements and the United States," in *The Papers of James Madison: Congressional Series*, ed. William T. Hutchinson and William M. E. Rachal, vol. 2 (Chicago: University of Chicago Press, 1962), 116; cf. Gérard de Rayneval to Jay, September 6, 1782, in *John Jay: The Winning of the Peace: Unpublished Papers, 1780–1784*, ed. Richard B. Morris, vol. 2 (New York: Harper and Row, 1980), 331–32.

19. Benjamin Franklin and Silas Deane to the Committee of Secret Correspondence, March 12, April 9, 1777, *RDC*, 2: 283–90; Arthur Lee to Florida Blanca, March 17, 1777, ibid., 290–91; Lee to the Committee of Secret Correspondence, March 18, 1777, ibid., 292–96; cf. *SL*, 8: 8; Stacy Schiff, *A Great Improvisation: Franklin, France, and the Birth of America* (New York: Henry Holt, 2006).

20. Nugent, *Habits of Empire*, 30.

21. Franklin to Robert Livingston, August 12, 1782, *RDC*, 5: 657; cf. Marquis de Lafayette to Adams, October 6, 1782, ibid., 800; Lafayette to Livingston, March 2, 1783, *RDC*, 6: 270.

22. Morris, *John Jay*, 451; cf. Adams to Livingston, October 31, November 8, 1782, *RDC*, 5: 839, 866; Jay to Livingston, September 18, 1782, ibid., 740; ibid., 849.

23. Adams, Franklin, Jay, and Laurens to Livingston, December 14, 1782, *RDC*, 6: 133; cf. provisional articles of peace: ibid., 96–100; Richard Oswald to Thomas Townshend, October 2, 1782, Morris, *John Jay*, 373.

24. *RDC*, 6: 466.

25. Nugent, *Habits of Empire*, 39–40; cf. Rayneval to Vergennes, December 25, 1782, *RDC*, 6: 166.

26. Adams, Franklin, Jay, and Laurens to Livingston, December 14, 1782, *RDC*, 6: 132; cf. Adams to Livingston, July 9, 1783, ibid., 530.

27. Samuel F. Bemis, *A Diplomatic History of the United States*, 5th ed. (New York: Holt, Rinehart and Winston, 1965), 82; Leckie, *From Sea to Shining Sea*, 8–9; Gordon S. Wood, *Empire of Liberty: A History of the Early Republic, 1789–1815* (New York: Oxford University Press, 2009), 634–35.

28. Washington to Madison, November 5, 1786, *GW*, 29: 51; *CR*, 55th Cong., 2nd sess., 6013; David P. Barash and Charles P. Webel, *Peace and Conflict Studies*, 3rd ed. (Washington: SAGE, 2014), 343.

29. Richard Beeman, Stephen Botein, and Edward C. Carter II, eds., *Beyond Confederation: Origins of the Constitution and American National Identity* (Chapel Hill: University of North Carolina Press, 1987).

30. Gordon to John Adams, September 7, 1782, in *Papers of John Adams*, ed. Gregg L. Lint, C. James Taylor, Margaret A. Hogan, Jessie May Rodrique, Mary T. Claffey, and Hobson Woodward, vol. 13 (Cambridge: Belknap Press, 2006), 450; Lee to Madison, April 3, 1790, *JMa:H*, 6: 11.

31. David Mayers, *Dissenting Voices in America's Rise to Power* (New York: Cambridge University Press, 2007), 13.

32. Nugent, *Habits of Empire*, 55–56; Jon Kukla, *A Wilderness So Immense: The Louisiana Purchase and the Destiny of America* (New York: Alfred A. Knopf, 2003), 113.

33. Jefferson to Livingston, April 18, 1802, *TJ:F*, 9: 364.

34. Mayers, *Dissenting Voices*, 17.

35. Madison to Charles Pinckney, November 27, 1802, *ASP:FR*, 2: 527.

36. Hamilton to Charles Cotesworth Pinckney, December 29, 1802, *AH*, 26: 71. Hamilton favored conquering Louisiana and Florida during the Quasi-War: Adams to Timothy Pickering, October 3, 1798, *The Works of John Adams*, ed. Charles F. Adams, vol. 8 (Boston: Little, Brown, 1853), 600.

37. *AC*, 7th Cong., 2nd sess., 183; cf. 94.

38. *Senate Journal*, 7th Cong., 2nd sess., 274.

39. Jefferson to Livingston, April 18, 1802, *TJ:W*, 4: 431; cf. Clifford L. Egan, "The United States, France, and West Florida, 1803–1807," *Florida Historical Quarterly* 47, no. 3 (1969): 227–52.

40. Jefferson to John Bacon, April 30, 1803, *TJ:W*, 8: 229; cf. E. Wilson Lyon, *Louisiana in French Diplomacy, 1759–1804* (Norman: University of Oklahoma Press, 1974), chap. 7.

41. Jefferson to Monsieur Dupont de Nemours, April 25, 1802, *TJ:LB*, 10: 318.

42. Livingston to Madison, April 11, 1803, *AC*, 7th Cong., 2nd sess., 1126.

43. T. Lothrop Stoddard, *The French Revolution in San Domingo* (New York: Houghton Mifflin, 1914), 327, 340; Philippe R. Girard, *The Slaves Who Defeated Napoleon: Toussaint Louverture and the Haitian War of Independence, 1801–1804* (Birmingham: University of Alabama Press, 2011).

44. Mayers, *Dissenting Voices*, 18.

45. Barbé-Marbois, *The History of Louisiana* (Philadelphia: Carey and Lea, 1830), 264; cf. 312–13.

46. Colin Elman, "Extending Offensive Realism: The Louisiana Purchase and America's Rise to Regional Hegemony," *American Political Science Review* 98, no. 4 (2004): 574; Barbé-Marbois, *History of Louisiana*, 276.

47. Stephen E. Ambrose, *Undaunted Courage: Meriwether Lewis, Thomas Jefferson, and the Opening of the American West* (New York: Simon and Schuster, 1996), 102.

48. H. M. Brackenridge, *Views of Louisiana* (Pittsburgh: Cramer, Spear and Richbaum, 1814), 69–70.

49. François-Xavier Martin, *The History of Louisiana, from the Earliest Period*, vol. 2 (New Orleans: A. T. Penniman, 1829), 205; cf. Brackenridge, *Views of Louisiana*, 85–88; Nugent, *Habits of Empire*, 54–55.

50. Walter Stahr, *John Jay: Founding Father* (New York: Continuum, 2005), 97.

51. Livingston to Madison, April 11, 1803, *AC*, 7th Cong., 2nd sess., 1126.

52. Livingston to Madison, April 13, 1803, ibid., 1130.

53. Livingston to Madison, April 17, 1803, ibid., 1134; Madison to Livingston and Monroe, April 18, 1803, ibid., 1135; Livingston and Monroe to Madison, May 13, 1803, ibid., 1147.

54. Alexander Hamilton, "Purchase of Louisiana," *New-York Evening Post*, July 5, 1803, *AH*, 26: 129–31; cf. Gilbert Lycan, *Alexander Hamilton and American Foreign Policy: A Design for Greatness* (Norman: University of Oklahoma Press, 1970), 417.

55. Pickering to Theodore Lyman, February 11, 1804, *Documents Relating to New England Federalism, 1800–1815*, ed. Henry Adams (Boston: Little, Brown, 1905), 346.

56. *AC*, 8th Cong., 1st sess., 465.

57. William Plumer Jr., *The Life of William Plumer* (Boston: Phillips, Samson, 1857), 285.

58. Peter J. Kastor, *The Nation's Crucible: The Louisiana Purchase and the Creation of America* (New Haven: Yale University Press, 2004), 4.

59. *AC*, 8th Cong., 1st sess., 461–62.

60. Charles W. Upham, *The Life of Timothy Pickering*, vol. 4 (Boston: Little, Brown, 1873), 79; Linda K. Kerber, *Federalists in Dissent: Imagery and Ideology in Jeffersonian America* (Ithaca, NY: Cornell University Press, 1980), 42.

61. Jefferson to John Breckinridge, August 12, 1803, *TJ:F*, 10: 7.

62. Alexander DeConde, *This Affair of Louisiana* (New York: Charles Scribner's Sons, 1976), 190–91; cf. 95–96.

63. Livingston and Monroe to Madison, May 13, 1803, *AC*, 7th Cong., 2nd sess., 1146; cf. Livingston to Madison, May 20, 1803, *ASP:FR*, 2: 561; Jackson to Jefferson, August 7, 1803, *AJ*, 1: 68.

64. Kastor, *Nation's Crucible*, 7; cf. DeConde, *This Affair of Louisiana*, 212, 252.

65. Senator John Pope of Kentucky labeled Florida's climate "more fatal to our people than the sword of a victorious enemy." *AC*, 11th Cong., 3rd sess., 40.

66. Nugent, *Habits of Empire*, 120; James G. Cusick, *The Other War of 1812: The Patriot War and the American Invasion of Spanish East Florida* (Gainesville: University Press of Florida, 2003), 316, n. 6; David J. Weber, *The Spanish Frontier in North America* (New Haven: Yale University Press, 1992), 298.

67. Nugent, *Habits of Empire*, 99.

68. Madison to Monroe, July 29, 1803, *ASP:FR*, 2: 627.

69. *AC*, 11th Cong., 3rd sess., 40.

70. Nugent, *Habits of Empire*, 128–29.

71. Ibid., 103.

72. Madison to Pinckney, Madison to Monroe, July 29, 1803, *ASP:FR*, 2: 614, 626.

73. Livingston to Madison, May 20, 1803, ibid., 561; Livingston and Monroe to Madison, June 7, 1803, ibid., 564; Isaac J. Cox, *The West Florida Controversy, 1798–1813* (Gloucester, MA: Peter Smith, 1967), 83.

74. *SL*, 2: 251–54.

75. Talleyrand to John Armstrong, December 21, 1804, *ASP:FR*, 2: 635; Livingston to Madison, June 20, 1804, *JMa:H*, 7: 124.

76. Madison to Monroe, April 15, 1804, *ASP:FR*, 2: 628.

77. Wanjohi Waciuma, *Intervention in Spanish Floridas, 1801–1813: A Study in Jeffersonian Foreign Policy* (Boston: Branden Press, 1976), 52; cf. *ASP:FR*, 2: 634.

78. Talleyrand to Armstrong, December 21, 1804, *ASP:FR*, 2: 635; Talleyrand to Chevalier de Santivanes, March 26, 1805, ibid., 659–60; Cox, *West Florida Controversy*, 102–38.

79. Madison to Armstrong and James Bowdoin, March 13, 1806, *JMa:H*, 7: 194; cf. Albert Gallatin to Jefferson, October 13, 1806, *AG*, 1: 311.

80. Jefferson to Madison, August 25, 1805, *TJ:F*, 10: 171; cf. Jefferson to Madison, September 16, 1805, ibid., 175; Jefferson to Madison, October 11, 1805, ibid., 176.

81. Rodrigo Botero, *Ambivalent Embrace: America's Troubled Relations with Spain from the Revolutionary War to the Cold War* (Westport, CT: Greenwood Press, 2001), 34.

82. See chapter 5.

83. Jefferson to Dearborn, August 12, 1808, *TJ:W*, 5: 338; cf. Jefferson to Gallatin, August 9, 11, 1808, ibid., 335, 336; Jefferson to Robert Smith, August 12, 1808, ibid., 337; Jefferson to Madison, August 12, 1808, ibid., 339.

84. Jefferson to Monroe, January 28, 1809, *TJ:W*, 5: 420; Jefferson to Madison, April 19, 1809, *TJ:F*, 11: 106; Jefferson to Madison, April 27, 1809, *TJ:LB*, 12: 276–77.

85. Smith to Wykoff, June 20, 1810, *TPUS* 9, 884; Waciuma, *Intervention in Spanish Floridas*, 140–42, 166; Nugent, *Habits of Empire*, 104–5; Rembert W. Patrick, *Florida Fiasco: Rampant Rebels on the Georgia–Florida Border, 1810–1815* (Athens: University of Georgia Press, 1954), 10.

86. Smith to Holmes, July 21, 1810, in Waciuma, *Intervention in Spanish Floridas*, 144; cf. Madison to Smith, July 17, 1810, *The Papers of James Madison: Presidential Series*, ed. J. C. A. Stagg, vol. 2 (Charlottesville, VA: University Press of Virginia, 1992), 419–21; Smith to Pinkney, June 13, 1810, *DC:ILN*, 1: 5–6.

87. Holmes to Smith, October 3, 1810, in Joseph B. Smith, *The Plot to Steal Florida: James Madison's Phony War* (New York: Arbor House, 1983), 66; cf. Stanley C. Arthur, *The Story of the West Florida Rebellion* (St. Francisville, LA: St. Francisville Democrat, 1935), 37–88, 105–24; Waciuma, *Intervention in Spanish Floridas*, 148–62; Robertson to Smith, July 6, 1810, *TPUS*, 9: 888–89; Holmes to Smith, July 31, August 8, 1810, ibid.: 889–91, 891–93.

88. *ASP:FR*, 3: 397; cf. 396; J. C. A. Stagg, *Borderlines in Borderlands: James Madison and the Spanish-American Frontier, 1776–1821* (New Haven: Yale University Press, 2009), 69–76, 83.

89. Frank L. Owsley Jr. and Gene A. Smith, *Filibusters and Expansionists: Jeffersonian Manifest Destiny, 1800–1821* (Tuscaloosa: University of Alabama Press, 2004), 63; Charles C. Griffin, *The United States and the Disruption of the Spanish Empire, 1810–1822* (New York: Columbia University Press, 1937), 106–15.

90. J. C. A. Stagg, "James Madison and George Mathews: The East Florida Revolution of 1812 Reconsidered," *Diplomatic History* 30, no. 1 (2006): 33; cf. Toulmin to Madison, October 31, November 6, 22, 28, December 6, 12, 1810, *TPUS*, 6: 128–30, 132, 135–39, 140–43, 149–51, 152–59; Stagg, *Borderlines in Borderlands*, 83–85; Cox, *West Florida Controversy*, 437–86; Waciuma, *Intervention in Spanish Floridas*, 171.

91. *SL*, 3: 471; cf. Stagg, *Borderlines in Borderlands*, 89–90.

92. Mathews and McKee were ordered to "pre-occupy *by force* the territory" if Britain moved to take it: Smith to Mathews and McKee, January 26, 1811, *ASP:FR*, 3: 571.

93. Mathews to Monroe, August 3, 1811, in Stagg, *Borderlines in Borderlands*, 105; Stagg, "James Madison and George Mathews," 45–47; 54; Patrick, *Florida Fiasco*, 84; Cusick, *Other War of 1812*.

94. Monroe to Mitchell, May 2, 1812, Stagg, *Borderlines in Borderlands*, 123; Monroe to Mitchell, May 27, 1812, *MPP*, 1: 510; cf. Monroe to Mathews, April 4, 1812, *ASP:FR*, 3: 572; Madison to Jefferson, April 24, 1812, *JMa:RF*, 2: 534; Stagg, "James Madison and George Mathews," 37–38, 49.

95. *AC*, 11th Cong., 3rd sess., 65–83.

96. *AC*, 12th Cong., 1st sess., 1683.

97. Gallatin to Monroe, May 8, 1813, *AG*, 1: 545; cf. House vote: *AC*, 12th Cong., 1st sess., 1685–86; Senate vote: ibid., 326; Patrick, *Florida Fiasco*, 151.

98. Madison's draft message to Congress, ca. December 8, 1812, Stagg, *Papers of James Madison: Presidential Series*, 5: 487; cf. speech of Hunter: *AC*, 13th Cong., 1st sess., 522; Senate vote: *AC*, 12th Cong., 2nd sess., 130; Patrick, *Florida Fiasco*, 253.

99. Cox, *West Florida Controversy*, 616–19; Senate vote: *AC*, 12th Cong., 2nd sess., 132.

100. Eustis to Pinckney, December 2, 1812, Patrick, *Florida Fiasco*, 223; cf. 214–18, 225–36; Stagg, *Borderlines in Borderlands*, 127; Nugent, *Habits of Empire*, 118; Owsley and Smith, *Filibusters and Expansionists*, 77–81.

101. Monroe to Gallatin, Adams, and Bayard, April 27, 1813, *Papers of James A. Bayard, 1796–1815*, ed. Elizabeth Donnan (Washington: Government Printing Office, 1915), 214–15.

102. Stagg, *Borderlines in Borderlands*, 176, 181.

103. Richard Rush, "Memo of a Cabinet Meeting," May 29, 1816, Stagg, *Borderlines in Borderlands*, 283, n. 49; cf. Madison to Jefferson, February 15, 1817, *JMa:RF*, 3: 34; James E. Lewis Jr., *The American Union and the Problem of Neighborhood: The United States and the Collapse of the Spanish Empire, 1783–1829* (Chapel Hill: University of North Carolina Press, 1998), 89.

104. William E. Weeks, *John Quincy Adams and American Global Empire* (Lexington: University Press of Kentucky, 1992), 54.

105. Ibid., 69; Stagg, *Borderlines in Borderlands*, 197.

106. Mark Jarrett, *The Congress of Vienna and Its Legacy: War and Great Power Diplomacy after Napoleon* (New York: I. B. Tauris, 2013), 198–99; Bagot to Castlereagh, February 8, 1818, in *Correspondence, Despatches, and Other Papers of Viscount Castlereagh*, ed. Charles W. Vane, vol. 11 (London: John Murray, 1853), 404–5; Weeks, *John Quincy Adams*, 77–78; Lewis, *American Union*, 123.

107. Weeks, *John Quincy Adams*, 57–58; cf. Owsley and Smith, *Filibusters and Expansionists*, 122–40.

108. *JQA:A*, 4: 39, 42; cf. Monroe, First Annual Message, *MPP*, 2: 14.

109. Monroe, Special Message to Congress, January 13, 1818, *MPP*, 2: 24.

110. Monroe to Jackson, December 28, 1817, Weeks, *John Quincy Adams*, 109; cf. 113; Calhoun to Jackson, February 6, September 8, 1818, *ASP:MA*, 1: 697; *AJ*, 2: 393.

111. Jackson to Monroe, June 2, 1818, *AJ*, 2: 378; Jackson to Gaines, August 7, 1818, *AJ*, 2: 384; Jackson to Monroe, January 6, August 10, 1818, ibid., 346, 385–87; Robert V. Remini, *Andrew Jackson and the Course of American Empire, 1767–1821* (New York: Harper and Row, 1981), 351–65.

112. Nugent, *Habits of Empire*, 122.

113. Onís to Adams, June 17, July 8, 1818, *ASP:FR*, 4: 495–96; Adams to Onís, July 23, 1818, ibid., 497–98; *JQA:A*, 4: 26, 79; Weeks, *John Quincy Adams*, 74, 117–18.

114. Monroe, Second Annual Message, *MPP*, 2: 40–41.

115. Adams to Erving, November 28, 1818, *JQA:F*, 6: 501–2; *JQA:A*, 4: 188; Weeks, *John Quincy Adams*, 55, 133, 151–55.

116. *JQA:A*, 4: 197–98.

117. Onís to Adams, February 1, 1819, *ASP:FR*, 4: 616; cf. Philip C. Brooks, *Diplomacy and the Borderlands: The Adams–Onís Treaty of 1819* (Berkeley: University of California Press, 1939), 136–39; *JQA:A*, 4: 208–9; Weeks, *John Quincy Adams*, 149.

118. *JQA:A*, 4: 274–75.

119. Griffin, *Disruption of the Spanish Empire,* 191–243.

120. Monroe, Special Message to Congress, March 8, 1822; *MPP*, 2: 116–18.

121. Weeks, *John Quincy Adams*, 72.

4. To the West

1. Richard B. Morris, *The Peacemakers: The Great Powers and American Independence* (New York: Harper and Row, 1965), 321–22.

2. Neville B. Craig, *The Olden Time*, vol. 2 (Cincinnati: Robert Clarke, 1876), 424–26; Reginald Horsman, *Expansion and American Indian Policy, 1783–1812* (East Lansing: Michigan State University Press, 1967), 20; Colin G. Calloway, "The Continuing Revolution in Indian Country," in *Native Americans in the Early Republic*, ed. Frederick E. Hoxie, Ronald Hoffman, and Peter J. Albert (Charlottesville: University of Virginia Press, 1999), 31.

3. David C. Hendrickson, *Union, Nation, or Empire: The American Debate over International Relations, 1789–1941* (Lawrence: University Press of Kansas, 2009), 159.

4. Knox to Washington, June 15, 1789, *ASP:IA*, 1: 13; U.S. Census Bureau, *Return of the Whole Number of Persons within the Several Districts of the United States* (Philadelphia: J. Phillips, 1793), 3. Disease and war had cut the Native American population from perhaps 250,000 a century earlier: Peter Wood, "From Atlantic History to a Continental Approach," in *Atlantic History: A Critical Appraisal*, ed. Jack P. Greene and Philip D. Morgan (New York: Oxford University Press, 2009), 422.

5. Calloway, "Continuing Revolution in Indian Country," 3; cf. 25.

6. Knox to Washington, July 7, 1789, *ASP:IA*, 1: 53.

7. Ibid., 53; cf. Knox to Putnam, May 22, 1792, *The Memoirs of Rufus Putnam*, ed. Rowena Buell (Boston: Houghton, Mifflin, 1903), 257–67; Reginald Horsman, "The Indian Policy of an 'Empire for Liberty,'" in Hoxie et al., *Native Americans and the Early Republic*, 46.

8. *GW*, 31: 396–403; cf. ibid., 32: 208, 34: 391.

9. Knox to Washington, July 7, 1789, *ASP:IA*, 1: 52.

10. Horsman, *Expansion and American Indian Policy*, 36.

11. Report of Secretary at War on Indian Hostilities, July 10, 1787, *JCC*, 32: 329; cf. Report of Secretary at War on Indian Affairs, July 20, 1787, *JCC*, 33: 388.

12. Report of Secretary at War on Indian Hostilities, July 10, 1787, *JCC*, 32: 331.

13. Schuyler to President of Congress, July 29, 1783, Papers of the Continental Congress, Item 153, Vol. 3, 603, National Archives, Washington, DC; cf. Schuyler to President of Congress, September 21, 1782, ibid., 593–95; Horsman, *Expansion and American Indian Policy*, 56.

14. Washington to James Duane, September 7, 1783, *GW*, 27: 133–40; Washington to the President of Congress, June 17, 1783, ibid., 17–18.

15. Knox to Washington, June 15, 1789, *ASP:IA*, 1: 13–14; cf. Knox to Washington, July 7, 1789, ibid., 53.

16. Report of Secretary at War on Indian Hostilities, July 10, 1787, *JCC*, 32: 331; Report of Secretary at War on Indian Affairs, July 20, 1787, *JCC*, 33: 389.

17. Knox to Washington, July 7, 1789, *ASP:IA*, 1: 54; cf. Knox to Washington, June 15, 1789, ibid., 13.

18. *JCC*, 27: 460–61; cf. October 1783 report on Northwest Native affairs: *JCC*, 25: 683–86.

19. *GW*, 32: 208.

20. Knox to Washington, July 7, 1789, *ASP:IA*, 1: 53–54; North Callahan, *Henry Knox, General Washington's General* (New York: Rinehart, 1958), 322.

21. *ASP:IA* 1: 82.

22. Knox to the Northwestern Indians, April 4, 1792, ibid., 230.

23. *GW*, 32: 205–8; cf. *GW*, 34: 386–92.

24. Douglas Hurt, *The Ohio Frontier: Crucible of the Old Northwest, 1720–1830* (Bloomington: Indiana University Press, 1998), 118; Colin G. Calloway, *The American Revolution in Indian Country* (New York: Cambridge University Press, 1995), 289. On Anglo-American fears of Native confederations: Robert M. Owens, *Red Dreams, White Nightmares: Pan-Indian Alliances in the Anglo-American Mind, 1763–1815* (Norman: University of Oklahoma Press, 2015).

25. James McHenry to Thomas Lewis, March 30, 1799, War Department, Letters Sent, Indian Affairs, Vol. A, 29–35, National Archives, Washington, DC; cf. Francis P. Prucha, *The Great Father: The United States Government and the American Indians* (Lincoln: University of Nebraska Press, 1984), 162–63; Horsman, *Expansion and American Indian Policy*, 83.

26. James Wilkinson, Benjamin Hawkins, and Andrew Pickens to Henry Dearborn, December 18, 1801, *ASP:IA*, 1: 659.

27. An Act to Regulate Trade and Intercourse with the Indian Tribes, *SL*, 1: 331.

28. An Act to Regulate Trade and Intercourse with the Indian Tribes, ibid., 138; cf. 329, 453; Anthony F. C. Wallace, *Jefferson and the Indians: The Tragic Fate of the First Americans* (Cambridge: Harvard University Press, 1999), 207; Francis P. Prucha, *American Indian Policy in the Formative Years: The Indian Trade and Intercourse Acts, 1790–1834* (Cambridge: Harvard University Press, 1962).

29. Knox to Washington, June 15, 1789, *ASP:IA*, 1: 13; Calloway, *American Revolution in Indian Country*, 3–4, 23; Horsman, *Expansion and American Indian Policy*, 107.

30. *GW*, 32: 208; Patricia N. Limerick, *The Legacy of Conquest: The Unbroken Past of the American West* (New York: W. W. Norton, 1987), 192; cf. Report of Secretary at

War on Indian Hostilities, July 10, 1787, *JCC*, 32: 328; Timothy Pickering to William Blount, March 23, 1795, *TPUS*, 4: 392.

31. Horsman, *Expansion and American Indian Policy*, 27–29, 69–72.

32. Knox to Washington, December 29, 1794, *ASP:IA*, 1: 543–44.

33. Ibid., 544.

34. Jefferson to Chastellux, June 7, 1785, *TJ:F*, 3: 419.

35. Dearborn to Benjamin Hawkins, May 24, 1803, Prucha, *Great Father*, 143.

36. Horsman, *Expansion and American Indian Policy*, 111.

37. Jefferson, "Hints on the Subject of Indian Boundaries," December 29, 1802, *TJ:W*, 9: 460–61; cf. Dearborn to Harrison, June 27, 1804, *WHH*, 1: 101.

38. Jefferson to Congress, January 18, 1803, *MPP*, 1: 352.

39. Jefferson to Jackson, February 16, 1803, *TJ:W*, 4: 464.

40. Jefferson to Hawkins, February 18, 1803, *TJ:F*, 9: 446–48.

41. Jefferson to Harrison, February 27, 1803, *WHH*, 1: 69–73; cf. Jefferson, "Hints on the Subject of Indian Boundaries," December 29, 1802, *TJ:W*, 9: 460–62.

42. Jefferson to Horatio Gates, July 11, 1803, *TJ:F*, 10: 13; cf. Jefferson to John Dickinson, August 9, 1803, ibid., 29–30; Jefferson to John Breckinridge, August 12, 1803, *TJ:LB*, 10: 410; Annie H. Abel, "The History of Events Resulting in Indian Consolidation West of the Mississippi River," in *Annual Report of the American Historical Association for the Year 1906*, vol. 1 (Washington: Government Printing Office, 1908), 244–48.

43. Jefferson, "Draft of an Amendment to the Constitution," *TJ:F*, 10: 6–7.

44. An Act Erecting Louisiana into Two Territories, and Providing for the Temporary Government Thereof, *SL*, 2: 289.

45. Jefferson to the Chiefs of the Upper Cherokees, May 4, 1808, *TJ:W*, 8: 213–15; Jefferson to the Deputies of the Cherokee Upper Towns, January 9, 1809, ibid., 228–30; Jefferson to the Deputies of the Cherokees of the Upper and Lower Towns, January 9, 1809, ibid., 230–32.

46. *TPUS*, 5: 142–46; Abel, "Indian Consolidation," 257.

47. Jefferson to the Chiefs of the Chickasaw Nation, March 7, 1805, *TJ:W*, 8: 199.

48. Dearborn to Return Meigs, March 25, 1808, William G. McLoughlin, *Cherokee Renascence in the New Republic* (Princeton: Princeton University Press, 1986), 129; Abel, "Indian Consolidation," 252–53.

49. Dearborn to Meigs, May 5, 1808, Abel, "Indian Consolidation," 254; Robert V. Remini, *Andrew Jackson and His Indian Wars* (New York: Viking, 2001), 115; Nancy Shoemaker, *American Indian Population Recovery in the Twentieth Century* (Albuquerque: University of New Mexico Press, 1999), 22.

50. Jefferson to the Chiefs of the Wyandots, Ottawas, Chippewas, Potawatomis, and Shawnees, January 10, 1809, *TJ:W*, 8: 234; cf. Jefferson to Captain Hendrick, the Delawares, Mohicans, and Munries, December 21, 1808, *TJ:LB*, 16: 452; Bernard W. Sheehan, *Seeds of Extinction: Jeffersonian Philanthropy and the American Indian* (Chapel Hill: University of North Carolina Press, 1973), 119–147.

51. Madison, First Inaugural Address, *MPP*, 1: 468.

52. Madison to William Wirt, October 1, 1830, *JMa:RF*, 4: 114; Abel, "Indian Consolidation," 255; Prucha, *American Indian Policy*, 160; Wallace, *Jefferson and the Indians*, 214.

53. Eustis to Neely, March 29, 1811, Horsman, *Expansion and American Indian Policy*, 162; Eustis to Hawkins, June 27, 1811, ibid., 160–61; cf. 119; Jefferson to Baron von Humboldt, December 6, 1813, *TJ:F*, 11: 353; Jefferson to Adams, June 11, 1812, *TJ:F*, 11: 255; Jefferson to the Chiefs of the Ottawas, Chippewas, Potawatomis, Wyandots, and Senecas of Sandusky, April 22, 1808, *TJ:W*, 8: 212; Abel, "Indian Consolidation," 268–69.

54. Sean M. O'Brien, *In Bitterness and in Tears: Andrew Jackson's Destruction of the Creeks and Seminoles* (Westport, CT: Praeger, 2003), ix–xv, 141–52; H. S. Halbert and T. H. Ball, *The Creek War of 1813 and 1814* (Chicago: Donohue and Henneberry, 1895), 143–76; Remini, *Andrew Jackson and His Indian Wars*, 62–79; Walter Nugent, *Habits of Empire: A History of American Expansion* (New York: Alfred A. Knopf, 2008), 118.

55. Horsman, "Indian Policy," 56; cf. Reginald Horsman, *The Origins of Indian Removal, 1815–1824* (East Lansing: Michigan State University Press, 1970), 8–9, 11–13; Crawford to Meigs, May 27, 1816, *ASP:IA*, 2: 110; McMinn to Crawford, October 25, 1816, *ASP:IA*, 2: 115; Jon Meacham, *American Lion: Andrew Jackson in the White House* (New York: Random House, 2008), 92; William E. Weeks, *John Quincy Adams and American Global Empire* (Lexington: University Press of Kentucky, 1992), 107.

56. Crawford to John Gaillard, March 13, 1816, *ASP:IA*, 2: 26–27.

57. *AC*, 14th Cong., 2nd sess., 78; *ASP:IA*, 2: 124; cf. Abel, "Indian Consolidation," 258; Horsman, "Indian Policy," 54; Horsman, *Expansion and American Indian Policy*, 147, 167.

58. Abel, "Indian Consolidation," 277; cf. Mary Stockwell, *The Other Trail of Tears: The Removal of the Ohio Indians* (Yardley, PA: Westholme, 2014); John P. Bowes, *Land Too Good for Indians: Northern Indian Removal* (Norman: University of Oklahoma Press, 2016).

59. Nugent, *Habits of Empire*, 120; cf. Francis P. Prucha, *American Indian Treaties: The History of a Political Anomaly* (Berkeley: University of California Press, 1997), 129.

60. Jackson to Monroe, March 4, 1817, *AJ*, 2: 281; cf. Jackson, Meriwether, and Franklin to Crawford, September 20, 1816, *ASP:IA*, 2: 105; Jackson to Calhoun, September 2, 1820, *AJ*, 3: 31–32; Remini, *Andrew Jackson and His Indian Wars*, 111–12; Meacham, *American Lion*, 151.

61. Cherokee Agency to the Commissioners, July 2, 1817, *ASP:IA*, 2: 142–43.

62. William M. Jurgelski, "A New Plow in Old Ground: Cherokees, Whites, and Land in Western North Carolina, 1819–1829" (PhD diss., University of Georgia, 2004), 117.

63. U.S. Commissioners to Graham, July 9, 1817, *AJ*, 2: 305; cf. Graham to Commissioners, August 1, 1817, *ASP:IA*, 2: 143; Jurgelski, "New Plow," 119.

64. Harlow G. Unger, *The Last Founding Father: James Monroe and a Nation's Call to Greatness* (Boston: Da Capo, 2009).

65. Calhoun to Speaker of the House of Representatives, December 5, 1818, *ASP:IA*, 2: 183–84; cf. Monroe, First Annual Message, *MPP*, 2: 16.

66. The Committee on Indian Affairs replaced temporary committees like the 1818 Select Committee on the Extinguishment of Indian Title to Certain Lands. Except for Troup, it was not chaired by a senator from east of the Appalachians until 1873; cf. Horsman, *Origins of Indian Removal*, 12–15.

67. Nicholas Guyatt, *Bind Us Apart: How Enlightened Americans Invented Racial Segregation* (New York: Basic Books, 2016); Ronald T. Takaki, *Iron Cages: Race and Culture in Nineteenth-Century America* (New York: Alfred A. Knopf, 1979), 80–107.

68. *CG*, 25th Cong., 2nd sess., Appendix, 470.

69. Walter A. McDougall, *Promised Land, Crusader State: The American Encounter with the World since 1776* (New York: Houghton Mifflin, 1997), 87–88.

70. Harry Ammon, *James Monroe: The Quest for National Identity* (Charlottesville: University of Virginia Press, 1990), 60.

71. Graham to Cass, March 23, 1817, *ASP:IA*, 2: 136; Abel, "Indian Consolidation," 289–91.

72. Wallace, *Jefferson and the Indians*, 218.

73. Monroe to Jackson, October 5, 1817, *AJ*, 2: 332.

74. Calhoun to Shelby and Jackson, May 2, 1818, *ASP:IA*, 2: 173; Calhoun to Shelby, July 30, 1818, ibid., 178.

75. Jackson to Shelby, August 11, August 25, 1818, *AJ*, 2: 387–88, 391.

76. Jackson and Isaac Shelby to Calhoun, October 30, 1818, ibid., 399–401; Remini, *Andrew Jackson and His Indian Wars*, 175–78.

77. *ASP:IA*, 2: 240; cf. Arthur H. DeRosier, *The Removal of the Choctaw Indians* (Knoxville: University of Tennessee Press, 1970), 46–47; Remini, *Andrew Jackson and His Indian Wars*, 198–205.

78. Path Killer, Charles Hicks, and Thomas Wilson to the Secretary of War, October 28, 1817, *ASP:IA*, 2: 146; cf. Cherokee Chiefs to McMinn, November 21, 1818, ibid., 487; James Mooney, *Myths of the Cherokee* (Mineola, NY: Dover, 1996), 106; Jurgelski, "New Plow," 131.

79. Calhoun to the Cherokee Delegation, February 11, 1819, ibid., 190; cf. Calhoun to Jackson, November 16, 1821, *AJ*, 3: 132; Calhoun to McMinn, March 16, December 29, 1818, *ASP:IA*, 2: 478, 480.

80. Royal G. Way, "The United States Factory System for Trading with the Indians, 1796–1822," *Mississippi Valley Historical Review* 6, no. 2 (1919): 235; cf. *AC*, 17th Cong., 1st sess., 317, 331, 343, 352; House debate and vote: ibid., 1791–1801.

81. John Marshall, *Johnson v. McIntosh*, February 28, 1823; cf. Lindsay G. Robertson, *Conquest by Law: How the Discovery of America Dispossessed Indigenous Peoples of Their Lands* (New York: Oxford University Press, 2005); Blake A. Watson, *Buying America from the Indians: "Johnson v. McIntosh" and the History of Native Land Rights* (Norman: University of Oklahoma Press, 2012).

82. *AC*, 18th Cong., 1st sess., 1164.

83. Monroe, Special Message to Congress, January 27, 1825, *MPP*, 2: 280.

84. Paul C. Nagel, *John Quincy Adams: A Public Life, A Private Life* (New York: Alfred A. Knopf, 1997), 296–323.

85. *JQA:A*, 7: 411.

86. Ibid., 89–90.

87. Barbour to John Cocke, February 3, 1826, *ASP:IA*, 2: 646–49; cf. *JQA:A*, 7: 113.

88. *JQA:A*, 7: 411.

89. *Report and Resolutions of the Legislature of Georgia with Accompanying Documents, January 23, 1827* (Washington: Gales and Seaton, 1827), 20–21; *JQA:A*, 7: 219, 220, 233; Barbour to Troup, January 29, 1827, *ASP:IA*, 2: 864; Report of Thomas H. Benton,

March 1, 1827, ibid., 869–72; Michael D. Green, *The Politics of Indian Removal* (Lincoln: University of Nebraska Press, 1982), 133.

90. Green, *Politics of Indian Removal*, 134–39. Adams also unsuccessfully sought further cessions from the Choctaw and Chickasaw: Jackson to Terrill, July 29, 1826, *AJ*, 3: 308–9; Remini, *Andrew Jackson and His Indian Wars*, 224.

91. *Acts of the General Assembly of the State of Georgia, Passed in Milledgeville at an Annual Session in November and December, 1827* (Milledgeville, GA: Camak and Ragland, 1827), 249; *Acts of the General Assembly of the State of Georgia, Passed in Milledgeville at an Annual Session in November and December, 1828* (Milledgeville, GA: Camak and Ragland, 1829), 88–89.

92. *RD*, 21st Cong., 1st sess., 318.

93. *Laws of the State of Mississippi; Embracing All Acts of a Public Nature from January Session 1824, to January Session 1838, Inclusive* (Baltimore: John D. Toy, 1838), 195–97.

94. Adams, Fourth Annual Message, *MPP*, 2: 416; cf. Annual Report of the Secretary of War, November 25, 1832, *ASP:MA*, 5: 21.

95. *RD*, 20th Cong., 1st sess., 820, 823.

96. Jackson to Monroe, March 4, 1817, *AJ*, 2: 279–80; cf. Remini, *Andrew Jackson and His Indian Wars*, 228; Meacham, *American Lion*, 93.

97. Eaton to Carroll and Coffee, May 20, 1829, Remini, *Andrew Jackson and His Indian Wars*, 227.

98. *RD*, 21st Cong., 1st sess., 318.

99. Ibid., 312.

100. Ibid., 1013.

101. Ibid., 998, 1011.

102. Ibid., 1070–71.

103. Ibid., 1079.

104. Ibid., 325.

105. Ronald Satz, *American Indian Policy in the Jacksonian Era* (Lincoln: University of Nebraska Press, 1975), 78.

106. David Mayers, *Dissenting Voices in America's Rise to Power* (New York: Cambridge University Press, 2007), 86–87; Donald B. Cole, *The Presidency of Andrew Jackson* (Lawrence: University Press of Kansas, 1993), 71.

107. Cole, *Presidency of Andrew Jackson*, 72–74; cf. 291, n. 51. House vote: *RD*, 21st Cong., 1st sess., 1135; cf. *RD*, 21st Cong., 1st sess., 383; cf. *SL*, 4: 412; Address of Cherokee Nation to the people of the United States, July 17, 1830, *Niles' Weekly Register*, August 21, 1830, Remini, *Andrew Jackson and His Indian Wars*, 254–55.

108. *JQA:A*, 8: 206.

109. *USSS*, 245: 240–42.

110. Ibid., 243–44; cf. Jackson to William Lewis, August 31, 1830, *AJ*, 4: 178–79.

111. *USSS*, 245: 261; cf. H. S. Halbert, "Story of the Treaty of Dancing Rabbit," in *Publications of the Mississippi Historical Society*, ed. Franklin L. Riley, vol. 6 (Harrisburg, PA: Harrisburg Publishing, 1902), 389; Satz, *American Indian Policy*, 65–66, 70–78; Ronald N. Satz, "The Mississippi Choctaw: From the Removal Treaty to the Federal Agency," in *After Removal: The Choctaw in Mississippi*, ed. Samuel J. Wells and Roseanna Tubby (Jackson: University Press of Mississippi, 1986), 4–8; DeRosier, *Removal of the Choctaw Indians*, 128.

112. Jackson to Coffee, April 7, 1832, *AJ*, 4: 430; cf. Green, *Politics of Indian Removal,* 176.

113. Remini, *Andrew Jackson and His Indian Wars*, 251.

114. *AJ*, 4: 483; Arrell M. Gibson, *The Chickasaws* (Norman: University of Oklahoma Press, 1971), 174–76; Cole, *Presidency of Andrew Jackson,* 111, 118; Prucha, *Great Father*, 83.

115. H. Niles, ed., *Niles' Weekly Register*, vol. 44 (Baltimore: Franklin Press, 1833), 256.

116. Anselm J. Gerwing, "The Chicago Indian Treaty of 1833," *Journal of the Illinois State Historical Society* 57, no. 2 (1964): 128.

117. Cass to Jackson, November 29, 1833, *RD*, 23rd Cong., 1st sess., Appendix, 10.

118. John Marshall, *Worcester v. Georgia*, March 3, 1832.

119. Jackson to Coffee, April 7, 1832, *AJ*, 4: 430; cf. Jackson to Wilson Lumpkin, June 22, 1832, *AJ*, 4: 451; Remini, *Andrew Jackson and His Indian Wars*, 257.

120. William Davis to Lewis Cass, March 5, 1836, in *Voices from the Trail of Tears*, ed. Vicki Rozema (Winston-Salem, NC: John F. Blair, 2007), 63.

121. Remini, *Andrew Jackson and His Indian Wars*, 265–68.

122. Cass to Thomas Jesup, May 19, 1836, *ASP:MA*, 7: 312; cf. Cole, *Presidency of Andrew Jackson,* 112; Mary Young, "The Creek Frauds: A Study in Conscience and Corruption," *Mississippi Valley Historical Review* 42 (1955): 411–37; Green, *Politics of Indian Removal,* 185; Remini, *Andrew Jackson and His Indian Wars*, 272–73; Prucha, *Great Father*, 81–82.

123. Cole, *Presidency of Andrew Jackson,* 110; cf. Anthony F. C. Wallace, *The Long, Bitter Trail: Andrew Jackson and the Indians* (New York: Hill and Wang, 1993), 87–88; Remini, *Andrew Jackson and His Indian Wars*, 238.

124. Mayers, *Dissenting Voices*, 98.

125. Wallace, *Long, Bitter Trail*, 93.

126. Remini, *Andrew Jackson and His Indian Wars*, 270; Prucha, *Great Father*, 87; Rozema, *Voices from the Trail of Tears*, 140; cf. 148.

127. J. W. Powell, *Nineteenth Annual Report of the Bureau of American Ethnology,* vol. 1 (Washington: Government Printing Office, 1900), 127; Winfield Scott, *Memoirs of Lieut.-General Scott*, vol. 1 (New York: Sheldon, 1864), 319; cf. Mayers, *Dissenting Voices*, 99–103; Meacham, *American Lion*, 318.

128. The entire as yet unassigned portion of the Louisiana Purchase was initially labeled "Indian country," gradually narrowing to modern-day Oklahoma over the succeeding decades: *SL*, 4: 729.

129. *RD*, 23rd Cong., 1st sess., 4774; cf. 4773.

130. *RD*, 23rd Cong., 1st sess., 4776.

131. Paul Frymer, *Building an American Empire: The Era of Territorial and Political Expansion* (Princeton: Princeton University Press, 2017), 5.

132. Cole, *Presidency of Andrew Jackson,* 116; Mayers, *Dissenting Voices*, 81; Remini, *Andrew Jackson and His Indian Wars*, 238, 277; Satz, *American Indian Policy*, 97.

133. Remini, *Andrew Jackson and His Indian Wars*, 277.

134. Mayers, *Dissenting Voices*, 105.

135. Alexis de Tocqueville, *Democracy in America*, trans. George Lawrence (New York: Harper and Row, 1966), 312.

136. Kevin Gover, "Address to Tribal Leaders," *Journal of American Indian Education* 39, no. 2 (2000): 4–6.

5. To the North

1. *JCC*, 1: 105–13.

2. What is now eastern Canada was named the Province of Quebec after France ceded it to Britain in 1763. The Constitutional Act of 1791 divided it into two provinces, Lower Canada and Upper Canada, roughly corresponding to modern-day Quebec and Ontario, respectively. The 1840 Act of Union recombined them into the Province of Canada, and in 1867 the British North America Act added New Brunswick and Nova Scotia to form the Dominion of Canada, which subsequently expanded to its modern proportions.

3. Marvin McInnis, "The Population of Canada in the Nineteenth Century," in *A Population History of North America*, ed. Michael R. Haines and Richard H. Steckel (New York: Cambridge University Press, 2000), 373.

4. John C. Miller, *Origins of the American Revolution* (Stanford: Stanford University Press, 1943); Robert Middlekauff, *The Glorious Cause: The American Revolution, 1763–1789* (New York: Oxford University Press, 2005); John Ferling, *Almost a Miracle: The American Victory in the War of Independence* (New York: Oxford University Press, 2007).

5. Gustave Lanctot, *Canada and the American Revolution, 1774–1783* (Cambridge: Harvard University Press, 1967), 21–29.

6. McInnis, "Population of Canada," 373; William Lerner, ed., *Historical Statistics of the United States: Colonial Times to 1970*, part 2 (Washington, DC: U.S. Department of Commerce, 1975), 1168.

7. William Duane, *Canada and the Continental Congress* (Philadelphia: Edward Gaskill, 1850), 4–6.

8. *JCC*, 2: 6870; James M. Callahan, *American Foreign Policy in Canadian Relations* (New York: Macmillan, 1937), 2; Lanctot, *Canada and the American Revolution*, 29, 37–38.

9. U.S. Declaration of Independence.

10. *JCC*, 2: 6870.

11. George M. Wrong, *Canada and the American Revolution: The Disruption of the First British Empire* (New York: Macmillan, 1935), 262; Richard B. Morris, *The Peacemakers: The Great Powers and American Independence* (New York: Harper and Row, 1965), 19; *JCC*, 14: 896–97; Joseph L. Davis, *Sectionalism in American Politics, 1774–1787* (Madison: University of Wisconsin Press, 1977), 26; H. James Henderson, *Party Politics in the Continental Congress* (New York: McGraw-Hill, 1974), 6, 261.

12. Edmund C. Burnett, *The Continental Congress* (New York: Macmillan, 1941), 113.

13. *JCC*, 1: 83.

14. Ibid., 88.

15. Duane, *Canada and the Continental Congress*, 4–6.

16. John H. Rhodehamel, ed., *The American Revolution: Writings from the War of Independence* (New York: Library of America, 2001), 75.

17. Lanctot, *Canada and the American Revolution*, 49, 62–75, 89–107; Wrong, *Canada and the American Revolution*, 282–88, 297–98.

18. Mark R. Anderson, *The Battle for the Fourteenth Colony: America's War of Liberation in Canada, 1774–1776* (Lebanon, NH: University Press of New England, 2013); Ferling, *Almost a Miracle*, 80–99.

19. Duane, *Canada and the Continental Congress*, 12–13.

20. *JCC*, 4: 149.

21. Wrong, *Canada and the American Revolution*, 260.

22. Duane, *Canada and the Continental Congress*, 12–13; Wrong, *Canada and the American Revolution*, 311–13.

23. Washington to Schuyler, May 17, 1776, *GW*, 5: 52; cf. Washington's June letters to John Hancock, ibid., 111–14, 120–21, 129–31, 142, 159–60.

24. *GW*, 11: 493; *BF*, 6: 454.

25. Articles of Confederation, art. 11.

26. Burnett, *Continental Congress*, 218; cf. 213–29, 248–58.

27. Michael Stephenson, *Patriot Battles: How the War for Independence Was Fought* (New York: HarperCollins, 2007), 32–33.

28. Wrong, *Canada and the American Revolution*, 315.

29. Washington to Continental Congress, December 23, 1777, *GW*, 10: 195; cf. Wayne Bodle, *The Valley Forge Winter: Civilians and Soldiers in War* (University Park: Pennsylvania State University Press, 2002), 39–40.

30. Willard M. Wallace, *Appeal to Arms: A Military History of the American Revolution* (New York: Harper and Brothers, 1951), 170.

31. Stephenson, *Patriot Battles*, 27; Wrong, *Canada and the American Revolution*, 354–55.

32. Washington to Thomas Nelson, February 8, 1778, *GW*, 10: 433; Washington to President of Congress, November 11, 1778, *GW*, 13: 224, 230; cf. Washington to President of Congress, September 12, 1778, *GW*, 12: 434–36; Burnett, *Continental Congress*, 371; Callahan, *Canadian Relations*, 7.

33. Lanctot, *Canada and the American Revolution*, 173–89; Ferling, *Almost a Miracle*, 290–93, 316–18, 446–47.

34. Henderson, *Party Politics*, 197; Burnett, *Continental Congress*, 291.

35. Washington to President of Congress, November 11, 1778, *GW*, 13: 224, 230; cf. Washington to Henry Laurens, November 14, 1778, ibid., 256.

36. Lanctot, *Canada and the American Revolution*, 178, 205; Wrong, *Canada and the American Revolution*, 356; Ferling, *Almost a Miracle*, 548.

37. *BF*, 6: 454; Lanctot, *Canada and the American Revolution*, 181–82.

38. *RDC*, 3: 302; Samuel F. Bemis, *A Diplomatic History of the United States*, 5th ed. (New York: Holt, Rinehart and Winston, 1965), 49; cf. Samuel F. Bemis, *American Foreign Policy and the Blessings of Liberty* (New Haven: Yale University Press, 1962), 113; Callahan, *Canadian Relations*, 8.

39. Bemis, *Diplomatic History*, 52; cf. 57; Bemis, *American Foreign Policy*, 114–28; Wrong, *Canada and the American Revolution*, 360–65; Walter Nugent, *Habits of Empire: A History of American Expansion* (New York: Alfred A. Knopf, 2008), 35–36.

40. Richard W. Maass, "'Difficult to Relinquish Territory Which Had Been Conquered': Expansionism and the War of 1812," *Diplomatic History* 39, no. 1 (2015): 70–97.

41. Carl von Clausewitz, *On War*, ed. Michael Howard and Peter Paret (Princeton: Princeton University Press, 1989), 605.

42. The British navy impressed more than fifteen thousand U.S. sailors from 1793 to 1812: Joshua Wolf, "'The Misfortune to Get Pressed': Impressment of American Seamen and the Ramifications on the United States, 1793–1812" (PhD diss., Temple University, 2015), 52; cf. Donald R. Hickey, *Don't Give Up the Ship! Myths of the War of 1812* (Chicago: University of Illinois Press, 2006), 20; John Quincy Adams to William Plumer, August 13, 1813, *JQA:F*, 4: 505; Jefferson to Madison, August 15, 1804, *TJ:F*, 10: 95; Madison to George Joy, May 22, 1807, *JMa:RF*, 2: 405.

43. Jefferson to Madison, August 4, 1805, *TJ:F*, 8: 374; Monroe to Madison, July 1, 1804, *JMo*, 4: 218.

44. Alfred T. Mahan, *The Influence of Sea Power upon the French Revolution and Empire, 1793–1812*, vol. 2 (Boston: Little, Brown, 1892), 355; cf. Reginald Horsman, *The Causes of the War of 1812* (Philadelphia: University of Pennsylvania Press, 1962), 56–57.

45. Tensions had run high since the previous June, when the H.M.S. *Leopard* fired on the U.S.S. *Chesapeake*, killing three, after it resisted being searched. The *Leopard* seized four deserters, including three formerly impressed Americans: Spencer C. Tucker and Frank T. Reuter, *Injured Honor: The Chesapeake–Leopard Affair, June 22, 1807* (Annapolis: Naval Institute Press, 1996); Hickey, *Don't Give Up the Ship*, 21.

46. Paul A. Gilje, *Free Trade and Sailors' Rights in the War of 1812* (New York: Cambridge University Press, 2013); Bradford Perkins, *Prologue to War: England and the United States, 1805–1812* (Los Angeles: University of California Press, 1961), 95; Troy Bickham, *The Weight of Vengeance: The United States, the British Empire, and the War of 1812* (New York: Oxford University Press, 2012), 21.

47. Adams to Harrison Otis, March 31, 1808, *JQA:F*, 3: 200.

48. *AC*, 11th Cong., 2nd sess., 581.

49. *AC*, 12th Cong., 1st sess., 1399.

50. Horsman, *Causes of the War of 1812*, 264.

51. Gordon S. Wood, *Empire of Liberty: A History of the Early Republic, 1789–1815* (New York: Oxford University Press, 2009), 655.

52. Monroe to John Taylor, June 13, 1812, *JMo*, 5: 206; Wilson Nicholas to Jefferson, February 4, 1810, in J. Jefferson Looney, ed., *The Papers of Thomas Jefferson, Retirement Series*, vol. 2 (Princeton: Princeton University Press, 2006), 195; Alan Taylor, *The Civil War of 1812: American Citizens, British Subjects, Irish Rebels, and Indian Allies* (New York: Alfred A. Knopf, 2010), 127.

53. Maass, "Expansionism and the War of 1812," 72.

54. Madison, Third Annual Message, *MPP*, 1: 494; Madison to the House of Representatives of the State of South Carolina, January 8, 1812, *JMa:RF*, 2: 524; cf. Madison, Fourth Annual Message, *MPP*, 1: 520. Discussion of Britain's maritime restrictions filled fifteen paragraphs of Madison's war message: *JMa:H*, 8: 192–200. Two months after the declaration of war Madison learned that Britain had provisionally repealed the Orders, but since British Foreign Secretary "Castlereagh had reserved the right to restore the system in May, 1813," Madison thought it "a trick to turn America from war": Perkins, *Prologue to War*, 421.

55. J. C. A. Stagg, *Mr. Madison's War: Politics, Diplomacy, and Warfare in the Early American Republic, 1783–1830* (Princeton: Princeton University Press, 1983), 23–24.

56. Donald R. Hickey, *The War of 1812: A Forgotten Conflict* (Chicago: University of Illinois Press, 2012), 44; Roger H. Brown, *Republic in Peril: 1812* (New York: W. W. Norton, 1971), 34; Wood, *Empire of Liberty*, 694–95.

57. Monroe to Russell, June 26, 1812, *DC:CR*, 1: 207; cf. George C. Daughan, *1812: The Navy's War* (New York: Basic Books, 2011), 39; Taylor, *Civil War of 1812*, 139; Scott A. Silverstone, *Divided Union: The Politics of War in the Early American Republic* (Ithaca, NY: Cornell University Press, 2004), 96; Wood, *Empire of Liberty*, 676.

58. David Mayers, *Dissenting Voices in America's Rise to Power* (New York: Cambridge University Press, 2007), 32; Horsman, *Causes of the War of 1812*, 236.

59. *AC*, 12th Cong., 1st sess., 711, 1388.

60. Winfield Scott, *Memoirs of Lieut.-General Scott*, vol. 1 (New York: Sheldon, 1864), 35; Stagg, *Mr. Madison's War*, 3; J. C. A. Stagg, "Enlisted Men in the United States Army, 1812–1815: A Preliminary Survey," *William and Mary Quarterly* 43, no. 4 (1986): 615–45; William B. Skelton, "High Army Leadership in the War of 1812: The Making and Remaking of the Officer Corps," *William and Mary Quarterly* 51, no. 2 (1994): 253–74; Jeffrey Kimball, "The Fog and Friction of Frontier War: The Role of Logistics in American Offensive Failure during the War of 1812," *Old Northwest 5* (1979/80): 323–43.

61. William G. Dean, "British Garrisons to 1871," in *Historical Atlas of Canada: The Land Transformed, 1800–1891*, ed. R. Louis Gentilcore, Don Measner, and Ronald H. Walder (Toronto: University of Toronto Press, 1993), 66; Lawrence S. Kaplan, "France and the War of 1812," *Journal of American History* 57, no. 1 (1970): 37.

62. Wood, *Empire of Liberty*, 659.

63. Jefferson to William Duane, August 4, 1812, *TJ:F*, 11: 265; cf. Jefferson to Thaddeus Kosciusko, June 28, 1812, ibid., 260.

64. Monroe to John Taylor, June 13, 1812, *JMo*, 5: 211.

65. *AC*, 12th Cong., 1st sess., 1397; cf. Perkins, *Prologue to War*, 284.

66. *AC*, 9th Cong., 1st sess., 555; *AC*, 11th Cong., 2nd sess., 580.

67. *AC*, 12th Cong., 1st sess., 447.

68. McInnis, "Population of Canada," 373; Robert Malcolmson, *A Very Brilliant Affair: The Battle of Queenston Heights, 1812* (Toronto: Robin Brass Studio, 2003), 14–16.

69. Stagg, *Mr. Madison's War*, 40; cf. Taylor, *Civil War of 1812*, 119.

70. Madison, "Political Observations," April 20, 1795, *JMa:RF*, 4: 498; Stagg, *Mr. Madison's War*, 38.

71. Stagg, *Mr. Madison's War*, 40.

72. *AC*, 12th Cong., 1st sess., 416; Lawrence S. Kaplan, "France and Madison's Decision for War in 1812," *Mississippi Valley Historical Review* 50, no. 4 (1964): 663.

73. Brown, *Republic in Peril*, 120; Perkins, *Prologue to War*, 427.

74. Horsman, *Causes of the War of 1812*, 236; cf. 169–71; *AC*, 12th Cong., 1st sess., 481; Julius W. Pratt, *Expansionists of 1812* (New York: Peter Smith, 1949), 166; Bradford Perkins, *The Cambridge History of American Foreign Relations*, vol. 1 (New York: Cambridge University Press, 1993), 138.

75. Clay to Thomas Bodley, December 18, 1813, *HC*, 1: 842; cf. *AC*, 11th Cong., 2nd sess., 580.

76. Monroe to John Taylor, June 13, 1812, *JMo*, 5: 207; cf. *Virginia Argus*, November 11, 1811; Pratt, *Expansionists of 1812*, 267.

77. Madison to Henry Wheaton, February 26, 1827, *JMa:RF*, 3: 555.

78. James A. Bayard to Andrew Bayard, May 2, 1812, "Papers of James A. Bayard, 1796–1815," in *Annual Report of the American Historical Association, 1913*, vol. 2, ed. Elizabeth Donnan (Washington, DC, 1915), 196.

79. Hugh Nelson to Charles Everett, December 16, 1811, Brown, *Republic in Peril*, 124.

80. Speech of Randolph: *AC*, 12th Cong., 1st sess., 533.

81. Gideon Granger to John Tod, December 26, 1811, Taylor, *Civil War of 1812*, 138.

82. *AC*, 12th Cong., 1st sess., 450, 712.

83. Liverpool to James Craig, April 4, 1810, Perkins, *Prologue to War*, 14.

84. Horsman, *Causes of the War of 1812*, 175–76, 266; Reginald Horsman, "Western War Aims, 1811–1812," *Indiana Magazine of History* 53, no. 1 (1957): 5–8.

85. Jefferson to Letue, November 8, 1808, *TJ:W*, 5: 384; cf. Jefferson to Joseph Cabell, February 2, 1816, *TJ:W*, 6: 544; Jefferson to Lafayette, May 14, 1817, *TJ:W*, 7: 66; Madison to Monroe, November 28, 1818, *JM:H*, 8: 420; William E. Buckley, *The Hartford Convention* (New Haven: Tercentenary Commission, 1934), 5; Dinah Mayo-Bobee, *New England Federalists: Widening the Sectional Divide in Jeffersonian America* (Madison, NJ: Fairleigh Dickinson University Press, 2017).

86. Speeches of Boyd: *AC*, 12th Cong., 1st sess., 521; Quincy: *AC*, 12th Cong., 2nd sess., 170; Miller and Culpepper: *AC*, 13th Cong., 2nd sess., 958, 1364; Mayers, *Dissenting Voices*, 40; Reginald C. Stuart, *Civil–Military Relations during the War of 1812* (Santa Barbara, CA: ABC-CLIO, 2009), 67; John R. Elting, *Amateurs, To Arms! A Military History of the War of 1812* (Chapel Hill: Algonquin Books, 1991), 8; Pratt, *Expansionists of 1812*, 164.

87. "Report and Resolutions of Connecticut on the Militia Question," August 25, 1812, in *State Documents on Federal Relations: The States and the United States*, ed. Herman V. Ames (Philadelphia: Department of History, University of Pennsylvania, 1911), 59–61; Wood, *Empire of Liberty*, 693.

88. Theodore Dwight, *History of the Hartford Convention* (New York: N. and J. White, 1833), 345–46, 357, 361, 370–71.

89. David C. Hendrickson, *Union, Nation, or Empire: The American Debate over International Relations, 1789–1941* (Lawrence: University Press of Kansas, 2009), 63.

90. Taylor, *Civil War of 1812*, 138; McInnis, "Population of Canada," 373.

91. Callahan, *Canadian Relations*, 66–67.

92. Jean-Claude Robert, "An Immigrant Population," in Gentilcore, Measner, and Walder, *Historical Atlas of Canada*, 21; R. Louis Gentilcore, Don Measner, and David Doherty, "The Coming of the Loyalists," ibid., 24; Wood, *Empire of Liberty*, 676.

93. *AC*, 9th Cong., 1st sess., 557.

94. Perkins, *Prologue to War*, 426.

95. Robert, "Immigrant Population," 21; Perkins, *Prologue to War*, 286; Taylor, *Civil War of 1812*, 8; Bickham, *Weight of Vengeance*, 12.

96. Nugent, *Habits of Empire*, 80; Pratt, *Expansionists of 1812*, 6; Reginald C. Stuart, *United States Expansionism and British North America, 1775–1871* (Chapel Hill: University of North Carolina Press, 1988).

97. J. C. A. Stagg, "Between Black Rock and a Hard Place: Peter B. Porter's Plan for an American Invasion of Canada in 1812," *Journal of the Early Republic* 19, no. 3 (1999): 387, 421.

98. *AC*, 12th Cong., 1st sess., 322–24.

99. Brown, *Republic in Peril*, 125, 124.

100. Taylor, *Civil War of 1812*, 139, 418.

101. F. A. Golder, "The Russian Offer of Mediation in the War of 1812," *Political Science Quarterly* 31, no. 3 (1916): 384, 382.

102. Monroe to Gallatin, Adams, and Bayard, April 15, 1813, *DC:CR*, 1: 213.

103. *AC*, 12th Cong., 2nd sess., 537.

104. Harper to Plumer, February 6, 1813, Pratt, *Expansionists of 1812*, 187.

105. *AC*, 13th Cong., 1st sess., 1073; cf. Pratt, *Expansionists of 1812*, 13, 188, 267.

106. Jefferson to Monroe, June 18, 1813, *TJ:W*, 6: 131; cf. Callahan, *Canadian Relations*, 79.

107. Monroe to Gallatin, Adams, and Bayard, June 23, 1813, *DC:CR*, 1: 212; Monroe to Adams and Bayard, January 1, 1814, *DC:CR*, 1: 216.

108. Jon Latimer, *1812: War with America* (Cambridge: Belknap Press, 2007), 3; cf. Donald R. Hickey, "What Was the British Perspective?" *Journal of the War of 1812* 11, no. 4 (2009): 7–15.

109. Perkins, *Prologue to War*, 426; cf. Mayers, *Dissenting Voices*, 37.

110. In contrast, the Red River settlement in Manitoba was home to only about four thousand at this time: McInnis, "Population of Canada," 373; cf. William L. Marr and Donald G. Paterson, *Canada: An Economic History* (Toronto: Gage, 1980), 42–116; Harold A. Innis, *Essays in Canadian Economic History* (Toronto: University of Toronto Press, 1956), 108–22; Harold A. Innis, *The Fur Trade in Canada: An Introduction to Canadian Economic History* (Toronto: University of Toronto Press, 1956).

111. John C. Dent, *The Last Forty Years: Canada since the Union of 1841*, vol. 1 (Toronto: George Virtue, 1881), 22–23.

112. Hunter's Lodge invasions in November and December 1838 ended disastrously: Major L. Wilson, *The Presidency of Martin Van Buren* (Lawrence: University Press of Kansas, 1984), 160.

113. Perkins, *Cambridge History*, 208.

114. Wilson, *Van Buren*, 147.

115. James C. Curtis, *The Fox at Bay: Martin Van Buren and the Presidency, 1837–1841* (Lexington: University of Kentucky Press, 1970), 180; cf. 177.

116. *CG*, 25th Cong., 2nd sess., 87.

117. Ibid., 103–4.

118. Ibid., 81.

119. Ibid., 77.

120. Wilson, *Van Buren*, 158–61.

121. *SL*, 5: 212; cf. Bemis, *Diplomatic History*, 223.

122. Wilson, *Van Buren*, 161, 147; Curtis, *Fox at Bay*, 178; cf. 175; Bemis, *Diplomatic History*, 223.

123. Curtis, *Fox at Bay*, 181.

124. Wilson, *Van Buren*, 161–62.

125. Dean, "British Garrisons," 66.

126. Curtis, *Fox at Bay*, 171; Ted Widmer, *Martin Van Buren* (New York: Henry Holt, 2005), 130–31.

127. *CG*, 25th Cong., 2nd sess., 82; cf. speech of Gray: ibid.

128. Ibid., 78.

129. Ibid., 79.

130. Ibid., 82, 79; cf. 87; speech of Clay: ibid.

131. Ibid., Appendix, 382–87.

132. Clay to George Featherstonhaugh, February 10, 1839, *HC*, 9: 284.

133. Widmer, *Van Buren*, 133, 88.

134. *Detroit Advertiser*, January 23, 1838, in Stuart, *United States Expansionism*, 132.

135. Stuart, *United States Expansionism*, 134.

136. Forsyth to Charles Bankhead, February 1836, *DC:CR*, 3: 4–6; Howard Jones, *To the Webster–Ashburton Treaty: A Study in Anglo-American Relations, 1783–1843* (Chapel Hill: University of North Carolina Press, 1977), 15–18.

137. *CG*, 25th Cong., 3rd sess., Appendix, 212–13; cf. *JB*, 3: 481–502.

138. *CG*, 25th Cong., 3rd sess., Appendix, 310, 314–15; cf. *CG*, 26th Cong., 1st sess., 322–24.

139. Francis M. Carroll, *A Good and Wise Measure: The Search for the Canadian–American Boundary, 1783–1842* (Toronto: University of Toronto Press, 2003), 217.

140. John Tyler to Daniel Webster, March 12, 1846, Jones, *Webster–Ashburton Treaty*, ix.

141. Pakenham to Aberdeen, August 1844, in James J. Barnes and Patience P. Barnes, *Private and Confidential: Letters from Ministers in Washington to Foreign Secretaries in London, 1844–67* (Selinsgrove, PA: Susquehanna University Press, 1993), 25.

142. Nugent, *Habits of Empire*, 158.

143. Ibid., 173–74.

144. *CG*, 29th Cong., 1st sess., 134.

145. Norman A. Graebner, *Empire on the Pacific: A Study in American Continental Expansion* (New York: Ronald Press, 1955), 3, 32, 143, 222.

146. David M. Pletcher, *The Diplomacy of Annexation: Texas, Oregon, and the Mexican War* (Columbia: University of Missouri Press, 1973), 107; Edward P. Crapol, *John Tyler, the Accidental President* (Chapel Hill: University of North Carolina Press, 2006), 146–47.

147. Nugent, *Habits of Empire*, 159; Robert Boyd, *The Coming of the Spirit of Pestilence: Introduced Infectious Diseases and Population Decline among Northwest Coast Indians, 1774–1874* (Seattle: University of Washington Press, 1999), 262.

148. Nugent, *Habits of Empire*, 175.

149. Charles G. Sellers, *James K. Polk: Continentalist, 1843–1846* (Princeton: Princeton University Press, 1966), 384; cf. Willard E. Ireland, "British Columbia's American Heritage," in *Historical Essays on British Columbia*, ed. J. Friesen and H. K. Ralston (Ottawa: Carleton Library, 1980), 113.

150. *MPP*, 4: 381.

151. Polk, First Annual Message, *MPP*, 4: 395.

152. *JP*, 1: 69, 82–83, 78.

153. *CG*, 25th Cong., 2nd sess., 168–69.

154. *CG*, 28th Cong., 2nd sess., Appendix, 137.

155. *CG*, 29th Cong., 1st sess., 297.

156. Ibid., 389.

157. *New York Morning News*, December 27, 1845.

158. *JP*, 1: 4; 64; cf. 80.

159. Ibid., 133; 159; cf. 155.

160. Ibid., 191.

161. *CG*, 28th Cong., 2nd sess., 135.

162. *CG*, 29th Cong., 1st sess., 133.

163. Ibid., 115; cf. speech of Parrish: ibid., 241.

164. *JP*, 1: 155.

165. McLane to Buchanan, February 3, 1846, Sellers, *Polk: Continentalist*, 380; cf. *JP*, 1: 209.

166. *JP*, 1: 453.

167. Pakenham to Aberdeen, June 13, 1846, in Barnes and Barnes, *Private and Confidential*, 35; cf. Stuart Anderson, "British Threats and the Settlement of the Oregon Boundary Dispute," *Pacific Northwest Quarterly* 66, no. 4 (1975): 153–60.

168. McInnis, "Population of Canada," 373; cf. Don Measner and Christine Hampson, "The Canadian Population, 1871, 1891," in Gentilcore, Measner, and Walder, *Historical Atlas of Canada*, 80–81.

169. W. T. Easterbrook and Hugh G. J. Aitken, *Canadian Economic History* (Toronto: Macmillan, 1958), 389.

170. Prime Minister Palmerston "led his government into an increasingly pragmatic, pro-Southern, position" when he expected the South to win, but as northern victory grew more likely he reined in prosouthern Cabinet members and Emperor Napoleon III: David Brown, *Palmerston: A Biography* (New Haven: Yale University Press, 2010), 452; cf. 451–55.

171. Glyndon Van Deusen, *William Henry Seward* (New York: Oxford University Press, 1967), 548.

172. Palmerston to Queen Victoria, January 20, 1865, George Earle Buckle, ed., *The Letters of Queen Victoria: A Selection from Her Majesty's Correspondence and Journal*, vol. 1 (London: John Murray, 1926), 248–49; cf. Brian Jenkins, *Fenians and Anglo-American Relations during Reconstruction* (Ithaca, NY: Cornell University Press, 1969), 40–42.

173. John M. Taylor, *William Henry Seward: Lincoln's Right Hand* (New York: HarperCollins, 1991), 252.

174. Donald Stoker, *The Grand Design: Strategy and the U.S. Civil War* (New York: Oxford University Press, 2010), 374; Jeremy Black, *America as a Military Power: From the American Revolution to the Civil War* (Westport, CT: Praeger, 2002), 136–78.

175. Allan R. Millet and Peter Maslowski, *For the Common Defense: A Military History of the United States of America* (New York: Macmillan, 1994), 248.

176. Dean, "British Garrisons," 66.

177. Peter Vronsky, *Ridgeway: The American Fenian Invasion and the 1866 Battle that Made Canada* (Toronto: Allen Lane, 2011), 3; Jenkins, *Fenians*, 42.

178. Jenkins, *Fenians*, 26, 28–33, 48.

179. Hereward Senior, *The Last Invasion of Canada: The Fenian Raids, 1866–1870* (Toronto: Dundurn Press, 1991), 48.

180. Bruce to Russell, October 31, 1865, in Jenkins, *Fenians*, 58.

181. Archibald to Russell, January 9, 1865, ibid., 43; cf. 34.

182. *New York Tribune*, November 16, 1865, ibid., 43.

183. Clarendon to Bruce, November 16, 1865, ibid., 63; cf. 23.

184. Ibid., 129.

185. Bruce to Russell, August 8, 1865, ibid., 51.

186. Bruce to Clarendon, April 17, 1866, ibid., 150.

187. Ibid., 44–46, 128–29.

188. Joe P. Smith, "American Republican Leadership and the Movement for the Annexation of Canada in the Eighteen-Sixties," *Report of the Annual Meeting of the Canadian Historical Association* 14, no. 1 (1935): 67, 70.

189. *CG*, 39th Cong., 1st sess., July 3, 1866, 3548; bill text: H.R. 754, 39th Cong. (1866).

190. Smith, "American Republican Leadership," 70–71; cf. Joe P. Smith, "The Republican Expansionists of the Early Reconstruction Era" (PhD diss., University of Chicago, 1933), 123–24.

191. Smith references Seward's April 1, 1861, memo to Lincoln as advocating "a programme of expansion in North and Central America," Smith, "American Republican Leadership," 67; it actually advocated using the threat of European interventions in the Western Hemisphere to inspire patriotism and avoid civil war. Its only mention of Canada reads, "I would seek explanations from Great Britain and Russia, and send agents into Canada, Mexico and Central America, to rouse a vigorous continental spirit of independence on this continent against European intervention," William H. Seward, "Some Thoughts for the President's Consideration," April 1, 1861, Reel 188, William Henry Seward Papers, Library of Congress. Smith also claims that Seward sent Robert Walker to spread proannexation propaganda in Montreal, Smith, "American Republican Leadership," 67–68; yet Seward wrote, "I see that some of the hostile presses in Canada report that Mr. Robert J. Walker has been engaged as an agent of this government in a plot for the annexation of Canada to the United States, and that he contradicts the allegation. . . . Mr. Walker's visit and sojourn in Canada have been without any previous direction from and without even the knowledge of this government. It is not believed here that he has engaged in any proceedings unfriendly to Canada or the British authority existing there." Seward to Adams, March 27, 1865, *FRUS: 1865*, vol. 1, 295.

192. Vronsky, *Ridgeway*, 25.

193. Bruce to Clarendon, January 9, 1866, ibid., 26; cf. Bruce to Clarendon, March 16, 1866, ibid.; Alexander Galt to George Brown, December 5, 1865, in Jenkins, *Fenians*, 107; Thornton to Stanley, August 18, 1868, ibid., 277; Thornton to Clarendon, July 26, 1869, ibid., 295.

194. Vronsky, *Ridgeway*, 27.

195. Seward to Reverdy Johnson, August 27, 1868, State Department: Foreign Dispatches to Great Britain, France, 1861–1869, 216–17, *WHSP*.

196. Thornton to Stanley, March 30, 1868, Jenkins, *Fenians*, 264; cf. 100; Thornton to Stanley, May 2, 1868, ibid., 271; Seward to Reverdy Johnson, August 27, 1868, State Department: Foreign Dispatches to Great Britain, France, 1861–1869, 216–17, *WHSP*.

197. Jenkins, *Fenians*, 272.

198. Ibid., 138; Senior, *Last Invasion*, 50–51.

199. Vronsky, *Ridgeway*, 27–30.

200. Hemans to Bruce, June 4, 1866, Jenkins, *Fenians*, 147; Vronsky, *Ridgeway*, 34–38.

201. Seward to Bruce, May 14, 1866, Jenkins, *Fenians*, 141.

202. Vronsky, *Ridgeway*, 243.

203. Jenkins, *Fenians*, 150.

204. Thornton to Clarendon, August 2, 1869, ibid., 295.

205. Ibid., 296.

206. Ibid., 302.

207. Allan Nevins, *Hamilton Fish: The Inner History of the Grant Administration* (New York: Dodd, Mead, 1936), 393.

208. *UG*, 20: 177; Nevins, *Fish*, 395.

209. Thornton to Clarendon, June 21, 1870, Jenkins, *Fenians*, 311.

210. Peter B. Waite, *The Life and Times of Confederation, 1864–1867: Politics, Newspapers, and the Union of British North America* (Toronto: University of Toronto Press, 1962), 273; cf. Fish to Grant, September 12, 1870, *UG*, 20: 294; Senior, *Last Invasion*, 56–57.

211. C. D. Howe, *The Canada Year Book 1948–49* (Ottawa: Edmond Cloutier, 1949), 154; Wayne Suttles, ed., *Handbook of North American Indians*, vol. 7 (Washington: Smithsonian Institution Press, 1990), 147; "Speech of Hon. Charles Sumner, of Massachusetts, on the Cession of Russian America to the United States" (Washington: Congressional Globe Office, 1867), 24–25; Russell Thornton, "Population History of Native North Americans," in *A Population History of North America*, ed. Michael R. Haines and Richard H. Steckel (New York: Cambridge University Press, 2000), 23; Nugent, *Habits of Empire*, 249; David E. Shi, "Seward's Attempt to Annex British Columbia, 1865–1869," *Pacific Historical Review* 47, no. 2 (1978): 220; J. M. Bumsted, *Reporting the Resistance: Alexander Begg and Joseph Hargrave on the Red River Resistance* (Winnipeg: University of Manitoba Press, 2003), 3; J. M. Bumsted, *The Red River Rebellion* (Winnipeg: Watson and Dwyer, 1996), 18.

212. Frank Golder, "The Purchase of Alaska," *American Historical Review* 25, no. 3 (1920): 411–25; Nikolay N. Bolkhovitinov, "The Crimean War and the Emergence of Proposals for the Sale of Russian America, 1853–1861," *Pacific Historical Review* 59, no. 1 (1990): 15–49; Stephen Haycox, *Alaska: An American Colony* (Seattle: University of Washington Press, 2002), 154–56; cf. "Speech of Hon. Charles Sumner," 8.

213. Ronald J. Jensen, *The Alaska Purchase and Russian–American Relations* (Seattle: University of Washington Press, 1975), 67–79.

214. Frederick Merk, *Manifest Destiny and Mission in American History* (New York: Alfred A. Knopf, 1963), 229.

215. Seward to Francis Vinton, May 23, 1867, State Department: Domestic Letters, vol. 2: 1868–1869, 452–54, WHSP; Seward to David Seymour, July 2, 1867, ibid., 456.

216. "Speech of Hon. Charles Sumner," 17.

217. Ibid., 24.

218. Report of Major General George H. Thomas, September 27, 1869, included in the Report of the Secretary of War, November 20, 1869, House Executive Documents, 41st Cong., 2nd sess., vol. 1, 119.

219. "Speech of Hon. Charles Sumner," 48.

220. Report of Major General George H. Thomas, 120.

221. "Speech of Hon. Charles Sumner," 15; Haycox, *Alaska*, 171.

222. Seward to Lovell H. Rosseau, August 7, 1867, State Department: Domestic Letters, vol. 2: 1868–1869, 469, WHSP; cf. "Speech of Hon. Charles Sumner," 15.

223. C. M. Clay to Seward, May 10, 1867, FRUS: 1867–68, vol. 1, 391.

224. Virginia H. Reid, *The Purchase of Alaska: Contemporary Opinion* (Long Beach, CA: Press-Telegram Printers, 1939), 20–34; Van Deusen, *William Henry Seward*, 537–41; Merk, *Manifest Destiny and Mission*, 229.

225. Eric T. L. Love, *Race over Empire: Racism and U.S. Imperialism, 1865–1900* (Chapel Hill: University of North Carolina Press, 2004), 32.

226. *New York Tribune*, April 1, 1867, George F. G. Stanley, *The Birth of Western Canada: A History of the Riel Rebellions* (Toronto: University of Toronto Press, 1960), 35; Love, *Race over Empire*, 33; Walter Stahr, *Seward: Lincoln's Indispensable Man* (New York: Simon and Schuster, 2013), 498.

227. Eduard de Stoeckl to Alexander Gorchakov, April 19, 1867, in Shi, "Seward's Attempt," 224; cf. Richard E. Neunherz, "'Hemmed In': Reactions in British Columbia to the Purchase of Russian America," *Pacific Northwest Quarterly* 80, no. 3 (1989): 101.

228. Willard E. Ireland, "British Columbia's American Heritage," in *Historical Essays on British Columbia*, ed. J. Friesen and H. K. Ralston (Ottawa: Carleton Library, 1980), 119; Van Deusen, *William Henry Seward*, 548–49.

229. Seward to Charles F. Adams, July 7, 1866, State Department: Foreign Dispatches to Great Britain, France, 1861–1869, 192–93, WHSP.

230. Shi, "Seward's Attempt," 222.

231. Neunherz, "Hemmed In," 102–5.

232. Allen Francis to Seward, April 23, July 2, 1867, Neunherz, "Hemmed In," 104, 107; cf. Shi, "Seward's Attempt," 222–23, 228, 231.

233. Charles F. Adams Jr., to Charles F. Adams, June 29, 1867, Shi, "Seward's Attempt," 224; cf. 228; Donald F. Warner, *The Idea of Continental Union: Agitation for the Annexation of Canada to the United States, 1849–1893* (Lexington: University of Kentucky Press, 1960), 129.

234. Shi, "Seward's Attempt," 231.

235. Calvin Pease and James G. Randall, eds., *The Diary of Orville Hickman Browning* (Springfield: Illinois State Historical Library 1933), 213.

236. Neunherz, "Hemmed In," 110; Shi, "Seward's Attempt," 232.

237. Bruce to Stanley, August 30, 1867, Shi, "Seward's Attempt," 231; cf. *CG*, 40th Cong., 2nd sess., 79; Lester B. Shippee, *Canadian–American Relations, 1849–1874* (New Haven: Yale University Press, 1939), 201; Nevins, *Fish*, 397.

238. Shi, "Seward's Attempt," 234.

239. "W. H. Seward Notes Made During Northwest Trip, 1869," Miscellaneous and Personal—Speeches and Proclamations, File Drawer 32, Folder 168, WHSP.

240. *CG*, 41st Cong., 2nd sess., 324.

241. Ibid., 325.

242. Dale Gibson, *Law, Life, and Government at Red River*, vol. 1 (Montreal: McGill-Queen's University Press, 2015), 204; Stanley, *Birth of Western Canada*, 13.

243. W. L. Morton, ed., *Alexander Begg's Red River Journal and Other Papers Relative to the Red River Resistance of 1869–1870* (Toronto: Champlain Society, 1956), 3–4; Bumsted, *Reporting the Resistance*, 9–16; Alexander Begg, *The Creation of Manitoba: or, A History of the Red River Troubles* (Toronto: A. H. Hovey, 1871).

244. Bumsted, *Red River Rebellion*, 30–31; Hamilton Fish, Diary, January 6, 1870, in Nevins, *Fish*, 386.

245. Stanley, *Birth of Western Canada*, 24.

246. *Correspondence and Papers Connected with Recent Occurrences in the North-West Territories* (Ottawa: I. B. Taylor, 1870), 80.

247. Bumsted, *Red River Rebellion*, 50, 116–17; Morton, *Begg's Red River Journal*, 86, 96, 240, 259.

248. Fish to Taylor, December 30, 1869, *The James Wickes Taylor Correspondence, 1859–1870*, vol. 3 (Altona, MB: D. W. Friesen and Sons, 1968), 97–98; cf. James Taylor to Grant, January 1871, *UG*, 20: 407–8.

249. Taylor to Chase, December 17, 1861, *Taylor Correspondence*, 21; Stanley, *Birth of Western Canada*, 36.

250. Taylor to N. W. Kittson, May 15, 1869, *Taylor Correspondence*, 71.

251. *UG*, 20: 337–38.

252. Fish, Diary, January 6, 1870, in Nevins, *Fish*, 386.

253. Fish to John Motley, January 14, 1870, Box 214, Hamilton Fish Papers, Library of Congress.

254. Fish, Diary, January 15, 1870, in Nevins, *Fish*, 387.

255. Nevins, *Fish*, 395–97.

256. *CG*, 41st Cong., 2nd sess., 2889.

257. Warner, *Continental Union*, 121–22; cf. *CG*, 41st Cong., 2nd sess., 2889.

258. *UG*, 20: 453; cf. Bumsted, *Red River Rebellion*, 198.

259. Nevins, *Fish*, 396.

260. Boutwell to Grant, July 29, 1870, *UG*, 20: 282.

261. Willard E. Ireland, "British Columbia's American Heritage," in *Historical Essays on British Columbia*, ed. J. Friesen and H. K. Ralston (Ottawa: Carleton Library, 1980), 119.

262. Nevins, *Fish*, 470–93; Rosemary Neering, *The Pig War: The Last Canada–U.S. Border Conflict* (Victoria, BC: Heritage, 2011).

263. George C. Herring, *From Colony to Superpower: U.S. Foreign Relations since 1776* (New York: Oxford University Press, 2008), 255.

264. Nevins, *Fish*, 384–87.

265. Bayard to Lionel Sackville-West, March 28, 1885, in *Canadian Military History: Selected Readings*, ed. Marc Milner (Mississauga, ON: Copp Clark Pitman, 1993), 8.

266. Callahan, *Canadian Relations*, 412; Warner, *Continental Union*, 216, 218, 234–35. Cummings's and Gallinger's proposals: *CR*, 52nd Cong., 1st sess., 1270; Warner, *Continental Union*, 240–41.

267. Warner, *Continental Union*, 213, 242.

6. To the South

1. John L. O'Sullivan, "Annexation," *United States Magazine and Democratic Review* 17, no. 85 (1845): 5.

2. Morfit to Forsyth, September 14, 1836, *USSS*, 24th Cong., 2nd sess., *Condition of Texas* (H.Doc. 35), 30.

3. Morfit to Forsyth, August 27, 1836, ibid., 12; cf. Andrés Tijerina, *Tejanos and Texas under the Mexican Flag, 1821–1836* (College Station: Texas A&M University Press, 1994), 22; B. R. Mitchell, *International Historical Statistics: The Americas, 1750–1993* (London: Macmillan, 1998), 35.

4. The U.S. economy grew by 1,270% over the same period: Andrés Reséndez, *Changing National Identities at the Frontier: Texas and New Mexico, 1800–1850* (New York: Cambridge University Press, 2005), 93–94.

5. Ibid.

6. Kinley J. Brauer, *Cotton versus Conscience: Massachusetts Whig Politics and Southwestern Expansion, 1843–1848* (Lexington: University of Kentucky Press, 1967).

7. Houston to William Murphy, May 6, 1844, *SH*, 4: 322.

8. Ibid., 323.

9. Jackson to Butler, December 9, 1831, February 25, 1832, *AJ*, 4: 380, 410; cf. Butler to Jackson, June 21, 1832, ibid., 450; Karl M. Schmitt, *Mexico and the United States, 1821–1973: Conflict and Coexistence* (New York: John Wiley and Sons, 1974), 38–41.

10. Frederick Merk, *Slavery and the Annexation of Texas* (New York: Alfred A. Knopf, 1972), 171.

11. Anson Jones, *Memoranda and Official Correspondence Relating to the Republic of Texas, Its History and Annexation* (New York: D. Appleton, 1859), 116.

12. Morfit to Forsyth, September 12, 1836, *USSS*, 24th Cong., 2nd sess., *Condition of Texas* (H.Doc. 35), 26–27.

13. Jackson, Message to Congress, December 21, 1836, *MPP*, 4: 1487; Morfit to Forsyth, September 10, 1836, in David M. Pletcher, *The Diplomacy of Annexation: Texas, Oregon, and the Mexican War* (Columbia: University of Missouri Press, 1973), 72–73.

14. Sam Houston, "Valedictory to the Texas Congress," December 9, 1844, *SH*, 4, 403; Houston to Murphy, May 6, 1844, *SH*, 4: 322; William C. Binkley, *The Expansionist Movement in Texas, 1836–1850* (Berkeley: University of California Press, 1925), chap. 5; Merk, *Slavery*, 172.

15. James Reilly to Jones, June 17, 1842, in Jones, *Memoranda*, 170.

16. See figure 1.2.

17. *CG*, 28th Cong., 1st sess., 482.

18. Buchanan, Speech on the Annexation of Texas, February 14, 1845, *JB*, 6: 100.

19. See figure 1.2; Pletcher, *Diplomacy of Annexation*, 58.

20. Smith to Jones, July 1, 1844, in Jones, *Memoranda*, 369.

21. Aberdeen to Bankhead, September 30, 1844, in Pletcher, *Diplomacy of Annexation*, 186; Justin H. Smith, *The Annexation of Texas* (New York: Barnes and Noble, 1941), 402–3.

22. Aberdeen to Elliot, December 31, 1844, in Pletcher, *Diplomacy of Annexation*, 187.

23. Smith to Jones, December 24, 1844, in Jones, *Memoranda*, 412.

24. Peel to Aberdeen, February 23, 1845, in Merk, *Slavery*, 165.

25. Ibid.

26. On race and the Texas Revolution: Alexander DeConde, *Ethnicity, Race, and American Foreign Policy: A History* (Boston: Northeastern University Press, 1992), 29–30.

27. Mitchell, *International Historical Statistics*, 137–38; Reginald Horsman, *Race and Manifest Destiny: The Origins of American Racial Anglo-Saxonism* (Cambridge: Harvard University Press, 1981), 213.

28. Tijerina, *Tejanos and Texas*, 137.

29. *CG*, 28th Cong., 2nd sess., Appendix, 212, 313.

30. *CG*, 28th Cong., 1st sess., Appendix, 764, 776, 771.

31. *CG*, 24th Cong., 1st sess., 394; *CG*, 28th Cong., 2nd sess., Appendix, 212, 313.

32. Merk, *Slavery*, 210.

33. Houston to William Murphy, May 6, 1844, *SH*, 4: 324.

34. Charles S. Sydnor, *The Development of Southern Sectionalism 1819–1848* (Baton Rouge: Louisiana State University Press, 1948).

35. Smith, *Annexation of Texas*, 68.

36. Nolan McCarty, Keith T. Poole, and Howard Rosenthal, "Congress and the Territorial Expansion of the United States," in *Party, Process, and Political Change in Congress: New Perspectives on the History of Congress*, ed. David W. Brady and Mathew D. McCubbins (Stanford: Stanford University Press, 2002), 392–451; cf. Barry R. Weingast, "Political Stability and Civil War: Institutions, Commitment, and American Democracy," in *Analytic Narratives*, ed. Robert H. Bates, Avner Greif, Margaret Levi, Jean-Laurent Rosenthal, and Barry R. Weingast (Princeton: Princeton University Press, 1998), 148–93.

37. Matthew Karp, *This Vast Southern Empire: Slaveholders at the Helm of American Foreign Policy* (Cambridge: Harvard University Press, 2016), 82–149.

38. *CG*, 27th Cong., 2nd sess., 174.

39. Merk, *Slavery*, 208.

40. James Reilly to Anson Jones, undated, in Jones, *Memoranda*, 231.

41. James M. Callahan, *American Foreign Policy in Mexican Relations* (Whitefish, MT: Kessinger, 2010), 18.

42. Smith, *Annexation of Texas*, 14–19.

43. *National Intelligencer*, May 4, 1843, in Merk, *Slavery*, 206; cf. Pletcher, *Diplomacy of Annexation*, 115; *National Intelligencer*, May 13, 1843, 173–75; Brauer, *Cotton versus Conscience*, 55–57.

44. Merk, *Slavery*, 127.

45. Hunt to R. A. Irion, January 31, 1838, in "Diplomatic Correspondence of the Republic of Texas: Part 1," *Annual Report of the American Historical Association for the Year 1907*, vol. 2 (Washington: Government Printing Office, 1908), 284–85.

46. Ibid., 287.

47. Glyndon Van Deusen, *William Henry Seward* (New York: Oxford University Press, 1967), 102.

48. Merk, *Slavery*, 210.

49. *CG*, 28th Cong., 1st sess., 607–11.

50. Jackson to Anthony Butler, October 19, 1829, *AJ*, 4: 79; Smith, *Annexation of Texas*, 27–28; Schmitt, *Mexico and the United States*, 58.

51. Schmitt, *Mexico and the United States*, 59.

52. Andrew Jackson, Eighth Annual Message, *MPP*, 3: 237.

53. Merk, *Slavery*, 45.

54. Pletcher, *Diplomacy of Annexation*, 73.

55. Merk, *Slavery*, 45.

56. *CG*, 24th Cong., 2nd sess., 83; Wharton to Houston, February 2, 1837, in "Diplomatic Correspondence of the Republic of Texas," 179.

57. Merk, *Slavery*, 6.

58. Tyler to Webster, October 11, 1841, in Smith, *Annexation of Texas*, 103; Pletcher, *Diplomacy of Annexation*, 86.

59. Smith, *Annexation of Texas*, 106.

60. Van Zandt to Jones, March 15, 1843, in Jones, *Memoranda*, 213.

61. Upshur to Nathaniel Tucker, October 26, 1843, in Merk, *Slavery*, 244.

62. John Tod to Jones, October 25, 1843, in Jones, *Memoranda*, 262.

63. Van Zandt to Jones, March 15, 1843, ibid., 213.

64. Pletcher, *Diplomacy of Annexation*, 73; cf. Charles M. Wiltse, *John C. Calhoun, Sectionalist, 1840–1850* (New York: Bobbs-Merrill, 1951), 199–216.

65. Calhoun to William King, August 12, 1844, *JC*, 5: 382–83.

66. Gen. J. P. Henderson to Jones, December 20, 1843, in Jones, *Memoranda*, 278; W. D. Miller to Jones, April 28, 1844, ibid., 346; J. H. Winchell to Jones, November 16, 1844, ibid., 402; G. W. Terrell to Jones, November 22, 1844, ibid., 405.

67. Van Zandt to Jones, April 19, 1843, in Pletcher, *Diplomacy of Annexation*, 116.

68. Van Zandt to Jones, August 12, 1843, in Jones, *Memoranda*, 244.

69. Thomas R. Hietala, *Manifest Design: American Exceptionalism and Empire* (Ithaca, NY: Cornell University Press, 2003), 40.

70. Merk, *Slavery*, 20.

71. Calhoun to King, August 12, 1844, *JC*, 5: 389–90.

72. *CG*, 28th Cong., 2nd sess., Appendix, 100; cf. Hietala, *Manifest Design*, 31, 54.

73. Merk, *Slavery*, 96.

74. David C. Hendrickson, *Union, Nation, or Empire: The American Debate over International Relations, 1789–1941* (Lawrence: University Press of Kansas, 2009), 166–70; Sanford Levinson and Bartholomew H. Sparrow, eds., *The Louisiana Purchase and American Expansion, 1803–1898* (New York: Rowman and Littlefield, 2005), chaps. 4, 5; Michael A. Morrison, *Slavery and the American West: The Eclipse of Manifest Destiny* (Chapel Hill: University of North Carolina Press, 1997), chap. 1.

75. *CG*, 35th Cong., 2nd sess., 967; cf. Hietala, *Manifest Design*, 49; Smith, *Annexation of Texas*, 346.

76. Schmitt, *Mexico and the United States*, 63.

77. Polk to William Polk, January 29, 1846, *JPC*, 11: 57–58.

78. *JP*, 1: 306–7.

79. Ibid., 392; cf. 390.

80. Ibid., 354; Schmitt, *Mexico and the United States*, 63.

81. *JP*, 1: 379.

82. Ibid., 384.

83. Ibid., 395–99; cf. *JP*, 2: 257; Polk to William Polk, October 2, 1846, *JPC*, 11: 337–38.

84. *JP*, 1: 437–38.

85. Ibid., 400; cf. 429, 436.

86. Ibid., 437–38.

87. Ibid., 495–97; cf. *JP*, 2: 16.

88. Polk, Third Annual Message, *MPP*, 4: 540; cf. Zachary Taylor, First Annual Message, *MPP*, 5: 20.

89. George L. Rives, *The United States and Mexico, 1821–1848*, vol. 2 (New York: Charles Scribner's Sons, 1913), 45–46.

90. John J. Mearsheimer, *The Tragedy of Great Power Politics* (New York: W. W. Norton, 2001), 238; Sean Lynn-Jones, "Realism and America's Rise: A Review Essay," *International Security* 23, no. 2 (1998): 157–82.

91. Polk thought California might be purchased for $15 million but was willing to pay up to $40 million: *JP*, 1: 34–35.

92. Polk, Third Annual Message, *MPP*, 4: 538; cf. Donald F. Stevens, *Origins of Instability in Early Republican Mexico* (Durham: Duke University Press, 1991), 11.

93. Henry W. Temple, "William H. Seward," in *The American Secretaries of State and Their Diplomacy*, ed. Samuel F. Bemis, vol. 7 (New York: Alfred A. Knopf, 1928), 105; cf. Stevens, *Origins of Instability*; Timothy J. Henderson, *A Glorious Defeat: Mexico and Its War with the United States* (New York: Hill and Wang, 2007), chaps. 1, 2.

94. *CG*, 29th Cong., 2nd sess., Appendix, 190.

95. Jeremy Black, *America as a Military Power: From the American Revolution to the Civil War* (Westport, CT: Praeger, 2002), 128; cf. W. A. DePalo, *The Mexican National Army, 1822–1852* (College Station: Texas A&M University Press, 1997).

96. William B. Skelton, "Professionalization in the U.S. Army Officer Corps during the Age of Jackson," *Armed Forces and Society* 1, no. 4 (1975): 443–71; William B. Skelton, *An American Profession of Arms: The Army Officer Corps, 1784–1861* (Lawrence: University Press of Kansas, 1992); Black, *America as a Military Power*, 112.

97. Black, *America as a Military Power*, 126–27.

98. Slidell to Buchanan, September 25, 1845, *JB*, 6: 264.

99. *JP*, 1: 71, 133; Polk to Louis McLane, June 22, 1846, *JPC*, 11: 216; *MPP*, 5: 2389; Merk, *Slavery*, 163; Rives, *United States and Mexico*, 45–46.

100. *JP*, 1: 133, 141, 395–99, 453.

101. Rives, *United States and Mexico*, 90–95.

102. George Bancroft to Polk, October 18, 1847, *JPC*, 13: 166; cf. Bancroft to Polk, November 18, 1847, *JPC*, 13: 198.

103. Horsman, *Race and Manifest Destiny*, 232.

104. Allan R. Millet and Peter Maslowski, *For the Common Defense: A Military History of the United States of America* (New York: Macmillan, 1994), 157.

105. Fred Anderson and Andrew Cayton, *The Dominion of War: Empire and Liberty in North America, 1500–2000* (New York: Viking, 2005), 283.

106. Reséndez, *Changing National Identities*, 32; David J. Weber, *The Mexican Frontier, 1821–1846: The American Southwest Under Mexico* (Albuquerque: University of New Mexico Press, 1982), 195.

107. Russell Thornton, "Population History of Native North Americans," in *A Population History of North America*, ed. Michael R. Haines and Richard H. Steckel (New York: Cambridge University Press, 2000), 28; Weber, *Mexican Frontier*, 206.

108. Weber, *Mexican Frontier*, 187–88, 206.

109. Ibid., 179.

110. Eugene D. Genovese, *The Political Economy of Slavery: Studies in the Economy and Society of the Slave South* (New York: Pantheon, 1965), 258.

111. *Federal Union*, November 10, 1846, in John H. Schroeder, *Mr. Polk's War: American Opposition and Dissent, 1846–1848* (Madison: University of Wisconsin Press, 1973), 55.

112. Boston *Advertiser*, September 26, 1846, in Brauer, *Cotton versus Conscience*, 208.

113. Schroeder, *Mr. Polk's War*, 152.

114. Brauer, *Cotton versus Conscience*, 210.

115. Ernest M. Lander, *Reluctant Imperialists: Calhoun, the South Carolinians, and the Mexican War* (Baton Rouge: Louisiana State University Press, 1980), 165, 160.

116. Schroeder, *Mr. Polk's War*, 71–72.

117. *JP*, 2: 350, 308.

118. Ibid., 350.

119. Ibid., 283, 289.

120. Ibid., 308; cf. 457–58.

121. Ibid., 76–77; cf. Polk to Archibald Yell, October 2, 1846, *JPC*, 11: 339.

122. *JP*, 2: 283, 349–50, 472. Polk also entertained the notion of annexing a strip of Sonora down to 31° and the Department of Tamaulipas but declined to demand them: *JP*, 3: 163–64.

123. Polk, Third Annual Message, *MPP*, 4: 538.

124. Ibid., 544; cf. *JP*, 3: 229–30.

125. "New Territory versus No Territory," *Democratic Review* 21 (October 1847): 291; Hietala, *Manifest Design*, 159.

126. Robert McCaa, "The Peopling of Mexico from Origins to Revolution," in Haines and Steckel, *Population History of North America*, 279; Michael R. Haines, "The White Population of the United States, 1790–1920," in Haines and Steckel, *Population History of North America*, 306.

127. Black, *America as a Military Power*, 126.

128. Ibid., 129.

129. Bancroft to Polk, May 18, 1847, *JPC*, 12: 261.

130. *JP*, 2: 339–40; *JP*, 3: 348.

131. Buchanan to James Shields, April 23, 1847, *JB*, 7: 287, 286.

132. Andrew Donelson to Polk, May 23, 1846, *JPC*, 11: 172; Donelson to Polk, March 13, 1848, *JPC*, 13: 365.

133. *Washington Daily Union*, January 4, 1848.

134. Calhoun to Thomas Clemson, June 15, 1847, in "Correspondence of John C. Calhoun," in *Annual Report of the American Historical Association for the Year 1899*, vol. 2, ed. J. Franklin Jameson (Washington: Government Printing Office, 1900), 734; cf. Calhoun to Andrew F. Calhoun, December 11, 1847, ibid., 741.

135. *JC*, 4: 308; cf. *CG*, 29th Cong., 2nd sess., Appendix, 356.

136. *JC*, 4: 310–11.

137. *JC*, 4: 410; cf. *CG*, 30th Cong., 1st sess., 98.

138. *CG*, 30th Cong., 1st sess., 429.

139. Ibid., 283.

140. *CG*, 28th Cong., 2nd sess., Appendix, 397; cf. 353–54.

141. *CG*, 29th Cong., 1st sess., Appendix, 201; cf. 184.

142. Polk, Third Annual Message, *MPP*, 4: 541.

143. Hietala, *Manifest Design*, 158.

144. *CG*, 29th Cong., 2nd sess., 516.

145. *CG*, 30th Cong., 1st sess., Appendix, 272; *CG*, 29th Cong., 2nd sess., Appendix, 363.

146. *CG*, 29th Cong., 2nd sess., Appendix, 133; cf. speech of Delano: ibid., 281.

147. *CG*, 29th Cong., 2nd sess., Appendix, 327.

148. Schroeder, *Mr. Polk's War*, 69.

149. *Charleston Mercury*, June 8, 1846, in Lander, *Reluctant Imperialists*, 12; cf. *Charleston Mercury*, May 25, 1846, in Horsman, *Race and Manifest Destiny*, 238.

150. Josiah C. Nott, *Two Lectures on the Connection between the Biblical and Physical History of Man* (New York: Bartlett and Welford, 1849), 36–38.

151. *Augusta Chronicle and Sentinel*, July 31, 1846, in Schroeder, *Mr. Polk's War*, 53.

152. Ralph W. Emerson, *The Journals and Miscellaneous Notebooks of Ralph Waldo Emerson*, ed. Ralph H. Orth and Alfred R. Ferguson, vol. 9 (Cambridge: Belknap Press, 1971), 430–31.

153. Walt Whitman, *The Gathering of the Forces*, ed. Cleveland Rodgers and John Black, vol. 1 (New York: G. P. Putnam's Sons, 1920), 247.

154. Horsman, *Race and Manifest Destiny*, 97, 209.

155. *SH*, 5: 34–35.

156. *Illinois State Register*, July 17, 1846, in John D. P. Fuller, *The Movement for the Acquisition of All Mexico: 1846–1848* (Cambridge, MA: Da Capo Press, 1969), 41.

157. *CG*, 30th Cong., 1st sess., 158; cf. speeches of Brown and Leigh: *CG*, 28th Cong., 2nd sess., Appendix, 96–97; *RD*, 24th Cong., 1st sess., 201.

158. Waddy Thompson, *Recollections of Mexico* (New York: Wiley and Putnam, 1847), 239; cf. 23, 204.

159. *CG*, 29th Cong., 2nd sess., Appendix, 131.

160. *CG*, 29th Cong., 2nd sess., 291. California's 1849 constitution allowed only Anglo-Americans to vote: Eric T. L. Love, *Race over Empire: Racism and U.S. Imperialism, 1865–1900* (Chapel Hill: University of North Carolina Press, 2004), 23.

161. *Philadelphia Public Ledger*, December 11, 1847, in Frederick Merk, *Manifest Destiny and Mission in American History* (New York: Alfred A. Knopf, 1963), 127; Pletcher, *Diplomacy of Annexation*, 555; cf. Andrew Lane to Polk, January 1, 1847, *JPC*, 12: 13.

162. *New York Herald*, October 28, 1847, in Hietala, *Manifest Design*, 160; cf. Richard B. Winders, *Mr. Polk's Army: The American Military Experience in the Mexican War* (College Station: Texas A&M University Press, 1997), 183.

163. *Louisville Democrat*, March 9, 1848, in Merk, *Manifest Destiny and Mission*, 151–52.

164. "New Territory versus No Territory," *Democratic Review* 21 (October 1847), 291; Hietala, *Manifest Design*, 159.

165. *JP*, 3: 276–77.

166. *CG*, 29th Cong., 2nd sess., Appendix, 191.

167. Amy S. Greenberg, *A Wicked War: Polk, Clay, Lincoln, and the 1846 U.S. Invasion of Mexico* (New York: Alfred A. Knopf, 2012), 259; Walter Nugent, *Habits of Empire: A History of American Expansion* (New York: Alfred A. Knopf, 2008), 215; Pletcher, *Diplomacy of Annexation*, chaps. 16, 17.

168. Although Polk entertained the Sierra Madre line as a maximum possible border—giving the United States Baja California, Sonora, Chihuahua, Coahuila, Nuevo León, and Tamaulipas—he judged it "doubtful whether this could be ever obtained by the consent of Mexico" and recognized that continuing the war would enflame domestic opposition "and thus lose the two provinces of New Mexico & Upper California, which were ceded to the U.S. by this treaty." *JP*, 3: 347–48.

169. *Washington Daily Union*, February 28, 1848, in Hietala, *Manifest Design*, 164–65; cf. *Washington Daily Union*, March 30, 1848.

170. *Louisville Democrat*, March 9, 1848, in Merk, *Manifest Destiny and Mission*, 151–52.

171. Letcher to Webster, October 22, 1850, *Senate Executive Documents*, 32nd Cong., 1st sess., vol. 10, 37.

172. Geoffrey Blainey, *The Causes of War* (New York: Free Press, 1988), 59.

173. Lewis Einstein, "Lewis Cass," in Bemis, *American Secretaries of State*, 6: 340–41.

174. Callahan, *Mexican Relations*, 260.

175. *New York Times*, January 25, 1860, in Pearl T. Ponce, "'As Dead as Julius Caesar': The Rejection of the McLane–Ocampo Treaty," *Civil War History* 53, no. 4 (2007): 350.

176. *CG*, 34th Cong., 1st sess., Appendix, 668.

177. Ponce, "McLane–Ocampo Treaty," 355.

178. *Augusta Sentinel*, February 24, 1860, in Ponce, "McLane–Ocampo Treaty," 351.

179. Callahan, *Mexican Relations*, 191.

180. Ibid., 193.

181. *CG*, 32nd Cong., 3rd sess., Appendix, 270.

182. Clyde A. Duniway, "Daniel Webster (Second Term)," in Bemis, *Secretaries of State*, 6: 98.

183. Webster to Fillmore, May 19, 1852, in *The Writings and Speeches of Daniel Webster*, vol. 18, ed. Fletcher Webster (Boston: Little, Brown, 1903), 532.

184. Callahan, *Mexican Relations*, 205.

185. Marcy to Gadsden, July 15 and October 22, 1853, *DC:IA*, 9: 134–44, 145.

186. Callahan, *Mexican Relations*, 224.

187. Ibid., 223; cf. 227–28; Paul N. Garber, *The Gadsden Treaty* (Gloucester, MA: Peter Smith, 1959).

188. Joseph C. G. Kennedy, *Population of the United States in 1860* (Washington: Government Printing Office, 1864), 568.

189. Einstein, "Lewis Cass," 324; cf. Cass to Forsyth, July 17, 1857, Callahan, *Mexican Relations*, 248.

190. Callahan, *Mexican Relations*, 254–59.

191. Einstein, "Lewis Cass," 337; cf. Callahan, *Mexican Relations*, 265.

192. Edward E. Dunbar, *The Mexican Papers* (New York: J. A. H. Hasbrouck, 1860), 98.

193. Ibid., 100.

194. Callahan, *Mexican Relations*, 270.

195. Ponce, "McLane–Ocampo Treaty."

196. Buchanan, Message to Congress, December 19, 1859; *JB*, 10: 359; cf. *JB*, 12: 249; Einstein, "Lewis Cass," 340–41; Callahan, *Mexican Relations*, 263.

197. Einstein, "Lewis Cass," 346.

198. Ibid., 343.

199. Cass to McLane, September 20, 1860, ibid., 344–45; cf. Cass to Faulkner, August 31, 1860, ibid., 344.

200. Callahan, *Mexican Relations*, 274.

201. John Bigelow to Seward, April 28, 1862, *Bigelow to Seward: Letters (Confidential), 1862–1866*, 43, *JBP*. The intervention initially included the British and Spanish fleets until the French ambition for regime change became known. Bigelow reported that British leaders came to see their participation "as a trap to engage them to stand by France in case of difficulty with us." Bigelow to Seward, June 25, 1863, ibid., 206.

202. Seward to William Dayton, September 24, 1861, March 3, 10, 31, July 11, 1862, State Department: Foreign Dispatches to Great Britain, France, 1861–1869, 248–49,

309, 315, 317, 344, *WHSP*; Seward to Charles Adams, February 19, 1862, ibid., 56; Seward to Horatio Perry, May 29, 1862, *FRUS*: 1862, 471; Bigelow to Seward, May 29, 1862, June 25, 1863, *Bigelow to Seward: Letters (Confidential), 1862–1866*, 57, 203–4, *JBP*.

203. Seward to Charles Adams, February 19, 1862, State Department: Foreign Dispatches to Great Britain, France, 1861–1869, 56, *WHSP*.

204. McCaa, "Peopling of Mexico," 279.

205. Seward to Corwin, April 6, 1861, *FRUS*: 1861, 67.

206. Callahan, *Mexican Relations*, 282–83; cf. Vinod K. Aggarwal, *Debt Games: Strategic Interaction in International Debt Rescheduling* (New York: Cambridge University Press, 1996), 130.

207. Seward to Corwin, June 7, 1862, *FRUS*: 1862, 748; Seward to Corwin, June 24, 1862, *FRUS*: 1862, 748–49; cf. Van Deusen, *Seward*, 366; Ernest N. Paolino, *The Foundations of the American Empire: William Henry Seward and U.S. Foreign Policy* (Ithaca, NY: Cornell University Press, 1973), 18.

208. Jefferson Davis, "Speech at Atlanta," February 16, 1861, in *The Papers of Jefferson Davis*, vol. 7, ed. Lynda L. Crist and Mary S. Dix (Baton Rouge: Louisiana State University Press, 1992), 44; Callahan, *Mexican Relations*, 281.

209. Perry to Seward, August 26, 1862, *FRUS*: 1862, 514; cf. Donald Stoker, *The Grand Design: Strategy and the U.S. Civil War* (New York: Oxford University Press, 2010), 20; Robert E. May, *The Southern Dream of a Caribbean Empire, 1854–1861* (Baton Rouge: Louisiana State University Press, 1973), 251; Callahan, *Mexican Relations*, 292; James M. Callahan, *Evolution of Seward's Mexican Policy* (Morgantown: West Virginia University, 1909), 21.

210. Matías Romero to Seward, July 9, 1864, *FRUS*: 1865–1866, vol. 2, 576–77.

211. M. M. McAllen, *Maximilian and Carlota: Europe's Last Empire in Mexico* (San Antonio: Trinity University Press, 2014), 183; cf. Box 80, Folder 4, *WHSP*. Juárez denied having made any such offer: Matías Romero to Seward, May 5, 1865, Juárez to Editor of the Diario, February 22, 1863, *FRUS*: 1865–1866, part 3, 496.

212. *FRUS*: 1865–1866, part 2, 262.

213. Seward to Adams, May 3, 1864, Callahan, *Mexican Relations*, 296; cf. Seward to Charles Adams, March 26, 1864, State Department: Foreign Dispatches to Great Britain, France, 1861–1869, 133, 135–36, *WHSP*; Frederic Bancroft, *The Life of William H. Seward*, vol. 2 (New York: Harper and Brothers, 1900), 430–31.

214. Bigelow to Seward, May 29, 1862, *Bigelow to Seward: Letters (Confidential), 1862–1866*, 53, *JBP*; cf. Bigelow to Seward, June 27, 1862, ibid., 66–67; John M. Taylor, *William Henry Seward: Lincoln's Right Hand* (New York: HarperCollins, 1991), 252; see figure 1.2.

215. Bigelow to Seward, March 9, 1865, *Bigelow to Seward: Letters (Confidential), 1862–1866*, 436, *JBP*; cf. Bigelow to Seward, circa June 1, 1865, ibid., 472.

216. Bigelow to Seward, April 21, 1865, ibid., 463; cf. Bigelow to Seward, March 10, 1865, ibid., 440.

217. Bigelow to Seward, October 19, 1865, ibid., 584; Callahan, *Mexican Relations*, 317; cf. Bigelow to Seward, December 21, 1865, January 5, 1866, *Bigelow to Seward: Letters (Confidential), 1862–1866*, 644–46, 684, *JBP*.

218. *CG*, 39th Cong., 1st sess., 3917.

219. Seward to Bigelow, September 6, November 6, 1865, *FRUS*: 1865–1866, vol. 3, 412, 489.

220. Bigelow to Seward, November 30, 1865, *FRUS: 1865–1866*, part 3, 490; Callahan, *Mexican Relations*, 316; cf. Callahan, *Seward's Mexican Policy*, 80; Dayton to Seward, April 22, 1864, *FRUS: 1864*, vol. 3, 76.

221. Seward to Bigelow, December 16, 1865, *FRUS: 1865–1866*, vol. 2, 429.

222. Joseph Wheelan, *Terrible Swift Sword: The Life of General Philip H. Sheridan* (Boston: Da Capo, 2012), 212–14; Millet and Maslowski, *For the Common Defense*, 251.

223. Lynn M. Case and Warren F. Spencer, *The United States and France: Civil War Diplomacy* (Philadelphia: University of Pennsylvania Press, 1970), 562.

224. Frederic Bancroft, "The French in Mexico and the Monroe Doctrine," *Political Science Quarterly* 11, no. 1 (1896): 39; cf. Donald B. Connelly, *John M. Schofield and the Politics of Generalship* (Chapel Hill: University of North Carolina Press, 2006), 184.

225. Bigelow to Seward, January 5, 1866, *John Bigelow Papers, Bigelow to Seward: Letters (Official), 1866*, New York Public Library, 4–5.

226. Seward to William Lawrence, July 21, 1866, State Department: Domestic Letters, Vol. 2: 1868–1869, 361 *WHSP*; Seward to Antonio López de Santa Anna Jr., November 8, 1866, ibid., 383.

227. *WHS*, 4: 122; cf. ibid., 320, 394–95, 406.

228. *CG*, 32nd Cong., 2nd sess., Appendix, 147.

229. Frederic Bancroft, "Seward's Ideas of Territorial Expansion," *North American Review* 167, no. 500 (1898): 84.

230. *WHS*, 3: 409.

231. Seward to Bigelow, March 28, 1865, *FRUS: 1865–66*, vol. 2, 388; Seward to Bigelow, September 6, 1865, *FRUS: 1865–66*, vol. 2, 413; cf. Paolino, *Foundations of the American Empire*, 11.

232. Callahan, *Mexican Relations*, 331; cf. 297; Van Deusen, *Seward*, 488; *CG*, 31st Cong., 1st sess., 267. Bigelow was of similar mind regarding "Spanish American states whose people belong to a different race from ours, who speak a different language, who profess a different religion and who have been trained under social and political institutions having very little in common with those of the United States." Callahan, *Seward's Mexican Policy*, 67. If it ever joined the United States, he wrote, "Mexico is to be conquered by immigration and not by the sword." Ibid., 56.

233. *WHS*, 5: 557.

234. "W. H. Seward Remarks Made during Trip to Mexico c. 1869," Miscellaneous and Personal—Speeches and Proclamations, File Drawer 32, Folder 113, *WHSP*.

235. *WHS*, 5: 580–81.

236. Kenneth E. Davison, *The Presidency of Rutherford B. Hayes* (Westport, CT: Greenwood Press, 1972), 200.

7. To the Seas

1. Eric Williams, *From Columbus to Castro: The History of the Caribbean* (New York: Random House, 1984), 361; cf. César J. Ayala, *American Sugar Kingdom: The Plantation Economy of the Spanish Caribbean, 1898–1934* (Chapel Hill: University of North Carolina Press, 1999), 16–17.

2. *CG*, 35th Cong., 2nd sess., 453–54; cf. speech of Hale: ibid., Appendix, 161; Van Buren to Cornelius Van Ness, October 2, 1829, *AIC*, 34; Buchanan to Saunders, June 17, 1848, ibid., 49.

3. *CG*, 35th Cong., 2nd sess., 543; cf. speech of Avery: ibid., 560; House Foreign Affairs Committee report: ibid., Appendix, 97.

4. *Tuskegee Republican*, May 13, 1858, in Robert E. May, *The Southern Dream of a Caribbean Empire, 1854–1861* (Baton Rouge: Louisiana State University Press, 1973), 14; cf. 16–17.

5. Walter Johnson, *River of Dark Dreams: Slavery and Empire in the Cotton Kingdom* (Cambridge: Harvard University Press, 2013), 304.

6. Van Buren to Van Ness, October 2, 1829, *AIC*, 34; cf. Jefferson to Monroe, October 24, 1823, *TJ:F*, 12: 320; Edward Everett to Eugéne de Sartiges, December 1, 1852, U.S. Department of State, *Correspondence on the Proposed Tripartite Convention Relative to Cuba* (Boston: Little, Brown, 1853), 34; Buchanan, Mason, and Soulé to Marcy, October 18, 1854, *DC:IA*, 7: 581; Buchanan, Second Annual Message, *MPP*, 5: 511.

7. *CG*, 35th Cong., 2nd sess., 453; cf. Rodrigo Botero, *Ambivalent Embrace: America's Troubled Relations with Spain from the Revolutionary War to the Cold War* (Westport, CT: Greenwood Press, 2001), 72.

8. Stevenson to John Forsyth, June 16, 1837, *AIC*, 39–40.

9. Madison to William Pinkney, October 30, 1810, *JMa:RF*, 2: 488; cf. Isaac J. Cox, "The Pan-American Policy of Jefferson and Wilkinson," *Mississippi Valley Historical Review* 1, no. 2 (1914): 223–28; Forsyth to Adams, November 20, 1822, *AIC*, 19; Adams to Forsyth, December 17, 1822, ibid., 20; Adams to Nelson, April 28, 1823, *JQA:F*, 7: 379; Jefferson to Monroe, October 24, 1823, *TJ:F*, 12: 318–21; Stevenson to Forsyth, June 16, 1837, *AIC*, 39–40; Webster to Campbell, January 14, 1843, ibid., 44; Buchanan to Romulus Saunders, June 17, 1848, ibid., 45–46.

10. Matthew Karp, *This Vast Southern Empire: Slaveholders at the Helm of American Foreign Policy* (Cambridge: Harvard University Press, 2016), 186–98.

11. Cuban slaveholders periodically favored annexation: Philip S. Foner, *A History of Cuba and Its Relations with the United States*, vol. 2 (New York: International Publishers, 1963), 9–19.

12. Forsyth to Adams, November 20, 1822, *AIC*, 19; cf. Forsyth to Aaron Vail, July 15, 1840, ibid., 41; Van Buren to Van Ness, October 2, 1829, ibid., 34.

13. Webster to Robert Campbell, January 14, 1843, ibid., 43–44.

14. Forsyth to Aaron Vail, July 15, 1840, ibid., 41–42; Abel Upshur to Washington Irving, January 9, 1844, ibid., 45.

15. Foner, *History of Cuba*, 1: 125; Isaac J. Cox, *The West Florida Controversy, 1798–1813* (Gloucester, MA: Peter Smith, 1967), 290–92; Cox, "Pan-American Policy," 222–23.

16. Robert Smith to Shaler, June 18, 1810, in James E. Lewis Jr., *The American Union and the Problem of Neighborhood: The United States and the Collapse of the Spanish Empire, 1783–1829* (Chapel Hill: University of North Carolina Press, 1998), 36; cf. Foner, *History of Cuba*, 1: 127–29.

17. Jackson to Monroe, June 2, 1818, *AJ*, 2: 378; cf. Randolph to Jackson, March 18, 1832, *AJ*, 4: 421.

18. Calhoun to Jackson, January 23, 1820, *AJ*, 4: 352.

19. Jefferson to Monroe, October 24, 1823, *TJ:F*, 12: 320.

20. Forsyth to Adams, November 20, 1822, February 10, 1823, *AIC*, 19, 20; Adams to Forsyth, December 17, 1822, ibid., 20; Adams to Nelson, April 28, 1823, *JQA:F*, 7: 381; Clay to Rufus King, October 17, 1825, *HC*, 4: 740; Van Buren to Van Ness, October 2,

1829, October 13, 1830, *AIC*, 34, 36; Forsyth to Vail, July 15, 1840, ibid., 41–42; Webster to Washington Irving, January 17, 1843, ibid., 42–43; Webster to Robert Campbell, January 14, 1843, ibid., 44.

21. Mary E. Snodgrass, *The Civil War Era and Reconstruction: An Encyclopedia of Social, Political, Cultural, and Economic History* (New York: Routledge, 2015), 487.

22. *CG*, 29th Cong., 1st sess., 92, 96.

23. *JP*, 3: 476–80, 482–83; cf. *JP*, 3: 446; Ángel Calderón de la Barca to Daniel Webster, August 2, 1850, *DC:IA*, 11: 529.

24. Saunders to Buchanan, December 14, 1848, *AIC*, 57; cf. Buchanan to Saunders, June 17, 1848, ibid., 47–50; Saunders to Buchanan, August 18, November 17, 1848, ibid., 55, 56.

25. Daniel Barringer to John Clayton, June 19, 1850, *DC:IA*, 11: 505–6; Calderón to Webster, August 2, 1850, ibid., 528–35; Webster to Fillmore, October 4, 1851, in *A Digest of International Law*, vol. 6, ed. John B. Moore (Washington, DC: Government Printing Office, 1906), 459; Webster to John Crampton, April 29, 1852, *AIC*, 8; Marcy to Buchanan, July 2, 1853, *DC:IA*, 7: 93–95; Buchanan to Marcy, November 1, 1853, ibid., 509; May, *Southern Dream*, 24–29. On southern filibustering in the 1850s: Johnson, *River of Dark Dreams*, 303–94; Amy S. Greenberg, *Manifest Manhood and the Antebellum American Empire* (New York: Cambridge University Press, 2005).

26. Everett to Eugéne de Sartiges, December 1, 1852, U.S. Department of State, *Correspondence on the Proposed Tripartite Convention Relative to Cuba* (Boston: Little, Brown, 1853), 34.

27. Fillmore, Third Annual Message, *MPP*, 11: 293.

28. Ibid., 22–23, 41.

29. *CG*, 33rd Cong., 1st sess., 637.

30. Ibid., 1024; Alexander Walker to A. G. Haley, June 15, 1854, in May, *Southern Dream*, 34; Robert E. May, *Manifest Destiny's Underworld: Filibustering in Antebellum America* (Chapel Hill: University of North Carolina Press, 2002).

31. *CG*, 33rd Cong., 1st sess., 1194, 1199–1200, 1298–1300.

32. Ibid., 647–48.

33. "No More Slave States," *New York Times*, October 2, 1854.

34. May, *Southern Dream*, 60; *CG*, 33rd Cong., 1st sess., 647–48.

35. Marcy to Soulé, April 3, 1854, *DC:IA*, 11: 177.

36. Soulé to Marcy, July 15, 1854, ibid., 798.

37. May, *Southern Dream*, 67; *CG*, 33rd Cong., 1st sess., 2178.

38. Buchanan to Marcy, July 14, 1853, *DC:IA*, 7: 497; Buchanan to Marcy, July 11, 1854, ibid., 555; Buchanan to Slidell, May 23, 1854, *JB*, 9: 200–201.

39. Buchanan, Mason, and Soulé to Marcy, October 18, 1854, *DC:IA*, 7: 584.

40. John McRae to J. F. H. Claiborne, June 7, 1855, in May, *Southern Dream*, 73.

41. May, *Southern Dream*, 164.

42. Buchanan to Fallon, December 14, 1857, *JB*, 10: 165.

43. Augustus Dodge to Marcy, July 12, 1855, *DC:IA*, 11: 874; cf. Barringer to Everett, January 5, 1853, ibid., 690; Soulé to Marcy, May 3, July 22, 1854, ibid., 771, 800; William Robertson to Marcy, July 5, 1855, ibid., 870; Dodge to Marcy, April 10, 1856, ibid., 903; Dodge to Pedro Pidal, November 24, 1856, ibid., 911; Dodge to Cass, August 22, 1857, November 19, 1858, January 5, 1859, ibid., 936, 959–60, 963–64; William Preston to Cass, March 9, April 25, July 3, 1859, March 6, 1860, ibid., 965–66, 970, 973, 978.

44. One alternative scheme would have seen the United States seize Cuba as payment for Spanish debt to U.S. citizens; another called for U.S. citizens to buy up $200 million of Spanish debt to British subjects, available for an 83 percent discount at the time, and demand Cuba as repayment: *CG*, 35th Cong., 2nd sess., 185, 296–97; Robert Toombs to W. W. Burwell, March 30, 1857, in *Annual Report of the American Historical Association for the Year 1911*, vol. 2, ed. Ulrich B. Phillips(Washington, DC, 1913), 399.

45. Preston to Cass, April 25, 1859, *DC:IA*, 11: 970; cf. Preston to Cass, October 23, 1859, ibid., 974.

46. Buchanan, Second Annual Message, *MPP*, 5: 511.

47. *CG*, 35th Cong., 2nd sess., 538.

48. Ibid., 453, 543; cf. 705; *CG*, 35th Cong., 1st sess., 461.

49. *CG*, 35th Cong., 2nd sess., 704; cf. speech of Wright: *CG*, 35th Cong., 1st sess., 461.

50. *CG*, 35th Cong., 2nd sess., 561.

51. Ibid., 538–39; ibid., Appendix, 111–13.

52. Foner, *History of Cuba*, 2: 123.

53. M. W. Cluskey, ed., *Speeches, Messages, and Other Writings of the Hon. Albert G. Brown* (Philadelphia: Jas. B. Smith, 1859), 593–95; cf. speech of Wright: *CG*, 35th Cong., 1st sess., 458–59.

54. *CG*, 35th Cong., 2nd sess., Appendix, 114; cf. speech of Kellogg: *CG*, 35th Cong., 2nd sess., 563.

55. *CG*, 35th Cong., 2nd sess., 1183–84; cf. 1188; speech of Dixon: ibid., 1335.

56. Ibid., Appendix, 164.

57. May, *Southern Dream*, 180.

58. William Newmarch, ed., *Journal of the Statistical Society of London*, vol. 23 (London: John William Parker and Son, 1860), 195.

59. *CG*, 35th Cong., 2nd sess., 539.

60. Ibid., Appendix, 114.

61. Ibid., Appendix, 166.

62. Ibid., Appendix, 160; cf. speech of Doolittle: *CG*, 35th Cong., 2nd sess., 967.

63. *CG*, 35th Cong., 2nd sess., 1181; cf. 1182–83.

64. Ibid., 1337–38.

65. Buchanan to Saunders, June 17, 1848, *AIC*, 49; cf. speeches of Quitman and Branch: *CG*, 34th Cong., 1st sess., 668; *CG*, 35th Cong., 2nd sess., Appendix, 99.

66. "Political Items from the Atlantic," *Sacramento Daily Union*, October 22, 1856.

67. *CG*, 35th Cong., 1st sess., Appendix, 461.

68. *CG*, 35th Cong., 2nd sess., 542.

69. Ibid., 1338.

70. Ibid., 1180–81; cf. Paul Frymer, *Building an American Empire: The Era of Territorial and Political Expansion* (Princeton: Princeton University Press, 2017), 205–11.

71. *CG*, 35th Cong., 2nd sess., 1385.

72. *CG*, 36th Cong., 1st sess., 2456.

73. Thomas H. McKee, *The National Conventions and Platforms of All Political Parties, 1789 to 1901* (Baltimore: Friedenwald Company, 1900), 109–11, 114–15; cf. Harold Holzer, ed., *The Lincoln–Douglas Debates* (New York: Fordham University Press, 2004), 153–54; "Farewell Speech of Hon. A. H. Stephens," July 2, 1859, in *Alexander H. Stephens in Public and Private*, ed. Henry Cleveland (Philadelphia: National Publishing,

1866), 645–46; May, *Southern Dream*, 186–87. Neither sectional bloc was entirely uniform: May, *Southern Dream*, 190–205.

74. August Belmont to Stephen Douglas, December 31, 1860, in Robert E. May, *Slavery, Race, and Conquest in the Tropics: Lincoln, Douglas, and the Future of Latin America* (New York: Cambridge University Press, 2013), 219; cf. *CG*, 36th Cong., 2nd sess., 651.

75. Lincoln to James Hale, January 11, 1861, in Roy P. Basler, ed., *The Collected Works of Abraham Lincoln*, vol. 4 (New Brunswick, NJ: Rutgers University Press, 1953), 172.

76. *CG*, 34th Cong., 1st sess., 668; G. Pope Atkins and Larman C. Wilson, *The Dominican Republic and the United States: From Imperialism to Transnationalism* (Athens: University of Georgia Press, 1998), 17.

77. Luis Martínez-Fernández, "Caudillos, Annexationism, and the Rivalry between Empires in the Dominican Republic, 1844–1874," *Diplomatic History* 17, no. 4 (1993): 575–77.

78. Atkins and Wilson, *Dominican Republic*, 16.

79. Martínez-Fernández, "Caudillos," 572–75, 579–81.

80. Atkins and Wilson, *Dominican Republic*, 18.

81. Sumner Welles, *Naboth's Vineyard: The Dominican Republic, 1844–1924*, vol. 1 (New York: Payson and Clarke, 1928), 353; Martínez-Fernández, "Caudillos," 592.

82. Smith to Seward, October 24, 1868, in Welles, *Naboth's Vineyard*, 1: 350; cf. 346–47; Martínez-Fernández, "Caudillos," 595.

83. Seward to Smith, November 17, 1868, in Welles, *Naboth's Vineyard*, 1; 352.

84. Andrew Johnson, Fourth Annual Message, *MPP*, 6: 689; cf. Welles, *Naboth's Vineyard*, 1: 356.

85. Eric T. L. Love, *Race over Empire: Racism and U.S. Imperialism, 1865–1900* (Chapel Hill: University of North Carolina Press, 2004), 28.

86. David M. Pletcher, *The Diplomacy of Trade and Investment: American Economic Expansion in the Hemisphere, 1865–1900* (Columbia: University of Missouri Press, 1998), 162–63.

87. *CG*, 40th Cong., 3rd sess., 317, 339, 340; cf. 337; Jacob D. Cox, "How Judge Hoar Ceased to Be Attorney-General," *Atlantic Monthly* 76, no. 454 (1895): 165.

88. Seward to Banks, January 29, 1869, in William J. Nelson, *Almost a Territory: America's Attempt to Annex the Dominican Republic* (Newark: University of Delaware Press, 1990), 64; cf. *CG*, 40th Cong., 3rd sess., 769.

89. Grant, "Reasons why San Domingo should be annexed to the United States," *UG*, 20: 74; cf. Grant's interview, March 29, 1870, *UG*, 20: 134; Love, *Race over Empire*, 47–48.

90. Grant, "Reasons why San Domingo should be annexed to the United States," *UG*, 20: 75.

91. Ibid., 76.

92. Fish to Babcock, July 13, 1869, Senate Executive Document 17, 41st Cong., 3rd sess., 79.

93. Frymer, *Building an American Empire*, 213.

94. Senate Executive Document 17, 41st Cong., 3rd sess., 98; Cox, "Judge Hoar," 166; Allan Nevins, *Hamilton Fish: The Inner History of the Grant Administration* (New York: Dodd, Mead, 1936), 271.

95. *Senate Documents*, 66th Cong., 1st sess., vol. 14 (Washington, DC: Government Printing Office, 1919), 207.

96. *UG*, 20: 123.

97. Nevins, *Fish*, 262.

98. Fish to George Bancroft, February 9, 1870, in Nevins, *Fish*, 313.

99. Nevertheless, Fish thought most Dominicans would have supported annexation: ibid., 315.

100. Ibid., 314.

101. *Senate Documents*, 66th Cong., 1st sess., vol. 14 (Washington, DC: Government Printing Office, 1919), 208.

102. *New York Herald*, March 26, 28, 1870, in Love, *Race over Empire*, 56, 57.

103. David Donald, *Charles Sumner and the Rights of Man* (New York: Alfred A. Knopf, 1970), 442–43.

104. Edward L. Pierce, ed., *Memoir and Letters of Charles Sumner*, vol. 4 (Boston: Roberts Brothers, 1893), 441; Moorfield Storey, *Charles Sumner* (Boston: Houghton Mifflin, 1900), 328.

105. *New York Herald*, March 25, 1870, *New York Tribune*, March 28, 1870, in Love, *Race over Empire*, 56.

106. *New York Times*, March 26, 1870, *New York Herald*, March 26, 1870, ibid., 58.

107. Nicholas Guyatt, "America's Conservatory: Race, Reconstruction, and the Santo Domingo Debate," *American Journal of History* 97 (May 2011): 976.

108. Henry B. Adams, "The Session," *North American Review* 111, no. 228 (1870): 58.

109. *UG*, 20: 171–72; cf. Nevins, *Fish*, 365–68; Cox, "Judge Hoar," 162–73; Carl Schurz, *The Reminiscences of Carl Schurz*, vol. 2 (New York: Doubleday, Page, 1908), 403.

110. *Senate Documents*, 66th Cong., 1st sess., vol. 14 (Washington, DC: Government Printing Office, 1919), 212.

111. *UG*, 20: 154; cf. Nevins, *Fish*, 326–27.

112. Nevins, *Fish*, 330–33. Like Cazneau and Fabens, Babcock owned land on the island and hoped annexation would make him rich: Atkins and Wilson, *Dominican Republic*, 24–25.

113. Ibid., 335, 318, 371; *Senate Documents*, 66th Cong., 1st sess., vol. 14 (Washington, DC: Government Printing Office, 1919), 216.

114. Grant to Baez, October 17, 1870, *UG*, 20: 311.

115. Ulysses Grant, Second Annual Message, *MPP*, 7: 99–101.

116. *CG*, 41st Cong., 3rd sess., 53.

117. Ibid., 227, 231.

118. Ibid., 225; cf. 226.

119. Ibid., 412.

120. Ibid., Appendix, 26, 29.

121. Ibid., Appendix, 30; cf. Cox to Schurz, February 21, 1871, in Love, *Race over Empire*, 67–68.

122. Tanisha M. Fazal, *State Death: The Politics and Geography of Conquest, Occupation, and Annexation* (Princeton: Princeton University Press, 2007), 138; cf. Frymer, *Building an American Empire*, 211–18.

123. *CG*, 41st Cong., 3rd sess., 416, 426.

124. Ulysses Grant, Eighth Annual Message, *MPP*, 7: 412–13.

125. Botero, *Ambivalent Embrace*, 92–93.

126. Howard W. Morgan, *William McKinley and His America* (Kent, OH: Kent State University Press, 2003), 253; *CR*, 55th Cong., 2nd sess., 3669, 3673.

127. They lost another 5,462 through disease: Richard F. Hamilton, *President McKinley, War and Empire*, vol. 2 (New Brunswick, NJ: Transaction Publishers, 2007), 94.

128. War Department, *Report on the Census of Cuba, 1899* (Washington, DC: Government Printing Office, 1900), 72, 81, 97.

129. Louis A. Pérez Jr., *Cuba between Empires, 1878–1902* (Pittsburgh: University of Pittsburgh Press, 1983), 4; Lester D. Langley, *Struggle for the American Mediterranean: United States–European Rivalry in the Gulf–Caribbean, 1776–1904* (Athens: University of Georgia Press, 1976), 166.

130. Nevins, *Fish*, 194; cf. 191–200, 231–33, 619–31.

131. Edward S. Mihalkanin, *American Statesmen: Secretaries of State from John Jay to Colin Powell* (Westport, CT: Greenwood Press, 2004), 196.

132. Richard H. Bradford, *The Virginius Affair* (Boulder: Colorado Associate University Press, 1980), 39–41, 59–63, 91–94, 126; Nevins, *Fish*, 667–94.

133. Grover Cleveland, Fourth Annual Message (second term), *MPP*, 9: 719.

134. Pletcher, *Diplomacy of Trade*, 168.

135. Blaine to Comly, December 1, 1881, *FRUS*: 1894, Appendix 2, 1159; cf. Walter S. Vail, ed., *The Words of James G. Blaine on the Issues of the Day* (Boston: D. L. Guernsey, 1884), 201, 213.

136. Edward P. Crapol, *James G. Blaine: Architect of Empire* (Wilmington, DE: Scholarly Resources, 2000), 9–10.

137. Pérez, *Cuba between Empires*, 31.

138. Ibid., 32–33.

139. Cleveland to Olney, July 16, 1896, *GC*, 448.

140. Ibid., 449; Grover Cleveland, Third Annual Message (second term), *MPP*, 9: 636; cf. Gerald G. Eggert, *Richard Olney: Evolution of a Statesman* (University Park: Pennsylvania State University Press, 1974), 260–62; Nick Cleaver, *Grover Cleveland's New Foreign Policy: Arbitration, Neutrality, and the Dawn of American Empire* (New York: Palgrave Macmillan, 2014), 159.

141. Grover Cleveland, "A Proclamation," *FRUS*: 1895, vol. 2, 1195; cf. Cleveland to Judson Harmon, September 21, 1896, *GC*, 459; Gresham to Hannis Taylor, March 14, 1895, *FRUS*: 1895, vol. 2, 1177; Duke of Tetuan to Taylor, May 16, 1895, ibid., 1184–85; Cleaver, *Cleveland's New Foreign Policy*, 147–96; Eggert, *Olney*, 257, 263.

142. Eggert, *Olney*, 269.

143. Olney to Cleveland, September 25, 1895, in Cleaver, *Cleveland's New Foreign Policy*, 153–54; Olney to Dupuy de Lôme, December 12, 1895, *FRUS*: 1895, vol. 2, 1216; Fitzhugh Lee to Day, November 23, 1897, *CR*, 55th Cong., 2nd sess., 3836; speech of Caffery: ibid., 3956–57; John L. Tone, *War and Genocide in Cuba, 1895–1898* (Chapel Hill: University of North Carolina Press, 2006), 57–68.

144. Olney to Enrique Dupuy de Lôme, April 4, 1896, *FRUS*: 1897, 542.

145. Ibid., 543–44; Dupuy de Lôme to Olney, June 4, 1896, *FRUS*: 1897, 548; Botero, *Ambivalent Embrace*, 86; Grover Cleveland, Fourth Annual Message (second term), *MPP*, 9: 719; Eggert, *Olney*, 267–69.

146. *SL*, 29, Appendix: 10; Cleaver, *Cleveland's New Foreign Policy*, 188.

147. Fareed Zakaria, *From Wealth to Power: The Unusual Origins of America's World Role* (Princeton: Princeton University Press, 1998), 154–64; Jeffrey W. Meiser, *Power and Restraint: The Rise of the United States, 1898–1941* (Washington, DC: Georgetown University Press, 2015), xiii.

148. McKee, *National Conventions and Platforms*, 303.

149. McKinley, First Inaugural Address, *MPP*, 10: 16.

150. George W. Auxier, "Middle Western Newspapers and the Spanish–American War, 1895–1898," *Mississippi Valley Historical Review* 26, no. 4 (1940): 529; cf. Richard F. Hamilton, *President McKinley, War and Empire*, vol. 1 (New Brunswick, NJ: Transaction Publishers, 2006), 109, 232; Robert Kagan, *Dangerous Nation* (New York: Vintage, 2006), 388–89.

151. John A. Garraty, *Henry Cabot Lodge: A Biography* (New York: Alfred A. Knopf, 1953), 183.

152. Cleveland to Olney, November 11, 1897, in Hamilton, *McKinley, War and Empire*, 1: 110; cf. Robert C. Hilderbrand, *Power and the People: Executive Management of Public Opinion in Foreign Affairs, 1897–1921* (Chapel Hill: University of North Carolina Press, 1981), 13–14.

153. Louis A. Pérez Jr., *Cuba: Between Reform and Revolution*, 5th ed. (New York: Oxford University Press, 2015), 131; cf. John L. Offner, *An Unwanted War: The Diplomacy of the United States and Spain over Cuba, 1895–1898* (Chapel Hill: University of North Carolina Press, 1992), 46–47.

154. Tone, *War and Genocide*, 210–23; cf. 158; Pérez, *Between Reform and Revolution*, 130–31.

155. John Sherman to Stewart Woodford, July 16, 1897, *FRUS*: 1898, 559.

156. A. C. Brice to Day, October 15, 1897, *FRUS*: 1898, 597; Joseph Springer to Day, October 20, 1897, ibid., 599; cf. Fitzhugh Lee to Day, November 23, December 7, 14, 1897, January 3, 15, 1898, *CR*, 55th Cong., 2nd sess., 3836; Brice to Day, November 17, December 17, 1897, January 18, 1898, Pulaski Hyatt to Day, December 14, 21, 1897, John Joba to Day, November 11, 1897, Walter Barker to Day, November 25, 1897, ibid., 3837; Barker to Day, December 8, 1897, January 27, February 17, March 14, 21, 24, 1898, ibid., 3838.

157. *CR*, 55th Cong., 2nd sess., 3877; cf. speech of Lodge: ibid., 3781–84; Hamilton, *McKinley, War and Empire*, 1: 149–69, 213–14; Tone, *War and Genocide*, 218–21; Kagan, *Dangerous Nation*, 391.

158. Woodford to Sherman, September 13, 1897, *FRUS*: 1898, 564; cf. Sherman to Dupuy de Lôme, June 26, August 24, November 6, 1897, *FRUS*: 1897, 507–10; Woodford to Sherman, September 13, 20, October 4, 5, 11, 1897, *FRUS*: 1898, 562, 567, 573, 576, 580; Offner, *Unwanted War*, 46–47.

159. William McKinley, First Annual Message, *MPP*, 10: 36, 33.

160. Day to Woodford, March 3, March 20, 1898, *FRUS*: 1898, 681, 692; Woodford to Sherman, March 25, 1898, ibid., 700–701; speeches of Turpie, Hoar, and Stewart: *CR*, 55th Cong., 2nd sess., 3549, 3835, 3903; Senate Foreign Relations Committee report: *CR*, 55th Cong., 2nd sess., 3773.

161. Sherman to Woodford, March 1, 1898, *FRUS*: 1898, 667–68; cf. Tone, *War and Genocide*, 216–17; Offner, *Unwanted War*, 80–81, 112.

162. *CR*, 55th Cong., 2nd sess., 2916–19; cf. speeches of Berry and Tillman, ibid., 3880, 3892; Woodford to McKinley, March 29, 1898, *FRUS*: 1898, 720; Offner, *Unwanted War*, 134.

163. *CR*, 55th Cong., 2nd sess., 3162–65.

164. Ibid., 3128–32.

165. Ibid., 3280–84.

166. Woodford to Sherman, March 21, 25, 1898, *FRUS*: 1898, 694, 700.

167. Woodford to McKinley, March 29, 1898, *FRUS*: 1898, 719; cf. 718; Day to Woodford, March 27, 28, 29, 1898, ibid., 711–12, 713, 718. Viewing Cubans as not "fit for self-government" and a U.S. protectorate as "very like the assumption of the responsible care of a mad-house," by mid-March Woodford personally saw annexation as the only path to peace: Woodford to McKinley, March 17, 1898, ibid., 687–88; cf. Woodford to McKinley, March 29, 1898, ibid., 720–21. He once raised the possibility of a purchase to Moret but acknowledged that most U.S. leaders rejected annexation: Woodford to McKinley, March 18, 1898, ibid., 690–91.

168. Woodford to Day, March 31, 1898, ibid., 726–27; Day to Woodford, April 4, 1898, ibid., 733; cf. Woodford to McKinley, March 24, 1898, ibid., 697.

169. H. H. Kohlsaat, *From McKinley to Harding: Personal Recollections of Our Presidents* (New York: Charles Scribner's Sons, 1923), 67.

170. *CR*, 55th Cong., 2nd sess., 3546–47; cf. speeches of Hoar and Fairbanks: ibid., 3835, 3845.

171. Ibid., 3497; cf. speeches of Mantle, Kenney, Lodge, Lindsay, and Gray: ibid., 3499–3501, 3547, 3781–84, 3790, 3841.

172. Ibid., 3774–75; cf. Langley, *American Mediterranean*, 165.

173. Speeches of Turpie, Lindsay, and Wellington: *CR*, 55th Cong., 2nd sess., 3548, 3789, 3952.

174. Walter LaFeber, *The New Empire: An Interpretation of American Expansion, 1860–1898* (Ithaca, NY: Cornell University Press, 1963), 384.

175. David Magie, *Life of Garret Augustus Hobart: Twenty-fourth Vice-President of the United States* (New York: G. P. Putnam's Sons, 1910), 174.

176. Hamilton, *McKinley, War and Empire*, 1: 118; Offner, *Unwanted War*, 234; cf. ix.

177. Henry S. Pritchett, "Some Recollections of President McKinley and the Cuban Intervention," *North American Review* 189, no. 640 (1909): 400–401.

178. Message, *FRUS*: 1898, 759; cf. *CR*, 55th Cong., 2nd sess., 3810, 3820–21.

179. Speeches of Lindsay, Turner, Teller, Wellington, Clark, Faulkner, and Clay: ibid., 3784, 3829, 3898, 3951, 3967, 3971, 3980.

180. Openly opposing annexation were Proctor (*CR*, 55th Cong., 2nd sess., 2919, 3983), Thurston (3164), Money (3284), Mason (3295), Allen (3413), Clay (3497), Stewart (3702, 4104), Butler (3732), Foraker (3780), Lodge (3783), Hoar (3786, 3835), Turner (3829), Gray (3841–42), Fairbanks (3842), Berry (3879–80), Tillman (3890), Wolcott (3893), Teller (3899), Cannon (3943), Wellington (3953), Caffery (3957), Hawley (3959), White (3961), Bate (3965), Pasco (3969), Wilson (3972), Elkins (3980), Pritchard (3984), Perkins (3985), and Davis (4017); cf. Lodge to Charles Francis Adams Jr., January 22, 1897, in Hamilton, *McKinley, War and Empire*, 1: 131. Annexation's lone proponent in the Senate was Gallinger, but in light of its widespread opposition he too favored independence: ibid., 3131.

181. *CR*, 55th Cong., 2nd sess., 3786, 3835; cf. speeches of Mason, Gray, Fairbanks, Berry, and Wolcott: ibid., 3295, 3842, 3846, 3879, 3893.

182. Ibid., 2919.

183. Ibid., 3164; cf. speeches of Tillman and Stewart: ibid., 3891, 3901.

184. Offner, *Unwanted War*, 130.

185. *CR*, 55th Cong., 2nd sess., 3958–59; cf. speech of Money: ibid., 3284.

186. Ibid., 3983.

187. Speeches of Stewart, Butler, and Pettus: ibid., 3703, 3730–33; in the House, Lentz, Bailey, McMillin, and Dinsmore: ibid., 3765–68, 3814–16.

188. Ibid., 3969; cf. speeches of Berry, Tillman, Stewart, White, and Teller: ibid., 3879, 3890, 3904, 3961, 4095.

189. Ibid., 3954; cf. *CR*, 55th Cong., 3rd sess., 325–30.

190. Margaret Leech, *In the Days of McKinley* (New York: Harper and Brothers, 1959), 188.

191. *CR*, 55th Cong., 2nd sess., 4228–29; 4244; *FRUS: 1898*, 819–20.

192. Protocol, *FRUS: 1898*, 824–25. U.S. demands: ibid., 820–21; Spanish acceptance: Duke of Almodóvar del Río to Day, August 7, 1898, ibid., 822–23.

193. McKinley, Instructions to the Peace Commissioners, September 16, 1898, *FRUS: 1898*, 906–7.

194. Speeches of Lindsay, Turner, Turpie, Stewart, Allen, and Stewart again: *CR*, 55th Cong., 2nd sess., 3784–90, 3830, 3839–40, 3902, 3944–45, 4029; cf. speeches of Hoar, Gray, and Fairbanks: ibid., 3833, 3842, 3846.

195. Day to Hay, October 8, 12, 22, 27, 1898, ibid., 924, 927, 930, 937; Day to McKinley, October 1, 1898, ibid., 916–17; Hay to Day, October 13, 25, 1898, ibid., 927, 932; H. Wayne Morgan, ed., *Making Peace with Spain: The Diary of Whitelaw Reid, September–December 1898* (Austin: University of Texas Press, 1965), 110.

196. Richard Olney, "The Growth of Our Foreign Policy," *Atlantic Monthly* (1900): 291; Cleveland to Olney, March 26, 1900, *GC*, 526–27.

197. Webster to Timoteo Haalilio and William Richards, December 19, 1842, *FRUS: 1894*, Appendix 2, 44; *CR*, 55th Cong., 2nd sess., 5786; John Tyler, Message to Congress Regarding U.S.–Hawaiian Relations, December 30, 1842, *MPP*, 4: 211–14; Merze Tate, *Hawaii: Reciprocity or Annexation* (East Lansing: Michigan State University Press, 1968), 117, 187, 206; David M. Pletcher, *The Diplomacy of Involvement: American Economic Expansion across the Pacific, 1784–1900* (Columbia: University of Missouri Press, 2001), 46–65.

198. *CR*, 55th Cong., 2nd sess., 5787; Seward to Edward McCook, September 12, 1867, Senate Committee on Foreign Relations, *Papers Relating to the Annexation of the Hawaiian Islands to the United States* (Washington, DC: Government Printing Office, 1893), 139; Sylvester K. Stevens, *American Expansion in Hawaii, 1842–1898* (New York: Russell and Russell, 1945), 108–40, 160–86.

199. Merze Tate, *The United States and the Hawaiian Kingdom: A Political History* (New Haven: Yale University Press, 1965), 155–93.

200. Pletcher, *Diplomacy of Involvement*, 250; William M. Morgan, *Pacific Gibraltar: U.S.–Japanese Rivalry over the Annexation of Hawai'i, 1885–1898* (Annapolis: Naval Institute Press, 2011), 200; cf. 216.

201. Morgan, *Pacific Gibraltar*, 221; ibid., 200–209.

202. George F. Hoar, *Autobiography of Seventy Years*, vol. 2 (London: Bickers and Son, 1904), 307–8.

203. William McKinley, First Annual Message, *MPP*, 10: 39.

204. *CR*, 55th Cong., 2nd sess., 5829; 5840; cf. speeches of Hitt, Newlands, Barrows, Howard, Linney: ibid., 5772, 5830, 5843–44, 5899, 5982.

205. Ibid., 5990–91, 6008; cf. speeches of Hitt, Henry, Barrows, Grow, Sulzer, Barham: ibid., 5774, 5840, 5844, 5890, 5905, 5913.

206. Ibid., 5989; cf. speeches of Alexander, Newlands, Henry, Barrows, Stewart, Pearce, Barham, Packer, and Lacey: ibid., 5785, 5829, 5840, 5844, 5892, 5893–95, 5913, 5931, 6008.

207. Ibid., 5846, 5775, 5771.

208. Ibid., 5908.

209. *Senate Reports*, 53rd Cong., 2nd sess., no. 227; cf. speeches of Sulzer, Gillett, CR, 55th Cong., 2nd sess., 5905, 5783; Morgan, *Pacific Gibraltar*, 221–22, 234.

210. CR, 55th Cong., 2nd sess., 5785; cf. 5786; speeches of Hitt, Henry, Linney, and Hull: ibid., 5772–73, 5839, 5982, 5983.

211. Ibid., 5844.

212. Thomas J. Osborne, *"Empire Can Wait": American Opposition to Hawaiian Annexation, 1893–1898* (Kent, OH: Kent State University Press, 1981), chap. 8.

213. CR, 55th Cong., 2nd sess., 5844; cf. speeches of Hitt, Gillett, Alexander, Walker, Pearson, Pearce, and Linney: ibid., 5772, 5782, 5785, 5795, 5835, 5894, 5982; Pletcher, *Diplomacy of Involvement*, 273–74.

214. CR, 55th Cong., 2nd sess., 6527; cf. speeches of Alexander, Henry, Barrows, Grow, Hamilton, Lacey, and Cummings: ibid., 5787, 5838, 5843, 5890, 5909, 6008, 6012.

215. Hugh Dinsmore of Arkansas alone rebutted arguments that annexation was necessary to deter a Japanese takeover of Hawaii and for U.S. coastal defense, though even he conceded its strategic advantages: ibid., 5776, 5779–80. He also tried to argue that Alaska offered a shorter route to Asia than Hawaii due to the earth's curvature, but this was effectively rebutted by Newlands and Grosvenor, among others: ibid., 5780, 5830, 5873.

216. Ibid., 5888; cf. speeches of Clardy, Dinsmore, Clark, Bland, Howard, Broussard, Meyer, Johnson, and Williams: ibid., 5775–76, 5778, 5792, 5842, 5903, 5937, 5987, 5998, 6013–14.

217. Ibid., 5974, 5792, cf. 5788, speeches of Gaines, Hitt, Clark, and Kitchin: ibid., 5774, 5775, 5790, 5932; *CS*, 5: 199, 204–5.

218. Ibid., 5998; cf. 5999; speeches by Bland, Hilborn, Broussard, Ball, Meyer, and Todd: ibid., 5841–42, 5927, 5937, 5977, 5987, 6009.

219. Ibid., 5903; cf. Morgan, *Pacific Gibraltar*, 178–79.

220. CR, 55th Cong., 2nd sess., 5845; cf. speeches of Dinsmore, Bell, Howard: ibid., 5778, 5832, 5904.

221. Ibid., 5982, 5967.

222. Ibid., 5790.

223. Ibid., 5791.

224. Ibid., 5833.

225. Ibid., 5792; cf. speeches of Dinsmore, Bland, Ball, and Johnson: ibid., 5777, 5842, 5977, 5998–99.

226. Ibid., 5791.

227. Speeches of Bland, Richardson, and Johnson: ibid., 5842, 5888, 5999.

228. Ibid., 5998.

229. Ibid., 5832–33; cf. speeches of Clark, Richardson, Kitchin, and Fitzgerald: ibid., 5788–92, 5888, 5932, 5967.

230. Ibid., 5910; cf. speeches of Hitt, Alexander, Newlands, Henry, Todd: ibid., 5773–74, 5786, 5831, 5838–40, 6010.

231. Ibid., 6012.

232. Stevens, *American Expansion in Hawaii*, 24–45; Tate, *Hawaiian Kingdom*, 1–18.

233. *CR*, 55th Cong., 2nd sess., 5788; cf. speeches of Gillett, Barrows, Grosvenor, Hull: ibid., 5783, 5844, 5880, 5983.

234. Ibid., 5879; cf. speech of Pearce: ibid., 5893.

235. Ibid., 5972; cf. speeches of Alexander and Pearce: ibid., 5787–88, 5896.

236. Ibid., 5930.

237. Ibid., 6010; cf. speech of Stewart: ibid., 5844.

238. Ibid., 5771; 6008; cf. 5775.

239. Ibid., 5831, 5830; cf. 5829, speeches of Alexander and Linney: ibid., 5787–88, 5982.

240. Ibid., 5989; cf. speeches of Hitt, Newlands, Henry, Grosvenor, Pearce, Barham, Danford, Bromwell, Packer, Berry, Hull: ibid., 5775, 5830–31, 5838, 5874, 5896, 5913, 5915, 5919, 5930, 5972, 5983.

241. Ibid., 6010.

242. Ibid., 5787.

243. Ibid., 5830; cf. speeches of Hitt and Pearce: ibid., 5775, 5897.

244. Ibid., 5982; cf. 5979

245. Ibid., 5930.

246. Ibid., 6008; cf. speeches of Henry, Bromwell, Packer, Linney, and Hull: ibid., 5837, 5919, 5930, 5982, 5983.

247. Ibid., 6017; cf. speech of Packer: ibid., 5930.

248. Ibid., 5783.

249. Ibid., 6008.

250. Ibid., 6019.

251. Ibid., 6522, 6525; cf. 6519, 6526, 6528; speech of Caffery: ibid., 6483.

252. Ibid., 6531; cf. speeches of Caffery, Mallory, Pettigrew, and Allen: ibid., 6484, 6577, 6622–23, 6634.

253. Ibid., 6534.

254. Ibid., 6484, 6486, 6611, 6620, 6705.

255. Speeches of Caffery, Bate, and Allen: ibid., 6484, 6525, 6643; cf. 6486, 6526.

256. Ibid., 6642; cf. speeches of Pettigrew and Allen: ibid., 6702.

257. Ibid., 6661.

258. Ibid., 6661, 6663; cf. 6662, speeches of Pettus, Lindsay, and Hale: ibid., 6573, 6666, 6708.

259. Ibid., 6702.

260. John A. S. Grenville, "American Naval Preparations for War with Spain, 1896–1898," *Journal of American Studies* 2, no. 1 (1968): 35; 43–44.

261. George Dewey, *Autobiography of George Dewey, Admiral of the Navy* (New York: Charles Scribner's Sons, 1913), 175.

262. Hamilton, *McKinley, War and Empire*, 2: 84; cf. 70; Tyler Dennett, *John Hay: From Poetry to Politics* (New York: Dodd, Mead, 1934), 190–91; Offner, *Unwanted War*, 199.

263. In one of the more remarkable tales of conquest, U.S. ships under Captain Henry Glass boldly cruised into Guam's harbor expecting a well-fortified enemy and

firing shots toward the fort of Santa Cruz. But the local Spanish officials rowed out to meet them apologizing that lack of ammunition prevented them from returning what they thought was a U.S. salute. Much to their surprise Glass informed them that the United States and Spain were at war, and they were now his prisoners. The local Spanish governor surrendered the following day: Leslie W. Walker, "Guam's Seizure by the United States in 1898," *Pacific Historical Review* 14, no. 1 (1945): 1–12.

264. Ernest R. May, *Imperial Democracy: The Emergence of America as a Great Power* (New York: Harcourt, Brace and World, 1961), 251; Lewis L. Gould, *The Presidency of William McKinley* (Lawrence: Regents Press of Kansas, 1980), 118; Offner, *Unwanted War*, 213–15; Leech, *Days of McKinley*, 283–86; McKinley, Instructions to the Peace Commissioners, September 16, 1898, *FRUS: 1898*, 904–8; cf. Morgan, *Making Peace with Spain*, 30–31, 233–38; Hamilton, *McKinley, War and Empire*, 2: 67–68.

265. César J. Ayala and Rafael Bernabe, *Puerto Rico in the American Century: A History since 1898* (Chapel Hill: University of North Carolina Press, 2007), 14, 29.

266. Henry K. Carroll, *Report on the Island of Porto Rico* (Washington, DC: Government Printing Office, 1899), 42.

267. *CR*, 56th Cong., 1st sess., 3692; Carroll, *Report*, 46, 51–52.

268. *CR*, 56th Cong., 1st sess., 3619.

269. Ibid., 3622; *CR*, 55th Cong., 3rd sess., 960; Allan Nevins, *Henry White: Thirty Years of American Diplomacy* (New York: Harper and Brothers, 1930), 136; cf. Walter LaFeber, *The Cambridge History of American Foreign Relations*, vol. 2 (New York: Cambridge University Press, 1993), 156, 158.

270. Julius W. Pratt, "American Business and the Spanish–American War," *Hispanic American Historical Review* 14, no. 2 (1934): 191; cf. 185–89, 196; Julius W. Pratt, *Expansionists of 1898: The Acquisition of Hawaii and the Spanish Islands* (Baltimore: Johns Hopkins University Press, 1936); Hamilton, *McKinley, War and Empire*, 2: xv, xvii, 93, 109–57. Decades later U.S. agricultural interests played a significant role finalizing Philippine independence: Thomas B. Pepinsky, "Trade Competition and American Decolonization," *World Politics* 67, no. 3 (2015): 387–422.

271. Pletcher, *Diplomacy of Involvement*, 285.

272. Thomas A. Bailey, "Dewey and the Germans at Manila Bay," *American Historical Review* 45, no. 1 (1939): 60–70; Dewey, *Autobiography*, 252–67.

273. Memorandum from Nakagawa, September 8, 1898, in James K. Eyre Jr., "Japan and the American Annexation of the Philippines," *Pacific Historical Review* 11, no. 1 (1942): 64.

274. Buck to Day, July 6, 1898, ibid., 59.

275. Ephraim K. Smith, "'A Question from Which We Could Not Escape': William McKinley and the Decision to Acquire the Philippine Islands," *Diplomatic History* 9 (1985): 369; cf. *Report of the Philippine Commission to the President*, vol. 1 (Washington, DC: Government Printing Office, 1900), 8; Hamilton, *McKinley, War and Empire*, 2: 75; Leech, *Days of McKinley*, 327–36.

276. Charles B. Elliott, *The Philippines to the End of the Military Regime* (Indianapolis: Bobbs-Merrill, 1916), 342; cf. Jacob G. Schurman, *Philippine Affairs: A Retrospect and Outlook* (New York: Charles Scribner's Sons, 1902), 2; Henry S. Pritchett, "Some Recollections of President McKinley and the Cuban Intervention," *North American Review* 189, no. 640 (1909): 400–401; Stuart C. Miller, *Benevolent Assimilation: The American Conquest of the Philippines, 1899–1903* (New Haven: Yale University Press, 1982), 14.

277. Elizabeth C. Hoffman, *American Umpire* (Cambridge: Harvard University Press, 2013), 174.

278. Hay to Day, October 14, 1898, *FRUS*: 1898, 928; Hamilton, *McKinley, War and Empire* 2: 81; cf. Governor Roosevelt's Letter of Acceptance, September 15, 1900, M. W. Blumenberg, ed., *Official Proceedings of the Twelfth Republican National Convention* (Philadelphia: Dunlap, 1900), 187.

279. H. C. Corbin to Major-General Merritt, August 17, 1898, *MPP*, 10: 217; cf. Hamilton, *McKinley, War and Empire*, 2: 75–76.

280. *CR*, 55th Cong., 3rd sess., 1450, 1480–84, 1530; cf. Hamilton, *McKinley, War and Empire*, 2: 83.

281. Joseph Wheeler, "Report on the Island of Guam, June 1900" (Washington, DC: Government Printing Office, 1900), 20; Ayala and Bernabe, *Puerto Rico*, 32.

282. Carroll, *Report*, 11.

283. Ibid., 36, 56; cf. 10; Ayala and Bernabe, *Puerto Rico*, 15, 20, 24, 26; Gordon K. Lewis, *Puerto Rico: Freedom and Power in the Caribbean* (New York: Monthly Review Press, 1963), 85–86.

284. Carroll, *Report*, 56–57.

285. *CR*, 56th Cong., 1st sess., 3685.

286. Ibid., 2105.

287. Ibid., 4054, 3681–82.

288. *CR*, 56th Cong., 1st sess., 4058, 3689; cf. speeches of Newlands, McClellan, Clay, ibid., 1994, 2067, 3682.

289. Speeches of Perkins, Ross, and Hamilton, ibid., 3635, 3683, 4052; cf. Lewis, *Puerto Rico*, 3–4; Bartholomew H. Sparrow, *The Insular Cases and the Emergence of American Empire* (Lawrence: University Press of Kansas, 2006), 58–64.

290. *CR*, 56th Cong., 1st sess., 3632.

291. Ibid., 3635, 3638; cf. 3636–37; speech of Dolliver: ibid., 4068.

292. Ibid., 3622.

293. Carroll, *Report*, 59.

294. Cf. speech of Lindsay: ibid., 3693.

295. José A. Cabranes, "Citizenship and the American Empire," *University of Pennsylvania Law Review* 127 (1978): 414–15; Juan R. Torruella, *The Supreme Court and Puerto Rico: The Doctrine of Separate and Unequal* (Dominican Republic: Editorial de la Universidad de Puerto Rico, 1988), 32–39.

296. *CR*, 56th Cong., 1st sess., 3608; cf. speeches of Newlands and Williams, ibid., 1994, 2162.

297. James H. Blount, *The American Occupation of the Philippines, 1898–1912* (New York: G. P. Putnam's Sons, 1912), 231–32; Paul A. Kramer, *The Blood of Government: Race, Empire, the United States, and the Philippines* (Chapel Hill: University of North Carolina Press, 2006); Love, *Race over Empire*, 7; cf. speech of Clay: *CR*, 56th Cong., 1st sess., 3681–82; Lanny Thompson, "The Imperial Republic: A Comparison of the Insular Territories under U.S. Dominion after 1898," *Pacific Historical Review* 71, no. 4 (2002): 565; Susan K. Harris, *God's Arbiters: Americans and the Philippines, 1898–1902* (New York: Oxford University Press, 2011), chaps. 1, 2.

298. Carl Schurz, "Thoughts on American Imperialism," *Century Magazine* (1898), in *CS*, 5: 481, 483, 505; cf. Schurz to McKinley, June 1, July 29, 1898, ibid., 472–76; Carl Schurz, *American Imperialism* (Boston: Dana Estes, 1899), 6, 13.

299. *CR*, 56th Cong., 1st sess., 3608, 3616.

300. *CR*, 55th Cong., 3rd sess., 922; *CR*, 56th Cong., 1st sess., 1520; cf. *CR*, 55th Cong., 3rd sess., 438, 1067, 1532; David S. Jordan, *Imperial Democracy* (New York, D. Appleton, 1899), 48.

301. *CR*, 55th Cong., 2nd sess., 6634; cf. 6642, 6712; speeches of Newlands and Lindsay: ibid., 5830–31, 6666–67.

302. Ibid., 6664.

303. *CR*, 56th Cong., 1st sess., 3622; cf. speech of Bate: ibid., 3613.

304. Ibid., 711; cf. speech of Lindsay: ibid., 3693.

305. Love, *Race over Empire*, xvii; Christopher Lasch, "The Anti-Imperialists, the Philippines, and the Inequality of Man," *Journal of Southern History* 24, no. 3 (1958): 323; cf. 319, 321, 330; Frederick Merk, *Manifest Destiny and Mission in American History* (New York: Alfred A. Knopf, 1963), 237–47.

306. Lasch, "Anti-Imperialists," 319, 322; Christina D. Burnett and Burke Marshall, "Between the Foreign and the Domestic: The Doctrine of Territorial Incorporation, Invented and Reinvented," in *Foreign in a Domestic Sense: Puerto Rico, American Expansion, and the Constitution*, ed. Christina D. Burnett and Burke Marshall (Durham: Duke University Press, 2001), 4; Julian Go, "Modes of Rule in America's Overseas Empire: The Philippines, Puerto Rico, Guam, and Samoa," in *The Louisiana Purchase and American Expansion, 1803–1898*, ed. Sanford Levinson and Bartholomew H. Sparrow (New York: Rowman and Littlefield, 2005), 209–29.

307. *CR*, 55th Cong., 3rd sess., 20; cf. 432–33, 493–502, 641, 783–84, 930, 963–68, 1064–67, 1070, 1384, 1430, 1445–47, 1530.

308. *CR*, 56th Cong., 1st sess., 4057; cf. speech of Teller: *CR*, 55th Cong., 3rd sess., 969.

309. *CR*, 56th Cong., 1st sess., 4070.

310. Ibid., 2105.

311. *CR*, 55th Cong., 3rd sess., 20; cf. 528, 561, 1342, 1348, 1445, 1479.

312. Ibid., 296; cf. 563–72, 838.

313. *CR*, 56th Cong., 1st sess., 4052.

314. Ibid., 1914; cf. speech of Cullom: ibid., 3617.

315. Ibid., 3637.

316. Ibid., 3629.

317. Ibid., 1062.

318. Ibid., 295; cf. 969, 1447.

319. *CR*, 56th Cong., 1st sess., 1057.

320. Ayala and Bernabe, *Puerto Rico*, 26, 28; Kramer, *Blood of Government*, 165.

321. Efrén R. Ramos, "Deconstructing Colonialism: The 'Unincorporated Territory' as a Category of Domination," in Burnett and Marshall, *Foreign in a Domestic Sense*, 115–16.

322. *Downes v. Bidwell*, 182 U.S. 287 (1901).

323. *Downes v. Bidwell*, 182 U.S. 287, 341–42 (1901).

324. *Hawaii v. Mankichi*, 190 U.S. 197–249 (1903); *Rassmussen v. United States*, 197 U.S. 516–36 (1905); cf. Dick Thornburgh, *Puerto Rico's Future: A Time to Decide* (Washington, DC: Center for Strategic and International Studies, 2007), 48–49.

325. Abbott L. Lowell, "The Status of Our New Possessions: A Third View," *Harvard Law Review* 13, no. 3 (1899): 176; cf. Burnett and Marshall, "Between the Foreign and the Domestic," 6.

326. Abbott L. Lowell, "The Colonial Expansion of the United States," *Atlantic Monthly* 83 (1899): 149–51.

327. Ibid., 152–53.

328. Gary Lawson and Guy Seidman, *The Constitution of Empire: Territorial Expansion and American Legal History* (New Haven: Yale University Press, 2004), 197; Rogers M. Smith, "The Bitter Roots of Puerto Rican Citizenship," in Burnett and Marshall, *Foreign in a Domestic Sense*, 378; cf. Sam Erman, *Almost Citizens: Puerto Rico, the U.S. Constitution, and Empire* (New York: Cambridge University Press, 2019); Thornburgh, *Puerto Rico's Future*, 46; Charles R. Venator-Santiago, *Puerto Rico and the Origins of US Global Empire: The Disembodied Shade* (New York: Routledge, 2015), 8–10, 45.

329. Hoffman, *American Umpire*, 175–76.

330. Philippine Autonomy Act, Pub. L. No. 64–240, 39 Stat. 545 (1916).

331. Chimène I. Keitner, "From Conquest to Consent: Puerto Rico and the Prospect of Genuine Free Association," in *Reconsidering the Insular Cases: The Past and Future of the American Empire*, ed. Gerald L. Neuman and Tomiko Brown-Nagin (Cambridge: Harvard University Press, 2015), 85; cf. *Balzac v. Porto Rico*, 258 U.S. 298–314 (1922).

332. Hoffman, *American Umpire*, 163–69.

333. Ernest R. May, *American Imperialism: A Speculative Essay* (New York: Atheneum, 1968), 14.

334. *FRUS: 1905*, 334.

335. Woodrow Wilson, "Address before the Southern Commercial Congress" in Mobile, AL, October 27, 1913; Welles, *Naboth's Vineyard*, 2: 277.

336. Lyndon B. Johnson, "Remarks in New York City at the Dinner of the Weizmann Institute of Science," February 6, 1964; Lyndon B. Johnson, "Remarks at the Democratic Congressional Dinner in the Washington Hilton Hotel," June 24, 1965; Lyndon B. Johnson, "Remarks to the 10th National Legislative Conference, Building and Construction Trades Department, AFL-CIO," May 3, 1965.

337. Paul A. Kramer, "Empires, Exceptions, and Anglo-Saxons: Race and Rule between the British and U.S. Empires, 1880–1910," *Journal of American History* 88, no. 4 (2002): 1316.

8. The International Implications of U.S. Annexation

Epigraph: Reginald Horsman, *Race and Manifest Destiny: The Origins of American Racial Anglo-Saxonism* (Cambridge, MA: Harvard University Press, 1981), 231.

1. *CR*, 55th Cong., 2nd sess., 2919.

2. Steven E. Lobell, Norrin M. Ripsman, and Jeffrey W. Taliaferro, eds., *Neoclassical Realism, the State, and Foreign Policy* (New York: Cambridge University Press, 2009); Melvin Small, *Democracy and Diplomacy: The Impact of Domestic Politics on U.S. Foreign Policy, 1789–1994* (Baltimore: Johns Hopkins University Press, 1996); James M. McCormick, ed., *The Domestic Sources of American Foreign Policy: Insights and Evidence*, 6th ed. (New York: Rowman and Littlefield, 2012); Helen V. Milner and Dustin Tingley, *Sailing the Water's Edge: The Domestic Politics of American Foreign Policy* (Princeton: Princeton University Press, 2015).

3. Peter J. Katzenstein, ed., *Between Power and Plenty: Foreign Economic Policies of Advanced Industrial States* (Madison: University of Wisconsin Press, 1978); Stephen D.

Krasner, *Defending the National Interest: Raw Materials Investments and U.S. Foreign Policy* (Princeton: Princeton University Press, 1978).

4. Colin Dueck, *Reluctant Crusaders: Power, Culture, and Change in American Grand Strategy* (Princeton: Princeton University Press, 2006); Kevin Narizny, *The Political Economy of Grand Strategy* (Ithaca, NY: Cornell University Press, 2007).

5. Kevin Narizny, "Both Guns and Butter, or Neither: Class Interests in the Political Economy of Rearmament," *American Political Science Review* 97, no. 2 (2003): 203–20; Rebecca U. Thorpe, *The American Warfare State: The Domestic Politics of Military Spending* (Chicago: University of Chicago Press, 2014).

6. Charles W. Ostrom Jr. and Brian L. Job, "The President and the Political Use of Force," *American Political Science Review* 80, no. 2 (1986): 541–66; Patrick James and John R. Oneal, "The Influence of Domestic and International Politics on the President's Use of Force," *Journal of Conflict Resolution* 35, no. 2 (1991): 307–32.

7. Gustavo A. Flores-Macías and Sarah E. Kreps, "Political Parties at War: A Study of American War Finance, 1789–2010," *American Political Science Review* 107, no. 4 (2013): 833–48; Kenneth A. Schultz and Barry R. Weingast, "The Democratic Advantage: Institutional Foundations of Financial Power in International Competition," *International Organization* 57, no. 1 (2003): 3–42.

8. Jeffrey W. Legro, *Rethinking the World: Great Power Strategies and International Order* (Ithaca, NY: Cornell University Press, 2005), chap. 3; Kevin Narizny, "Rational Idealism: The Political Economy of Internationalism in the United States and Great Britain, 1870–1945," *Security Studies* 12, no. 3 (2003): 1–39.

9. Helen V. Milner and Dustin H. Tingley, "The Political Economy of U.S. Foreign Aid: American Legislators and the Domestic Politics of Aid," *Economics and Politics* 22, no. 2 (2010): 200–232.

10. Jeffrey W. Meiser, *Power and Restraint: The Rise of the United States, 1898–1941* (Washington, DC: Georgetown University Press, 2015); Scott A. Silverstone, *Divided Union: The Politics of War in the Early American Republic* (Ithaca, NY: Cornell University Press, 2004); Fareed Zakaria, *From Wealth to Power: The Unusual Origins of America's World Role* (Princeton: Princeton University Press, 1998); Miriam F. Elman, "The Foreign Policies of Small States: Challenging Neorealism in Its Own Backyard," *British Journal of Political Science* 25, no. 2 (1995): 171–217; Jack Snyder, *Myths of Empire: Domestic Politics and International Ambition* (Ithaca, NY: Cornell University Press, 1991).

11. Peter Trubowitz, *Politics and Strategy: Partisan Ambition and American Statecraft* (Princeton: Princeton University Press, 2011).

12. Peter Trubowitz, *Defining the National Interest: Conflict and Change in American Foreign Policy* (Chicago: University of Chicago Press, 1998).

13. Lawrence R. Jacobs and Benjamin I. Page, "Who Influences U.S. Foreign Policy?" *American Political Science Review* 99, no. 1 (2005): 107–23.

14. Henry R. Nau, *Conservative Internationalism: Armed Diplomacy under Jefferson, Polk, Truman, and Reagan* (Princeton: Princeton University Press, 2013); Michael C. Desch, "America's Liberal Illiberalism: The Ideological Origins of Overreaction in U.S. Foreign Policy," *International Security* 32, no. 3 (2007/08): 19; Walter R. Mead, *Special Providence: American Foreign Policy and How It Changed the World* (New York: Routledge, 2002); Walter A. McDougall, *Promised Land, Crusader State: The American Encounter with the World since 1776* (New York: Houghton Mifflin, 1997).

15. Stephen M. Saideman, *The Ties that Divide: Ethnic Politics, Foreign Policy, and International Conflict* (New York: Columbia University Press, 2001); Alexander DeConde, *Ethnicity, Race, and American Foreign Policy: A History* (Boston: Northeastern University Press, 1992).

16. Robert D. Putnam, "Diplomacy and Domestic Politics: The Logic of Two-Level Games," *International Organization* 42, no. 3 (1988): 460.

17. David A. Lake, *Hierarchy in International Relations* (Ithaca, NY: Cornell University Press, 2009), 15.

18. David A. Lake, *Entangling Relations: American Foreign Policy in Its Century* (Princeton: Princeton University Press, 1999); David A. Lake, "Escape from the State of Nature: Authority and Hierarchy in World Politics," *International Security* 32, no. 1 (2007): 47–79; David Sylvan and Stephen Majeski, *U.S. Foreign Policy in Perspective: Clients, Enemies, and Empire* (New York: Routledge, 2009).

19. Charles Lipson, "International Cooperation in Economic and Security Affairs," *World Politics* 37, no. 1 (1984): 14.

20. Nuno P. Monteiro, *Theory of Unipolar Politics* (New York: Cambridge University Press, 2014); Nuno P. Monteiro, "Unrest Assured: Why Unipolarity Is Not Peaceful," *International Security* 36, no. 3 (2011/12): 9–40.

21. Hilde E. Restad, *American Exceptionalism: An Idea that Made a Nation and Remade the World* (New York: Routledge, 2015); Godfrey Hodgson, *The Myth of American Exceptionalism* (New Haven: Yale University Press, 2009); Seymour M. Lipset, *American Exceptionalism: A Double-Edged Sword* (New York: W. W. Norton, 1996).

22. Echoing recent attention to race in studies of American political development: Desmond King and Rogers M. Smith, "Racial Orders in American Political Development," *American Political Science Review* 99, no. 1 (2005): 75–92; Joseph Lowndes, Julie Novkov, and Dorian T. Warren, eds., *Race and American Political Development* (New York: Routledge, 2008).

23. William Kristol and Robert Kagan, "Toward a Neo-Reaganite Foreign Policy," *Foreign Affairs* 75, no. 4 (1996): 18–32; Robert Kagan, "The Benevolent Empire," *Foreign Policy* 111 (1998): 24–35.

24. Stephen G. Brooks, "Can We Identify a Benevolent Hegemon?" *Cambridge Review of International Affairs* 25, no. 1 (2012): 27–38; Christopher Layne, "The Unipolar Illusion Revisited: The Coming End of the United States' Unipolar Moment," *International Security* 31, no. 2 (2006): 7–41.

25. Samuel P. Huntington, "The Lonely Superpower," *Foreign Affairs* 78, no. 2 (1999): 48; cf. Francis Fukuyama, *America at the Crossroads: Democracy, Power, and the Neoconservative Legacy* (New Haven: Yale University Press, 2006), 111–13.

26. Layne, "Unipolar Illusion Revisited," 19.

27. Keir A. Lieber and Gerard Alexander, "Waiting for Balancing: Why the World Is Not Pushing Back," *International Security* 30, no. 1 (2005): 109–39.

28. John M. Owen IV, "Transnationalism, Liberalism and American Primacy; or, Benignity Is in the Eye of the Beholder," in *America Unrivaled*, ed. G. John Ikenberry (Ithaca, NY: Cornell University Press, 2002), 239–59.

29. Susan K. Harris, *God's Arbiters: Americans and the Philippines, 1898–1902* (New York: Oxford University Press, 2011); Paul A. Kramer, *The Blood of Government: Race, Empire, the United States, and the Philippines* (Chapel Hill: University of North Carolina

Press, 2006); Tony Smith, *America's Mission: The United States and the Worldwide Struggle for Democracy in the Twentieth Century* (Princeton: Princeton University Press, 1994).

30. Greg Grandin, *Empire's Workshop: Latin America, the United States, and the Rise of the New Imperialism* (New York: Henry Holt, 2006); Michael C. Desch, *When the Third World Matters: Latin America and United States Grand Strategy* (Baltimore: Johns Hopkins University Press, 1993); Walter LaFeber, *Inevitable Revolutions: The United States in Central America* (New York: W. W. Norton, 1993).

31. Theodore Roosevelt, Fourth Annual Message, *MPP*, 10: 831–32.

32. Alexander Cooley and Hendrik Spruyt, *Contracting States: Sovereign Transfers in International Relations* (Princeton: Princeton University Press, 2009), chap. 4; Lake, *Entangling Relations*; Daniel Nexon and Thomas Wright, "What's at Stake in the American Empire Debate," *American Political Science Review* 101, no. 2 (2007): 253–71; Robert H. Wade, "The Invisible Hand of the American Empire," *Ethics and International Affairs* 17, no. 2 (2003): 77–88.

33. G. John Ikenberry, *Liberal Leviathan: The Origins, Crisis, and Transformation of the American World Order* (Princeton: Princeton University Press, 2011); G. John Ikenberry, "Institutions, Strategic Restraint, and the Persistence of American Postwar Order," *International Security* 23, no. 3 (1998/99): 43–78; Carla Norloff, *America's Global Advantage: U.S. Hegemony and International Cooperation* (New York: Cambridge University Press, 2010); Richard W. Maass, Carla Norloff, and Daniel W. Drezner, "Correspondence: The Profitability of Primacy," *International Security* 38, no. 4 (2014): 188–205.

34. John M. Owen IV, *The Clash of Ideas in World Politics: Transnational Networks, States, and Regime Change, 1510–2010* (Princeton: Princeton University Press, 2010); Mark L. Haas, *The Ideological Origins of Great Power Politics* (Ithaca, NY: Cornell University Press, 2004), 6–8.

35. Abraham F. Lowenthal, ed., *Exporting Democracy: The United States and Latin America* (Baltimore: Johns Hopkins University Press, 1991); Smith, *America's Mission*, chap. 3.

36. Sebastian Rosato, "The Flawed Logic of Democratic Peace Theory," *American Political Science Review* 97, no. 4 (2003): 590–91; Lindsey A. O'Rourke, *Covert Regime Change: America's Secret Cold War* (Ithaca, NY: Cornell University Press, 2018).

37. Stephen Kinzer, *Overthrow: America's Century of Regime Change from Hawaii to Iraq* (New York: Henry Holt, 2006); Robert S. Litwak, *Regime Change: U.S. Strategy through the Prism of 9/11* (Baltimore: Johns Hopkins University Press, 2007).

38. Desch, "America's Liberal Illiberalism," 7.

39. LaFeber, *Inevitable Revolutions*, 22.

40. John S. Mill, "A Few Words on Non-Intervention," in *The Collected Works of John Stuart Mill*, ed. John M. Robson, vol. 21 (Toronto: University of Toronto Press, 1984), 119; John Rawls, *The Law of Peoples* (Cambridge: Harvard University Press, 1999), 93; cf. Immanuel Kant, "Perpetual Peace," trans. Lewis W. Beck, in *Kant on History*, ed. Lewis W. Beck (Upper Saddle River, NJ: Prentice Hall, 2001); Michael W. Doyle, "Liberalism and World Politics," *American Political Science Review* 80, no. 4 (1986): 1155–62.

41. Kant, "Perpetual Peace," 86; cf. Kenneth N. Waltz, "Kant, Liberalism, and War," *American Political Science Review* 56, no. 2 (1962): 333; Michael Doyle, "Kant, Liberal Legacies, and Foreign Affairs," pt. 1, *Philosophy and Public Affairs* 12 (1983): 206.

42. *USSS*, 66th Cong., 1st sess., *Treaty of Peace with Germany* (S.Doc. 76), 42.

43. Niall Ferguson, *Empire: The Rise and Demise of the British World Order and the Lessons for Global Power* (New York: Basic Books, 2002), xxii; cf. Uday S. Mehta, *Liberalism and Empire: A Study in Nineteenth-Century British Liberal Thought* (Chicago: University of Chicago Press, 1999); Jennifer Pitts, *A Turn to Empire: The Rise of Imperial Liberalism in Britain and France* (Princeton: Princeton University Press, 2005).

44. Russell Thornton, *American Indian Holocaust and Survival: A Population History since 1492* (Norman: University of Oklahoma Press, 1987); Andrew Bell-Fialkoff, "A Brief History of Ethnic Cleansing," *Foreign Affairs* 72, no. 3 (1993): 110–21.

45. Michael Mann, *The Dark Side of Democracy: Explaining Ethnic Cleansing* (New York: Cambridge University Press, 2005), 2; cf. Bernard Yack, "Popular Sovereignty and Nationalism," *Political Theory* 29, no. 4 (2001): 517–36; Paulina O. Espejo, "Paradoxes of Popular Sovereignty: A View from Spanish America," *Journal of Politics* 74, no. 4 (2012): 1053–65.

46. Paul Frymer, *Building an American Empire: The Era of Territorial and Political Expansion* (Princeton: Princeton University Press, 2017).

47. Thomas R. Hietala, *Manifest Design: American Exceptionalism and Empire* (Ithaca, NY: Cornell University Press, 2003), 164.

48. Eric T. L. Love, *Race over Empire: Racism and U.S. Imperialism, 1865–1900* (Chapel Hill: University of North Carolina Press, 2004), 23.

49. Richard F. Bensel, *Sectionalism and American Political Development, 1880–1980* (Madison: University of Wisconsin Press, 1984), xix.

50. Trubowitz, *Defining the National Interest*, 27, 23.

51. Ibid., 20.

52. Rogers Smith, *Civic Ideals: Conflicting Visions of Citizenship in U.S. History* (New Haven: Yale University Press, 1997); Reginald Horsman, *Race and Manifest Destiny: The Origins of American Racial Anglo-Saxonism* (Cambridge: Harvard University Press, 1981); Love, *Race over Empire*; Michael H. Hunt, *Ideology and U.S. Foreign Policy* (New Haven: Yale University Press, 1987), chap. 3; Samuel P. Huntington, *Who Are We? The Challenges to America's National Identity* (New York: Simon and Schuster, 2005).

53. Hans Kohn, *The Idea of Nationalism: A Study in Its Origins and Background* (New York: Macmillan, 1944); Liah Greenfeld, *Nationalism: Five Roads to Modernity* (Cambridge: Harvard University Press, 1992); Rogers Brubaker, "The Manichean Myth: Rethinking the Distinction between 'Civic' and 'Ethnic' Nationalism," in *Nation and National Identity: The European Experience in Perspective*, ed. Hanspeter Kriesi, Klaus Armingeon, Hannes Siegrist, and Andreas Wimmer (Zurich: Verlag Ruegger, 1999), 55–72.

54. Smith, *Civic Ideals*, 1; cf. Lon Kurashige, *Two Faces of Exclusion: The Untold History of Anti-Asian Racism in the United States* (Chapel Hill: University of North Carolina Press, 2016).

55. Taras Kuzio, "The Myth of the Civic State: A Critical Survey of Hans Kohn's Framework for Understanding Nationalism," *Ethnic and Racial Studies* 25, no. 1 (2002): 20–39.

56. Nikhil P. Singh, *Race and America's Long War* (Oakland: University of California Press, 2017); Zoltan Hajnal and Michael U. Rivera, "Immigration, Latinos, and White Partisan Politics: The New Democratic Defection," *American Journal of Political Science* 58, no. 4 (2014): 773–89.

57. Monty G. Marshall, Ted R. Gurr, and Keith Jaggers, *Polity IV Project, Political Regime Characteristics and Transitions, 1800–2013: Dataset Users' Manual* (Vienna, VA: Center for Systemic Peace, 2014); Barbara Wejnert, *Diffusion of Democracy: The Past and Future of Global Democracy* (New York: Cambridge University Press, 2014); John Markoff, *Waves of Democracy: Social Movements and Political Change*, 2nd ed. (New York: Routledge, 2016).

58. Benedict Anderson, *Imagined Communities: Reflections on the Origin and Spread of Nationalism* (New York: Verso, 1983); Ernest Gellner, *Nations and Nationalism* (Ithaca, NY: Cornell University Press, 1983); E. J. Hobsbawm, *Nations and Nationalism since 1780: Programme, Myth, Reality* (New York: Cambridge University Press, 1990).

59. Ernest Gellner, "Nationalism and Xenophobia," in *New Xenophobia in Europe*, ed. Bernd Baumgartl and Adrian Favell (London: Kluwer Law International, 1995), 6–9; cf. Henri Tajfel, "Social Psychology of Intergroup Relations," *Annual Review of Psychology* 33 (1982): 1–39; Jonathan Mercer, "Anarchy and Identity," *International Organization* 49, no. 2 (1995): 229–52.

60. Craig Parsons, *A Certain Idea of Europe* (Ithaca, NY: Cornell University Press, 2003); Raymond Taras, *Xenophobia and Islamophobia in Europe* (Edinburgh: Edinburgh University Press, 2012); Baumgartl and Favell, *New Xenophobia*.

61. Stephen G. Brooks, *Producing Security: Multinational Corporations, Globalization, and the Changing Calculus of Conflict* (Princeton: Princeton University Press, 2005); Patrick J. McDonald, *The Invisible Hand of Peace: Capitalism, the War Machine, and International Relations Theory* (New York: Cambridge University Press, 2009); John Mueller, *Retreat from Doomsday: The Obsolescence of Major War* (New York: Basic Books, 1989); William C. Wohlforth, "The Stability of a Unipolar World," *International Security* 24, no. 1 (1999): 5–41.

62. Zeev Maoz and Bruce Russett, "Normative and Structural Causes of Democratic Peace, 1946–1986," *American Political Science Review* 87, no. 3 (1993): 624–38; Bruce M. Russett, *Grasping the Democratic Peace: Principles for a Post–Cold War World* (Princeton: Princeton University Press, 1993); James Lee Ray, *Democracy and International Conflict: An Evaluation of the Democratic Peace Proposition* (Columbia: University of South Carolina Press, 1995).

63. Rosato, "Flawed Logic."

64. John M. Owen IV, *Liberal Peace, Liberal War* (Ithaca, NY: Cornell University Press, 1997); Ido Oren, "The Subjectivity of the 'Democratic' Peace: Changing U.S. Perceptions of Imperial Germany," *International Security* 20, no. 2 (1995): 147–84; Christopher Layne, "Kant or Cant: The Myth of the Democratic Peace," *International Security* 19 (1994): 5–49.

65. Erik Gartzke, "The Capitalist Peace," *American Journal of Political Science* 51, no. 1 (2007): 166–91; McDonald, *Invisible Hand of Peace*; Michael Mousseau, "The Social Market Roots of Democratic Peace," *International Security* 33, no. 4 (2009): 52–86; Michael Mousseau, "The Democratic Peace Unraveled: It's the Economy," *International Studies Quarterly* 57, no. 1 (2013): 186–97.

66. Paul K. Huth, *Standing Your Ground: Territorial Disputes and International Conflict* (Ann Arbor: University of Michigan Press, 1996); John A. Vasquez and Marie T. Henehan, *Territory, War, and Peace* (New York: Routledge, 2011).

67. Douglas M. Gibler, *The Territorial Peace: Borders, State Development, and International Conflict* (New York: Cambridge University Press, 2012); Douglas M. Gibler,

"Bordering on Peace: Democracy, Territorial Issues, and Conflict," *International Studies Quarterly* 51, no. 3 (2007): 509–32.

68. Gibler, *Territorial Peace*, 167.

69. Sharon Korman, *The Right of Conquest: The Acquisition of Territory by Force in International Law and Practice* (Oxford: Clarendon Press, 1996); Mark W. Zacher, "The Territorial Integrity Norm: International Boundaries and the Use of Force," *International Organization* 55, no. 2 (2001): 215–50; Tanisha M. Fazal, *State Death: The Politics and Geography of Conquest, Occupation, and Annexation* (Princeton: Princeton University Press, 2007), 44–54; Boaz Atzili, *Good Fences, Bad Neighbors: Border Fixity and International Conflict* (Chicago: University of Chicago Press, 2012), 10–30.

70. Stephen A. Kocs, "Territorial Disputes and Interstate War, 1945–1987," *Journal of Politics* 57, no. 1 (1995): 159; William J. Dixon, "Democracy and the Peaceful Settlement of International Conflict," *American Political Science Review* 88, no. 1 (1994): 15.

71. Michael C. Desch, "War and Strong States, Peace and Weak States?" *International Organization* 50, no. 2 (1996): 237–68; Boaz Atzili, "When Good Fences Make Bad Neighbors: Fixed Borders, State Weakness, and International Conflict," *International Security* 31, no. 3 (2006/07): 139–73.

72. George W. Egerton, *Great Britain and the Creation of the League of Nations: Strategy, Politics, and International Organization, 1914–1919* (Chapel Hill: University of North Carolina Press, 1978), 203; Stephen C. Schlesinger, *Act of Creation: The Founding of the United Nations* (Boulder, CO: Westview, 2003).

73. Fazal, *State Death*, 47.

74. William W. Burke-White, "Crimea and the International Legal Order," *Survival* 56, no. 4 (2014): 65–80.

75. Mark L. Haas, "A Geriatric Peace? The Future of U.S. Power in a World of Aging Populations," *International Security* 32, no. 1 (2007): 112–47; Michael Beckley, "China's Century? Why America's Edge Will Endure," *International Security* 36, no. 3 (2011/12): 41–78.

76. Barry R. Posen, *Restraint: A New Foundation for U.S. Grand Strategy* (Ithaca, NY: Cornell University Press, 2014); Stephen G. Brooks and William C. Wohlforth, *America Abroad: The United States' Global Role in the 21st Century* (New York: Oxford University Press, 2016).

77. John Boyd Orr, Nobel Lecture, December 12, 1949.

INDEX

Page numbers in italics refer to figures, tables, and maps.

Milton Keynes UK
Ingram Content Group UK Ltd.
UKHW012001160823
426985UK00001B/60